THE OXFORD BOOK OF THEATRICAL ANECDOTES

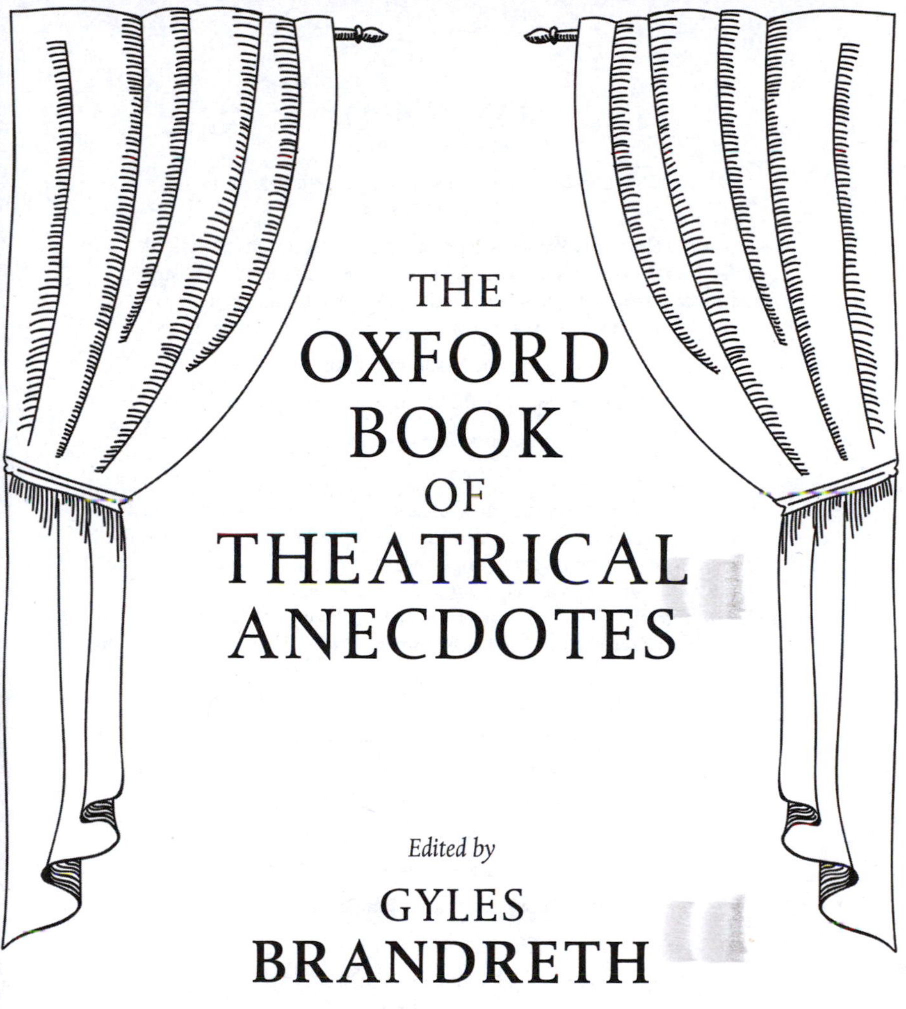

THE OXFORD BOOK OF THEATRICAL ANECDOTES

Edited by

GYLES BRANDRETH

OXFORD
UNIVERSITY PRESS

OXFORD
UNIVERSITY PRESS

Great Clarendon Street, Oxford, OX2 6DP,
United Kingdom

Oxford University Press is a department of the University of Oxford.
It furthers the University's objective of excellence in research, scholarship,
and education by publishing worldwide. Oxford is a registered trade mark of
Oxford University Press in the UK and in certain other countries

First Edition published in 2020

Impression: 4

Published in the United States of America by Oxford University Press
198 Madison Avenue, New York, NY 10016, United States of America

British Library Cataloguing in Publication Data
Data available

Library of Congress Control Number: 2020934896

ISBN 978–0–19–874958–5

Printed and bound in Great Britain by
Clays Ltd, Elcograf S.p.A.

For Michèle
whom I met at an audition in 1968,
and who, on stage, in the wings,
backstage, in the gallery, the circle and the stalls,
has been my best friend and good companion
ever since

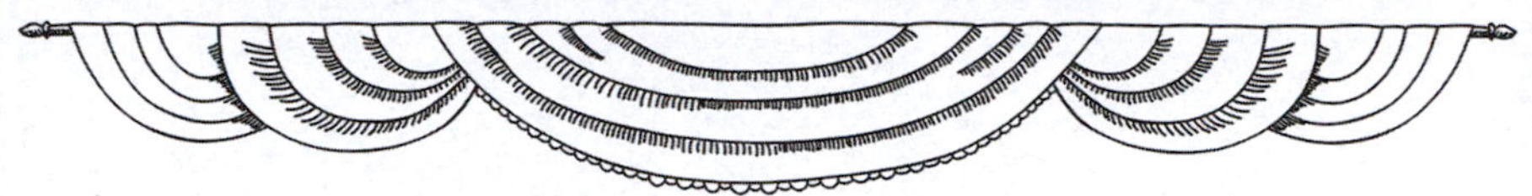

CONTENTS

ACKNOWLEDGEMENTS

'For all, our thanks'

HAMLET

INDEX

'As index to the story we late talk'd of'

RICHARD III

What is an anecdote? According to my favourite dictionary—the *Concise Oxford*, fourth edition, given to me for my twelfth birthday in 1960, but still a valued companion sixty years on—an anecdote is a 'narrative of detached incident', the story of a stand-alone moment.

For that same birthday, in 1960, I was taken to the Old Vic theatre in London to see my first *Romeo and Juliet*. It was directed by Franco Zeffirelli and starred a young Judi Dench as Juliet. I went with my parents. It turned out that Judi Dench's parents were there, too. When Juliet came on and said to the Nurse (played by Peggy Mount), 'Where are my father and my mother, Nurse?' a reassuring voice called out from the stalls, 'Here we are, darling, in Row H.' I have been collecting theatrical anecdotes ever since. (You will find that one, authenticated by Dame Judi, on p. 668.)

When I go to the theatre, which is often, I am almost willing the unexpected to happen. I was at the Royal Shakespeare Theatre in Stratford-upon-Avon in 1974 when the late, great Nicol Williamson, in the middle of a schools' matinée of *Macbeth*, kicked a wooden stool across the stage in a fury and bellowed at the noisy children in the stalls to 'belt up or get out'. My wife was at the Criterion Theatre in London, some years later, to see Williamson leave the stage six minutes after starting a performance of his one-man show about the actor John Barrymore, remarking to the audience as he departed, 'I don't want to do this anymore.' In the event, he was back on stage the following night, explaining that the part was 'overwhelming' and he didn't want to play it if he was feeling under par. On another occasion, in New York, Williamson punched a fellow actor at the curtain call, apparently because he had misheard the actor who had whispered as the curtain fell, 'That's a wrap.'

That story reminds me of the charming, wiry, one-armed Irish character actor David Kelly, who first came to notice playing the title role in Samuel Beckett's *Krapp's Last Tape* at the Abbey Theatre in Dublin in 1959. Later, when he played the part in New York, he relished the review that appeared beneath the headline: 'At last the *Krapp* we have been waiting for'. And *that* reminds me of the matinée my wife and I attended at the Abbey, during which another fine Irish actor, Norman Rodway, in a Restoration romp, tripped on stage as he made his entrance and tore a ligament—causing the abandonment of the play because there was no understudy.

I was not there at *Cyrano de Bergerac* at the Bristol Old Vic when the dashing matinée idol Peter Wyngarde's wig was set alight by a candle and the actor hopped frantically around the stage before eventually yanking off his flaming head of hair to reveal to his aghast admirers that, actually, he was bald. More traumatically, I was at the Mermaid Theatre in London on the first night of William Trevor's *The Old Boys* starring the mighty Sir Michael Redgrave, who had a lifelong terror of first nights. Halfway through the play the earpiece that was feeding him his lines slipped its moorings and clattered to the floor, leaving the great actor bereft and speechless.

I wish I had been there when Redgrave's near-contemporary Sir Ralph Richardson was appearing in Brighton in the pre-London run of Joe Orton's *What the Butler Saw*, and, mid-performance, tottered down to the front of the stage and enquired, loudly and with a certain urgency, 'Is there a doctor in the house?' A man in the circle identified himself. Sir Ralph looked up and said, 'Terrible play, isn't it, doctor?', before tottering back upstage and carrying on with it.

I got to know Sir Ralph in the 1970s when I was artistic director of the Oxford Theatre Festival. He was both full of good sense ('Acting is the ability to keep an audience from coughing,' he liked to say) and gloriously eccentric. More than once he was found scrabbling on all fours in a dark corner of the wings, moaning plaintively, 'Has anyone seen my talent? It's small, but it used to be quite shiny.' Hoping to persuade him to appear in a play about a missionary, in which he would be the only human character, the rest being wild animals ('Oh,' he purred, 'I know Anna Massey's going to make a lovely giraffe'), I entertained him to lunch at Rules' restaurant in Covent Garden. His attention was caught by a man he appeared to recognize on the far side of the dining room. 'Oh, is that you, Stanley?' he called out. 'Oh, Stanley Jackson, my old friend! Good to see you—but how you've changed! You've gone all bald and you've shaved off your moustache. And your face was such a lovely, round, jolly face. Now it's all long and lugubrious.' At this point, the man across the room interrupted Sir Ralph's flow to say, 'I'm not Stanley Jackson.' 'Oh,' cried Richardson, 'changed your name as well, have you?'

Around the same time in the 1970s, Sir Ralph's good friend, Sir John Gielgud, came to Oxford for me to recreate some golden moments from his celebrated *Richard II*. When I marvelled at how he managed to cry at exactly the same point each time he performed a particular speech, he murmured apologetically, 'Bladder too near my eyes, I'm afraid.' Sir John was a walking encyclopaedia of theatre lore. He told me that as a boy he had been there when his great-aunt, Ellen Terry, delivered the immortal line, 'Let us find a nosy cook.' On his last first night in the West End, Gielgud, aged 80, briefly forgot his lines, stamped his foot impatiently until the prompt came and then carried on. Gielgud's whole life revolved around the theatre and he continued working almost until his death, aged 96, in 2000. As I learnt when I wrote his biography, work to him was everything and, even in his nineties, he would become anxious and impatient if his partner spent too long on the telephone. 'Get off the line, Martin,' he'd plead. 'My agent may be trying to get through.'

Rex Harrison ('sexy Rexy', six-times-married actor and film star, always admired but not always loved within his profession, and knighted less than a year before his death) carried on working until three weeks before he died, aged 82, in 1990, playing in Somerset

Maugham's *The Circle* on Broadway. He had pancreatic cancer, but preferred to be on stage than off. He used to say, 'Nobody is as interesting to spend an evening with as a really good part.' I met him by chance towards the end of his life and only because he was partially blind. He was coming out of the Ritz Hotel in London and bumped into me at the foot the steps. He was going to the Caprice restaurant nearby and we walked there together. When we arrived, he enquired, 'Why have you brought me here, young man?' I explained to him that I hadn't, but he seemed happy to talk to me all the same. He told me that at his first-ever appearance on stage, at the Liverpool Playhouse, he had only had one line. He had to run on and say excitedly, 'It's a baby—fetch a doctor.' Unfortunately, he ran on and said, 'It's a doctor—fetch a baby.'

I was a friend of Patrick Garland, who directed Harrison in the 1981 revival of the musical *My Fair Lady*, in which the star, now in his seventies, reprised his most famous role as the irascible Professor Henry Higgins. Harrison's poor eyesight meant that on more than one occasion he walked off the stage straight into the orchestra pit, and his advanced years made him insist on having Cathleen Nesbitt play his mother in the revival as she had done in the original production. Nesbitt, however, was now in her nineties, uncertain of her lines (occasionally convinced she was in a revival of *Camelot* rather than *My Fair Lady*) and quite frail. There were regular scuffles in the wings as she and Rex Harrison tussled over which of them should have access to the performance-enhancing oxygen cylinder first.

I was a friend, too, of the stout character actor Peter Bull, who played Pozzo in the original London production of *Waiting for Godot* in 1955—'the play', as one critic famously put it, 'in which nothing happens, twice.' Peter Bull's mother brought her best friend to the opening night, but all Mrs Bull could think to say when she reached her son's dressing room at the conclusion of the ground-breaking drama was 'Gladys thought the brass-work in the stalls beautifully polished.' Bull also recalled standing on stage and hearing a lady in the front row whisper to her neighbour, 'I do wish the fat one would go away.'

One or two of these stories feature in the pages that follow, but not all of them—and for a reason. This is *The Oxford Book of Theatrical Anecdotes* and, quite rightly, at the Oxford University Press they have high standards. To qualify for inclusion here an anecdote has to have what the auction houses call 'provenance'. We need to know where it comes from: who reported the anecdote first and how reliable a witness are they? There are lots of fun stories I might have liked to have included, but couldn't in the end, because I could not find a credible original written source to give the anecdote the validity the OUP quite properly demands.

For example, there is a famous story concerning two actors noted for their fondness for the bottle: Wilfred Lawson, a Yorkshire-born character actor who died aged 66 in 1966, and Richard Burton, the Welsh actor and film star who died aged 58 in 1984. In the 1950s, so the story goes, Lawson bumped into Richard Burton in the Salisbury pub in St Martin's Lane before suggesting, after copious amounts of alcohol, that they go together to the New Theatre nearby to see the play. Lawson was in it, but did not make his appearance until Act Two. The bibulous duo found seats up at the front of the gallery. When Act One finished they went to the bar, had more drinks and then settled down for Act Two. After a few minutes, Lawson nudged Burton and said, cheerily, 'You'll like this bit. This is where I come on.'

Did it ever happen? If it did, in later years Burton said he had no memory of it.

There is another story that is sometimes told about Wilfred Lawson—or Robert Newton or Richard Burton or Peter O'Toole or any number of other actors who appeared in Shakespeare and had reputations as drinkers. In this anecdote, an actor playing the title role in *Richard III* comes onto the stage at the opening of the play clearly the worse for wear. As with a hiccup he completes the line, 'Now is the winter of our discontent…' an audience member calls out, 'You're drunk!' With a chuckle, the actor immediately responds: 'If you think I'm drunk, wait until you see the Duke of Buckingham!'

It turns out that is an anecdote that has been told about many a player going back several generations before that of Wilfred Lawson or Robert Newton, at least as far as to the era of John Junius Booth (1821–83), who was a notorious drinker—regularly to be heard calling from the stage to the prompt corner, 'What's the line? What's the line?', occasionally to be heard calling, 'What's the play?' Booth was an English actor who went to America. His co-workers did their best to save him from himself. Before a performance, to keep him from the bottle they would lock him in his dressing-room and take away the key. Booth, however, anticipated them by getting the theatre call-boy to go out and buy him a bottle of whisky—so that, before the performance, the call-boy could stand outside the star dressing-room holding the opened bottle and Booth could drink from it from inside the locked dressing-room by pushing a paper straw through the keyhole.

It's a story that has been handed down the years, but is true? Does it stand up? The paper drinking straw was not patented until 1888, five years after Booth's death. Perhaps he used a rye grass straw (it's possible)—or perhaps the story, as with so famous of the best-loved theatrical tales, is simply apocryphal.

John Junius Booth had two sons of note: the younger was John Wilkes Booth, perhaps the most notorious actor in history, a well-regarded Romeo, a Confederate sympathizer deeply opposed to the abolition of slavery, who, aged 26, assassinated President Abraham Lincoln at the Ford Theatre in Washington, DC, on 14 April 1865;

the older was Edwin Booth, regarded by many as the most distinguished American Hamlet of the nineteenth century. Happily, the anecdote about how the actor-brother of the actor who assassinated President Lincoln later saved the life of the son of President Lincoln *can* be authenticated.

It happened in late 1864 or early 1865, and Robert Lincoln told the story in a 1909 letter to Richard Watson Gilder, editor of *The Century Magazine*:

> *The incident occurred while a group of passengers were late at night purchasing their sleeping car places from the conductor who stood on the station platform at the entrance of the car. The platform was about the height of the car floor, and there was of course a narrow space between the platform and the car body. There was some crowding, and I happened to be pressed by it against the car body while waiting my turn. In this situation the train began to move, and by the motion I was twisted off my feet, and had dropped somewhat, with feet downward, into the open space, and was personally helpless, when my coat collar was vigorously seized and I was quickly pulled up and out to a secure footing on the platform. Upon turning to thank my rescuer I saw it was Edwin Booth, whose face was of course well known to me, and I expressed my gratitude to him, and in doing so, called him by name.*

The fact that, by sheer chance, he had saved the life of Abraham Lincoln's son, not knowing at the time who he was, was reckoned to have been of considerable comfort to Edwin Booth, whose family name had been so blighted by his brother's assassination of the president. Robert Lincoln's letter is what gives this seemingly incredible anecdote its credibility. By drawing them from reliable sources I trust that most of the anecdotes that feature in the pages that follow have the required 'provenance'.

Edwin Booth's final performance, aged 58, was as Hamlet in 1891. Three years earlier, in 1888, he had founded the Players Club in New

York, as a private gentleman's club for performing, literary, and visual artists and their friends and associates. A comparable club had been formed in London, half a century before, in 1831, and many members of the Garrick Club feature as star players in this book—Charles Kean, Sir Henry Irving, Sir Herbert Beerbohm Tree, Sir Laurence Olivier, Sir John Gielgud, and Sir Donald Sinden among them. Though I am not a member of the Garrick (my son is; my father was), much of the research for the older anecdotes in this collection was undertaken in the club's library—thanks to Donald Sinden, who loved the theatre, his club, and a theatrical anecdote in equal measure.

I first encountered Donald Sinden when I was about fifteen and a pupil at Bedales, a coeducational boarding school in Hampshire. My best friend at Bedales (where the list of theatrical parents ran from Oscar Wilde to Laurence Olivier to Peter Hall) was a boy called Simon Cadell, who came from a theatrical family, and whose father, a theatrical agent, had Donald Sinden as a star client. The best of the vintage stories in this collection are ones to which he introduced me. I collaborated with Sir Donald on his books about the theatre, performed with him occasionally (not an easy undertaking: he was a natural scene-stealer), admired him hugely (he was a lovely man; his range was considerable; his theatrical 'presence' totally compelling), and think of him every time I take to the stage in any capacity. He once gave me a masterclass in elocution, explaining that 'it's your vowels that give you volume and your consonants that give you clarity.' Before any performance I now warm up with an exercise he taught me, standing in front of my dressing-room mirror, taking a deep breath, and repeating his mantra: 'Hip bath, hip bath, lavatory, lavatory, bidet, bidet, douche.' And after the show, too, I follow Sinden's advice, by not reading the reviews. 'If it's good, it's good,' he told me. 'If it isn't, you'll know.'

Three or four years ago, in London, at the opening of his show *Young Frankenstein,* I asked author, director, actor Mel Brooks, then 91 and a little hard of hearing, what he felt about critics. 'They're very noisy at night,' he said. 'You can't sleep in the country because of them.' 'No', I said, 'critics not crickets.' 'Oh, critics!' cried Mel. 'What good are they? They can't make music with their hind legs.'

I have been blessed to know great men of the theatre like Mel Brooks and Donald Sinden. I have known critics, too. When I was at Oxford University in the late 1960s I met the celebrated Kenneth Tynan, a fine critic and the first Literary Manager of the National Theatre, but best remembered now as the first person to say 'fuck' on television. (He also created the 'nude review' *Oh, Calcutta!* after the first night of which the dancer and actor Robert Helpmann is said to have remarked, 'The trouble with naked dancing is that not everything stops when the music stops.')

One of my good friends at Oxford was Michael Coveney, who went on to become a drama critic of note. As students, I directed and he choreographed a production of *Cinderella* for the OUDS (Oxford University Dramatic Society). We cast a young Eliza Manningham-Buller as our Fairy Queen. She went on to become the head of MI5. We offered a beautiful young girl called Michèle Brown a part in the chorus, but she turned us down, opting instead to appear in someone else's production of *Twelfth Night* as Viola. She went on to become my wife and, along with Donald Sinden, has been my principal collaborator in compiling this collection.

Michèle and I have been going to the theatre together since 1968 and, since then, have also been involved in producing or co-producing a score of shows on tour and in the West End. We know a lot of actors and a number of directors, too—though in the pages that follow you will find many more stories about actors than directors. (On the whole, actors are more noticeable than directors. Actors are accustomed to being in the spotlight: directors belong in the semi-darkness of the stalls.) In the 1970s we put on the première of William Douglas-Home's play *The Dame of Sark* and persuaded Celia Johnson to take the leading role. She was a remarkable actress, who brought an emotional quality to every part she played without, I think, knowing quite how she did it. Visiting her dressing-room before a performance, I always found her, specs perched lightly on the tip of her nose, either finishing off the crossword or playing a game of Patience. Some years later I asked her if she could remember who had directed the play. She couldn't. I told her. 'Oh really?' she asked. 'Are you sure?' I then asked her to name her favourite director. 'Oh,' she said lightly, waving away the question, 'I've worked with so many.' 'But you must have a favourite?' 'Er... um... not really.' 'Are there any you remember?' She gave a small, tinkly laugh. 'I don't think so.' And *that* story about Dame Celia reminds me of the one about Dame Edith Evans, who, spotting a young man sitting in the stalls on the first day of rehearsal, asked who he was. 'That's the director, Dame Edith,' she was told. 'Ah well,' she replied, 'I dare say we'll find him something to do.'

As well as producing plays, I have appeared in a few. I found myself at the Duchess Theatre in the West End in a show called *Zipp!* in early 2002 and the reality of life in the theatre was brought home to me when for several performances, after a series of severe rainstorms, we had to negotiate onstage buckets strategically placed to catch the water leaking through the theatre roof. When I played Lady Bracknell in a musical version of *The Importance of Being Earnest* at the Riverside Studios in London in 2011, I was so dazzled and amused by the performance of Edward Pethebridge (a hilarious and definitive Canon Chasuble) that I dared not look at him on stage for fear of 'corpsing'—see p. 700 to find how Samuel Pepys disapproved of 'corpsing'. When I played Malvolio in *Twelfth Night* in Edinburgh in 2007 I was struck by the fact that I had difficulty learning the lines for the scene in which Olivia's steward is imprisoned and visited by Feste disguised as the cleric, Sir Topas. I knew that many other, rather more distinguished, actors had found this scene difficult to memorize—Sir Donald Sinden and Sir Donald Wolfit among them. Indeed, Wolfit was of the opinion that the scene must have been written by some other hand: 'If I can't learn it, Shakespeare didn't write it,' he maintained.

There are a lot of stories about Sir Donald Wolfit here—and about Sir Frank Benson and Sir Laurence Olivier—simply because these great men of the theatre seem to have more stories told about them in their day than seem to be being told about actors of later generations. Sir John Gielgud features more here than does Sir Michael Redgrave, not because one was a greater actor than the other, but simply because more people have recorded more anecdotes about one than the other. It seems it is the personality of the individual, rather than their fame or genius, that gives rise to the quantity and quality of anecdotes about them. (Are today's actors more serious-minded and consequently a tad duller than those of yesteryear? I pass no judgement here. As Lady Bracknell says, 'I merely desire information.')

Playwright, composer, lyricist, actor, and director Sir Noël Coward is in the book, of course, but not with either of the 'Coward stories' that my friend, the brilliant Bonnie Langford (whose father, Baron Hardup, I have played to her Cinderella, twice) believes to be true, simply because I have been unable to find a reliable written source for either of them. Bonnie, as a little girl, appeared in a musical version of *Gone with the Wind* at the Theatre Royal, Drury Lane, in 1972. To many in the audience, her star turn as the five-year-old 'Bonnie' stole the show, but Noël Coward was not impressed, saying tartly as the curtain fell: 'Two things should have been cut. The second act and that child's throat.'

But did he say it? Bonnie is convinced he did, but if he did, he was repeating an old line. In 1968, four years earlier, Dick Richards published a little book called *The Wit of Noël Coward*, and there, on page thirteen, is exactly the same line—word for word—attributed to Coward but in relation to a different child in a different production on another continent.

There is an alternative version of this same anecdote attributed to Coward. Here the story revolves around the live horse that featured in the Drury Lane *Gone with the Wind*. On the opening night, the horse did rather more than break wind on stage during the show, apparently prompting Coward to remark, 'Nothing wrong with the show that couldn't be fixed by shoving the child's head up the horse's arse.'

If he said it at all (and it sounds a bit overly vulgar for the fastidious Master), no one recorded him saying it at the time—so it does not feature in *The Oxford Book of Theatrical Anecdotes*, however much we might want it to. Nor is Coward here after a performance of David Storey's 1971 play *The Changing Room*, in which the actors playing rugby players after a match all took off their clothes on stage, and Coward was said to have voiced his disappointment in the nudity with the quip: 'I didn't pay good money to see fourteen acorns and a chipolata.'

And while on the subject of *The Changing Room*, the actors in the play expressed alarm during the previews because they could hear the sound of metallic clicking from the darkened auditorium at key moments in the production and feared it might be lunatic protestors who had arrived at the theatre armed and were now in the stalls cocking their rifles. It turned out to be the noise of opera glasses hitting spectacle lenses at the moment the lads on stage stripped off…And then there's the story of the time Cicely Cooper, the sister of Dame Gladys Cooper, appeared at the Duchess Theatre playing the small part of the maid and expressed concern that the audience was hissing her whenever she came on. It transpired, audience members were merely whispering to one another, 'That's

Cissie Cooper, Gladys Cooper's sister!' It's one of my favourite stories, but I doubt very much that it's true.

You will find some of your favourite theatrical anecdotes here, but only if I could find a solid source for them. I hope you will find plenty of surprises, too. Spoilt for choice, I have tried to select anecdotes that are revelatory as well as interesting or amusing. I want these 'narratives of detached incident' to be six-hundred or so glimpses of the theatre as it has evolved over the past six-hundred years—from the age of Shakespeare when boys played the women's parts to the time of the Restoration when actresses were all too often regarded as strumpets to the modern era when many of them want to be called 'actors' not 'actresses' (see Denise Gough on p. 420); from the early nineteenth century heyday of Ira Aldridge (the first Shakespearean actor of African American heritage to win international acclaim), to our own time when black actors are regularly cast in traditionally white roles but where it's almost unimaginable for a role such as Othello to be played by a white actor. (The last two white actors of note to play the Moor of Venice were Sir Laurence Olivier and Sir Donald Sinden. Sir Patrick Stewart did play the part in Washington, DC, in 1997, but in a production where all the other parts were played by black actors.)

My own instinct is that any actor should be allowed to tackle any part. Glenda Jackson's King Lear was a *tour de force*. How I wish I had seen Sarah Bernhardt's Hamlet. I am not Jewish, but I would love to play Shylock. I am neither royal nor Danish nor a spirit, but I have had a go at Claudius and the Ghost in *Hamlet*. For me that's the thrill of live theatre: anything goes and anything may happen.

The *Hamlet* in which I appeared at the Park Theatre in 2017 was directed by Simon Evans and David Aula, in a version edited by them and Imogen Bond—to whom I am indebted for some of the most recent anecdotes featured here. Thanks for other anecdotes go to Peter Rankin, Aleks Sierz, and too many of my theatre friends for me to be able to acknowledge them individually. The list could be infinite because stories keep coming my way. The other day, for example, I met the actress Joanna McCullum, who told me a story about Sir Donald Wolfit I had not heard before. When Joanna's mother, the celebrated Googie Withers, took over from Peggy Ashcroft in Terence Rattigan's *The Deep Blue Sea* in the West End in the early 1950s, she chanced to encounter Wolfit, who congratulated her on the fine reviews she had received. He then asked which was the day of her midweek matinée. 'It's on a Thursday,' she told him. 'Excellent,' said Wolfit. 'That means you can come to see my Lear on Wednesday.'

Repeating this story to my friend Martin Jarvis prompted him to tell his Googie Withers story. Martin and Googie appeared together in 1976 at the Chichester Festival Theatre in a production of *The Circle* by Somerset Maugham. The part of Lord Porteous was played by Bill Fraser, who found it difficult to resist the temptation to amuse the audience with a certain amount of comical mugging, not always in keeping with the role. When, at one matinée, Googie Withers caught him letting his top row of dentures fall onto his lower lip to get a laugh, she cornered him in the wings and said to him, quietly, 'Remember, Bill, you're supposed to be playing a peer, not on the end of one.'

Returning to Wolfit for a moment, when he was starting out, almost a century ago, playing Salanio in *The Merchant of Venice* at Consett in County Durham, he was disconcerted to find find four women sitting in the front row, each with a baby at her breast. During the interval the stage manager explained that the front row was reserved for nursing mothers so that 'they should not be over-looked'. According to Wolfit's biographer, playwright and Oscar-winning screenwriter Ronald Harwood (author of *The Dresser*), at a theatre on the outskirts of Birmingham, as Portia said, 'The quality of mercy is not strained', a loud voice rang out from the gallery, 'Well, good night all,' and heavy boots clumped down the gallery steps. At the Theatre

Royal, Whitehaven, performing *The Bells* to a hostile audience, an older actor called out to the young Wolfit, 'Get up stage, you fool!', as a cascade of empty beer bottles landed at his feet.

Much more recently, at the Trafalgar Studios in London in 2018, midway through a performance of the drama *Killer Joe*, the actor playing the lead, Orlando Bloom, stopped the show—twice—to berate a member of the audience for using an iPad. According to one eyewitness, the *Lord of the Rings* star let fly with some pretty fruity language and the temperature in the theatre—already hot, thanks to the weather—rose still further. I wish I had been there. As you can tell, I am drawn to a drama at the drama.

In my book, theatre is often best when the unexpected occurs. If you want to see something flawless, buy a box set. In the movies, no one 'dries', no one 'corpses', no one enters late or drunk or in the middle of the wrong scene. No one fluffs their lines and you only get to see what the director wants you to see. It is a film, a fixed record of something pre-packaged and polished to perfection. The theatre is different. The theatre is live and electric: it is happening before your very eyes in the here and now, that's the essence of it. And when something goes awry, it's a powerful reminder of just that.

As for the matter of audience interruptions, it's an old challenge but has been given a new twist, thanks to modern technology. As well as Bloom's tirade at the Trafalgar Studios, another story that made the headlines a year or so ago featured the cast of a touring production of *Titanic the Musical* raging from the stage at two audience members who were preoccupied watching England's World Cup penalty shoot-out while the icy tragedy was being played out on stage; the guilty duo in the front stalls were so engrossed in the football they even cheered at the scoring of each England goal.

Of course, if you don't want your audience fiddling with their mobiles during your play, make your performance so compelling that they won't. The theatre is not there for the actors, or the writers, or the directors: it is there for the audience—and, as the groundlings made plain in Shakespeare's day, an audience likes to make its presence felt. In the pages that follow, you will find plenty of boisterous audience participation in Act Five. Directors and playwrights are the focus of Act Four. During the interval, you can eavesdrop on fellow audience members and theatre critics, past and present. But before then, first and foremost, we have our players, appearing in chronological order, and ready now to take the stage.

Welcome to *The Oxford Book of Theatrical Anecdotes*. Enjoy the show.

Gyles Brandreth

2020

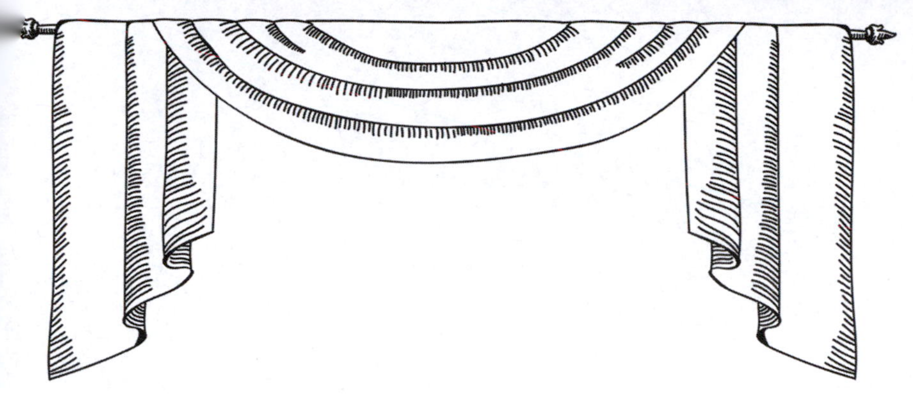

ACT ONE

PLAYERS FROM WILLIAM SHAKESPEARE TO HENRY IRVING

'The actors are at hand and by their show you shall know all'

A MIDSUMMER NIGHT'S DREAM

WILLIAM SHAKESPEARE
(1564–1616)

1

We think of Shakespeare, primarily, as the great dramatist—and in this book the playwrights don't come centre stage until Act Four—but Shakespeare, of course, was also a professional actor: at the end of the sixteenth century, one of the Lord Chamberlain's Men, and later, in the reign of King James I, one of the King's Men. His plays feature in many of the anecdotes in this collection and lines of his provide the chapter headings. Shakespeare himself features in only a few anecdotes—and none of them seem very reliable. But, as he has the Sea Captain remind us in Twelfth Night, *'what great ones do, the less will prattle of.'*

MR. WILLIAM SHAKESPEARE was borne at Stratford-upon-Avon in the County of Warwick. His father was a Butcher, and I have been told heretofore by some of the neighbours, that when he was a boy he exercised his father's Trade, but when he kill'd a Calfe he would doe it in a high style, and make a Speech. There was at this time another Butcher's son in this Towne that was held not at all inferior to him for a naturall witt, his acquaintance and coetanean [contemporary], byt dyed young.

This William, being inclined naturally to Poetry and acting, came to London, I guesse about 18: and was an Actor at one of the Playhouses, and did acte exceedingly well.

SOURCE
John Aubrey, *Brief Lives* (set down between 1669 and 1696)

2

Concerning Shakespear's first appearance in the playhouse. When he came to London, he was without money and friends, and being a stranger he knew not to whom to apply, nor by what means to support himself.—At that time coaches not being in use, and as gentlemen were accustomed to ride to the playhouse, Shakespear, driven to the last necessity, went to the playhouse door, and pick'd up a little money by taking care of the gentlemen's horses who came to the play; he became eminent even in that profession, and was taken notice of for his diligence and skill in it; he had soon more business than he himself could manage, and at last hired boys under him, who were known by the name of Shakespear's boys: Some of the players accidentally conversing with him, found him so acute, and master of so fine a conversation, that struck therewith, they recommended him to the house, in which he was first admitted in a very low station, but he did not long remain so, for he soon distinguished himself, if not as an extraordinary actor, at least as a fine writer. His name is printed, as the custom was in those times, amongst those of the other players, before some old plays, but without any particular account of what sort of parts he used to play: and Mr Rowe says, 'that tho' he very carefully enquired, he found the top of his performance was the ghost in his own Hamlet.'

SOURCE
Theophilus Cibber, *The Lives of the Poets of Great Britain and Northern Ireland to the time of Dean Swift* (1753)

3

It is well known that Queen Elizabeth was a great admirer of the immortal Shakspeare, and used frequently (as was the custom with persons of great rank in those days) to appear upon the stage before the audience, or to sit delighted behind the scenes, when the plays of our bard were performed. One evening, when Shakspeare himself was personating the part of a King, the audience knew of her Majesty being in the house. She crossed the stage when he was performing, and, on receiving the accustomed greeting from the audience, moved politely to the poet, but he did not notice it! When behind the scenes, she caught his eye, and moved again, but still he would not throw off his character, to notice her: this made her

Majesty think of some means by which she might know, whether he would depart, or not, from the dignity of his character, while on the stage. Accordingly, as he was about to make his exit, she stepped before him, dropped her glove, and re-crossed the stage, which Shakspeare noticing, took up, with these words, immediately after finishing his speech, and so aptly were they delivered, that they seemed to belong to it:

'And though now bent on this high embassy,
Yet stoop we to take up our *Cousin's* glove!'

He then walked off the stage, and presented the glove to the Queen, who was greatly pleased with his behaviour, and complimented him upon the propriety of it.

SOURCE
Anon., *Dramatic Table Talk* (sometimes ascribed to Richard Ryan) (1825)

RICHARD BURBAGE
(1567–1619)

4

Which is your Burbage now?
Your best actor?

Ben Jonson, *Bartholomew Fair* (1614)

Richard Burbage, the most famous tragedian of his day, was the original interpreter of some of Shakespeare's greatest characters, including Hamlet, Othello, King Lear, and Richard III.

Upon a tyme when Burbidge played Richard III, there was a citizen grone soe farr in liking with him, that before shee went from the play shee appointed him to come that night unto hir by the name of Richard the Third. Shakespeare overhearing their conclusion went before, was intertained and at his game ere Burbidge came. Then message being brought that Richard the Third was at the dore, Shakespeare caused returne to be made that William the Conqueror was before Richard the Third. Shakespeare's name William.

SOURCE
Diary of John Manningham 1602–03, ed. J. Bruce (1868)

CHARLES HART (1625–1683) & JOSEPH HAINES (1638–1701)

5

Charles Hart, once a boy player with the King's Men, became a leading heroic actor of the Restoration. Joe Haines was a comedian, singer, sometime fortune-teller, and one of the first English Harlequins. This is an early example of 'upstaging', a feature of many theatrical anecdotes.

About this time [1673] there happened a small pique between Mr Hart and Joe, upon the account of his late negotiation in France, and there spending the company's money to so little purpose, or, as I may properly say, to no purpose at all. There happened to be one night a play called 'Cataline's Conspiracy,' wherein there was wanting a great number of senators. Now Mr Hart, being chief of the house, would oblige Joe to dress for one of these senators, although his salary, being fifty shillings a week, freed him from any such obligation. But Mr Hart, as I said before, being sole governor of the playhouse, and at a small variance with Joe, commands it, and the other must obey. Joe being vexed at the slight Mr

Hart had put upon him, found out this method of being revenged upon him. He gets a scaramouch dress, a large full ruff, makes himself whiskers from ear to ear, puts on a long merry cap, a short pipe in his mouth, a little three-legged stool in his hand, and in this manner follows Mr Hart on the stage, sets himself down behind him, and begins to smoke his pipe, laugh and point at him, which comical figure put all the house in an uproar, some laughing, some clapping, and some hallooing. Now Mr Hart, as those who knew him can aver, was a man of that exactness and grandeur on the stage, that let what would happen, he'd never discompose himself or mind anything but what he then represented, and had a scene fallen behind him he would not at that time look back to see what was the matter; which Joe knowing, remained still smoaking; the audience continued laughing; Mr Hart acting and wondering at this unusual occasion of their mirth—sometimes thinking it some disturbance in the house; again, that it might be something amiss in his dress. At last, turning himself towards the scenes, he discovered Joe in the aforesaid posture; whereupon he immediately goes off the stage, swearing he would never set foot on it again unless Joe was immediately turned out of doors; which was no sooner spoke than put in practice.

SOURCE
R. Wewitzer, *Dramatic Remains*, quoted in W. Clark Russell, *Representative Actors* (1888)

THOMAS BETTERTON
(?1635–1710)

6

Thomas Betterton was one of the principal actors of the Restoration theatre, making a particular success of Shakespearean roles such as Hamlet and Lear. The son of an under-cook to King Charles I, his dramatic powers overcame the disadvantages of a low voice, small eyes, and an ungainly figure.

Archbishop Tillotson was very well acquainted with Betterton, and continued that acquaintance even after he was in that high station. One day when Betterton came to see him at Lambeth, that prelate asked him how it came about that after he had made the most moving discourse that he could, was touched deeply with it himself, and spoke it as feelingly as he was able, yet he could never move people in the church near so much as the other did on the stage?

'That,' says Betterton, 'I think is easy to be accounted for: 'tis because you are only *telling* them a story, and I am *showing* them facts.'

SOURCE
Joseph Spence, *Observations, Anecdotes, and Characters of Books and Men*, ed. James M Osborn (1966)

7

Not only was Betterton's range of characters unlimited, but the number he 'created' was never equalled by any subsequent actor of eminence—namely, about one hundred and thirty! In some single seasons he studied and represented no less than eight original parts—an amount of labour which would shake the nerves of the stoutest among us now.

His brief relaxation was spent on his little Berkshire farm, whence he once took a rustic to Bartholomew Fair for a holiday. The master of the puppet-show declined to take money for admission—'Mr Betterton,' he said, 'is a brother actor!' Roger, the rustic, was slow to believe that the puppets were not alive; and so similar in vitality appeared to him, on the same night, at Drury Lane, the Jupiter and Alcmena in *Amphitryon,* played by Betterton and Mrs Barry, that on being asked what he thought of them, Roger, taking them for puppets, answered, 'They did wonderfully well for rags and sticks.'

SOURCE

Dr John Doran, *Their Majesties' Servants: Annals of the English Stage from Betterton to Kean,* ed. and rev. R. W. Lowe (3 vols, 1888)

EDWARD KYNASTON
(?1640–1706)

8

Actresses first appeared on the English stage during the Restoration period. Edward Kynaston was one of the last boy-players of female roles. He played Juliet to Betterton's Romeo on several occasions.

Tho' as I have before observ'd, Women were not admitted to the Stage, 'till the return of King Charles yet it could not be so suddenly supply'd with them, but that there was still a Necessity, for some time, to put the handsomest young Men into Petticoats; which Kynaston was then said to have worn, with Success; particularly in the Part of Evadne, in the *Maid's Tragedy,* which I have heard him speak of; and which calls to my Mind a ridiculous Distress that arose from these sort of Shifts, which the Stage was then put to—the King coming a little before his usual time to a Tragedy, found the Actors not ready to begin, when his Majesty not chusing to have as much Patience as his good Subjects, sent to them, to know the Meaning of it; upon which the Master of the Company came to the Box, and rightly judging that the best Excuse for their Default would be the true one, fairly told his Majesty that the Queen was not shav'd yet: The King, whose good Humour lov'd to laugh at a Jest, as well as to make one, accepted the Excuse, which serv'd to divert him, till the male Queen cou'd be effeminated. In a word, Kynaston, at that time, was so beautiful a Youth, that the Ladies of Quality prided themselves in taking him with them in their Coaches, to Hyde-Park, in this Theatrical Habit, after the Play; which in those Days, they might have sufficient time to do, because Plays then were us'd to begin at four a-Clock; The Hour that People of the same Rank, are now going to Dinner—Of this Truth, I had the Curiosity to enquire, and had it confirm'd from his own Mouth, in his advanc'd Age: And indeed, to the last of him, his handsomeness was very little abated.

SOURCE
An Apology for the Life of Colley Cibber (1740), ed. B. R. S. Fone (1968)

NELL GWYNN
(1650–1687)

9

Eleanor 'Nell' Gwynn was a fine comic actress and the mistress of King Charles II. Samuel Pepys, who called her 'pretty, witty Nell', was one of her many admirers.

...so great performance of a comical part was never, I believe, in the world before as Nell hath done this, both as mad girle, and then, most and best of all, when she comes in like a young gallant; and hath the motions and carriage of a spark, the most that ever I saw any man have. It makes me, I confess, admire her.

SOURCE
Samuel Pepys on Nell Gwynn's performance as Florimel in Dryden's *Mayden Queene*, *Diary* (2 March 1667)

ELIZABETH KNEPP
(d.1681)

10

Elizabeth Knepp (or Knipp) was another of Pepys's favourites. This anecdote, and the one that follows, show that actresses at the time could expect no privacy in their dressing rooms.

. . . to the King's house and there, going in, met with Knipp, and she took us up into the tiring-rooms and to the women's shift, where Nell was dressing herself and was all unready, and is very pretty, prettier than I thought. And so walked all up and down the house above, and then below into the scene-room, and there sat down, and she gave us fruit: and here I read the questions to Knipp, while she answered me, through all her part of 'Flora's Figaries,' which was acted today. But, Lord! To see how they were both painted would make a man mad, and did make me loathe them; and what base company of men comes among them, and how lewdly they talk! and how poor the men are in clothes, and yet what a show they make on the stage by candle-light, is very observable. But to see how Nell cursed, for having so few people in the pit, was pretty.

SOURCE
Diary of Samuel Pepys (5 October, 1667)

BECK MARSHALL
(*fl.* 1663–1667)

11

Rebecca 'Beck' Marshall was another of the first female performers on the English stage to be admired both by Samuel Pepys and Charles II. With her older sister, Anne, she was a mainstay of the King's Company, established, under Charles II's patronage by Thomas Killigrew, who built the King's Playhouse in Drury Lane. Beck Marshall also appeared for one season with the other authorized theatre company of the period, the Duke's Company, established by Sir William Davenant, under the patronage of Charles II's brother, the Duke of York, later King James II. Beck was noted for her feuds with Nell Gwynn and, on more than one occasion, for seeking the protection of the King.

The 'tiring rooms of the actresses were then open to the fine gentlemen who frequented the house. They stood by at the mysteries of dressing, and commented on what they beheld and did not behold, with such breadth and coarseness of wit, that the more modest or least impudent ladies sent away their little handmaidens. The dressing over, the amateurs lounged into the house, talked loudly with the pretty orange girls, listened when it suited them, and at the termination of the piece crowded again into the 'tiring room of the most favourite and least scrupulous of the actresses. Among these gallants who thus oscillated between the pit and the dressing bowers of the ladies, was a Sir Hugh Middleton. On the second Saturday of February 1667, Sir Hugh was among the joyous damsels dressing for the play, behind the stage of old Drury. The knight was so unpleasantly critical on the nymphs before him, that one of them, sharp-tongued Beck Marshall, bade him keep among the ladies of the Duke's House, since he did not approve of those who served the King. Sir Hugh burst out with a threat, that he would kick, or what was worse, hire his footman to kick, her. The pretty but angry Rebecca nursed her wrath all Sunday; but on Monday she notified the ungallant outrage to the great champion of insulted dames, the King. Nothing immediately came of it; and on Tuesday, there was Sir Hugh glowering at her from the front of the house, and waylaying her, as she was leaving it with a friend. Sir Hugh whispers a ruffianly-looking fellow, who follows the actress, and presses upon her so closely, that she is moved by a double fear—that he is about to rob, and perhaps stab her. A little scream scares the bravo for a minute or so. He skulks away, but anon slinks back; and, armed with the first offensive missile he could pick up in a Drury Lane gutter, he therewith anoints the face and hair of the much-shocked actress, and then, like the valiant fellows of his trade, takes to his heels. The next day, sweet as Anadyomene rising from the sea, the actress appeared before the King, and charged Sir Hugh with being the abettor of this gross outrage. How the knight was punished, the record in the State Paper Office does not say; but about a fortnight later a royal decree was issued, which prohibited gentlemen from entering the 'tiring rooms of the ladies of the King's Theatre. For some nights the gallants sat ill at ease among the audience; but the journals of the period show that the nymphs must have been as little pleased with this arrangement as the fine gentlemen themselves, who soon found their way back to pay the homage of flattery to the most insatiable of goddesses.

SOURCE

Dr John Doran, *Their Majesties' Servants: Annals of the English Stage from Betterton to Kean*, ed. and rev. R. W. Lowe (3 vols, 1888)

ELIZABETH BOUTWELL (*fl.* 1670s, d.1715) & ELIZABETH BARRY (1658–1713)

12

Elizabeth Boutwell (Boutell) was celebrated for playing the virtuous Queen Statira opposite Beck Marshall as the more malevolent Roxanna—a part also played by Elizabeth Barry in Nathaniel Lee's The Rival Queens *(1677). Boutwell was described by Edmund Curll in* The History of the English Stage *(1741) as 'a very considerable actress; she was of low Stature, had very agreeable Features, a good Complexion, but a Childish Look. Her Voice was weak, tho' very mellow; she generally acted the young, innocent Lady whom all the Heroes are mad in Love with; she was a Favourite of the Town.' Barry, sometime mistress of John Wilmot, 2nd Earl of Rochester, was described by the playwright John Dennis (1658–1734) as 'that incomparable Actress changing like Nature which she represents, from Passion to Passion, from Extream to Extream, with piercing Force and into Easy Grace.'*

This story is told by Campbell, in his 'Life of Mrs. Siddons,' of Mrs Boutwell. 'She was,' he says, 'the original *Statira* of Lee's "Alexander," and acted the "Rival Queens" successively with Mrs. Marshall and Mrs. Barry. Once when playing with the latter of the ladies, she was in danger of dying on the stage in earnest. Before the curtain drew up the two Queens, *Statira* (Boutwell) and *Roxana* (Barry) had a real rivalship about a lace veil, which was at last awarded to the former by the property-man. This decision so enraged *Roxana* that she acted her part rather too naturally, and in stabbing *Statira* sent her dagger, though it was a blunted one, through Mrs. Boutwell's stays, about a quarter of an inch into the flesh.'

SOURCE
W. Clark Russell, *Representative Actors* (1888)

SUSANNAH MOUNTFORT (*c.*1667–1703) & ANNE BRACEGIRDLE (1671–1748)

13

When the King's Company and the Duke's Company merged in 1682 to form the United Company, two of the leading ladies were Anne Bracegirdle and Susannah Mountfort—whose husband, the actor William Mountfort, was the presumed lover of Mrs Bracegirdle and, in 1692, murdered by a jealous rival in consequence.

Discretion contributed not a little to make her [Anne Bracegirdle] the Cara, the Darling of the Theatre; for it will be no extravagant thing to say, scarce an audience saw her that were less than half of them lovers, without a suspected favourite among them.

SOURCE
Colley Cibber, 'The Romantick Virgin', in *Apology for the Life of Colley Cibber* (1740), ed. B. R. S. Fone (1968)

14

The most interesting performance of Ophelia that I have met with on record, was that of Mrs Susannah Mountfort...Mrs Mountfort, during her last years, became deranged, but, as her disorder was not outrageous, she was not placed under any rigorous confinement, but was suffered to walk about her house. One day, in a lucid interval, she asked what play was to be performed that evening, and was told it was to be 'Hamlet'. Whilst she was on the stage she had acted Ophelia with great applause; the recollection struck her, and, with all that cunning which is so frequently allied to insanity, she found means to elude the care of her attendants, and got to the theatre, where, concealing herself till the scene where Ophelia was to make her appearance in her mad state, she pushed upon the stage before the person appointed to play the character, and exhibited a representation of it that astonished the performers as well as the audience. She exhausted her vital powers in this effort, was taken home, and died soon after.

SOURCE
Thomas Campbell, *Life of Mrs Siddons* (1834)

COLLEY CIBBER
(1671–1757)

15

Actor, dramatist, Poet Laureate and sometime manager of Drury Lane Theatre, Colley Cibber's adaptation of Shakespeare's Richard III *held the stage for more than a hundred years. Cibber's version contained the famous line, 'Off with his head—so much for Buckingham'. John Verbruggen (d.1708) created the roles of Loveless in Vanbrugh's* The Relapse *and Mirabell in Congreve's* The Way of the World. *He married Susannah Mountfort after William Mountfort's murder in 1692.*

Cibber and Verbruggen were two dissipated young fellows, who determined, in opposition to the advice of friends, to become great actors. Much about the same time, they were constant attendants upon Downes, the prompter of Drury-lane, in expectation of employment. What the first part was, in which Verbruggen distinguished himself, cannot now be known. But Mr Richard Cross, late prompter of Drury-lane theatre, gave me the following history of Colley Cibber's first establishment as a hired actor. He was known only, for some years, by the name of Master Colley. After waiting impatiently a long time for the prompter's notice, by good fortune he obtained the honour of carrying a message on the stage, in some play, to Betterton. Whatever was the cause, Master Colley was so

After a few hums and haws, and a disposing of my hair, so that it might stand on end, 'like quills upon the fretful porcupine,' I supposed my father's ghost before me, 'arm'd *cap à piè,'* and off I started.

'Angels and ministers of grace defend us! (*He wiped the razor.*)
Be thou a spirit of health, or goblin damn'd (*He strapped it.*)
Bring with thee airs from heav'n, or blasts from hell! (*He shaved on.*)
Thou com'st in such a questionable shape,
That I will speak to thee. I'll call thee Hamlet!
King, Father, Royal Dane!—O, answer me!
Let me not burst in ignorance.' (*He lathered again.*)

I concluded with the usual

'Say, why is this? wherefore? what should we do?'

but still continued in my attitude, expecting the praise due to an exhibition, which I was booby enough to fancy was only to be equalled by himself. But, to my eternal mortification, he turned quick upon me, brandished the razor in his hand, and thrusting his half-shaved face close up to mine, he made such horrible mouths at me, that I thought he was seized with insanity, and I shewed more natural symptoms of being frightened at him than at my father's Ghost. 'Angels and ministers! yaw! whaw! maw!' However, I soon perceived my vanity by his ridicule. He finished shaving, put on his wig, and, with a smile of good-nature, he took me by the hand. 'Come,' said he, 'young gentleman,—eh, let us see now what we can do.' He spoke the speech—*how* he spoke it, those who have heard him never can forget. 'There,' said he, 'young gentleman; and when you try that speech again, give it more *passion*, and less *mouth*.'

SOURCE
James Boaden, *Memoirs of Mrs Siddons* (1827)

26

The Garrick Club in London, founded in 1831, was named in Garrick's honour. Its archives contain this letter from him to a lady who was hoping to interest the great actor in a young man with ambitions for the stage.

To Her Grace the Duchess of Portland: 29th October, 1767

I shall always be happy to obey your Grace's commands, but our Company at present is so full and all the Parts dispos'd of, that I could not without great injustice to those Actors I have already engag'd, employ the person you recommend.

I have given Mr Collins the best advice in my Power, and appris'd him that I should be ready at the End of the season to examine his qualifications for the stage. If your Grace will permit me to speak my mind, I think he has the most unpromising Aspect for an Actor I ever saw. A small pair of unmeaning Eyes stuck on a round unthinking face are not the most desirable requisites for a Hero or a fine Gentleman. However I will give him a Tryal if he is unemployed at that time of the year so if he can be of the least service to me or himself I shall most certainly obey Your Grace's Commands.

SOURCE
Letter from David Garrick to the Duchess of Portland, presented to the Garrick Club in 1935 by Raymond Massey

27

The friendship between David Garrick and the slightly older Samuel Johnson was profound, but it was not always easy. It ended well, however.

When Garrick was one day mentioning to me Dr Johnson's illiberal treatment of him, on different occasions; 'I question,' said he, 'whether, in his calmest and most dispassionate moments, he would allow me the high theatrical merit which the public have been so generous as to attribute to me.' I told him that I would take an early opportunity to make the trial, and that I would not fail to inform him of the result of my experiment. As I had rather an active curiosity to put Johnson's disinterested generosity fairly to the test, on this apposite subject, I took an early opportunity of waiting on him, to hear his verdict on Garrick's pretensions to his great and universal fame. I found him in very good and social humour; and I began a conversation which naturally led to the mention of Garrick. I said something particular on his excellence as an actor; and I added, 'But pray, Dr. Johnson, do you really think that he deserves that illustrious theatrical character, and that prodigious fame, which he has acquired?' 'Oh, Sir,' said he, 'he deserves every thing that he has acquired for having seized the very soul of Shakspeare; for having embodied it in himself; and for having expanded its glory over the world.' I was not slow in communicating to Garrick the answer of the Delphic oracle. The tear started in his eye—'Oh! Stockdale,' said he, 'such a praise from such a man! *this* atones for all that has passed.'

SOURCE
Johnsonian Miscellanies, ed. George Birkbeck Hill (2 vols, 1897)

SAMUEL FOOTE
(1719–1788)

28

Samuel Foote was an actor, playwright, and theatre manager who, notoriously, lost his leg in a riding accident in 1766 and used his subsequent disability to comic effect. Famously, he put his talent for caricature and mimicry to good use in the plays he wrote as well as in the performances he gave—off stage as well as on.

They are remarkable in Dublin, when pleased, to continue applauding till the curtain falls, often not suffering the play to finish. This was a compliment frequently paid to Mr Sheridan [actor and father of playwright Richard Brinsley Sheridan].

Foote once said to that gentleman, very seriously, 'My dear Sheridan, I wish you would relieve yourself of a great deal of labour and trouble!'

'In what manner!' says Sheridan, 'do inform me, and I shall be obliged to you.'

'Why,' says Foote, 'instead of Richard the Third, act King Henry in that tragedy.'

'Good God, Mr. Foote! Why should I relinquish Richard, where you are a witness I get such universal applause!—Give me your reason.'

'O'!' says Foote, 'the best reason in the world; for if you will perform Henry instead of Richard, the play will finish in the first act, and the players may all go home in good time to supper.'

SOURCE
Tate Wilkinson, *Memoirs of His Own Life* (1791)

29

I made a visit with him [Garrick] by his own proposal to Foote at Parson's Green; I have heard it said he was reserved and uneasy in his company; I never saw him more at ease and in a happier flow of spirits than on that occasion.

Where a loud-tongued talker was in company, Edmund Burke declined all claims upon attention, and Samuel Johnson, whose ears were not quick, seldom lent them to his conversation, though he loved the man, and admired his talents: I have seen a dull damping matter-of-fact man quell the effervescence even of Foote's unrivalled humour.

But I remember full well, when Garrick and I made him the visit above-mentioned poor Foote had something worse than a dull man to struggle with, and matter of fact brought home to him in a way, that for a time entirely overthrew his spirits, and most completely frighted him from his propriety. We had taken him by surprise, and of course were with him some hours before dinner, to make sure of our own if we had missed of his. He seemed overjoyed to see us, engaged us to stay, walked with us in his garden, and read to us some scenes roughly sketched for his Maid of Bath. His dinner was quite good enough, and his wine superlative: Sir Robert Fletcher, who had served in the East Indies, dropt in before dinner and made the fourth of our party: When we had passed about two hours in perfect harmony and hilarity, Garrick called for his tea, and Sir Robert rose to depart: there was an unlucky screen in the room, that hid the door, and behind which Sir Robert hid himself for some purpose, whether natural or artificial I know not; but Foote, supposing him gone, instantly began to play off his ridicule at the expence of his departed guest. I must confess it was (in the cant phrase) *a way that he had,* and just now a very unlucky way, for Sir Robert bolting from behind the screen, cried out—'I am not gone, Foote; spare me till I am out of hearing; and now with your leave I will stay till these gentlemen depart, and then you shall amuse me at their cost, as you have amused them at mine.'

SOURCE
Richard Cumberland, *Memoirs* (1806)

PEG WOFFINGTON
(1720–1760)

30

Margaret 'Peg' Woffington was an Irish actress who became one of the favourites of the London stage, noted for comic and 'breeches' roles in which she appeared as a man. She appeared frequently with Charles Macklin and David Garrick, the most celebrated of her several lovers.

Upon their return from Dublin, Mrs Woffington lodged in the same house with Macklin; and as Garrick often visited there, there was a constant course of society between the parties; a fourth visitor, too, sometimes made his appearance, but in *private*—who was a Noble Lord, now living, and who was much enamoured with Miss Woffington's many agreeable qualifications. It, however, unfortunately happened one night, that Garrick had occupied Miss Woffington's chamber when his Lordship took it in his head to visit his favourite Dulcinea. A loud knocking at the door announced his arrival; when Garrick, who had always a proper presentiment of danger about him, jumped out of bed, and gathering up his clothes as well as he could, hurried up to Macklin's apartments for security.

Macklin was just out of his first sleep when he was roused by his friend, who told him the particular cause of disturbing him, and requested the use of a bed for the remainder of the night. But what was Garrick's surprise, when, on reviewing the articles of his dress which he brought up with him, 'in the alarm of fear,' he found he had left his scratch wig below in Miss Woffington's bed-chamber! Macklin did all he could to comfort him—the other lay upon tenter-hooks of anxiety the whole night.

But to return to his Lordship: he had scarcely entered the apartment, when finding something entangle his feet in the dark, he called for a light, and the first object he saw was this unfortunate scratch! which taking up in his hand, he exclaimed with an oath, 'Oh! Madam, have I found you out at last? So here has been a lover in the case!' and then fell to upbraiding her in all the language of rage, jealousy, and disappointment. The lady heard him with great composure for some time, and then, without offering the least excuse, 'begged of him not to make himself so great a fool, but give her her wig back again.' 'What! Madam, do you glory in your infidelity? Do you own the wig then?'—'Yes to be sure I do,' said she: 'I'm sure it was my money paid for it, and I hope it will repay me with money and reputation too.' This called for a farther explanation. At last she very coolly said, 'Why, my Lord, if you will thus desert your character as a man, and be prying into all the little peculiarities of my domestic and professional business, know that I am soon to play a breeches part,* and that wig, which you so triumphantly hold in your hand, is the very individual wig I was practicing in a little before I went to bed: and so, because my maid was careless enough to leave it in your Lordship's way—here I am to be plagued and scolded at such a rate, as if I was a common prostitute.'

This speech had all the desired effect: his Lordship fell upon his knees, begged a thousand pardons, and the night was passed in harmony and good humour.

* *A breeches role is one where an actress plays a man's part or a part that requires her to dress as a man.*

SOURCE

Thomas Davies, *Memoirs of David Garrick*, ed. Stephen Jones (2 vols, 1808)

31

This agreeable actress (Peg Woffington) in the part of *Sir Harry* coming into the Green room said pleasantly, In my conscience, I believe half the men in the house take me for one of their own sex. Another actress reply'd, It may be so, but in my conscience, the other half can convince them to the contrary.

SOURCE
W. R. Chetwood, *A General History of the Stage* (1749)

JOHN MOODY
(1727–1812)

32

John Moody was born in Cork in Ireland, the son of a hairdresser named Cochran. When he took to the stage, he changed his name to 'Moody' in the hope of being taken for an Englishman—as a consequence of which he became known as 'Irish Moody'. He appeared in London at Drury Lane, in theatres throughout the British Isles, and at Kingston in Jamaica where his roles included Hamlet, Romeo, and King Lear. He created the role of Lord Burghley in Sheridan's play The Critic, *in 1779.*

Among the traits of stupidity put to the account of actors, by which droll unrehearsed effects have been produced on the stage, there is none that is supposed to convey greater proof of stupidity than that which distinguished the actor who originally represented Lord Burghley in *The Critic*. The names of several players are mentioned, each as being the hero of this story; but the original Lord Burghley, or Burleigh was Irish Moody, far too acute an actor to be suspected for a fool. When Sheridan selected him for the part, the manager declared that Moody would be sure to commit some ridiculous error, and ruin the effect. The author protested that such a result was impossible; and according to the fashion of the times, a wager was laid, and Sheridan hurried to the performer of the part to give him such instructions as should render any mistake beyond possibility.

Lord Burghley has nothing to say, merely to sit awhile; and then, as the stage directions informed him, and as Sheridan impressed it on his mind, 'Lord Burghley comes forward, pauses near Dangle, shakes his head, and exit.' The actor thoroughly understood the direction, he said, and could not err. At night he *came* forward, *did* pass near Dangle, shook his—Dangle's—head, and went solemnly off.

SOURCE

Cornhill Magazine (1867), quoted in W. Clark Russell, *Representative Actors* (1888)

GEORGE ANNE BELLAMY
(1727–1788)

33

George Anne Bellamy (so christened because of the clergyman's impaired hearing of the proposed name Georgiana) was the illegitimate daughter of an Irish peer who came to London and scored a particular success playing in Romeo and Juliet *opposite David Garrick. Plays were then performed in contemporary dress, as this anecdote—involving the Irish actors Spranger Barry and Thomas Sheridan and her rival Fanny Furnival—illustrates.*

Early in the [Dublin] season, the tragedy of 'All for Love, or the World well Lost,' was revived; in which Barry and Sheridan stood unrivalled in the characters of Antony and Ventidius. The getting it up produced the following extraordinary incidents. The manager, in an excursion he had made during the summer to London, had purchased a superb suit of cloaths that had belonged to the Princess of Wales, and had been only worn by her on her birth-day. This was made into a dress for me to play the character of Cleopatra; and as the ground of it was silver tissue, my mother thought that by turning the body of it in, it would be a no unbecoming addition to my waist, which was remarkably small. My maid-servant was accordingly sent to the theatre to assist the dresser and mantua-maker in preparing it; and also in sewing on a number of diamonds; my Patroness [Mrs Butler] not only having furnished me with her own, but borrowed several others of her acquaintance for me. When the women had finished the work, they all went out of the room, and left the door of it indiscreetly open.

Mrs Furnival, who owed me a grudge, on account of my eclipsing her, as the more favourable reception I met with from the public... accidentally passed by the door of my dressing-room in the way to her own, as it stood open. Seeing my rich dress thus lying exposed, and observing no person by to prevent her, she stepped in, and carried off the Queen of Egypt's paraphernalia, to adorn herself in the character of Octavia, the Roman matron, which she was to perform. By remarking from time to time my dress, which was very different from the generality of heroines, Mrs Furnival had just acquired taste enough to despise the black velvet in which those ladies were usually habited. And without considering the impropriety of enrobing a Roman matron in the habiliments of the Egyptian queen; or perhaps not knowing that there was any impropriety in it, she determined, for once in her lifetime, to be as fine as myself, and that at my expense. She accordingly set to work to let out the cloaths, which, through my mother's economical advice, had been taken in.

When my servant returned to the room, and found the valuable dress, that had been committed to her charge, missing, her fright and agitation were beyond expression. She ran like a mad creature about the theatre, enquiring of everyone whether they had seen any thing of it. At length she was informed that Mrs Furnival had got possession of it. When running to that lady's dressing-room, she was nearly petrified at beholding the work, which had cost her so much pains, undone. My damsel's veins, unfortunately for

Mrs Furnival, were rich with the blood of the O'Bryens. And though she had not been blest with so polished an education as such a name was entitled to, she inherited at least the *Spirit* of the Kings of Ulster. Thus qualified for carrying on an attack even of a more important nature, she at first demanded the dress with tolerable civility; but meeting with a peremptory refusal, the blood of her great fore-fathers boiled within her veins, and without any more ado, she fell tooth and nail upon poor Mrs Furnival. So violent was the assault, that had not assistance arrived in time to rescue her from the fangs of the enraged Hibernian nymph, my theatrical rival would probably have never had an opportunity of appearing once in her life adorned with *real* jewels.

When I came to the theatre, I found my servant dissolved in tears at the sad disaster; for notwithstanding her heroic exertions, she had not been able to bring off the cause of the contest. But so far was I from partaking of her grief, that I could not help being highly diverted at the absurdity of the incident. Nothing concerning a theatre could at that time affect my temper. And I acknowledge I enjoyed a secret pleasure in the expectation of what the result would be. I sent indeed for the jewels; but the lady, rendered courageous by Nantz, and the presence of her paramour, Morgan, who was not yet dead, she condescended to send me word, that I should have them after the play.

In this situation I had no other resource than to reverse the dresses, and appear as plain in the character of the luxurious Queen of Egypt, as Antony's good wife, although the sister of Caesar, ought to have been. In the room of precious stones, with which my head should have been decorated, I substituted pearls; and of all my finery I retained only my diadem, that indispensible mark of royalty.

Every transaction that takes place in the theatre, and every circumstance relative to it, are as well known in Dublin as they would be in a country town. The report of the richness and elegance of my dress had been universally the subject of conversation, for some time before the night of performance; when, to the surprize of the audience, I appeared in white satin. My kind patroness, who sat in the stage-box, seemed not to be able to account for such an unexpected circumstance. And not seeing me adorned with the jewels she had lent me, she naturally supposed I had reserved my regalia till the scene in which I was to meet my Antony.

When I had first entered the green-room, the manager, who expected to see me splendidly dressed, as it was natural to suppose the inchanting Cleopatra would have been upon such an occasion, expressed with some warmth his surprise at a disappointment, which he could only impute to caprice. Without being in the least discomposed by his warmth, I coolly told him, 'that I had taken the advice Ventidius had sent me by Alexis, and had parted with both my cloaths and jewels to Antony's wife.' Mr Sheridan could not conceive my meaning; but as it was now too late to make any alteration, he said no more upon the subject. He was not however long at a loss for an explanation; for going to introduce Octavia to the Emperor, he discovered the jay in all her borrowed plumes. An apparition could not have more astonished him. He was so confounded, that it was some time before he could go on with his part. At the same instant Mrs Butler exclaimed aloud, 'Good Heaven, the woman has got on my diamonds!' The gentlemen in the pit concluded that Mrs Butler had been robbed of them by Mrs Furnival; and the general consternation, occasioned by so extraordinary a scene, is not to be described. But the house observing Mr Sheridan to smile, they supposed there was some mystery in the affair, which induced them to wait with patience till the conclusion of the act. As soon as it was finished, they bestowed their applause upon Antony and his faithful veteran; but as if they had all been animated by the same mind, they cried out, 'No more Furnival! No more Furnival!' The fine dressed lady, disappointed of the acclamations she expected to receive on account of the grandeur of her habiliments, and thus hooted for the impropriety of her conduct, very prudently called fits to her aid, which incapacitated her from appearing again.

SOURCE
George Anne Bellamy, *An Apology for the Life of George Anne Bellamy* (1785)

34

Mrs Bellamy played Alicia in 'Jane Shore' in presence of the King of Denmark (who was then on a visit to George III), who, wearied with very fast living, was in a sound sleep during one of her finest scenes. The angry lady had to exclaim, 'Oh, thou false lord!' and she drew near to the slumbering monarch, and shouted it close to his ears with such astounding effect that he started up, rubbed his eyes, became conscious of what was going on, and how it had come about, and remarked that he would not have such a woman for his wife though she had no end of kingdoms for a dowry.

SOURCE
Cornhill Magazine (1863), quoted in W. Clark Russell, *Representative Actors* (1888)

HENRY MOSSOP
(?1729–?1774)

35

An Irish actor who enjoyed initial success alongside Garrick at Drury Lane until jealousy of Garrick proved his undoing. At the time of these anecdotes Mossop was in charge of the Smock Alley Theatre in Dublin.

I was one night witness to an untoward circumstance at Smock-alley Theatre. Congreve's 'Mourning Bride' was the tragedy; Mossop was Osmin, and a subordinate actor, Selim: Selim being stabbed by Osmin, should have remained dead on the stage, but seized with a fit of coughing, he unluckily put up his hand and loosened his stock, which set the audience in a burst of laughter. The scene over, the enraged manager and actor railed at his underling for daring to appear alive when he was dead, who, in excuse, said he must have choked had he not done as he did: Mossop replied, 'Sir, you should choke a thousand times, rather than spoil my scene.'

At a period when the payments were not very ready at the Smock-alley treasury, one night Mossop, in Lear, was supported in the arms of an actor who played Kent, and who whispered him, 'If you don't give me your honour, Sir, that you'll pay me my arrears this night, before I go home, I'll let you drop about the boards.' Mossop alarmed, said 'Don't talk to me now.' 'I will,' said Kent, 'I will; I'll let you drop.' Mossop was obliged to give the promise, and the actor thus got his money, though a few of the others went home without theirs.

SOURCE
John O'Keefe, *Recollections of the Life of John O'Keefe* (1826)

JAMES WILLIAM DODD
(*c.*1734–1796)

36

A London-born actor and member of David Garrick's company, Dodd won wide acclaim for his portrayal of characters such as Sir Andrew Aguecheek in Twelfth Night *and as the original Sir Benjamin Backbite in* The School for Scandal.

There was a gossiping anecdote told of Dodd, for the truth of which I will not be answerable. He sojourned in lodgings near the theatre with a *chère amie* belonging to the company. This perhaps he might have found to be a snug arrangement in the summer months, if the tranquillity of the *téte-à-téte* had not been daily disturbed by discussing frivolous points, upon which the fond pair very furiously differed; insomuch that the gentleman was wont to enforce his arguments more by missiles than by metaphors; in short, he threw chairs, tables, and chimney-piece crockery all about the room. In the heat of one of these domestic fracas, which happened at an early dinner upon a shoulder of mutton, while Dodd clattered, and the *chère amie* screamed, the landlord rushed upon the scene of action in hopes, if he could not prevent a further breach of the peace, to hinder their breaking more of his property. 'How dare you, mister,' ejaculated Dodd, who was brandishing the shoulder of mutton in his hand, 'obtrude into our apartments while we are *rehearsing*?'—'Rehearsing!' cried the enraged landlord, while the broken bits of sham china were crunching under his feet, 'I could have sworn you were fighting.'—'No, sir,' said Dodd; 'we were rehearsing the supper scene in "Catherine and Petruchio, or the *Taming of a Shrew*." '—'Why, it does look,' observed his landlord, giving a glance round the room, 'as if you had been trying to tame a shrew, sure enough.' 'Don't you know, fellow,' asked Dodd, sternly, 'that we are advertised to act the parts this very night?'—'Not I, truly,' returned the host—'Then go downstairs, sir,' cried the comedian, 'and read the bill of the play; and read it every morning, sir, to prevent your repeating this impertinence.' History records not whether the landlord read the playhouse bill; but it sets forth that he did not forget *his own*.

SOURCE
W. Clark Russell, *Representative Actors* (1888)

THOMAS WESTON
(1737–1776)

37

Comedy rather than tragedy was Weston's forte: by several accounts, his performance as Abel Drugger was as good as his Richard III was bad.

You should have seen Weston. It was impossible, from looking at him, for any one to say that he was acting. You would suppose they had gone out and found the actual character they wanted, and brought him upon the stage without his knowing it. Even when they interrupted him with peals of laughter and applause, he looked about him as if he was not at all conscious of having anything to do with it, and then went on as before. In Scrub, Dr Last, and other parts of that kind, he was perfection itself. Garrick would never attempt Abel Drugger after him. There was something peculiar in his face; for I knew an old schoolfellow of his who told me he used to produce the same effect when a boy, and when the master asked what was the matter, his companion would make answer, 'Weston looked at me, sir!'

SOURCE
William Hazlitt, *The Round Table: Northcote's Conversations, Characteristics, and Miscellania*, ed. W. Carew Hazlitt (1903)

38

In *The Rival Candidates* [by Sir Henry Bate Dudley, 1775], this year he spoke the epilogue in the company of a big dog, nearly as high as his waist, which he led by the ring in its collar. It is a most engaging beast and stares up into its droll companion's face, while he is speaking, with an almost human expression; the latter stroked him with so much condescension that it is obvious to all that they are kindred spirits. On the second occasion on which I saw the play

Weston, for the first time, wearied of speaking this epilogue and refused to appear; the audience took this in very bad part, and 'Epilogue! Epilogue!' resounded from all the throats which had done their best to wake Richard the Third from the dead; but still Weston did not appear. Several persons left the boxes, but I had made up my mind to await the outcome of the matter. Suddenly there came a shower, first of pears, then oranges, and next quart bottles, on to the stage, one of them, containing, I should think, three quarts, striking one of the glass chandeliers; and it looked like turning into a riot, when Weston came on the stage with Dragon (that is the dog's name) as calmly as though he were always called for like this. There was a little hissing here and there, but this soon died down. Now there is a passage in the epilogue, in which, I believe, he is speaking of the critics, where he addresses the dog thus: 'But why do you put your tail between your legs, Dragon, they will not hurt you?' On the spur of the moment, without detriment either to rhyme or couplet, Weston altered the passage into: 'And why do you put your tail between your legs, you tom-fool? They won't throw any bottles at your head.' The situation was saved at a very critical juncture by this excessively witty alteration, so aptly expressed in rhyme. There was no end to the clapping and shouting. But Weston did not move a muscle, his face being as expressionless as a brick, not the least trace of pleasure or complacency, no more than on the face of his four-footed friend.

SOURCE
Lichtenberg's Visits to England as Described in His Letters and Diaries, trans. Margaret L. Mare and W. H. Quarrell (1938)

WILLIAM BENSLEY
(1738–1817)

39

'He had the fine poetical enthusiasm', declared Charles Lamb, 'the rarest faculty among players.' It was put to the test in the following incident.

He had to play Henry VI in 'Richard the Third.' After the monarch's death in the early part of the play, he had to appear for a moment or two as his own ghost, in the fifth act. The spirits were at that time exhibited *en buste* by a trap. Now our Henry was invited out to supper, and being anxious to get there early, and knowing that little more than his shoulders would be seen by the public, he retained his black velvet vest and bugles, but discarding the lower part of his stage costume, he drew on a jaunty pair of new, tight, nankeen pantaloons, to be as far dressed for his supper company as he could. When he stood on the trap, he cautioned the men who turned the crank not to raise him as high as usual, and of course they promised to obey. But a wicked low comedian was at hand, whose love of mischief prevailed over his judgment, and he suddenly applied himself with such goodwill to the winch, that he ran King Henry up right to a level with the stage; and moreover, gave his majesty such a jerk that he was forced to step from the trap onto the boards to save himself from falling. The sight of the old Lancastrian monarch in a costume of two such different periods—mediaeval above, all nankeen and novelty below—was destructive of all decorum both before the stage and upon it. The audience emphatically 'split their sides,' and as for the tyrant in the tent, he sat bolt upright, and burst into such an insane roar that the real Richard could not have looked more frantically hysterical had the deceased Henry actually visited him in the spirit.

SOURCE
Dr Doran, *Table Traits*, quoted in W. Clark Russell, *Representative Actors* (1888)

TATE WILKINSON
(1739–1803)

40

This anecdote, from an early biography of David Garrick, serves as an introduction to the young Tate Wilkinson, who later became a successful actor and theatre manager and published his own volume of memoirs.

One morning a letter was brought in at Southampton Street, introducing a young man who wished to go on the stage. Garrick received him kindly, listened to his declamation, which was poor enough, and comforted the aspirant by telling him that his shyness was a very good sign of success. This young fellow had hung about the green-room in Covent Garden, and for all his shyness was a pert, forward, impudent *gamin,* whose precocious talents of mimicry had been overpraised by friends. He offered to 'take off' some of the well-known actors, to show the manager his gifts. 'Nay, now,' said Garrick, in his peculiar mixture of hesitation and repetition, which made his 'talk' a favourite subject of imitation. 'Nay, now, sir, you must take care of this; for I used to call myself the first at this business.' But the young fellow knew the manager's weak place. He began, leading off with Foote. The likeness amused the manager immensely, and the performance was repeated. 'Hey, now! now—what—all,' went on Mr Garrick. 'How—really this—this—is—why, well, well, well, do call on me on Monday, and you may depend on my doing all I can for you.' This broken style of speech was Mr Garrick's characteristic when addressing his inferiors, and was, in fact, his *managerial* manner, and may have been found very useful in helping him to any positive declaration. It was not a bad auxiliary for one who was asked for so much, and had to refuse so much.

On the Monday the youth came again, and was welcomed warmly. He was told that inquiries had been made about his widowed mother, and that he was to be put on the books at thirty shillings a week—a fortune indeed. The youth's name was Tate Wilkinson, who has left behind a very curious history of himself and other players, which is a mass of truth, blunders, and falsehoods—a mass, too, of meanness, vanity, and egotism.

SOURCE
Percy Fitzgerald, *Life of David Garrick*, rev. edn (1899)

MR AND MRS MATTOCKS
(d.1804 and 1746–1826, respectively)

41

He was a theatrical manager; she was more famous as an actress, formerly Isabella Hallam.

Mattocks was manager of the Portsmouth Theatre at this time—his company consisted of Mrs Mattocks, Mrs Kennedy, Whitfield, Booth, Wheeler, Perry, Dutton, Townshend, &c., the latter I remember a student at Dublin College. Mrs Mattocks, agreeable to what was due to her professional talents (which were of the first order), imagined that her name being up, must fill the house each time she played.—One night, on which the opera of the 'Maid of the Mill' was to be acted, she walked from her dressing-room and looked through the curtain, and on seeing a half-empty house, returned, sat down, and sent for Mattocks;—he came, she told him to dismiss the house for that she certainly would not play:—he, with his usual politeness, and calm good-humour, seemed to acquiesce, and to approve of her spirited determination, at the same time expressing himself rather angry at the want of taste in the public, thus exceeding her in his remarks upon such neglect.

This matrimonial colloquy took up about twenty minutes.—'Make yourself easy, my dear,' he said, 'for I'll go this instant, and dismiss the house.'—He left her, and walking leisurely towards the front of the stage, gave the Prompter the private order to ring the band into the orchestra, and begin the Overture. He was obeyed; he then ordered the curtain to ring up,—and up it went. Mrs Mattocks, by this time, having heard musicals which she did not expect, ventured to quit her dressing-room, and go towards the stage, where, to her astonishment and vexation, she heard the full chorus of,

'Free from sorrow, free from strife,
Oh! How blest the miller's life!'—&c.

Angry with Mattocks, she reproached him for the deception he had put upon her, when he with mildness said, 'Come with me down to the wing, and throw your eye round the house, then try what you can say on this occasion.'—She complied, looked out, and saw the theatre, boxes, pit, and gallery, all full;—before the conclusion of the first scene, it was an overflow. The fact was, it happened to be a very fine evening—the King had been on the water, and on the ramparts, and all the people out on their walks and rambles, boating and sailing, every one eager to have even a distant sight of his Majesty.—Mrs Mattocks was, perhaps, right, but the manager, who well knew the danger of what is called 'dismissing a house,' was aware of this; and, in reality, it is wiser for actors, if there is only as much in the theatre as will pay for the lights, never to dismiss an audience; it throws a damp upon the public spirit and feelings, and many persons, after such a circumstance, will keep from a theatre, always doubting whether the night they fix on to go to the play, there will be any play at all.

Mrs Mattocks recovered her good-humour, and performed the charming Patty with all her usual delightful and delighting powers.

SOURCE
John O'Keefe, *Recollections of the Life of John O'Keefe* (1826)

SARAH SIDDONS
(1755–1831)

42

According to the critic William Hazlitt (1778–1830), 'She was Tragedy personified. She was the stateliest ornament of the public mind. She was not only the idol of the people, she not only hushed the tumultuous shouts of the pit in breathless expectation, and quenched the blaze of surrounding beauty in silent tears but to the retired and lonely student, through long years of solitude, her face has shone as if an eye had appeared from Heaven.' Fanny Burney (1752–1840) noted in her diary: 'I found her the Heroine of a Tragedy—sublime, elevated and solemn. In face and person truly noble, and commanding in manners quiet and stiff; in voice, deep and dragging; and in conversation, formal, sententious, calm and dry.' Sarah Siddons came from a theatrical family—she was the sister of John, Charles, and Stephen Kemble—and, without question, the leading tragic actress of the late eighteenth century.

How much more pleasantly people tell their history in social converse than in formal writing. I remember Mrs Siddons describing to me the same scene of her probation on the Edinburgh boards with no small humour. The grave attention of my Scottish countrymen, and their canny reservation of praise till they were sure she deserved it, she said, had well-nigh worn out her patience. She had been used to speak to animated clay; but she now felt as if she had been speaking to stones. Successive flashes of her elocution, that had always been sure to electrify the South, fell in vain on those Northern flints. At last, as I well remember, she told me she coiled up her powers to the most emphatic possible utterance of one passage, having previously vowed in her heart, that if this could not touch the Scotch, she would never again cross the Tweed. When it was finished, she paused, and looked to the audience. The deep silence was broken only by a single voice exclaiming, *'That's no bad!'* This ludicrous parsimony of praise convulsed the Edinburgh audience with laughter. But the laugh was followed by such thunders of applause, that, amidst her stunned and nervous agitation, she was not without fears of the galleries coming down.

SOURCE
Thomas Campbell, *Life of Mrs Siddons* (1834)

43

I was at Edinburgh one year when she was electrifying the Northern metropolis with many characters, and with none more than this. One of her fellow-performers, Mr Russell, told me an instance of her power in the part. A poor fellow who played the Surveyor, in 'Henry VIII,' was met by Mr Russell coming off the stage, having just received the Queen Katherine's (Siddons's) rebuke, *'You were the Duke's surveyor, and lost your office on the complaint o' the tenants.'* The mimetic unjust steward was perspiring with agitation. 'What is the matter with you?' said Mr Russell. 'The matter!' quoth the other, 'that woman plays as if the thing were in earnest. She looked on me so through and through with her black eyes, that I would not for the world meet her on the stage again.'

SOURCE
Thomas Campbell, *Life of Mrs Siddons* (1834)

44

She took her professional farewell of the stage on the 29th of June, 1812. The play was 'Macbeth.' At an early hour a vast crowd assembled around the theatre of Covent Garden, and, when the doors were opened, the struggle for places became a service of danger. After the sleep-walking scene, in the tragedy, the applause of the spectators became ungovernable: they stood on the benches, and demanded that the performance of the piece should not go further than the last scene in which she appeared. As this wish seemed to be felt by the great majority, the actor Chapman came forward, and signified that it should be complied with.

SOURCE
Thomas Campbell, *Life of Mrs Siddons* (1834)

45

From intense devotion to her profession she derived a peculiarity of manner, of which I have the fullest belief she was not in the least conscious, unless reminded of it;—I mean the habit of attaching dramatic tones and emphasis to common-place colloquial subjects. She went, for instance, one day, into a shop at Bath, and, after bargaining for some calico, and hearing the mercer pour forth an hundred commendations of the cloth, she put the question to him, '*But will it wash?*' in a manner so electrifying as to make the poor shopman start back from his counter. I once told her this anecdote about herself, and she laughed at it heartily, saying, 'Witness truth, I never meant to be tragical.'

SOURCE
Thomas Campbell, *Life of Mrs Siddons* (1834)

46

One night, when Mrs Siddons had occasion to drain 'the poisoned cup,' a ruffian bawled out, to the overthrow of all order in the rest of the house, 'That's right, Molly; soop it up, ma lass.' Once during her engagement, the evening being hot, Mrs Siddons was tempted by a torturing thirst to avail herself of the only relief to be obtained at the moment. Her dresser, therefore, dispatched a boy in great haste to 'fetch a pint of beer for Mrs. Siddons.' Meanwhile the play proceeded, and on the boy's return with the frothed pitcher, he looked about for the person who had sent him on his errand, and not seeing her, inquired, 'Where is Mrs. Siddons?' The scene-shifter whom he questioned, pointing his finger to the stage, where she was performing the sleeping-scene of *Lady Macbeth*, replied, 'There she is.' To the horror of the performers, the boy promptly walked on to the stage close up to Mrs Siddons, and with a total unconsciousness of any impropriety, presented the porter! Her distress may be imagined; she waved the boy away in her grand manner several times without effect. At last the people behind the scenes, by dint of beckoning, stamping, &c., succeeded in getting him off with the beer, while the audience were in an uproar of laughter, which the dignity of the actress was unable to quell for several minutes.

SOURCE
Life of Mathews, quoted in W. Clark Russell, *Representative Actors* (1888)

47

From the moment she assumed the dress she became the character, she never chatted or coquetted by the green-room fire but placed herself where no word of the play could escape her, or the illusion for a moment be destroyed.

SOURCE
William Robson, *The Old Playgoer* (1846)

GEORGE FREDERICK COOKE
(*c*.1756–1812)

48

One of London's leading players, Cooke was persuaded to become one of the first English actors to tour America, where his early performances won him widespread acclaim. Soon, however, his 'old complaint' began to get the upper hand and the bottle, which had dogged much of his career in England, hastened his end. William Dunlap, his biographer, reports his attendance at a dinner where he was 'full of wine, life and whim, the very spirit of the party surrounding him'.

Among the guests was a young and distinguished actor, who, enlivened by surrounding circumstances, descanted rather fully upon his own talents. Cooke led him on, praised him, made him praise himself, until having worked him up to the point he wished, he asked him who had been his model?

'Mr—, Sir; I have studied him in Hamlet, Sir, and in Benedict—but his Romeo—did you see my Romeo—there was—himself: when he says, turning to Juliet, which brings his back to the audience,

'There is more peril in thine eye—'

then whirling round and making a lunge at the audience,

'—than twenty
'Of *their* swords—.'

'—there, Sir, is a fine instance of suiting the action—ha, Sir?'

'I see you have studied your profession attentively, and taken lessons from great actors; you have everything from nature that can be wished; you have person, manner, voice—every requisite to make a great actor; and you have acquired great knowledge of the profession, very great indeed, Sir, and now I would advise one thing.'

'What is that, Sir.'

'Forget all you have learned as quick as possible.'

SOURCE
Memoirs of George Frederick Cooke, Esq., ed. William Dunlap (1813)

JOHN PHILIP KEMBLE
(1757–1823)

49

Kemble was an actor-manager of distinction and the brother of the even more celebrated Sarah Kemble Siddons. His appearance was not striking and he was plagued by asthma, complaining how frequently he was 'drawing on his chest and finding the cheque dishonoured'. Many actors of his time were also gifted musically. Kemble was not one of them.

A translation of the popular French piece, 'Richard Coeur de Lion', was produced at Drury Lane Theatre on the twentieth of October [1786], with the original music by Grétry. Miss Romanzini (afterwards Mrs Bland) sang the pretty chanson, 'The Merry Dance', with great naiveté and effect. The character of Richard was acted by Mr John Kemble, who, though he had not a singing voice, got through the two-part song, on which the plot hinges, better than expected. At one of the rehearsals of the piece Kemble, who had got the tune of it tolerably well, being very deficient in keeping the time, Mr Shaw, the leader of the band, impatiently exclaimed, 'Mr. Kemble, that won't do at all!—you *murder* time abominably!'—'Well, Mr. Shaw,' replied Kemble, 'it is better to *murder* it, than to be continually *beating* it as you are.'

SOURCE
W. T. Parke, *Musical Memoirs* (1830)

50

Kemble turned his head so slowly that people might have imagined he had a stiff neck, while his words followed so slowly that he might have been reckoning how many words he had got by heart.

SOURCE
Leigh Hunt, *Critical Essays on Performers in the London Theatre* (1807)

JOSEPH MUNDEN
(1758–1832)

51

Munden was a successful comic actor who appeared in London at Covent Garden, the Haymarket Theatre, and Drury Lane. He was admired by the public, but not universally loved within the acting profession.

Munden had an unpleasant way of discouraging, if not extinguishing, the flame of ambition in the youthful dramatic author's breast. During a green-room reading of a comedy he would sit making hideous faces, and when the three or five acts were concluded, plaintively remark, 'My precious eyes, sir, but where's the comedy?'

Munden had a foolish way of boasting of his ignorance. 'I never read any book but a play,' said this son of a poulterer; 'no play but one in which I myself acted, and no portion of that play but my own scenes.' When this was told to Charles Lamb, he said, 'I knew Munden well, and I *believe* him.'

SOURCE
W. Clark Russell, *Representative Actors* (1888)

MRS DOROTHEA (DORA) JORDAN
(1761–1816)

52

Dora Jordan was an Anglo-Irish actress, noted for her artistry, her beauty (her legs were reckoned the loveliest ever seen on an actress), and the fact that she was, for twenty years while he was Duke of Clarence, the mistress of the future King William IV. Together they had ten children, all of whom took the surname FitzClarence, and were, of course, the first cousins of Queen Victoria who loved the theatre and asked her prime minister, Lord Melbourne, about Mrs Jordan.

Lord M talked of Mrs Jordan; I thought he couldn't remember her, but he said he did perfectly, and remembers going to see her act in '13 with Madame de Stael, who was delighted with her, she had a beautiful voice, and sang all those songs without music delightfully' exceedingly lively, and seemed always in the highest spirits on the stage; Lord M continued, that her real forte was in such characters as a 'Chamber Maid', though she acted latterly Lady Teazle and even Juliet, but it was the same thing…Her singing 'used to produce an electrical effect'.

Lord M (also said) it was a very curious thing, her acquaintance with the late King, which he thinks began as early as '82, for that he was not very fond of the Theatre though he always used to be there when she acted; and Peak, the Treasurer of either Drury Lane or Covent Garden, told Lord M, that the King used to always come himself to receive her salary—which was paid regularly to him; Mrs Jordan was very good natured, Lord M said, and George IV liked her, and used to go and dine with them.

SOURCE

Journal of Queen Victoria, 28 December 1838, quoted by Claire Tomalin, *Mrs Jordan's Profession* (1994)

53

Little she is and yet not insignificant in her figure, which, although short, has a certain roundness and embonpoint which is very graceful. Her voice is harmony itself…and it has certain little breaks and undescribable (sic) tones which in simple archness have a wonderful effect, and I think (without exception even of Mrs Siddons) she has the most *distinct* delivery of any actor or actress I ever heard.

Her face I could not see, owing to the amazing bunch of hair she had pulled over her forehead, but they tell me it is expressive, but not very pretty; her figure is such as I have described, and uncommonly pretty in boy's clothes, which she goes into in the 3rd act. Her action is *odd*; I think there is something foreign in it, at least it is a little *outré*, which however was probably affected for the character—for nothing could suit it better.

SOURCE
Letter from Mary Tickell, October 1785, quoted by W. Fraser Rae, *Sheridan: A Biography* (1896)

54

In due course, the Duke of Clarence abandoned Mrs Jordan. In October 1811, when she was on tour playing Nell in The Devil to Pay, *he wrote to her proposing a meeting. She knew what lay in store and was much distressed.*

With that kindness that always marked her conduct, she would not withdraw her name from the bills, though such was her state, when she arrived at the theatre, from continual hysterics, that we may literally say, she was saturated in sorrow... In her scene with Jobson... Nell laughs immoderately, on which Jobson remarks, 'Why Nell, the conjurer has not only made you drunk, but he has made you laughing drunk.' When Mrs Jordan attempted to laugh, she burst into tears; and the actor, with great presence of mind, altered the text by saying, 'Nell, the conjurer has not only made thee drunk, he has made thee *crying* drunk,' and thus brought her through the scene. As soon as the play was over, she was put into a travelling chariot in her Nell's dress, and started to keep her appointment with her royal lover.

SOURCE
William Oxberry, *Dramatic Biography and Histrionic Anecdotes* (1835)

ROBERT ELLISTON
(1774–1831)

55

Like so many of the leading players in the eighteenth and nineteeth centuries, Robert Elliston was both a theatre manager and an actor.

He was a man whose pomposity and majesty in private life were absolutely amazing; but he was a great actor for all that and an intelligent manager. For example, King George IV was a most theatrical man in all he did, and when his coronation took place he dressed all his courtiers and everybody about him in peculiarly dramatic costumes—dresses of Queen Elizabeth's time. It was all slashed trunks and side cloaks, etc. Of course, the dukes, earls and barons were particularly disgusted at the way they had to exhibit themselves, and as soon as the coronation ceremonies were over these things were thrown aside and sold, and Elliston bought an enormous number of them. He was then the lessee of the Surrey Theatre, where he got up a great pageant and presented 'The Coronation of George IV.' He had a platform made in the middle of the pit, and in one scene he strutted down among the audience in the royal robes; at which, with some good-natured chaff, there was a tremendous round of applause. For the moment Elliston became so excited that he imagined he was really the King himself, and spreading out his arms he said, amid silence: 'Bless you, my people!'

SOURCE
Lester Wallack, *Memories of Fifty Years* (1889)

56

Poor Elliston at last was so overcome with the gout that he could not act at all. He was then lessee of Drury Lane and my father was his stage-manager, appearing in Elliston's old parts, Captain

THOMAS A. COOPER

(1776–1849)

59

One of the first English-born actors to become an American citizen, Thomas Cooper was an outstanding exponent of the new style of acting evolved by the Kembles and became the leading tragedian of the American stage. George Barrett was another English-born actor, eighteen years Cooper's junior.

In the company of the old Chestnut Street Theatre at this epoch was a young actor, Mr George Barrett, called generally 'Gentleman George.' He was a juvenile actor of great local repute in Philadelphia, and moved among all the young swells of that day. He was to play Laertes in 'Hamlet' with Cooper, who arrived from Baltimore too late for rehearsal; so George went to his dressing-room in order to ascertain the arrangement of the fencing match in the last scene. Mr Cooper was morose, and said, 'Go to the prompter, sir, and find out!' When the fencing began Barrett would not let Cooper disarm him, and the audience could see this fact and became excited. Finally, Barrett, with sword down, stood quietly to be run through by Cooper. When the curtain fell Cooper started up in a towering passion, and exclaimed to Barrett, 'What did you mean by your conduct, sir?' Drawing himself up to his full height, six feet two inches, Barrett replied, 'Go to the prompter, sir, and find out!'

SOURCE
Mrs John Drew, *Autobiographical Sketch* (1900)

JOSEPH GRIMALDI
(1778–1837)

60

Grimaldi was an English actor, comedian, and dancer, who became the most popular British entertainer of his day. The young Charles Dickens was one of his many admirers and, as 'Boz', edited (or possible entirely wrote) Grimaldi's posthumous memoirs, published in 1838. Starring in pantomimes at Drury Lane, Covent Garden, and Sadler's Wells, Grimaldi was the original 'Clown Joey' and his catchphrase, 'Here we are again!', still occasionally features in pantomimes today.

Aside from his comic talents and fine singing voice, Grimaldi was an innovator, widely acknowledged as the father of modern 'slap and motley.' It was Grimaldi who overhauled the Clown's appearance from the rustic booby that had remained more-or-less unaltered since the sixteenth century, to the heavily made-up and colourfully-attired clowns that we are familiar with today. The new make-up left not a centimetre of skin exposed—not even in the nostrils or inside of the lips—and, as such, it implied a much stricter division between the man and the mask, an impenetrability that acted as a kind of invitation to speculate about what they might have concealed. Was there, perhaps, a division in Grimaldi himself? Rumours to this effect arose during the initial success of *Mother Goose*: the King of Clowns, it was reported, was subject to debilitating bouts of offstage depression, reports he himself chose to confirm with a punning quip, 'I am GRIM ALL DAY, but I make you laugh at night.' A series of anecdotes followed that prefigured Dickens' biographical portrait in black-and-white, the most famous of which dates from the 1820s and involves a visit to the surgeon, John Abertheny. Grimaldi, hoping to find a cure for his depression, asks Abertheny for advice, and unaware of his client's identity, the surgeon prescribes the diversions of 'relaxation and amusement':

'But where shall I find what you require?' said the patient. 'In genial companionship,' was the reply; 'perhaps sometimes at the theatre;—go and see Grimaldi.' 'Alas!' replied the patient, 'that is of no avail to me; I am Grimaldi.'

SOURCE
Andrew McConnell Stott, *The Public Domain Review* (2011)

RICHARD JONES
(1778–1851)

61

The elegance and finery of William Lewis, actor-manager of Covent Garden Theatre from 1773 to 1809, led to him being nicknamed 'Gentleman' Lewis. He encouraged younger light comedians, like Jones, to emulate his style.

In 1809 Richard Jones made his *début* at Covent Garden, in Macklin's comedy of *Love à la Mode,* as Squire Groom. Lewis attended behind the scenes to witness his *protégé's* first attempt. When the cue was given for his entrance, Jones became transfixed with fear, and instead of giving the 'view halloo,' was struck dumb. Lewis perceiving the dilemma of the new actor, roared, 'Yoicks! yoicks!' The audience hearing those well-known sounds exclaimed, 'A second Lewis!' Slapping Jones on the back, Lewis told him to go in and win. Jones, lacking courage, dashed on the stage amid the most deafening plaudits; and as he paced about in his jockey-dress—thus showing off his slim, tall, and well-formed person—minutes absolutely elapsed before he could utter a word for the applause. His success was most complete, and Jones remained in London as the true successor of Lewis as long as the legitimate drama had a home.

SOURCE
Recollections of an Actor, quoted in W. Clark Russell, *Representative Actors* (1888)

FANNY ALSOP
(1782–1821)

62

Frances 'Fanny' Alsop was the daughter of Dora Jordan by Richard Daly, the manager of the Smock Alley Theatre of Dublin. The critic William Hazlitt went to see her Rosalind in As You Like It *in October 1814.*

A lady of the name of Alsop, a daughter of Mrs Jordan (by a former husband), has appeared at Covent Garden theatre, in the character of Rosalind. Not only the circumstances of her relationship to that excellent actress, but the accounts in the papers raised our curiosity and expectations very high. We were unwillingly disappointed. The truth is, Mrs Alsop is a very nice little woman, who acts her part very sensibly and cleverly, and with a certain degree of arch humour, but no more like her mother, 'than I to Hercules'. When we say this, we mean no disparagement to this lady's talents, who is a real acquisition to the stage in correct and chaste acting,—but simply to prevent comparisons, which can end only in disappointment. Mrs Alsop would make a better Celia than Rosalind.—Mrs Jordan's excellencies were all natural to her; it was not as an actress, but as herself, that she charmed everyone. Nature had formed her in the most prodigal humour, and when nature is in the humour to make a woman all that is delightful, she does it most effectually.

chief, by the name of Alantenaida, as the highly finished card left at my house had it. I repaired to the hotel, and was conducted up stairs to the folding-doors of the hall, when the servants left me. I entered, aided by the feeble light of the room; but at the remote end I soon perceived something like a forest of evergreens, lighted up by many rays from floor-lamps, and surrounding a stage or throne; and seated in great state was the chief. I advanced, and a more terrific warrior I never surveyed. Red Jacket or Black Hawk was an unadorned, simple personage in comparison. Full dressed, with skins tagged loosely about his person, a broad collar of bear-skin over his shoulders, his leggings, with many stripes, garnished with porcupine quills; his moccasins decorated with beads; his head decked with the war-eagle's plumes, behind which flowed massive black locks of dishevelled horse-hair; golden-colored rings pendant from the nose and ears; streaks of yellow paint over the face, massive red daubing about the eyes, with various hues in streaks across the forehead, not very artistically drawn. A broad belt surrounded his waist, with tomahawk; his arms, with shining bracelets, stretched out with bow and arrow, as if ready for a mark. He descended his throne and rapidly approached me. His eye was meteoric and fearful, like the furnace of the cyclops. He vociferously exclaimed, Alantenaida! the vowels strong enough. I was relieved; he betrayed something of his raucous voice in imprecation. It was Kean. An explanation took place. He wished to know the merits of the representation. The Hurons had honored him by admission into their tribe, and he could not now determine whether to seek his final earthly abode with them for real happiness, or return to London, and add renown to his name by performing the Son of the Forest. I never heard that he ever afterwards attempted, in his own country, the character. He was wrought up to the highest pitch of enthusiasm at the Indian honor he had received, and declared that even Old Drury had never conferred so proud a distinction on him as he had received from the Hurons. My visit was of some time. After pacing the room, with Indian step, for an hour or more, and contemplating himself before a large mirror, he was prevailed upon to change his dress and retire to rest. A day or two after, he sailed for Europe, with his Indian paraphernalia.

The professional receipts of Kean during his engagement in New York, were, I believe, at least equal to those for a like number of nights which he received at the acme of his renown in London. His average income for some twelve or fifteen years was not less than ten thousand pounds per annum. He rescued Old Drury from bankruptcy, yet he is said to have been often in need, and died almost penniless. There was no one special extravagance chargeable to him; but he was reckless in money matters, and figures entered not into his calculations. He had a helping hand for all applications, and he never forgot his early friends.

SOURCE
John W. Francis, *Old New York* (1858)

69

Craven's Head Tavern, Drury-lane, William Oxberry, a Drury Lane comedian, was the host. Edmund Kean loved a social glass, and never forgot old companions of his former wanderings. Star now of the dramatic hemisphere, he still indulged in his former habits. Oxberry held a musical club at this tavern weekly, at which Edmund Kean presided. A club-night happened to fall upon a 'Richard the Third' night at Drury. 'What's to be done?' thought Oxberry; 'the chair will be vacant.' Visitors were wont to crowd the Craven's Head to look at the town's wonder, Kean—a thing to remember and talk about—especially for those who were privileged to hear him sing. 'The Jolly Dogs' (our clubbites' name) became as difficult to enter as the 'Carlton' or 'United Service' of our day.

of public admiration the invasion ceased to be spoken of. He acted two nights at Leicester, and on a half-holiday, my cousin Birch having sent a note to excuse me and his eldest son from the afternoon's callings-over at my father's request, Tom Birch and myself were smuggled into a chaise, and reached Leicester in time for the play—'Richard III'. The house was crowded. John Kemble and H. Harris, son of the Patentee of Covent Garden, sat in the stage box immediately behind us. I remember John Kemble's handkerchief strongly scented of lavender, and his observation, in a very compassionate tone, 'Poor boy! He is very hoarse.' I could form little judgment of the performance, which excited universal enthusiasm, and in the tempest of which we were of course borne along. In subsequent engagements with my father we became playfellows, and off the stage W. H. West Betty was a boy with boys, as full of spirits, fun, and mischief as any of his companions, though caressed, fondled, and idolized by peeresses, and actually besieged for a mere glimpse of him by crowds at his hotel door. An instance of the 'madness that ruled the hour' was given at Dunchurch, where he stopped to dine and sleep, being prevented from acting at Coventry in Passion Week by Cornwallis, Bishop of Lichfield and Coventry. One of the leading families in the country, who were on their way to Coventry to see him were stopped by the news at Dunchurch. The lady begged and entreated the landlord to get her a sight of 'the young Roscius.' She would 'give anything.' The landlord unwilling to disoblige his patrons, suggested that there was but one way in which her wish could be gratified: 'Mr. and Mrs. Betty and their son were just going to dinner, and if she chose to carry in one of the dishes she could see him, but there was no other way.' The lady, very grateful in her acknowledgements, took the dish, and made one of the waiters at table. I mention this as one among the numerous anecdotes of his popularity. The

Prince of Wales made him handsome presents, and in short he engrossed all tongues.

SOURCE
Macready's Reminiscences, ed. Sir F. Pollock (1876)

WILLIAM CHARLES MACREADY
(1793–1873)

72

Macready was the chief rival of Kean in the early nineteenth century. A great tragedian, he was known for the lengthy pauses he developed for dramatic effect—known still, among older actors, as 'a Macready pause'. Although he had no great love for his profession, he did much for it, insisting on adequate rehearsals, for example, and restoring the texts of Shakespeare's plays, by then often corrupted. A somewhat earnest actor and manager, Macready nevertheless could see humour in the theatre, as his Journals *and* Reminiscences *show.*

My experience of country theatres never presented me with any scenes resembling the barn of Hogarth's Strolling Players, but it was not altogether without its whimsical expedients and ludicrous mishaps. On the first representation of the grand Ballet of Action of Macbeth I was most busily and anxiously engaged in looking after the working of the machinery, which was very complicated, and urging on the performers. In the scene after Duncan's murder there was scarcely three minutes' time for Macbeth and Lady Macbeth to wash the blood from their hands. Macbeth, poor Conway, on rushing from the stage in an agony of despair, exclaimed, 'Oh! My dear sir, my dresser is not here! What shall I do?' (the old man with water, soap, and towel was at the opposite side). There was not an instant for reflection. 'Here,' I cried, 'come here:' dragging him up to the gentlemen's first dressing-room, where he plunged his hands into a jug of water. 'There is no towel, my dear sir!' in continued agony he cried. I snatched up the first semblance of cloth that lay to hand, with which he dried his half-washed hands, and dashed back to the stage again. With the water and cloth in my hands I met at the foot of the stairs Lady Macbeth in equal perplexity, who hastily availing herself of the ready aid, rushed back to her place on the stage. The jug &c., I hastily deposited in my own room, and returned to watch the closing of the scene. The curtain fell that night with much applause on our barbarous violation of Shakespeare, and I went to my lodgings through a deep snow, insensible to the cold from the satisfaction I felt in the success of the evening. The next morning the acting manager met me with a very grave countenance, foretelling 'the nature of a tragic volume,' and opened his tale of woe with,—'Sir, I am very sorry to tell you, there are thieves in the theatre!' 'Good heavens!' I answered, 'is it possible? Let every inquiry be made, that they may be punished, or at least turned out of the place. What has been stolen?' 'Why, sir, Mr. Simkin's breeches! When he went to dress himself at the end of the evening, his breeches were gone, and he was obliged to walk home to his lodgings through the snow without any.' I desired the strictest search and inquiry to be made, and no pains spared to detect the offender. After a little time, however, a thought crossed me, and I asked the manager what kind of small clothes they were. When he told me they were brown kerseymere, it flashed across me that I had seized them for Conway's towel, and had thrown them under the table in my own room. The injury was repaired, but the story of Simkin's small clothes was for some time repeated as against my impetuosity.

SOURCE
Macready's Reminiscences, ed. Sir F. Pollock (1876)

73

Macready's support for James Sheridan Knowles led to the latter's Virginius *being staged at Covent Garden in 1820. Both of them triumphed, Macready confirming his reputation. Then the play toured the English provinces.*

One of the most ludicrous attempts to follow out the stage directions of the author at the least possible expense that I ever had the ill-luck to witness was at Kendal. The *corps dramatique* arrived in the town too late for the rehearsal of 'Virginius,' and I had to undergo during the two first acts a succession of annoyances in the scenic deficiencies and in the inaccuracies of the players. My unhappy temper was severely tried under the repeated mortifications I experienced, but in the third act of the play, where Siccius Dentatus should be discovered on a bier with a company of soldiers mourning over it, I saw the old man, who represented the Roman Achilles, lying on the ground, and two men standing near. This was too absurd! the body having to be borne off in sight of the audience. I positively refused to go on. 'Oh, pray, Sir,' urged the manager, 'go on: the men have rehearsed the scene, and you will find it all right.' In vain I represented that the men 'could not carry off the old man.' 'Oh, yes, indeed, Sir,' reiterated the manager, 'they perfectly understand it.' There was nothing for it but submission. After some delay the scene was drawn up, and disclosed the three as described. On I went and uttered my lamentation over the prostrate veteran, but when I gave the order 'Take up the body, bear it to the camp'—to my agony and horror the two men, stooping down, put each an arm under the shoulder of the dead Dentatus, raised him upon his feet, he preserving a corpse-like rigidity, his eyes closed, and his head thrown back, and arm-in-arm the trio marched off at the opposite side of the stage amid roars of laughter from the convulsed spectators.

SOURCE
Macready's Reminiscences, ed. Sir F. Pollock (1876)

74

William Robertson was manager of the Lincoln circuit.

Louth, November 29. Walked with Mr Robertson to the theatre, which answers also the double purpose of a Sessions House; it is not the worst I have seen. Dressed in magistrates' room—'quite convenient'. When ready to go on the stage, Mr Robertson appeared with a face full of dismay; he began to apologise, and I guessed the remainder. 'Bad house?' 'Bad Sir, there's no one!' 'What? nobody at all?' 'Not a soul, sir—except the Warden's party in the boxes.' 'What the d—l! not one person in the pit or gallery?' 'Oh, yes, there are one or two.' 'Are there five?' 'Oh, yes, five.' 'Then go on; we have no right to give ourselves airs, if the public do not choose to come and see us; go on at once!' Mr Robertson was astonished at what he thought my philosophy, being accustomed, as he said, to be 'blown up' by his *Stars*, when the houses were bad. I never acted Virginius better in all my life—good taste and earnestness.

SOURCE
The Journals of Macready (1832–51), ed. J. C. Trewin (1967)

75

January 17. In going through the box-office heard a woman inquiring for something entertaining for children. Brownell mentioned that Mr Macready and Dowton would play on Monday. 'Oh, no' she replied, 'they are very good actors, but I want something entertaining for children; when will *Aladdin* be done?' So much for Bath taste!

SOURCE
The Journals of Macready (1832–51), ed. J. C. Trewin (1967)

76

To Bath, March 6 . . . [*In the stage-coach*] Captain Bourchier [*a passenger*], as I soon learned his name to be, talked much; among other subjects mentioned young Kean's success at Bath, told me that he knew him, and that his dresses cost him £300 per annum, that he was very pleasant, and related many amusing stories about the theatre. One of Macready, who is a good actor, but he can never play without applause. He went on one night to play and no notice was taken of him, on which he said to the manager, 'I cannot get on, if they do not applaud me'. Upon which the manager went round and told the audience that Mr Macready could not act if they did not applaud him. When Macready reappeared, the applause was so incessant as to disconcert him, and he observed, 'Why, now I cannot act, there is so much applause'. I told him I rather discredited the story, 'In short,' I observed, 'perhaps I ought to apologise to you for allowing you to tell it without first giving you my name—my name is Macready.' He was very much confused, and I as courteous in apologising as I could be.

Bath, March 8 . . . [*Virginius*] The Icilius (a Mr Savile) was either half-stupidly drunk, or, as is very probable, a born ass. Virginia would have made an excellent representation of Appius' cook, as far as appearance went, added to which she seemed to think that she was playing Virginius, not Virginia, and fortified herself for some extraordinary efforts by a stimulant which was too easily detected on a near approach to her. The whole business was most slovenly—and last year this play was actually a *pattern* of correctness. Therefore last year there was a loss on the theatre, and now there is a considerable profit. So much for the judgement and taste of a Bath public. Pshaw! It is all quackery . . .

Exeter, March 18 . . . Between the third and fourth acts [of *Virginius*] the manager came into my room to apologise for a delay of some

story than in the matter, and he has embellished the whole circumstances with a great many fictitious variations, not the less amusing because untrue, but which are pardonable enough in such a work as Mr Mathews, the materials of which are acknowledged to have been made up as much of fiction as of truth. He says that on the occasion alluded to, I played Hamlet, and in the celebrated soliloquy, 'To be or not to be' the similarity of the sound of the words reminding the audience of the Negro melody, 'Opossum Up a Gum Tree', they loudly called for it, and this polite request Mr Mathews makes me accede to in the following language: 'Well, den, ladies and gemmen, you like "Opossum Up a Gum Tree" better den you like *Hamlet*? Me sing him to you', which I, according to the anecdote, did three or four times, much to the exquisite edification of my black hearers, and then resumed my part of the pensive prince. The truth, however, is that I never attempted the character of Hamlet in my life, and I need not say that the whole of the ludicrous scene so well and so humorously described by Mr Mathews never occurred at all.

SOURCE

Herbert Marshall and Mildred Stock, *Ira Aldridge: The Negro Tragedian* (1958)
(Quoted from *Memoir and Theatrical Career of Ira Aldridge, the African Roscius*, Anonymous, London, 1849)

82

Aldridge toured extensively and was especially popular in Prussia and Russia. This is how one audience member received his Othello in St Petersburg in 1858.

I am firmly convinced that after Aldridge it is impossible to see Othello performed by a white actor, be it Garrick himself. A present-day white European, as compared to the African, with his leonine and at the same time childlike nature, is more like Iago, a tamer of wild animals!...Seeing before one the tamed Othello in the net of the tamer, seeing the wild lion in the power of the educated

European (the Iago of contemporary history), one involuntarily thinks of the many generations of black people suffering under the whip of American slave-traders, and one remembers that daring and good woman who decided, once and for all, to stamp their brows with the mark of Cain. All this has been represented by Shakespeare so truthfully, so powerfully, that, without the slightest exaggeration—one risks hating all his white heroes, or at least, the Venetians that surround Othello, not excluding, possibly, even Desdemona herself. It is a pity that even she is not black!

SOURCE
Herbert Marshall and Mildred Stock, *Ira Aldridge: The Negro Tragedian* (1958)
(Quoted from K Zvantsev, *Ira Aldridge, a Biographical Essay*)

WALTER LACY
(1809–1898)

83

Walter Lacy was a noted character actor who became Professor of Elocution at the Royal Academy of Music.

My chief work in London was at the Princess's, where, in Mr Maddox's time, I often played twenty-four parts a week, such as the Gamin in 'The Angel of the Attic,' Charles Paragon in 'The Little Devil,' Alfred Highflyer, and Bounce in the 'Ojibbeway Indians.' On one occasion a laughable incident occurred. A party of Ojibbeways in the pit-box became suddenly so excited at witnessing my scalping Oxberry, as the 'ring-tailed roarer of the backwoods,' that uttering a war-whoop, they prepared to make a rush for the stage, but seeing me take the low comedian's wig off only, they all burst into peal after peal of laughter. With Charles Kean, I started a team of three—i.e.

Rouble (original) in the 'Prima Donna,' Chateau Renaud in the 'Corsican Brothers,' and Alfred Highflyer in a 'Roland for an Oliver,' and ran them three months. These were brilliantly contrasted characters, affording splendid opportunity for an artist to establish himself. Of such an opportunity the severity of my early training, and the various experience of my career, enabled me to take full advantage. The author was to have ridden the middle horse, but owing to a difference with the management, my name was put in the cast at three days' notice. Fortunately I remembered being in a theatre in Paris in Louis Philippe's time (where I observed Dion Boucicault in a side box), when a man entered the parterre with hair and beard black as night, the hair cut close to the skull. I at once said to myself, 'If ever I play a Frenchman, *that* shall be the head.' It was odd that author, actor, and model should come together! I ordered the wig; wrote to Angelo, who, with prompt kindness came up from Brighton to his chambers in Curzon Street, where, after we had discussed a brief luncheon, we took off our coats, and in two hours I was able to master the combat with rapiers. After the first act of the 'Prima Donna,' Charles Kean came to my dressing-room to congratulate me on my 'make-up' and acting in Rouble; and at the conclusion of the 'Corsican Brothers' I was cheered by the whole house. The manager and manageress were delighted, and Mr Bayle Bernard came on the stage with the late Douglas Jerrold to compliment me on the 'originality and finish of my acting.' Next morning, Charles Mathews and Madame Vestris called me to their carriage in the middle of Regent Street, and heartily congratulated me, Charles Mathews saying, 'If that isn't a Frenchman, I don't know what is.' My make-up hit the house, and was the keynote of the new rendering of the part.

SOURCE

Letter from Walter Lacy to W. Clark Russell, quoted in *Representative Actors* (1888)

CHARLES KEAN
(1811–1868)

84

The son of Edmund Kean, Charles Kean was meticulous about production standards. These recollections come from Squire Bancroft who appeared with Kean's company as a young actor.

He was easily upset, when acting, by even a trifling noise. Years ago, in a seaport town he visited, a habit prevailed among the occupants of the gallery of cracking nuts throughout the performance. This played havoc with Kean when he acted there. On the following morning he called those who travelled with him together, and after loudly bewailing his sufferings and anathematising the gallery boys, gave instructions to his followers to go into the town and buy up every nut within its walls, either in the shops or on the quays. This was done. The result for the two following evenings was perfect success, crowned by the chuckles of the tragedian.

But oh, the third night! The fruiterers, perplexed by the sudden and unaccountable demand for nuts, had sent to Covent Garden and other sources for a plentiful supply to meet its hoped-for continuance; the demand fell off, there was a glut in the local market, the nuts so deluged the town that they were sold more abundantly and cheaper than ever. Crack!—crack!—crack! was the running fire throughout the succeeding performances, and the rest of Kean's engagement was fulfilled in torment.

The carpenters of country theatres always dreaded Charles Kean's advent among them, for, in his earlier days on the stage, when he rehearsed, he would steadily go through his own scenes just as at night. During this time silence was strictly ordered to be observed all over the theatre; a creaking boot, a cough, a sneeze, the knocking of a hammer, would distress the tragedian beyond measure.

'Is there anything wrong in the room, sir?' said she.

'Nothing at all. Go away,' I replied.

'Well, sir,' she continued, 'there's a policeman at the door, and he says as 'ow there's a crazy old man in your room, a-flingin' of his 'arnds and a-goin' on hawful, and there's a crowd of people across the street a-blockin' up the way.'

I turned towards the window, and to my horror I found that I had forgotten to put down the curtain, and, as it seemed to me, the entire population of London was taking in my first-night. I had been unconsciously acting with the lights full up, to an astonished audience who had not paid for their admission. As I tore off my wig and beard a shout went up. Quickly pulling down the curtain, I threw myself in a chair, overcome with mortification at the occurrence. In a few minutes the comical side of the picture presented itself, and I must have laughed for half an hour. I had been suffering from an attack of nervous dyspepsia, consequent upon the excitement of the past week, and I firmly believe that this continuous fit of laughter cured me.

SOURCE
Joseph Jefferson, *Autobiography* (1890)

LAURA KEENE
(*c*.1830–1873)

91

An English-born actress, Laura Keene was the first woman in America to become a theatre manager, although her greatest claim to fame lies in a very different quarter.

Though she made no lasting impression on the American theatre and though her popularity and success declined long before she quit the stage, her name is associated with the careers of many great stars of the American theatre, her acting was a worthy example of feminine charm and emotionalism, and her name is forever linked with American history because she was the star of the play being presented in Ford's Theatre the night Abraham Lincoln was assassinated, and she was the one who recognized John Wilkes Booth as he made his escape and who, it is said, held the dying President's head in her lap until he was carried from the theatre.

SOURCE
Garff B. Wilson, *A History of American Acting* (1966)

JOHN COLEMAN
(1832–1904)

92

This is an anecdote about a worthy actor whose heyday was in the 1860s, but who made a memorable appearance in Stratford at the turn of the twentieth century.

Up to this time [Frank] Benson had, for some years, been responsible for the Annual Birthday Festival at Stratford-on-Avon, but now the season at the Lyceum stood in the way, and as he was under contract to the Memorial Theatre Company Benson was placed in a somewhat difficult position. Then it was that John Coleman, who had a version of Pericles of his own brew and which for years he had been endeavouring to get produced, hearing of Benson's dilemma, prevailed upon him to agree that his Pericles should form the fare for the coming celebration at Stratford. So it happened that John Coleman appeared on Shakespeare's birthday as the Prince of Tyre at the Memorial Theatre at Stratford-on-Avon. He must then have been not far short of eighty and was perhaps not even a name to a great number of people, but to those with any knowledge of stage history he was a conspicuous figure about 1860, though perhaps not in the very front rank. He was a man of some literary ability. In addition to this version of Pericles he was responsible for several theatrical publications, including a life of Phelps and another of himself in two volumes. He was a tragedian of some distinction with an honourable record. But, of course, it was unfortunate that Benson's Lyceum season should have resulted in a version of Pericles, a play of which the authorship has often been in doubt, and that it should have been presented in this guise; also that the leading part should have been taken by an actor, however worthy, who was long since past his prime.

Benson sent down to Stratford-on-Avon, from his Lyceum company, Lilian Braithwaite, Lily Brayton, Oscar Asche, Harcourt Williams, H. A. Tongue, H. O. Nicholson and myself. In the opening scene of this version John Coleman was supposed to be a handsome youth shipwrecked and cast up by the waves on the shore. I wish I could picture for you this youth as presented by poor old John. He had naturally an old man's figure: the paunch, bent knees and pouched and baggy neck. He wore pink fleshings covering his poor old body and finishing as mittens on his hands. Green wool was stuck on here and there to represent sea-weed. He wore a golden flowing wig, the join of which was not coloured to his face. The local hairdresser had sprinkled his heavy white moustache and shaggy eyebrows with gold powder, which shook off as he walked. He eschewed grease paint and his wrinkled old countenance was tinged with rouge and he wore a beard on his chin, which was no match for his moustache. And this was the 'golden youth' at whom Mariana had to gaze, spellbound by his beauty!

SOURCE
O. B. Clarence, *No Complaints* (1943)

EDWIN BOOTH
(1833–1893)

93

From a noted theatrical family, for thirty years, Edwin Booth was the leading classical actor of the American stage, reckoned by some as the finest Hamlet of the nineteeth century. During his record-breaking run as Hamlet at the Winter Garden Theater in New York, his younger brother, John Wilkes Booth (who, a year later, in 1865, was to assassinate Abraham Lincoln), confided, 'Between ourselves, he is Hamlet—melancholy and all.' Edwin was dogged by this disposition throughout his life, through domestic grief (his first wife died early, his second went mad), the shame of his brother's crime, and financial catastrophes.

In 1845 the Booths were living on North Front Street, but a year later moved to a home on Exeter Street, where a spacious arbor in the back yard served as a theatre in which many ambitious youths who grew to be prominent actors played their first parts. There they performed, before select juvenile audiences, classic and romantic dramas with the female rôles left out. Edwin organized the company and was its manager. Booth's [his father] disapproval soon forced them to move to a cellar in Triplet Alley.

The cellar was under a hotel kept by John Lutz (afterward associated with Laura Keene), who knew nothing of the rental arrangements they had made with his Negro janitor by promising him all the pennies he collected at the door. The admission fee was three cents for reserved seats, one cent for standing room, and there was no free list. Edwin was the star, George L. Stout was prompter and leading man, and Sleepy Clarke, as he was called, was stage manager. Other company members included Theodore Hamilton, Summerfield Barry, Samuel Knapp Chester, and Henry Stuart, who was to be known professionally as Stuart Robson.

Stage properties and funds to promote the venture were obtained by borrowing surreptitiously from their elders. Robson's mother had an old iron stove which was not in use, and the others pointed out to him that he might add something to the treasury by turning it into cash. The fact that his mother never spared the rod on a certain part of his anatomy made him hesitate, but the sale was finally accomplished and the money used to buy an abandoned set piece from a resort at Fell's Point. By some such means, they financed also the purchase of an old nag at the horse market and hired an organ-grinder to fill in as orchestra.

Edwin, whose great desire was to be a clown in a circus, was advertised to perform a daring equestrian act on the opening night, but when they got the old nag into the ring and Edwin was lifted onto his back the horse refused to budge. Efforts to force him into action had no effect, until a rasping tune from the hand organ sent him gallivanting around the circle. One boy's father owned a livery stable, and unknowingly, furnished feed for the animal, who grew so fat that they had to remove a partition to get him out. An account of these Triplet Alley days was given by George L. Stout in his *Recollections:*

> It was in this cellar that Edwin Booth made his first appearance as *Richard III,* and a tragedy indeed it turned out to be. He was anxious to get armour and finally solved the puzzle by getting pieces of oilcloth and covering them with large spangles cut from the gabardine worn by his father as *Shylock.* He cut up the garment and transferred the spangles without detection, and had made beautiful armour. Unfortunately, just about this time the old man had a sudden call to play *Shylock,* and in looking over his wardrobe discovered the loss. He went at once to Wilkes and began thrashing him without more ado, promising to keep up until told who did the mischief. On this hint, Wilkes spoke, and confessed that Edwin was responsible, moreover, that he was at the moment wearing the stolen ornaments. The old man lost no time in hastening to the cellar, but

> was held up at the door by the janitor, who refused to let him pass without the tribute of three cents. Whereupon Booth pitched into the negro and fought his way to the cellar, his anger now at boiling point. Edwin was just saying, "A horse! A horse! My kingdom for a horse!" before an entranced audience, when he heard the well known voice. With a lightning appreciation of his father's form blocking the door, he made a wild dash for the window. He got half way through when the armour stuck, and the old man began to 'lay on' with a vigor that produced realistic shrieks from *Richard* who was on the other side of the window being tugged vigorously by a policeman, who thought he was climbing out of the window with burglarious spoils! Between his father and the policeman, poor Edwin was literally torn with contending emotions.

The plays were so well patronized by the boys and girls of the neighbourhood that they were kept up for several weeks, and the Negro often took in more than a dollar at each performance. But rivalry among members of the company divided them and led to much trouble. Robson and Hamilton organized another group, claimed all the stage properties they had scraped together, and stole the set. Edwin and his associates fought them and got it back. They foiled further attempts with clubs and sticks, and moved it, when not in use, to a secret hiding place.

SOURCE
Stanley Kimmel, *The Mad Booths of Maryland* (1940)

94

As a means of gaining truth and conviction in his performances, Booth tried to 'think himself' into his roles. He attempted, imaginatively, to *become* the characters so he could better understand how they felt. On nights when he could not sleep, he let the moods of his roles 'flood through his mind.' Before a performance, he tried to

chapter-heading of some grand old romance: it thrilled, and was intended to thrill...

I can only speak of Irving's entrances, but I believe that with Edmund Kean an entrance was also something to experience...

To prepare for this entrance in *The Bells,* the entire first fifteen minutes of the play conspired.

The talk all hovered around the thought of the man who was coming, and about other things somehow connected with him.

The storm raging outside the house; the sudden blowing open of a window in the next room, which smashed a whole trayful of crockery and glass as it swung open—the looking at the clock which told of the overdue traveller—the slow, quiet talk which mumbled on—and, above all, the queer 'hurry music,' as it is called, which was astonishingly dramatic: all these things led up to the first point to be made, and made with decision: 'Here is the man!' And now watch what he will do—better still, how he will do it—best of all, watch his face and figure, and follow what it is these are hinting at.

Irving once on, the shout of applause going up he lowers his arms, he lowers his head, he relaxes his force all over, seems to turn it off to an almost dead calm, while the applause rolls on and up. Twice, maybe three times, he, as it were, shifts one foot (his right I think it was), and by this slight and meaningless gesture a limit is being reckoned to the applause which goes on and on—no other motion, except that the foot in shifting sends a slight vibration also without significance, through the whole person before us—and then as the applause dies away, at the first sign of it dying, the actor clips it off by a sudden gesture of awakening from his long and patiently-endured ordeal—flings cap and whip to right and left, and begins to shed his coat, his muffler, as his wife and daughter run to help him off with them.

SOURCE
Edward Gordon Craig, *Henry Irving* (1930)

97

Henry Irving's first entrance in *The Bells*. The printed version states that:

> *(Mathias is seen passing the window. The door opens. Lights up. Chord.)*
>
> MATHIAS: It is I.

Of course you needed to be an actor-manager to arrange for all the lights to be turned up and the full orchestra to strike a chord on your entrance. Gordon Craig, in his biography of Irving, remarks upon his idiosyncratic pronunciation and says that his first line sounded like 'Tsi' ('t's I). Years later Baliol Holloway, who had seen the great man in *The Bells*, explained that he only did that out of necessity because, as he had been seen through the window, the entire audience expected the arrival of their hero and were prepared to greet him with a storm of applause. He had no time to say the full 'It is I'. So the opening of the door, the lights up, the chord, 'Tsi' were simultaneous, a fraction of a second before the applause.

SOURCE
Donald Sinden, *Laughter in the Second Act* (1985)

98

Bram Stoker (1847–1912), now famous as the author of Dracula, *was celebrated in his day as general manager to Henry Irving and his company at the Lyceum. Stoker first met Irving in Dublin in 1876.*

Here in a dining room, amid a dozen friends, a man in evening dress stood up to recite a poem with which we had all been familiar from our schooldays, which most if not all of us had ourselves recited at some time.

But such was Irving's commanding force, so great was the magnetism of his genius, so profound was the sense of his dominance that I sat spellbound. Outwardly I was as of stone; nought quick in me but receptivity and imagination. That I knew the story and was even familiar with its unalterable words was nothing. The whole thing was new, re-created by a force of passion which was like a new power. Across the footlights amid picturesque scenery and suitable dress, with one's fellows beside and all around one, though the effect of passion can convince and sway it cannot move one personally beyond a certain point. But here was incarnate power, incarnate passion, so close that one could meet it eye to eye, within touch of the outstretched hand. The surroundings became non-existent; the dress ceased to be noticeable; recurring thoughts of self-existence were not at all. Here was indeed Eugene Aram as he was face to face with his Lord; his very soul aflame in the light of his abiding horror. Looking back now, I can realise the perfection of art with which the mind was led and swept and swayed hither and thither as the actor wished. How a change of tone or time denoted the personality of the 'Blood-avenging Sprite'—and how the nervous, eloquent hands slowly moving, outspread fanlike, round the fixed face—set as doom, with eyes as inflexible as Fate—emphasised it till one instinctively quivered with pity! Then came the awful horror on the murderer's face as the ghost in his brain seemed to take external shape before his eyes, and enforced on him that from his sin there was no refuge. After this climax of horror the Actor was able by art and habit to control himself to the narrative mood whilst he spoke the few concluding lines of the poem.

Then he collapsed half-fainting.

There are great moments even to the great. That night Irving was inspired. Many times since then I saw and heard him—for such an effort eyes as well as ears are required—recite that poem and hold audiences, big or little, spellbound till the moment came for the thunderous outlet of their pent-up feelings; but that particular vein

I never met again. Art can do much; but in all things even in art there is a summit somewhere. That night for a brief time in which the rest of the world seemed to sit still, Irving's genius floated in blazing triumph above the summit of art. There is something in the soul which lifts it above all that has its base in material things. If once only in a lifetime the soul of a man can make wings and sweep for an instant into mortal gaze, then that 'once' for Irving was on that, to me, ever memorable night.

As to its effect I had no adequate words. I can only say that after a few seconds of stony silence following his collapse I burst out into something like a violent fit of hysterics.

Let me say, not in my own vindication but to bring new tribute to Irving's splendid power that I was no hysterical subject. I was no green youth; no weak individual, yielding to a superior emotional force. I was as men go a strong man—strong in many ways. If autobiography is allowable in a work of reminiscence, let me say here what has to be said of myself.

In my earlier years I had known much illness. Certainly till I was about seven years old I never knew what it was to stand upright. This early weakness, however, passed away in time and I grew into a strong boy. When I was in my twentieth year I was Athletic Champion of Dublin University. When I met Irving first I was in my thirtieth year. I had been for ten years in the Civil Service, and was then engaged on a dry-as-dust book on *The Duties of Clerks of Petty Sessions.* I had edited a newspaper, and had exercised my spare time in many ways—as a journalist; as a writer; as a teacher. In my college days I had been Auditor of the Historical Society—a post which corresponds to the Presidency of the Union in Oxford or Cambridge—and had got medals, or certificates, for History, Composition and Oratory. I had been President of the Philosophical Society; I had got University Honours in pure Mathematics. I had won numerous silver cups for races of various kinds—for rowing, weight-throwing, and gymnastics.

I had played for years in the University football team, where I had received the honour of a 'cap'! When, therefore, after his recitation I became hysterical, it was distinctly a surprise to my friends; for myself surprise had no part in my then state of mind. Irving seemed much moved by the occurrence.

On piecing together the causes of his pleasure at finding an understanding friend, and his further pleasure in realising that that friend's capacity for receptive emotion was something akin in forcefulness to his power of creating it, I can now have some glimpse of his compelling motive when he went into his bedroom and after a couple of minutes brought me out his photograph with an inscription on it, the ink still wet:

'My dear friend Stoker. God bless you! God bless you!!

Henry Irving. Dublin, December 3, 1876'

In those moments of our mutual emotion he too had found a friend and knew it. Soul had looked into soul! From that hour began a friendship as profound, as close, as lasting as can be between two men.

SOURCE
Bram Stoker, *Personal Reminiscences of Henry Irving* (1906)

99

When on our Western tour in 1899–1900 we visited Kansas City for three nights, playing in the Opera House afterwards destroyed by fire. At that time limelight for purposes of stage effect had been largely superseded by electric light, which was beginning to be properly harnessed for the purpose. It was much easier to work with and cheaper, as every theatre had its own plant. Irving, however, preferred the limelight of calcium light, which gives softer and more varied effects, and as it was not possible to get the necessary gas-tanks in many places we took with us a whole railway wagon-load of them. These would be brought to the theatre with the other paraphernalia of our work. As we had so much stuff that it was not always possible to find room for it, we had to leave some of the less perishable goods on the sidewalk. This was easy in Kansas City, as the theatre occupied a block and its sidewalks were wide and not much used except on the main street. Accordingly the bulk of our gas-tanks were piled up outside. The scarlet colour of the oxygen tanks evidently arrested the attention of a local reporter and gave him ideas. On the morning after the first performance his paper came out with a sensational article to the effect that at last the treasured secret was out: Henry Irving was in reality a dying man, and was only kept alive by using great quantities of oxygen, of which a wagon-load of tanks had to be carried for the purpose. The reporter went on to explain how, in order to investigate the matter properly, he had managed to get into the theatre as a stage hand and had seen the tanks scattered about the stage. Further, he went on to tell how difficult it was to get near Irving's dressing-room as rude servants ordered away any one seen standing close to the door. But he was not to be baffled. He had seen at the end of the act Irving hurry into his room to be reinvigorated. He added, with an inconceivable *naïveté,* that precautions were taken to prevent the escape of the life-giving oxygen—*for even the keyhole was stopped up.*

SOURCE
Bram Stoker, *Personal Reminiscences of Henry Irving* (1906)

100

On one occasion there was a man with whom we had some business dealings and who, to say the least of it, did not impress any of us favourably. Irving was very outspoken about him, so much so that I remonstrated, fearing lest he might let himself in for an action for libel. I also put it that we had not sufficient data before us to justify so harsh a view. Irving listened to me patiently and then said:

SARAH BERNHARDT
(1845–1923)

109

Perhaps the most celebrated and versatile actress of her time, Sarah Bernhardt was as triumphant in London in 1879 in Phèdre as in New York a year later as Marguerite in La Dame aux Camélias. *In later life she even played Hamlet. Numerous stories circulated about her eccentricities, many of which were well founded. Here Mrs Patrick Campbell, who played Mélisande to Bernhardt's Pelléas, in a production of Maurice Maeterlinck's play, describes some unscripted business.*

Her company indiscreetly told me that Madame Sarah had never been known to make fun or to laugh on the stage.

In a tobacconist's shop I saw a tobacco pouch made in the shape of a fish, and painted to represent one. I bought it, took it to the theatre, and tied it down to a bit of canvas at the bottom of the well at the Fountain.

At the performance, when Sarah came to the second act and stood by the *fontaine des aveugles*, she spied the fish and began improvising about *les poisons là*.... She stooped gracefully over the edge to take the fish out; as it was tied, she nearly lost her balance. Without concern she went on calmly with her part. I laughed, spoiling my lovely little scene.

When the curtain fell Sarah did not allude to what had happened, neither did I. The next day when we lunched together she had a strange, preoccupied expression on her face. Later, at the matinée, when we came to the Cave scene, at the point where she tenderly takes my hand and helps me over the rocks, she took hold of my hand, hard—squash—she held a raw egg in hers.

I did not smile, but with calm dignity I went on with my part. I can see now the tears of laughter trickling down her cheeks, and her dear body shaking with merriment as I grew more and more dignified to the end of the scene.

Her company told me afterwards, almost with awe, that Madame must love me very, very much.

SOURCE
Mrs Patrick Campbell, *My Life and Some Letters* (1922)

110

Although feeling feverish one day Bernhardt disregarded her doctor's orders not to go on that evening in L'Étrangère *at the Gaiety Theatre. He was furious but insisted that she at least took 'a prescription in case of a relapse'.*

The opium I had taken in my potion made my head rather heavy. I arrived on the stage in a semi-conscious state, yet delighted with the applause I received. I walked as though I were in a dream, and could scarcely distinguish my surroundings. The house itself I only saw through a luminous mist. My feet glided without effort over the carpet, and my voice sounded to me far away—very far away. I was in that delicious stupor that one experiences after chloroform, morphine, opium, or hasheesh.

The first act went off very well, but in the third act, just when I was to tell the Duchesse de Septmonts (Croizette) all the troubles that I, Mrs Clarkson, had gone through during my life, just as I should have commenced my interminable story, I could not remember anything. Croizette murmured by first phrase for me, but I could only see her lips move without hearing a word. I then said, quite calmly:—

'The reason I sent for you here, madame, is because I wanted to tell you my reasons for acting as I have done, but I have thought it over and have decided not to tell you them today.'

Sophie Croizette gazed at me with a terrified look in her eyes; she then rose and left the stage, her lips trembling and her eyes fixed upon me all the time.

'What's the matter?' everyone asked, when she sank almost breathless into an arm-chair.

'Sarah has gone mad!' she exclaimed. 'I assure you she has gone stark mad. She has cut out the whole of her scene with me.'

'But how?' everyone asked.

'She has cut out two hundred lines,' said Croizette.

'But what for?' was the eager question.

'I don't know. She looks quite calm.'

The whole of this conversation, which was repeated to me later on, took much less time than it does now to write it down. Coquelin had been told, and he now came on to the stage to finish the act. The curtain fell. I was stupefied and desperate afterwards on hearing all that people told me. I had not noticed that anything was wrong, and it seemed to me that I had played the whole of my part as usual, but I was really under the influence of opium. There was very little for me to say in the fifth act, and I went through that perfectly well. The following day the accounts in the papers sounded the praises of our company, but the piece itself was criticised. I was afraid at first that my involuntary omission of the important part in the third act was one of the causes of the severity of the Press. This was not so, however, as all the critics had read and re-read the piece. They discussed the play itself, and did not mention my slip of memory.

SOURCE
The Memoirs of Sarah Bernhardt, ed. Sandy Lesberg (1977)

111

Stories innumerable have been told about Sarah Bernhardt; of her extravagance, her love for reclame, her tornado-like rages (these with many grains of truth in them), of her cruelty (invariably false), and of her numerous caprices and escapades; but of her kindness, her generosity, her whole-hearted sympathy in sickness or distress, few have cared to tell except those who have known her personally, and if such tales were even briefly recorded they would form a volume of inconvenient size.

I remember, during a performance in London, one of the scene-shifters, new to the theatre, falling backwards down a concealed stairway and injuring himself severely.

Sarah sent for doctors and did all that was to be done at once, and after the curtain fell I came to bid her good night,

'He is going on all right,' I said. 'You can go home quite satisfied.'

Sarah looked surprised. 'But I'm not going home.'

'You are going to stay here?'

'Of course.'

'All night?'

'Yes.'

'But the man is being well cared for: you may be sure that he has everything he wants.'

'I shall be sure if I stay here,' said Sarah simply.

'If I go home I shall not.'

SOURCE

W. Graham Robertson, *Time Was: The Reminiscences of Graham Robertson* (1931)

112

Towards the end of her supreme period critics began to weary because she appeared so much in the clap-trap, stagy dramas of Sardou, though whenever she was seen in work worthy of her she resumed all her old sovereignty. They began to carp at what had charmed them for so long and to say that the much-hymned 'golden voice'—a soft chant, little above a whisper, yet of a penetrating and bewildering sweetness—was a trick commonly practised by High

Church curates, that it was no natural tone but a false voice. Who ever said that it was not?

Sarah Bernhardt herself told me that she had hit upon this false voice as a means of saving her natural voice, which was, in her youth, easily exhausted; that she achieved it—as does the curate—by pitching the voice up in the head and producing it through the nose, and that, by alternating it with her natural utterance, she could come safely through long tirades which otherwise would have left her speechless.

But to produce a false voice and to use it beautifully are two different things; with the curate it is sing-song and dull monotony, from the lips of Sarah Bernhardt it was the cooing of doves, the running of streams, the falling of soft spring rain. And its carrying power!

SOURCE
W. Graham Robertson, *Time Was: The Reminiscences of Graham Robertson* (1931)

113

One evening I was sitting with Madame Sarah in her dressing-room at the theatre, watching her make up. This always fascinated me—it was absorbing to note the subtle touches with which she changed her own delicate features into the sensual, heavy-lipped face of Theodora, the olive-tinted mask of Lorenzaccio or the fragile semplance of Napoleon's ill-fated son. This evening Sarah was gradually resolving into Cleopatra, and, as final details were being added, Mrs Campbell entered.

Sarah was absorbed for the moment and could spare little attention: she was painting her hands, staining the finger-tips and palms with the dusky red of henna. Mrs Campbell watched with some impatience; she had business to discuss and was in a hurry.

'Why do you take so much trouble?' she said at last. 'What you are doing will never show from the front. Nobody will see it.'

'I shall see it,' replied Sarah slowly. 'I am doing it for myself. If I catch sight of my hand it will be the hand of Cleopatra. That will help me.'

She never spared trouble—in fact, I do not think she realised the meaning of the word. Nothing connected with her art was a trouble; she would always give her best.

SOURCE

W. Graham Robertson, *Time Was: The Reminiscences of Graham Robertson* (1931)

114

In 1907 she was ill, she began to feel her marvellous powers failing her; in 1908 she discovered the cause and underwent an operation in Paris.

On her next visit to London I called on her with a friend and, missing her, was coming down the stairs of the hotel when I saw the well-known figure in advance of me 'There she is,' I said, but my friend looked incredulous. 'That is not Sarah Bernhardt—that is a young girl.' Nevertheless it was Sarah.

That night I saw her in 'Phedre' at her very best, wonderful as ever before, and I went round to speak with her after the play. Many old friends were with her, Jean Richepin—whose play, 'Le Chemineau,' was then running at His Majesty's Theatre—George Clairin, and others.

I stared at her, my astonishment absolutely banishing my manners. 'But—but it's ridiculous,' I blurted out.

'Yes,' said Sarah, gravely looking at herself in a long mirror. 'Yes, it's ridiculous. That is the word. I can hardly believe it yet. I feel that I have been summoned before le bon Dieu and he has said to me, "Well Sarah Bernhardt, you have been a very good girl on the whole—you have made the most of your time—you shall have your youth back again."'

For there she stood, the slender, pathetically lovely Phaedra of old, a miracle for all men to see.

SOURCE

W. Graham Robertson, *Time Was: The Reminiscences of Graham Robertson* (1931)

WILLIAM TERRISS
(1847–1897)

115

Known as 'Breezy Bill', Terriss was one of the most popular players of his day, a fine Shakespearean actor, but best known for swashbuckling roles, such as Robin Hood, and the melodramas staged at the Adelphi Theatre in the Strand. Ellen Terry said that when he was given presents by the audience, which happened every night, he gave them straight to the call boy or the gas man. At the age of 50, he was murdered at the stage-door of the Adelphi by a demented small-part actor with an imagined grievance.

Irving, who had a very warm corner in his heart for William Terriss, used to be immensely amused at the almost effortless way in which he could sweep a great audience before him, often without having taken the trouble to dive very deeply into the inner meaning of the text. On one occasion at rehearsal the great man, who was listening to him declaim magnificently, stopped the scene and mischievously asked, 'Bill, my boy, what do those last two lines mean?' 'What do you say, guv'nor?' said Terriss. 'The last two lines—what do they mean, my boy?' 'Oh! the last two lines—well—what about them?' 'What do they mean?' came the enquiry again. 'Oh! the lines,' again replied Terriss, 'you want to know what they do mean?' 'Yes,' said Irving, 'what do they mean?' 'Well, guv'nor, they mean, of course, they mean—' Here he paused. 'Well, Bill, what *do* they mean?' 'Oh, well,' said the ever-undefeated Bill, 'so help me goodness, guv'nor, I'm blowed if I know what they *do* mean.' 'No, I thought not,' retorted Irving, joining in the shout of laughter which the very frank reply brought forth.

SOURCE
Sir Seymour Hicks, *Me and My Missus* (1939)

ELLEN TERRY
(1847–1928)

116

Bram Stoker, Henry Irving's manager at the Lyceum Theatre in London and, later, famously, the author of Dracula, *said of her: 'Ellen Terry is a great actress, the greatest of her time; and she will have her niche in history. She is loved by everyone who ever knew her. Her presence is a charm, her friendship a delight; her memory will be a national as well as a personal possession.' Her son, Edward Gordon Craig, said 'Even with her head in a bag she would have captured the house'. Born into a notable theatrical family, Ellen Terry became the most celebrated Shakespearean actress of her day, playing for many years opposite Irving in his company at the Lyceum. She played Juliet at the Lyceum in 1882 and the following was found on the fly-leaf of her copy of the play.*

Get the words into your remembrance first of all. Then, (as you have to convey the meaning of the words to *some* who have ears, but don't hear, and eyes, but don't see) put the words into the simplest vernacular. Then exercise your judgment about their sound.

So many different ways of speaking words! Beware of sound and fury signifying nothing. Voice unaccompanied by imagination, dreadful. Pomposity, rotundity.

Imagination and intelligence absolutely necessary to realize and portray high and low imaginings. Voice, yes, but not mere voice production. You must have a sensitive ear, and a sensitive judgment of the effect on your audience. But all the time you must be trying to please *yourself*.

Get yourself into *tune*. Then you can let fly your imagination, and the words will seem to be supplied by yourself. Shakespeare supplied by oneself! Oh!

Realism? Yes, if we mean by that real feeling, real sympathy. But people seem to mean by it only the realism of low-down things.

To act, you must make the thing written your own. You must steal the words, steal the thought, and *convey* the stolen treasure to others with great art.

SOURCE
From *Four Lectures on Shakespeare*, ed. Christopher St John (1932)

117

The Terry family was a large one. Ellen's sisters Kate, Marion, and Florence, were all fine actresses.

All the Terrys had very bad memories. Marion, at the end of her life, used to go to play the big scene from *Lady Windermere's Fan*, with my aunt Mabel Terry-Lewis, her niece, at charity matinées, and I remember my mother trying to hear her go through her words at our house. She kept making endless mistakes, although she had known the part for many years. However, they all had a lot of skillful ways of covering their lapses of memory, as many old actors do. Irene Vanbrugh, in her last performance, had the same trouble, but she would shout or stamp her foot or look at the other actor, making it seem as if he was the one who had dried up. This was a much more common occurrence in my days as a youthful playgoer. The prompter was often a good deal in evidence, particularly on first nights, and the audience did not mind, they thought it was all part of the fun. When I saw Ellen Terry as the Nurse in Doris Keane's *Romeo and Juliet* in 1919 she could hardly remember a word, and Basil Sydney and Leon Quartermaine, who were playing Romeo and Mercutio respectively, whispered every line in her ear, and then she said the line herself and it sounded as if she had just thought of it. One would have thought it would have made her nervous, but she still had confidence in her charisma and in the audience, and managed to enchant them just the same.

SOURCE
Sir John Gielgud, *An Actor and His Time* (1979)

118

Though I may seem like myself to others, I never *feel* like myself when I am acting, but some one else, so nice, and so young and so happy, and always-in-the-air, light and bodyless.

SOURCE
Ellen Terry and Bernard Shaw: A Correspondence, ed. Christopher St. John (1933)

119

She was large and lovely and gracious and opulent and untidy with everything falling out of her voluminous handbag.

SOURCE
Gwen Ffrangcon-Davies, *The Times* (26 January 1991)

120

She was an extremely beautiful girl and as innocent as a rose. When Watts kissed her, she took for granted she was going to have a baby.

SOURCE
George Bernard Shaw, quoted in S. Winsten, *Days with Bernard Shaw* (1949)

MADGE KENDAL
(1849–1935)

121

With Sir John Hare, Madge Kendal had a long and successful partnership at the St James's Theatre in London, where Pinero's play, The Squire, *was produced in 1881.*

'The Squire' was unquestionably one of the greatest triumphs of the Hare and Kendal management and created a phrase which was current for a long time in the newspapers that it 'wafted the scent of the hay over the footlights,' so perfect a picture was it of country life.

Its production created a sensation, for its plot was everywhere assumed to have been borrowed without admission from Thomas Hardy's *Far from the Madding Crowd*. Mr Pinero, as he then was, stated emphatically that he had never read the novel so that the similarity of the stories was merely one of those coincidences which if not frequent are not unknown either in the theatre or in literature.

The result of this acrimonious discussion was that, one night, when the curtain went up, I noticed in a private box Mr Hardy himself, Sir George Lewis, presumably his solicitor, and Mr Comyns Carr who had come to see the play and discover how far the plot of 'The Squire' agreed with the novel.

The trouble arose through Mr Hare having mislaid the manuscript among the hundreds he had received. Mr Comyns Carr lost his temper at the delay in receiving an answer and asked for the play.

Eventually, Mr Hare wrote that he did not like it as 'Mrs. Kendal did not like her part.'

Alas! I had never even seen the manuscript.

Some considerable time later Mr Hare did find the manuscript and he and Mr Comyns Carr became good friends again.

In the second act of 'The Squire' I wore an evening dress, the material for which I searched carefully to get, as it had a thread of yet the Elgin Room at the British Museum was never inconveniently crowded.

The admiration, I suppose, must have been merely a passing fashion, for when later on the Beauty went upon the stage where all who would might see her, she never commanded a large following. Certainly she was not a good actress yet neither was she a bad one, and that is saying much.

Her voice and speech were beautiful, and when she had beautiful words to say she said them simply, not chopping them up with 'business' or strangling them with 'suppressed emotion.' Her Rosalind is one of my pleasant memories. She gave no 'performance', no new readings; she was not coquettish or hoydenish, she did *not* sing the 'Cuckoo' song, she did so few stupid things that the part began to play itself and at times the true Rosalind stood before us. In short, she gave Shakespeare a chance, and the poor man really came through very well. One bit of original business I remember which I have never noticed in another Rosalind. She carefully avoided all vulgar clowning in passages referring to her male attire, but when she spoke the line—'Here, on the skirts of the forest, like fringe on a petticoat,' she put out her hand with a perfectly natural gesture to pick up her own petticoat, and finding none, paused awkwardly for half a second.

She also provided the only Audrey that I have ever seen on the stage. In appearance exactly right, an apple-cheeked maid with a touch of rustic dignity, shy in manner, her awe of Touchstone only overcome by her deep curiosity. The line—'Is it honest in deed and word—is it a true thing?'—usually drawled with a leer between two bites at a property turnip, came earnestly, falteringly, with the intent gaze of a puzzled child and with a child's reluctance to put a grave thought into words. It brought no foolish laugh, but made the little figure of Audrey live.

SOURCE

W. Graham Robertson, *Time Was: The Reminiscences of Graham Robertson* (1931)

RICHARD MANSFIELD
(1854–1907)

131

Hugely versatile, playing in Gilbert and Sullivan operas and Shakespeare, Richard Mansfield achieved international success with his dual role as Dr Jekyll and Mr Hyde (first performed in Boston in 1887). He was also the first to introduce Shaw to American audiences with Arms and the Man *(1894) and* The Devil's Disciple *(1897).*

His major productions were lavishly mounted and prepared with scrupulous attention to every detail. And each detail was supervised by the intense, high-strung star whose explosions, when things went wrong, were the terror of managers and fellow performers. Once the production was prepared, however, and once the actor was ready to perform, he lost himself in the role he was playing. An incident which occurred in 1894 during his production of *Scenes and Incidents from the Life of Napoleon Bonaparte* illustrates his power of absorption and concentration. Shortly before the curtain rose Mansfield had exploded in fury when a stage hand had accidentally dropped a broom against his dressing room door. But during the performance, when Mansfield was waiting in the wings to begin the crucial scene at Waterloo, a supernumerary stumbled over a stack of rifles and sent them clattering to the floor. The cast was petrified, expecting a titanic outburst. But Mansfield did not move or blink an eye. He appeared not even to have heard the noise—so absorbed was he in the thoughts and feelings of his imaginary situation.

SOURCE
Garff B. Wilson, *A History of American Acting* (1966)

LUDWIK SOLSKI
(1855–1954)

132

This anecdote dates from 1957 when Sir Laurence Olivier was on tour in Eastern Europe with a Stratford-upon-Avon production of Titus Andronicus.

In Warsaw there was an imposing statue outside the Theatre and Larry [Olivier] asked who it was.

'That' said the Polish dramaturg in deference, 'that is the great, great Polish actor Solski.'

'Really. What sort of roles did he play?'

'Everything. All his life he played everything. When he was eighty he again played Hamlet.'

'Hamlet—at eighty! Must've been quite a hole left behind when he died.'

'Yes,' was the fatalistic reply. 'And what relief.'

SOURCE
Tarquin Olivier, *My Father Laurence Olivier* (1992)

MRS BERNARD BEERE
(1856–1915)

133

'A woman capable of such wit and aplomb', said Madge Kendal, 'should have this anecdote told to her credit.'

I only met her once. This was at a large bazaar which was attended by everybody who was anybody, and at which I was asked to preside at the photograph stall. Mrs Beere had just made a sensational success in 'As in a Looking Glass,' an adaptation of the novel of the same name, and her photograph was in every shop window, so that I knew her well by sight.

As I stood at my stall, this lady, beautifully dressed—she was a striking figure, for she was very tall—came slowly up to me and raising her lorgnette and staring at me fixedly said, in a supercilious tone, 'Are you selling *your* photographs, Mrs. Kendal?'

'No,' I replied, 'but I have some excellent ones of Mrs. Bernard Beere.'

'Show me some,' she drawled.

I took up a few small photographs which were retailed in the shops at a shilling each.

'Very good,' she said, 'How much are they?'

'Five pounds each,' I replied in my blandest tones. 'I'll take this one,' she rejoined. 'How cheap!'

Several years afterwards, when the Garrick Theatre was being built by Sir W. S. Gilbert for Sir John Hare, a delay occurred because water was struck when they were digging for the foundations of the stage.*

Not anticipating such an accident Sir John Hare had engaged certain members of his company for the opening play on a given date. Among them was Mrs Bernard Beere.

When it was decided that the opening of the theatre must be postponed, Sir John Hare informed Mrs Beere.

'Water under the stage,' she replied, 'has nothing to do with me,' and she claimed that her salary should begin on the appointed date.

* *At the time, Gilbert said that he didn't know 'whether to continue with the building or sell the fishing rights.'*

SOURCE

Dame Madge Kendal, *Madge Kendal* (1933)

once received a telegram from Pa which read: 'Can you play Rugby week beginning November 3rd. F.R. Benson.'

This placed the actor in a quandary: should he travel north, or learn his lines in *The Merry Wives of Windsor*, or start training as a wing three-quarter?

SOURCE
Ronald Harwood, *Sir Donald Wolfit* (1971)

137

Sport in the country makes me think, too, of Sir Frank Benson. I suppose no actor who ever lived has been such an all-round athlete as this old 'Varsity Blue. It is said of him, that if he were debating which of two actors to engage for a certain part, the slightly inferior artist, if he was a fine cricketer, would most certainly have obtained the coveted honour of employment under the Bensonian banner.

I have heard, though I cannot vouch for the story, that Sir Frank's contracts with his artists were always worded: 'To play the Ghost in "Hamlet" and keep wicket,' or 'To play Laertes and field cover-point'; and it was said that no Polonius need apply unless he happened to be a first-class wicket-keeper.

SOURCE
Sir Seymour Hicks, *Me and My Missus* (1939)

138

And always there was our 'hostess manageress', our good fairy, who shared our joys and sorrows, that winsome and cheerful lady, Mrs Benson, Lady Benson as she is now, and still as sprightly and vivacious as she was when I was one of the company with whom she was universally popular. I have already referred to the fable about games in the Benson company—'wanted a Laertes and centre forward'—'good bowler for Roderigo'. This was all rubbish, of course, but Benson did believe in keeping the body in training as well as the mind. There were few weeks either in winter or summer without a cricket, hockey, or football match and occasionally water polo. I remember a game of rugby on the race-course at Cork, when Benson—who got his blue for the three mile at Oxford—took a pass and was speeding on towards the opposite goal with that wonderful springy stride and his long hair streaming behind, when a voice rang out, 'Begorra Mike! Hamlet's in!'

SOURCE
O. B. Clarence, *No Complaints* (1943)

139

Benson himself, of course, rigidly attended and supervised all rehearsals. At midday Charles Richmond, his dresser and factotum would appear with a large bag of buns for a short lunch interval. It was an established practice that anyone who was late for rehearsal had to subscribe a shilling to the 'Bun Fund'. A young lady was late one day and was told of this. She didn't understand and Mr Benson explained to her that the sum of one shilling would be deducted from her salary. She said, 'Oh, Mr Benson! I don't get any salary'. I suppose she was a pupil. What my salary was I have no idea; more perhaps than I was worth, but I know it wasn't much because when I left the company after four years I was then only getting what is known as a living wage. There were not many managers at that time who paid people while they were learning their business.

SOURCE
O. B. Clarence, *No Complaints* (1943)

140

Benson reverenced Stratford as a place where, he told a last-night audience, 'it is your privilege and mine to help to reawaken the sleeping soul of England.' Pre-war Stratford was un-commercialised and all who came were caressed by its spell in spring and summer;

productions from the gallery at His Majesty's. For some reason we talked about Duse. Chaplin described an occasion on which he saw her act. He began to imitate the actor who had appeared that night with Duse. He whipped out a chair and sat astride it and began to jabber bogus Italian. In a brilliant mime, he showed how the actor was enthralling the audience with a long speech when suddenly the curtains behind began to move and a little old lady came out very quietly and glided across the stage and put her hands towards the fire. Duse. And at this point the poor actor who had seemed so remarkable a moment before was completely blotted out.

SOURCE
Sir John Gielgud, *An Actor and His Time* (1979)

CHARLES HAWTREY
(1858–1923)

143

The leading London comedian of his day, Hawtrey created a style that was widely imitated. He became manager of Her Majesty's Theatre in 1885 and of the Comedy in 1887.

He was always just in—or just out of—some awful money muddle, and either worried to death or else in the greatest good humour.

He seemed to spend half his life rushing about to get money to stave off creditors, and there is a characteristic true story of how he once dealt with a writ-server. He received the man in his most fascinating Hawtrey manner, accepted the writ gracefully, and insisted on giving the bewildered visitor one of his best cigars.

'Are you doing anything this evening?' he asked presently. 'Have you seen my play?'

The man replied, no, he hadn't seen Hawtrey's play.

'Then, my dear fellow, you must—I insist,' he exclaimed. 'I will get you two seats.'

He disappeared into the adjoining office, calling to his secretary, and then returned with an envelope.

'There you are, my dear chap, two for to-night,' he said.

The man, overcome by Hawtrey's charm, stammered all the grateful thanks he could think of, and took his departure. What he said when, later, he opened the envelope and found the writ inside it, I do not know!

SOURCE
Gladys Cooper, *Gladys Cooper* (1931)

C. AUBREY SMITH
(1863–1948)

144

C. Aubrey Smith was a former English Test cricketer who became a successful stage actor until he left Britain for Hollywood where he became the acknowledged leader of the British film community there.

It was not customary in Cardiff to play a mid-week matinée, but we did, and our little company of seven outnumbered the paid admissions by the margin of one! Aubrey Smith claimed we had set a record. Henry Miller countered that he had been with a touring company which had topped the paid audience by two to one. 'What was the play?' demanded Aubrey testily. '*Henry IV, Part II*,' was the answer. I remember the old cricketer's reply, 'Good God, sir, that play has a cast of thirty—two to one means an audience of fifteen. Ours is the victory—by a margin of nine, sir, nine!'

Aubrey Smith was then in his late fifties, handsome, rugged, a monolith of probity, wildly miscast as a philandering husband. In spite of his excellent performance, those who saw the play knew for certain that the virtue of Miss Carson as the other woman was never in jeopardy. Aubrey, a great cricketer, had captained the English Eleven on two tours. He was an ardent golfer too, and in the wings while waiting for his entrances he would practice short approaches with his stick and a ball of paper. On one occasion during a performance he chipped his paper ball through a window of the setting onto the stage. He was terribly cut up about it. I whispered that nobody would notice. He was one of those people who cannot whisper and replied in a resonant tone, 'I know, but I shanked my shot!' It was always his custom to clear his vocal cords before an entrance. Sometimes the audience would be puzzled to hear offstage a distant voice booming 'Hip bath! Hip bath! Hip bath!'

SOURCE
Raymond Massey, *A Hundred Different Lives* (1979)

FRED TERRY
(1863–1933)

145

A member of the distinguished Terry family, whose members included Dame Ellen Terry and Sir John Gielgud, Fred was a handsome romantic actor, especially acclaimed for his role as Sir Percy Blakeney in The Scarlet Pimpernel.

He once mounted a production of *Romeo and Juliet* for his daughter Phyllis. He had intended to act Mercutio, but became ill during rehearsals and finally directed the play without appearing in it himself. A shy young actor, engaged to play the part of Paris, was given an elaborate Carpaccio costume to wear—parti-coloured tights and an Italianate wig falling to his shoulders. Some of the older members of the company, with whom he shared a dressing-room, mischievously drew attention to the inadequacy of his make-up, and finally persuaded him to add mascara to his eye-lashes, rouge to his lips, and a dangling pearl to his right ear. Deeply self-conscious in all this finery, the young man slunk timidly on to the stage at the dress parade and bashfully announced himself. Fred, who was asleep in the darkness of the stalls, woke suddenly, rammed his glasses on to his nose, and, roaring with laughter, shouted out, 'My God, it's a tart I once slept with in Bury St. Edmunds!'

SOURCE
Sir John Gielgud, *Distinguished Company* (1972)

MRS BEERBOHM TREE
(1863–1937)

146

Helen Maud Holt was always known professionally as Mrs Beerbohm Tree or Lady Tree. An educated woman, an accomplished actress and a successful manager, she was twenty when she married Herbert Beerbohm Tree in 1883 and continued her career for twenty years after his death in 1917. Tree was a known philanderer, who fathered a number of children outside his marriage. One evening, when her husband was late home, Helen was said to have said, 'Ah, Herbert, late again? Another confinement in Putney?' On another occasion, she discovered him dining tête-à-tête with the young and handsome male actor, Esme Percy, and closing the

HELP IT, it would be a best-seller. But you couldn't. Besides, you don't know. I do.

SOURCE

George Bernard Shaw, letter 19 December 1938, *Bernard Shaw and Mrs Patrick Campbell: Their Correspondence*, ed. Alan Dent (1952)

MAY WHITTY
(1865–1948)

158

Born in Liverpool, May Whitty enjoyed success as an actress in London, New York, and Hollywood. Married to the actor-manager Ben Webster, their only daughter, Margaret Webster, was born in the USA in 1905. In 1918, May Whitty became the first actress to be made a Dame, in recognition of her charitable work during the First World War.

[After a 6-month tour of Canada in 1931–2, Donald] Wolfit spent four hectic days in New York, then in the unsteady grip of Prohibition; he was looked after by Dame May Whitty who plied him with a home-made brew 'which she made in her bathroom from grapes and other mysterious ingredients'. This no doubt contributed to the fact that he found New York 'bewildering'.

SOURCE

Ronald Harwood, *Sir Donald Wolfit* (1971)

SEYMOUR HICKS
(1871–1949)

159

Hicks was an actor, entertainer, playwright, and producer, who often appeared with his celebrated wife, Ellaline Terriss. He appeared in London's first-ever revue, Under the Clock, *in 1894 and was much admired for his performance as Scrooge in* A Christmas Carol. *Acting from the age of nine, he began his professional career at the age of sixteen, in 1887.*

1887 was just at the end of what is known in the theatrical profession as the lesser palmy days. It was at this time that every piece perpetrated by any kind of author was tried out at a matinée. I often prompted four new productions a week. This gave amateur playwrights an opportunity of paying to see their absolute rubbish performed by professional actors, while distinguished amateurs often had the impertinence to appear in any classic parts supported by a first-class London company, many of whom were obliged through lack of means to subject themselves to this, the greatest possible indignity.

As may be supposed, most of these performances were thrown on anyhow, and so many amusing things occurred at them that if ever members of my profession happened to be dull or in doubt as to how to spend a happy afternoon, it became the fashion for them to go and have a good laugh at some anæmic Richard the Third, or enjoy some atrocious nonsense labelled a 'New and Original play in four Acts.' One of these poor souls played Hamlet, with a cast of many of the best actors in London, his only qualification for the part being that he was the son of rich parents, his father having made his money in a flourishing carrier's business. The matinée must have cost £500 in salaries alone. The laughter commenced on Hamlet's entrance, and continued merrily throughout the afternoon, a mighty roar arising when the King (was it by accident or design?) misquoted his lines to the Queen, and instead of saying, 'Full thirty journeys hath the sun and moon,' etc., substituted for them, 'Full thirty times has *Pickford's van* gone round.' A week later the melancholy matinée-giver left England for the Cape of Good Hope.

SOURCE
Sir Seymour Hicks, *Me and My Missus* (1939)

160

Of course there were occasionally good matinée productions, but they were few and far between. One, I remember, was of an historical drama that went smoothly enough until almost the very end of the last act, when there came one of the biggest unintentional laughs I have ever heard in a theatre.

The scene was a dungeon, and in it, chained to the wall, was a Royalist hero on the eve of execution. The heroine entered to bid him farewell, and a scene was enacted between the pair in which the withers of the audience were wrung watching as they did the parting of a devoted man and woman. The main object of the heroine's arrival in addition to saying her last good-bye, was that she brought for her lover's use a small phial of poison with which he would cheat the hangman on the morrow and spare himself the indignity of a public execution. In the nervousness of a first performance, however, the lady who played the heart-broken girl forgot this part of the plot entirely, and left without handing over the all-important means of escape. The actor realized her mistake when it was too late. She had gone; in vain he called for her return, but she came not. In vain he walked to the prompt corner, but, as is usual when a prompter is really wanted, he was not there. The situation was a hopeless one, and he stood in the centre of the stage, beginning his last farewell to the world without the faintest notion of how he was to get out of it. No sword, no gun, no poison, no anything. The actors and actresses in the audience were quick to see his dilemma, and waited with sympathetic eagerness to see what he would do. The inspiration of genius came to him, and with tragic intensity he declared:

'And so to-night I die. Yes. Never, oh never shall it be said that the last of the De Courceys fell by the hand of the paid executioner; no, never! never!' And suddenly, with a convulsive twitch of the head and the raising of his arm, he fell prone and cried, 'Thank God! I have broken my neck!'

SOURCE
Sir Seymour Hicks, *Me and My Missus* (1939)

161

Of me, the critics usually said: 'He seemed to perspire more than usual on this occasion'; a notice of this kind drew from the then Mr Arthur Pinero the remark, 'Seymour, I'm not sure they are wrong. If I were you I shouldn't advertise "Doors open at eight," I should alter it to "Pores open at nine"'.

SOURCE
Sir Seymour Hicks, *Me and My Missus* (1939)

EDWARD GORDON CRAIG
(1872–1966)

162

Edward Gordon Craig and his sister Edith were the children of Ellen Terry. Before becoming an innovative designer and director, Craig had been an actor with Henry Irving's company at the Lyceum Theatre.

We were sitting round the Green Room (E.T. [Ellen Terry] not there) while Irving read us his version of this play. It began at twelve o'clock, I see, and ended at two-fifteen. I and Ben Webster were seated side by side on some sort of a seat or bench which looked out through the window, across Burleigh Street, to the public house opposite. And as we settled into our places to listen to Irving reading, the vision of the public house came upon us. It made no immediate effect, but there it was.

Then Irving's voice began to inform us of the words of this play which, it occurred to me (looking at the public house), I could quite easily read to myself later on, without his taking all this trouble to read it to us. I began to puff and blow a little—gently. The words entered into my ears now and then, in a sort of corkscrew way which somehow irritated me—my eyes still on the public house. Those chaps in there, drinking beer…I began to move restlessly. Irving's voice went on and on. Ben Webster gave me a poke in the ribs with his elbow. What did he do that for? Men drinking beer…On goes the voice, on goes the beer. Something began to stir in me which I believe is called 'the devil.' But the result was not devilish, it was merely idiotic. I began to titter. Can one be drunk by thinking of beer and so lose control over some organ or other? My speech was all right, but I hadn't to use that. Looking was all right—I could see. I think it was the hearing that was troublesome. Irving's voice went on and on, and at last I was almost overcome by a desire to roar with laughter. The scene 'Public House'—the voice 'Irving doing the play'—these not of a piece. I bottled up the laughter with thoughts of the beer; but it became worse, and I let out a squeak with a pop. Irving, you know, was a saint: otherwise he would have risen up and told me to leave the room. I didn't laugh, but by this time I was gasping. Ben Webster gave me a kick on the leg, which didn't mend matters. I wanted to kick him back, but that would have meant catastrophe. Then I frowned. I frowned hard and in doing so, lowered my head and began to breathe heavily through my nose. My lips were sealed—no more squeaks. But I did not hear another word. All Irving's beautiful speech was lost on me, and the reading came to an end and I think I must have given him a glance out of the corner of my eye. And then he went out of the room, nobly—and I had no further desire to laugh—suicide was the thought then.

SOURCE
Edwin Gordon Craig, *Index to the Story of My Days* (1957)

GERALD DU MAURIER
(1873–1934)

163

Gerald du Maurier—often described as the first and finest exponent of naturalistic acting—was noted for parts such as Bulldog Drummond and the master-cracksman Raffles. He was not one to take his profession too seriously. A. A. Milne said, 'When one knew him, one knew that the stage meant nothing to him but a means of getting money; he never pretended otherwise.'

Nobody on the stage was ever safe when Gerald was present: he would go to the most appalling lengths, and take infinite time and trouble with his experiments. Nothing pleased him more than a successful joke, and, back in his dressing-room, he would rock with laughter until the tears ran down his cheeks, while he told the story of one of his latest shock discoveries. He would invent strange contraptions with string, and place them under the tablecloth, then press some sort of bulb and the plates and cups and saucers would jump about in undignified fashion before their respective owners, who were trying to look as if they were really eating eggs and bacon; there were rolls filled with cotton wool, bananas made of soap, and apples that squeaked a protest when moved; there were cushions that uttered significant and unmistakable sounds when sat upon, collapsible knives and forks that crumpled in the hand, tumblers that melted at the first drop of liquid.

He even once went to the trouble of staging that well-known Chinese torture of the drip of water... and made scientific arrangements for a drop to fall periodically from above on to the forehead of a wretched and innocent performer, who was tied by his part to sit in a certain chair and conduct a very serious conversation for many minutes on end.

SOURCE
Daphne du Maurier, *Gerald: A Portrait* (1934)

BERT WILLIAMS
(1874–1922)

164

Egbert Austin Williams was born in the Bahamas and died in New York. W. C. Fields, who appeared on stage with him, described him as 'the funniest man I ever saw—and the saddest man I ever knewn.' He holds a special place in theatre history.

Bert Williams was one of the biggest stars of his day and the first black man to have his name in lights over the marquee. At one performance at the St Louis Orpheum, Lionel Barrymore exclaimed to the stage manager, 'Isn't he great!' The manager had to admit it: 'He's a good nigger and knows his place.' Just then Williams came offstage and said as he walked by, 'Yes, he's a good nigger and he knows his place and his place is dressing room Number One'.

SOURCE
Ken Bloom, *Show and Tell* (2016)

LILLAH McCARTHY
(1875–1960)

165

In 1953, the Australian actor Trader Faulkner bought the Stella Maris*—a houseboat moored on the Thames at Chelsea, where among others, he entertained Lillah McCarthy, English actress, theatre manager, and, from 1906 to 1918, wife of the director and playwright Harley Granville-Barker.*

There were many friends who loved to visit us on the houseboat.

Probably long forgotten now was Bernard Shaw's admired leading lady, Lillah McCarthy, first wife of theatrical legend Harley Granville-Barker. Lillah was very grand, very Victorian and was of the generation that succeeded Henry Irving and Ellen Terry. All I remember of her now was that she was large, imposing, and a friend of my mother's (Lillah had known Diaghilev and Pavlova and was part of that glittering theatrical pre-first world war generation). It was always a treat to listen to and learn from Lillah.

One day we received word that Lillah wanted to visit the *Stella Maris* for afternoon tea—something extremely unwise at her age and with her degree of infirmity—but the request was tantamount to a Royal Command.

On the agreed day, tea was prepared and Lillah's faithful 'help' brought her by taxi to the moorings.

That afternoon the Thames was raging and the houseboats were creaking and wrenching at their moorings. With the assistance of two of the longshoremen we managed to get Lillah to the top of the narrow gangway leading down to the *Esperance*. Two more heftys were then summoned and the ancient Lillah, paralysed with terror, was laboriously hoisted down and across to the front door of the *Stella Maris*. Having finally got her inside, I suggested a cup of tea.

'Tea?' she bellowed, in true Shavian style. 'Not bloody likely. A large neat whisky, if you please!'

Amid what turned out to be a riotous afternoon party, we handed out whiskies to each of the four longshoremen who had helped to hoist our illustrious guest aboard, as Lillah continued to regale us with stories of her friendships with Bernard Shaw, Henry Irving and other glittering luminaries of her day.

Of course, I'd never seen Lillah perform onstage, but her exit from the *Stella Maris* had a style and grandeur about it that I'll wager matched Sarah Bernhardt's. When the time came, the four hefty longshoremen eased her out the front door and onto our gangway. Manipulating her along the narrow gangplank, up onto the pontoon and up to the waiting taxi in Cheyne Walk was a feat of muscular magic. By now a crowd had gathered. All it needed was for Bernard Shaw and her ex-husband Harley Granville Barker to suddenly appear to complete the scene.

'Goodbye, dear audience!' she boomed. 'I doubt this performance will be repeated, and it could well be my last.'

Indeed it was. She died a few weeks later.

SOURCE
Trader Faulkner, *Inside Trader* (2012)

ERNEST THESIGER
(1879–1961)

166

The cast also included Ernest Thesiger, a great character who constantly referred to his great friend 'Dear Queen Mary', with whom he used to do crochet work. He was very old by the end of his career and enjoyed telling the story of someone who stared hard at him in the tube and eventually said, 'Excuse me, but weren't you Ernest Thesiger?'*

* *Postscript supplied to the editor by Sir Donald Sinden: 'Ernest told me this story, but claimed that he replied, "Madam, I was."'*

SOURCE
Derek Salberg, *My Love Affair with a Theatre* (1978)

JOHN BARRYMORE
(1882–1942)

167

A member of the celebrated Drew and Barrymore families, John ('Jack') Barrymore was an American actor who played in comedy and the classics and became a film star, as well known for his drinking, his four divorces, and his eventual bankruptcy as for his triumphs on stage and screen. 'He had a wild soul, and no one could discipline him', said a colleague. The actor, writer, and director Willie Collier (1864–1944) said that he liked Barrymore too much ever to fire him for his misbehaviour, tardiness, or eccentricity—but his resolve was certainly tested on the opening night of the London run of The Dictator.

The Dictator proved so popular in America that in 1905 Mr Frohman [the New York producer] suggested that Collier take the company to England. Marie Tempest, another Frohman star, was at this time appearing most successfully at the Comedy Theatre, a London playhouse controlled by Frohman. It was the producer's novel intention that Collier and Miss Tempest make a trans-Atlantic interchange, each artist to appear for a four weeks' season at the other's stand. Instead of four weeks, Miss Tempest played for a year in New York, and Collier for more than a year in London.

On the opening night in London, and with much at stake for Collier, two of his actors put him in a fine predicament. Jack, of course, was the worse offender.

At the rise of the curtain on *The Dictator*, Collier, as Travers, is found in desperate need of a new name to cover his identity as a fugitive from the law. Ordinarily, in the play, one of his actors, in the role of Bowie, comes on-scene to sell his name to Travers for twenty-five thousand dollars. But tonight the actor appeared with alcoholic hauteur, and when Collier asked, 'By the way, what is your name, the one I am to purchase?' he refused point-blank to tell it. Nor could Collier, as Travers, squeeze the name 'Bowie' out of his suddenly obstinate actor. He wheedled him, but the actor refused any information. In fact he made an exit, leaving the first-nighters in ignorance of his identity. Finally Collier improvised, saying, 'Of course I know his name. Knew it right along. Happened to meet his wife. She told me it was "Bowie."'

Hardly had Collier hauled himself out of this pit than Jack arrived on-stage to make matters worse, far worse.

The first entrance of the wireless operator was important for a proper understanding of the play. The business provided that Jack give Collier a wireless dispatch written on two long sheets of paper. Collier would read the report aloud, thus advising the audience of the why, when, and wherefore of the action.

Jack appeared on cue, but had in his hand only a small fragment torn from a menu card, a triangle about the size of a Cape of Good Hope postage stamp. He offered this tiny absurdity to the astounded Collier with the usual dialogue, 'Here, Chief, is the dispatch.'

Collier, his eye upon the scrap of paper, improvised, 'But where is the real dispatch? The longer one?'

Jack also improvised. 'Here it is, sir. Or have your eyes gone back on you again?'

'Go to the wireless room,' said the desperate Collier, 'and bring the *first* dispatch. There are two sheets of it. Remember? That's the one I want to read. Not this piece of confetti.'

'But this *is* the first dispatch,' Jack insisted. 'I took it down myself, word for word. Put on your bifocals.'

Collier knew that the long, plot-point speech he was supposed to deliver hardly could be accepted by a London audience as being read from the menu-fragment.

'Look,' he said, then added under his breath, 'if you don't go for the prop, I'll break your leg!' Then, so that the audience might hear, 'Someone is trying to double-cross us. Go back and look again. I'm sure you will find the genuine message.'

'But I *know* this is the one, sir,' Jack insisted. 'It was sent by a well-known female impersonator.'

'Then have her, or him, send us another.'

'But,' Jack said, 'he, or she, can't. He, or it, just died.' He wiped away a tear, and sniffled, 'Are you going to the funeral?'

'No,' said Collier. 'how can I?'

'Why not, sir?'

'Because,' said Collier, 'I haven't got a black dress!' He barked, 'Now go for the other message.' He added under his breath, 'It's a terrible thing to be stranded in London. Catch on?'

Jack went off-stage, leaving Collier to ad lib once again for almost half a minute. Then Barrymore re-appeared to present Collier with exactly the same triangular bit of paper!

'Sir, I have had this authenticated,' and he held up the little scrap. 'It was not written by the late female impersonator, but by the very clever fellow who engraves the Lord's Prayer on the heads of pins.'

There was no other course for Collier than to take the miserable paper, hurriedly edit down his regular speech, and hope for the best. But Willie barely had reached the close of his abridged reading when the actor who hitherto had refused to give the name 'Bowie,' entered unexpectedly to shout: 'I've decided to tell you my name. It's John P. Murphy!'

SOURCE
Gene Fowler, *Good Night, Sweet Prince* (1944)

168

This story, relating to another play at another time, is typical of the anecdotes that illustrate Barrymore's bad behaviour.

Some weeks afterward, and in another city, he lost his temper entirely. It was at the end of the first act. At this point in the play Peter [the character played by Barrymore] picked up the Duchess of Towers' bouquet. After looking at it tenderly for a long moment, he pressed the flowers to his lips. Then he murmured, '*L'amour.*' It was one of the most touching scenes in the play. It sent the ladies into near-swoons.

On this particular evening some girl in the gallery, hysterical with delight, giggled. Jack called out: 'Damn it! If you think you can play this better than I can, come on down and do it.'

He hurled the bouquet into the audience. It struck a woman in the face. The curtain fell. Barrymore stomped off-stage to his dressing-room to lock himself inside it.

Sounds of outrage came from the audience. Miss [Constance] Collier was dismayed to hear high-pitched voices filtering through the curtain. The actors stood in their places on the stage as if paralyzed. Then the manager of the theatre, purple and blowing, charged round from the pass-door.

'I'll bring a damage suit against you!' he shouted at Miss Collier. 'Barrymore has ruined the reputation of my theatre. I'll not allow you to fulfil your engagement for the remainder of the week. My God! Nobody is safe with this man. I'll have him barred from every…'

He paused to regain his wind. The actress took this opportunity to beg the manager to allow the curtain to rise for the second act. He said no. The audience would throw things.

'They're sitting out there now, desperate and waiting,' he said. 'Peek out at 'em. You'll see. They're like a sheriff's posse.'

Miss Collier did peer out to observe the audience waiting as if to exercise some terrible judgment. She finally persuaded the manager to allow the curtain to rise. He recommended that Miss Collier make a speech of apology and offer to return all box-office moneys to the patrons. She declined to do this.

'All right then,' the manager warned, 'but if you're killed, don't say I didn't tell you.'

There had been half an hour's delay. Jack refused to come out of his dressing-room. No threats could move him. Finally Miss Collier informed him that he really had injured an inoffensive woman in the audience, and that the victim's eye had been bandaged.

'In that case,' Barrymore said, 'ring up the curtain.'

The curtain rose for the second act. It seemed remarkable that so few persons had left the theatre or asked for their money back. There was the type of quietness that obtains before a prison riot. The slight plop of a moth against a spotlight slide sounded like a howitzer shell in the challenging silence.

Jack's entrance did not occur until halfway through the second act. Ordinarily, before this appearance of Peter, there were moments of laughter or hand-clapping. Tonight there was no laughter, no applause. Silence.

The cast was terrified. The suspense led Miss Collier to issue whispered instructions of an 'abandon ship' nature. She admonished the crew to lower the curtain the moment the audience began to tear Jack apart.

The moment arrived, and Jack arrived with the moment. He entered with profound self-assurance. He was casual. He might have been on his way to a church, so poised was he. And now the presence that mysteriously was his on any stage, and always would be strangely his, spread its electric influence over the whole house.

He received the wildest sort of applause. Cheers even, and the waving of women's kerchiefs.

It is said that the manager of the theatre sank to his knees, either to pray or to keep from collapsing on his face. No one was sued. The play could have gone on for weeks to capacity business in that city.

SOURCE
Gene Fowler, *Good Night, Sweet Prince* (1944)

169

One of Barrymore's biggest successes was his 1925 Hamlet *in London.*

One thing that enchanted Jack with the *Hamlet* play was the physical leeway it permitted the actor. 'You can play it standing, sitting, lying down, or, if you insist, kneeling. You can have a hangover. You can be cold-sober. You can be hungry, overfed, or have just fought with your wife. It makes no difference as regards your stance or your mood. There are, within the precincts of this great role, a thousand Hamlets, any one of which will keep in step with your whim of the evening. Why, one night in London, after I had been overserved with Scotch at the home of—never mind her name—I got halfway through my "To Be" soliloquy when it became expedient to heave-ho, and quickly. I sidled off to the nearest folds of the stage draperies and played storm-at-sea. I then resumed the soliloquy. After the performance one of the fine gentlemen who had sponsored me for membership in the Garrick Club confided: "I say, Barrymore, that was the most daring and perhaps the most effective innovation ever offered. I refer to your deliberate pausing in the midst of the soliloquy to retire, almost, from the scene. May I congratulate you upon such imaginative business? You seemed quite distraught. But it was effective!" To which I replied: "Yes, I felt slightly overcome myself."'

SOURCE
Gene Fowler, *Good Night, Sweet Prince* (1944)

170

There was always a feeling of good humour and good fellowship on tap. I was explaining one day to the girls who carry on the body of Ophelia in the burial scene that, owing to the extraordinary and suggestive lighting of Robert E. Jones, they would not be recognized as having appeared in earlier scenes. I cautioned them that they should remember that in this scene they were virgins. One of them said to me: 'My dear Mr. Barrymore, we are not character actresses, we are extra ladies.' This is the spirit in which the whole production was done.

SOURCE
John Barrymore, *Confessions of an Actor* (1926)

SYBIL THORNDIKE
(1882–1976)

171

'Lively, passionate, argumentative', said John Gielgud of Sybil Thorndike. Her faith, her Socialism, and her long marriage to the actor and director Lewis Casson were all important to her. Her long association with the Old Vic under Lilian Baylis began in 1914. Her career encompassed Greek tragedy and contemporary comedy, Shakespeare, Chekhov, and Shaw. Famously, she created Shaw's Saint Joan in 1924. Earlier, in a letter to her father, she told of an incident while on tour with Ben Greet's company in America.

Then we went to the Spanish Mission—the monks are too adorable and showed us all over the monastery—all the allowable parts that is—some parts females aren't allowed in—and what do you think?—Ben Greet has given them 2 boxes for a performance of *Everyman*—the Superior let them come because B.G. said it was a religious service and not a play proper at all.

...The monks all came to the show last night with their nice bare feet and their sweet simple faces. We had the shock of our lives when Death came on—we thought they'd be awfully impressed, instead of which they all burst right out laughing—just like I do—at the wrong time. We were absolutely flabbergasted, till some one told us that in the mediaeval times Death was often the comedy character, just as the Devil was, and that no true Catholic could treat them seriously—so here were these darling old monks being truly mediaeval—never having changed in feeling since those long-back times. It gave me a great cheer and a lump in my throat. You see they used to play this very play, Father, in the Churches in the Middle Ages, one almost felt these old dears were reincarnated from them.

SOURCE
Russell Thorndike, *Sybil Thorndike* (1921)

172

A spiritual moment of a different kind, again from her time with the Ben Greet Company, on tour in America and playing in The Comedy of Errors *on a college campus.*

Normally she kept away from alcohol, which tended to go to her head. On this hot day, weighed down by her heavy costume and the long wait before her entrance, she drank two mint juleps, wandered off, and fell asleep in a nearby field. When her cue came it took ten minutes to find her. Eventually she was gleefully chaired back to the stage by a group of students. Greet's reaction is not recorded, but from that day on she never drank alcohol before a performance.

SOURCE
Jonathan Croall, *Sybil Thorndike: A Star of Life* (2008)

173

In 1921 she played Lady Macbeth in a special gala performance at the Odeon Theatre in Paris.

It was a tough assignment: Sybil had not played the part since 1915.... Edy Craig [director and designer, and Ellen Terry's daughter] insisted she borrow the dresses Ellen Terry had worn, as they were 'now beautifully supple and will almost play the part by themselves.' One of these, sewn all over with real green beetle wings, had been a sensation at the Lyceum, and immortalised in a portrait by John Singer Sargent. 'The instant I put on Ellen Terry's dress something happened to me' Sybil recalled. 'Not a tremble, not a quake.' When Hackett lost his way in the banquet scene, she hurled him across the stage, while whispering his lines in his ear. Afterwards she told him: 'Don't thank me, thank Ellen's dress.' Despite this hitch, it had been a satisfying occasion. 'I felt ten feet high that day,' she said later. 'Under great emotional stress I always feel enormously tall. It's a strange feeling: I seem to be on a higher plane, looking down on the audience from a vast height.'

SOURCE
Jonathan Croall, *Sybil Thorndike: A Star of Life* (2008)

174

Ralph Richardson said of Sybil Thorndike: 'She could act with a tailor's dummy and bring it to life.' He first worked with her at the Old Vic soon after she had been made a Dame in 1931.

'I was much in awe,' Ralph Richardson recalls. 'Dame Sybil was the first great star I had played with. Five minutes before the curtain went up I wondered if I dared pay court and wish her well. I went to the door of her dressing-room, but I was afraid to knock in case she was communing with herself before that big part. Then I heard a buzz of talk inside, and tapped. "Come in, Ralph dear," Sybil said. "Won't you have a bun? There isn't really time for introductions." She was feeding half-a-dozen schoolgirls with buns a few moments before the performance.'

SOURCE
Elizabeth Sprigge, *Sybil Thorndike Casson* (1971)

175

Dame Sybil opened in April 1951 in N. C. Hunter's Waters of the Moon *with Dame Edith Evans at the Haymarket Theatre. The play ran for a couple of years.*

All things considered, they got on remarkably well together though later in the run Frith Banbury had on Dame Edith's [Edith Evans] advice to reprimand Dame Sybil for overacting at one matinée: 'Yes,' replied Sybil, 'I was rather naughty on Saturday afternoon, but I had two grandchildren in front and I was determined that they should know exactly what the play was about. Consequently much underlining... However I've pulled myself together now and if you come again I think you'll find all is in order.'

This was the only occasion on which Dame Edith and Dame Sybil ever did a prolonged run together, and while Dame Edith cascaded from a great height ('like Royalty opening a bazaar', said Tynan) Dame Sybil contented herself by playing Schumann on the stage and, when the grandchildren weren't in front, capturing the few good scenes she did have almost by stealth...

Twenty years later I asked Dame Edith what she remembered of it all: 'Sybil I always envied for having so many relatives. She had the dressing room above mine, and all I ever seemed to hear was the tramp of children's feet.' Legend has it that when the play had been running successfully for a year, the Tennent management announced to Edith that she'd be getting a whole new wardrobe from Balmain. 'Good,' said Edith, 'but you'd better do something for Sybil too, what about a new cardigan?'

SOURCE
Sheridan Morley, *Sybil Thorndike: A Life in the Theatre* (1977)

176

In 1935 she appeared in Robert Morley's Short Story *alongside Marie Tempest, a fine light comedienne though regarded by some as 'a monstrous tartar of a woman'.*

Yet if Sybil lacked style, she certainly had steel. 'Marie could be a bitch,' she remarked later, with rare directness. 'She would try to make you her slave, and if you gave way she despised you and treated you like dirt.' She also hated other actors getting all the audience's attention, and would try to upstage them. She tried it on with Sybil, sitting at her desk making scratching noises with her pen at the wrong moment. Sybil countered this by placing blotting paper there at the next performance. Another night she played with a handkerchief downstage while Sybil had a scene upstage that got several laughs. Sybil responded the next night by playing a game of patience on the floor during Marie Tempest's scene, so bringing the attention back to her. As they went off-stage together the older woman whispered: 'You're a very clever actress, aren't you!' To which Sybil replied: 'Not especially, darling, but clever enough to act with you.' They then became good friends.

SOURCE
Jonathan Croall, *Sybil Thorndike: A Star of Life* (2008)

177

Here she is on tour in Australia in Enid Bagnold's The Chalk Garden *in 1958.*

Sybil still liked to play the occasional trick on stage, such as crossing her eyes at Jane as they were about to play a scene together, or tickling the palm of her hand as she held it, making it difficult for her not to giggle. Patricia Kennedy recalls: 'Once or twice she crossed her eyes at me—but always in the middle of one of her own speeches.' But Lewis' playfulness was much more extreme. One night, having heard that someone thought him 'a bit past it', he came on at the next performance in full juvenile make-up—fair hair, blue eye-shadow, doll cheeks and cupid-bow lips—and flounced about the stage, while the other actors tried desperately to carry on normally. Sybil was furious at this unprofessional conduct, and was heard raging at him in the dressing-room afterwards, forcing him to apologise to the management and company.

SOURCE
Jonathan Croall, *Sybil Thorndike: A Star of Life* (2008)

178

In 1960 she appeared with Marie Lohr and other veteran actresses in Noël Coward's Waiting in the Wings, *a play about a group of elderly actresses living in a retirement home. Dame Sybil had occasional problems with her lines which lead Coward to nickname her 'Fluffy Damesy'.*

The play ran until February, then toured for several weeks. Legend has it that at one performance one elderly actress dried, the prompter gave the line, then gave it again, after which someone said: 'We know the line dear, but who says it?'

SOURCE
Jonathan Croall, *Sybil Thorndike: A Star of Life* (2008)

179

Her final stage appearance was at the theatre named after her, the Thorndike in Leatherhead, in John Graham's There was an Old Woman. *She turned 87 during the run.*

Another cast member, Barbara Laurenson, recalls: 'There were no histrionics, no displays of ego. Sybil was dignified, undemanding, almost unassuming.' There were humorous moments. At the point where a stage direction read 'Old Woman hovers in the background', Philip Grout saw Sybil making strange hand movements. When he asked what she was doing, she replied: 'I'm hoovering.'

She also had problems with her lines, telling Patricia: 'I'm worried about the play. I love it, but such speeches I've got. These ruddy words to be learned nearly finish me.' She would hit herself and say, 'Silly bloody fool, can't remember anything!' She would exercise her memory by trying to memorise the names of the shops in the street. Grout recalls another method: 'I went to her hotel before the opening to hear her words. She had six coins laid out in a row, and she would only move a coin away if she got a page or a section perfect. I was amazed by her desire for perfection.'

SOURCE
Jonathan Croall, *Sybil Thorndike: A Star of Life* (2008)

180

How fitting it was that her very last public appearance should have been at the Old Vic on its farewell night [in 1974]. At the end of the performance, she was wheeled down the aisle in her chair, to smile and wave for the last time to the people sitting in the theatre she had always loved so well. Lively, passionate, argumentative, always travelling, acting, learning a new language or a new poem, a magnificent wife and mother, she was surely one of the rarest women of our time. 'Oh, Lewis,' she cried once, 'if only we could be the first actors to play on the moon.'

SOURCE
Sir John Gielgud, *An Actor and His Time* (1979)

181

Sybil continued to support many causes, great and small. She became a trustee of the Theatre Girls' Club in Soho, which provided accommodation for unemployed or low-paid actresses—two-thirds of the profession were reckoned to be out of work at this time. She was on the board of the Council for the Abolition of the Death Penalty, an issue about which she felt strongly. She opened sales of work and church bazaars, and made radio appeals for the Invalid Children's Aid Association and the Homes of St Giles for British Lepers. According to Emlyn Williams, when one of her daughters took a phone call from a family friend, she said: "They're not in. Daddy is reading Shakespeare sonnets to the blind and Mummy's playing Shakespeare to the lepers."

SOURCE
Jonathan Croall, *Sybil Thorndike: A Star of Life* (2008)

BALIOL HOLLOWAY
(1883–1967)

182

Regarded by some as the finest Falstaff, Othello, and Richard III of his time, according to Sir Donald Sinden, Holloway's long experience in the theatre left him with an enviable sense of stagecraft.

I went off to consult my old friend Baliol Holloway, by then aged eighty-four, who had spent the whole of his theatrical career in the classical repertoire. In his minute flat in Thayer Street, 'Ba' gave me a two-hour lesson in the art of the aside:

> An aside must be directed to a given seat in the theatre—a different seat for each aside, some in the stalls, some in the circle. Never to the same seat twice—the rest of the audience will think you have a friend sitting there. If you are facing to the right immediately before the aside, then direct it to the left of the theatre, and vice versa. Your head must crack round in one clean movement, look straight at the occupant of the seat, deliver the line and crack your head back to exactly where it was before. The voice you use must be different from the one you are using in the play. If loud, then soft; if soft, then loud; if high, then low; if low, then high; if fast, then slow; if slow, then fast. During an aside, no other characters must move at all—the time you take does not exist for them.

'Ba' and I practiced what he preached, using a scene from—I think—*Still Waters Run Deep* in which two characters speak in asides for twenty or more lines, until he was satisfied that I could do it. It worked and it was a proud moment when 'Ba' later saw a performance and congratulated me.

SOURCE
Donald Sinden, *A Touch of the Memoirs* (1982)

183

Soon after the turn of the century Ba read in a theatrical newspaper that a leading man was required for a stock company in Northampton. In answer to his letter an appointment was made for the following Saturday. Ba put on his best suit, caught the train to Northampton, asked his way to the theatre and presented himself outside the manager's office. 'Come in,' a voice bellowed. Standing behind a desk was a portly man with his jacket off, braces supporting his trousers and a bowler hat on his head.

'My name is Holloway sir—Baliol Holloway.'

'Yes, well I'm glad you've come, 'olloway—I want you to start Monday.' He then opened a drawer, took out six scripts and threw them one by one on the desk: 'There you are; Monday night; Tuesday night. Wednesday matinée same as Monday. Wednesday night. Thursday night. Friday night. Saturday matinée same as Thursday. Saturday night. Six wonderful parts 'olloway. Monday night's the best one—forty-two rounds [rounds of applause] in it. And you've got the best line in the play: I'll give it to you. "I may be only a trooper, Kendrick, but I would rather be a trooper—ten times rather—than an ensign with an 'eart as black as Villiers." Brings the house down, 'olloway. Good luck.'

Considerably shaken, Ba found himself some digs and started to swot up his six leading parts over the weekend. On Monday night he opened and at the end of the performance the manager appeared in his dressing room. 'Not bad 'olloway, not bad. Thirty-six out of the forty-two. But 'olloway, "'eart as black as Villiers"—what 'appened to it?'

'I don't know, sir,' said Ba. 'I shouted it as loudly as I could.'

'SHOUTED IT!? It's yer right arm. YOU DROPPED IT!...Look, I'll give it to you again: "I may be only a trooper, Kendrick, but I would rather be a trooper—*ten times rather*—[the manager here raised his arm ominously and pointed] than an ensign with an 'eart as black as Villiers." Hold it; keep yer arm up there till they do applaud.'

SOURCE
Donald Sinden, *Laughter in the Second Act* (1985)

TOM WALLS
(1883–1949)

184

Tom Walls is best known for the farces he presented and starred in with Ralph Lynn and others at London's Aldwych Theatre, among them A Cuckoo in the Nest *by Ben Travers.*

Rehearsals of the *Cuckoo,* which began five days after I had first met Tom Walls, gave me my first experience of some of his singular methods as actor-producer. For the first two of the three-weeks rehearsal he sat and directed the rest of the company, including his understudy. At the beginning of the third week he resigned himself, with a groan of effort, to participation in the acting. But during the past fortnight he had, of course, been much too busy to study his lines; and when the play started out on its one week's probation at some provincial theatre his performance was liable to hiatus. This didn't embarrass him at all. He would cross to the prompt corner and rally the dittering stage-manager with a rasping and resounding aside—'Come on, Bobbie—let's have it, can't you?' He had no compunction or shame about this. He took a contemptuous view of audiences as the best of times. But it is only fair to say that on first nights in London he was not only word-perfect but gave what was probably his best performance of the entire run of a play. 'In every play there's only one show that really matters,' he used to say; a candid admission of his cynical outlook on the whole concern.

SOURCE
Ben Travers, *Vale of Laughter* (1957)

LAURETTE TAYLOR

(1884–1946)

185

Born in New York, of Irish descent, Laurette Taylor was an American stage actress and silent film star now best remembered for her performance in Tennessee Williams' The Glass Menagerie *in 1944, alongside Eddie Dowling who also co-directed the play. After her death, Williams said of Laurette Taylor, 'There was a radiance about her art which I can compare only to the greatest lines of poetry, and which gave me the same shock of revelation as if the air about us had been momentarily broken through by light from some clear space beyond us.' On the Broadway opening of the play the cast took 24 curtain calls. Then:*

After the curtain came down for the last time, Taylor threw her arms around Dowling.

'Eddie, I can't remember anything,' she said. 'Does it look like a success?'

I said, 'Well, Laurette, you must have left your hearing aids home because there's never been such…'

She said, 'Well, I never pay attention to applause. But the quiet during the performance, Eddie. What is the quiet?'

'We learned from thirteen or fourteen weeks in Chicago, Laurette, about the quiet.'

'But,' she said, 'New York isn't Chicago. They're intelligent in New York.'

I said, 'Laurette, this isn't a matter of intelligence. These are basic emotions, my dear girl, and haven't you caught on yet to the kind of play we're doing?'

She said, 'Oh, don't give me all that nonsense.' She said, 'Why wasn't there some reaction to my funny lines? I didn't get one so-and-so.'

I said, 'Well, you'll find out very soon.'

The number of people who came backstage to see the actors was so large that the Playhouse's safety curtain had to be lifted to allow the euphoric spillover crowd to loiter onstage. 'It was like after a World Series game when they come down out of the stands. That's what it was,' Dowling said. He continued, 'We went on for a long time after... I don't suppose there's been a hit since like it. Certainly, no actress before or since has ever made the impression this woman made. She's a legend along with Bernhardt and Duse, and all out of that little play.'

SOURCE
John Lahr, *Tennessee Williams: Mad Pilgrimage of the Flesh* (2014)

186

As the lights faded out on Dowling, they faded in on Laurette Taylor as Amanda, the matriarch of the hapless Wingfield family, entering upstage into the apartment's dining room. The reception for Taylor, who had made her Broadway debut in 1903 at the age of sixteen and had been a full-fledged star for more than thirty years, was deafening. On the eve of her sixty-first birthday, she was returning to Broadway after a five-year hiatus. Her rustication was the aftermath of an Actors' Equity suspension for drunkenly disrupting and closing a play. The death of her playwright husband, Hartley Manners, in 1928, had sent Taylor 'on the longest wake in history,' as she liked to joke. 'She'd closed many a show on opening night. The managers despised her, and they thought I was crazy entirely to have anything to do with her,' Dowling said. Management might have been wary of Taylor—'the alcoholic of alcoholics,' as she was known on the Rialto—but the public's loyalty was rock solid. 'Nothing like this we'd ever heard before. And so it thwarted the action a little bit, and it threw her. It really threw her,' Dowling recalled about the barrage of applause that greeted Taylor. To fill the stage time and to settle the audience, Taylor brushed the hair out of her eyes and talked into the telephone. 'It's Amanda,' she said, holding the receiver in her hand—vamping until the applause died down—'It's Amanda. And I've got to talk to you.' Finally the audience grew quiet. 'This was just about the time I came through the door and said, "Ma, I've got good news for you",' Dowling recalled. 'Instead of giving me the right answer, she took me into the second act.'

SOURCE
John Lahr, *Tennessee Williams: Mad Pilgrimage of the Flesh* (2014)

GODFREY TEARLE
(1884–1953)

187

Born in New York and brought up in England, Godfrey Tearle was the son of the British actor-manager George Osmond Tearle (1852–1901) and the American actress Marianne 'Minnie' Conway (1852–1896). In 1893, he made his stage debut as young Prince Richard, Duke of York, in his father's production of Richard III *and in 1908 he appeared in his first film as Romeo in* Romeo and Juliet. *Remembered on screen for his appearance in Alfred Hitchcock's 1935 version of* The 39 Steps, *on film he was often cast as the quintessential English gentleman, while on stage he was a noted Shakespearean actor, and knighted for his services to the theatre not long before his death.*

Hidden away in Godfrey's entry in *Who's Who in the Theatre* is the most delightful sequence. Between 1904 and 1906 he toured in his own company playing Hamlet, Othello, Shylock, Brutus, Romeo and Sir Peter Teazle. Years later at His Majesty's Theatre he is playing Marcellus in *Hamlet*, Ludovico in *Othello*, Lorenzo in *The*

Merchant, Octavius in *Julius Caesar* and Trip in *The School for Scandal*. Big fish in little ponds to little fish in big ponds.

He told me that in *Antony and Cleopatra* in 1946 at the Piccadilly Theatre, the young actor playing his servant Eros was suddenly taken ill and an unprepared replacement was pushed on at the last moment to assist in removing Antony's armour. Godfrey spoke: 'Unarm, Eros; the long day's task is done. Off, pluck off.' The young replacement looked aghast. 'I'm so sorry,' he said and retired from the scene.

SOURCE
Donald Sinden, *A Touch of the Memoirs* (1982)

GLADYS COOPER
(1888–1971)

188

Gladys Cooper was a British actress whose long career began in musical comedy and pantomime in the Edwardian era and took in theatre management, films, and television. Popular on both sides of the Atlantic, in such plays as J. M. Barrie's Peter Pan *in London just after the First World War and Enid Bagnold's* The Chalk Garden *in New York nearly 40 years later, these stories come from her autobiography.*

At Drury Lane I got to know a delicious type of old-time actor, who, according to his own story, had in the 'sixties (or perhaps it was the 'fifties, I forget) created 'a furore' in nearly all the best parts Shakespeare wrote. If you believed him he had been, in his time, about the most marvellous Hamlet, Iago, Julius Caesar, Jew in *The Merchant*, and so on, ever to walk the stage.

He was a great talker, and one night, recounting some of his alleged triumphs, he was proceeding, 'From the moment I make my appearance on the stage I always forget everything but my part. I leave my own personality behind me—I am Hamlet, Romeo, Othello, Anthony, as the case may be, the theatre disappears, the audience vanishes—I am...' when one of his irritated listeners interrupted:

'Yes, I have noticed that,' remarked the interrupter.

'You have noticed what?' demanded the old actor.

'That your audience vanishes,' was the unkind but deserved reply.

SOURCE
Gladys Cooper, *Gladys Cooper* (1931)

189

It may be heretic of me, but I am inclined to hold and maintain that *Peter Pan* is really more of a play for grown-ups than for children. Hook is a terrifying character. When children are asked 'Do you believe in fairies?' they are egged on to call out 'Yes' by the elders. When I played in the piece we did as big business in the evenings with adult audiences as in the afternoons with children.

It is fatal to introduce children to the back of the stage after you have asked them to believe in *Peter Pan*. One afternoon a small boy was brought to my dressing-room. He looked at me suspiciously for some moments and then he said: 'Well, now fly.' There absolutely does not seem to be any adequate answer to that sort of demand.

SOURCE
Gladys Cooper, *Gladys Cooper* (1931)

190

An actor I knew was playing a very tragic part in a drama, and in one scene he is discovered sitting at a table in a country inn. He has ordered some food and the maid brings in a plate and sets before him what is supposed to be a mutton chop. The actor usually turns from the table as she approaches, to say his lines. One night they could not find the 'property' chop, so a small brown gingerbread biscuit was put upon the plate. The maid placed it before the unfortunate actor, who was so petrified at what he beheld before him that, instead of declaiming to the air the line 'Oh, God, how long will it last?' (meaning his agony of mind) he addressed the words to the biscuit. A roar of laughter went up from the whole audience and a ribald voice from the gallery shouted 'Cheer up, guv'nor! It's treasury night to-morrow—you'll 'ang out.'

SOURCE
Gladys Cooper, *Gladys Cooper* (1931)

EDITH EVANS
(1888–1976)

191

Reckoned by many the greatest actress of the first two-thirds of the twentieth century, her phrasing of 'A handbag?' *as Lady Bracknell in* The Importance of Being Earnest *has passed into legend. She is remembered, too, for her Millimant in Congreve's* The Way of the World *and her Rosalind in* As You Like It. *Peter Ustinov described a wartime production of Sheridan's* The Rivals *in which they both appeared. In the orchestra were former members of the Berlin Philharmonic, under their leader, Lance-Corporal Professor Doktor*

Strietzel, as well as sometime members of the Vienna Philharmonic, led by Private Professor Doktor Stiasny.

The play, performed in garrison theatres in very flimsy yet evocative sets, assuring a rapid continuity of action, opened in Salisbury, and was an instant success. One distinguished admiral was even compelled to admit to Edith Evans, 'By Jove, I'm embarrassed to say that this is the first play by Shakespeare I've seen since Richard of Bordeaux!'

One drawback to these garrison theatres was that there was no method of concealing the orchestra. Its members sat on the same level as the audience. It was merely the actors who were elevated. I noticed on the first night that the orchestra made use of a miniature chessboard in order to while away the time during the histrionics, and often musicians crept forward like troops in a dugout to make some snide move. As far as I could understand it was a permanent championship, Berlin versus Vienna.

I hoped and prayed that Edith Evans wouldn't notice what was going on, but on the fourth night, during a brilliant tirade, she stopped dead. One eye had alighted on the tiny chessboard just as an Austrian viola player had spotted a crack in the enemy defence, and was creeping forward on all fours to deliver the *coup de grâce*.

She faltered, fumbled, and then, with superb dramatic instinct, she looked at me and said, in a tone of pained surprise, 'What did you say?'

Determined not to be placed on the defensive, I invented a little Sheridan: 'Madam, though the humours of Bath be but a diversion to our contumely, I will not presume on your generosity to the extent of belittling those very qualities which, while they do us but scant justice before the evil tongues of the town, nevertheless becalm the odious, and bring success to fools.'

Neither I nor the audience knew what on earth I was talking about, but I said it, or something like it, with immense conviction, with the result that our exit was rewarded by a burst of spontaneous applause.

Poor Edith was livid, and kept referring to the chess playing as a 'Gilbertian situation'. After the show, I accosted Professor Strietzel. To soften the blow somewhat (for after all, he *was* a lance corporal, and I had seen how hostile he had become towards poor Private Stiasny) I told him he had never played better than on that night.

His face lit up.

'You are a *real* musician,' he counter-flattered, 'tonight, for ze *först* time, ze Boccherini was good, alzo I still have trouble mit ze Mozart und ze Dittersdorf.'

'Yes,' I replied reasonably, 'but even there, I noticed a distinct improvement.'

'Even there, even there!' he agreed.

'There's only one thing... one criticism.'

'Ach!' His face darkened once again in anticipation of some searing words of truth.

'The game of chess,' I said.

He bridled like a frisky horse. 'Are you serious?' he asked quietly.

'I'm afraid so. There has to be an end to it. It is frightfully distracting for the actors. We can see your every move down there, and—'

'It distracts you?' he enquired, all innocence and soft surprise.

'Yes,' I said.

'No!' he roared. 'You are too fine an artist to be distracted. It's zis voman!'

'Now come on!' I snapped, simulating crossness. 'She's a most distinguished actress and a wonderful person—'

'It's not as zough it vas a big chessboard,' he shouted, and then his voice became dramatically diminutive. 'It vas a little chessboard.' His two index-fingers reduced its imaginary size to about one inch square.

'The smaller the chessboard the greater the distance you have to travel to make a move, and the greater the distraction for us,' I declared.

He knew a checkmate when he saw it, and retired from the scene of battle.

The next night, Edith found it hard to concentrate, which was unlike her, being a creature of a ferocious inner discipline, and usually impervious to external influence. As soon as I hobbled on the stage in the guise of my gouty paterfamilias, I saw what was happening.

The orchestra, deprived of its chessboard, had now arranged the lights from its music-stands so that its members were lit from beneath, and they now followed Edith's every move in this ghostly light, looking for all the world like war-criminals following the arguments of their advocate with misgiving and resignation.

Once again, at the end of the performance, I was compelled to accost Profession Strietzel.

'Tonight,' I said sternly, 'it was not so good.'

He was in surly temper.

'Once again,' he grumbled, 'you give proof of your musicianship. Stiasny is like a mule so stubborn. The Boccherini vas one Funeral March, not one minuet. A disgrace. The Mozart vas a little better, and the Dittersdorf superb. The rest—'

'I have a criticism.'

'Please.' He smiled like a head-waiter confronted with a fly in the mayonnaise.

'Why do you follow Edith Evans with your eyes in a manner calculated to disturb any performer, any artist?'

What was left of his smile faded, and he became controlledly rational.

'First, it vas the chessboard. Correct me if I am wrong. Chess ve shouldn't play…'

'That is correct.'

'So ve leave the chessboard at home. Vot else can ve do? Ve follow the play. Ve look at the voman.'

Suddenly the constriction of his voice and the coolness of his presentation of the facts deserted him. He shouted volcanically: 'You think it gives us *pleasure* to vatch zis voman? Ve, who have seen Paula Wessely at her height!'

I tried to top him in bluster, but he lowered his voice to a kind of lugubrious mutter, at the same time looking into the distance to lend a cosmic significance to his words.

'You know, ven ve left Germany, mit concentration-camps and persecution, ve thought ve would come to a land vere ve could breathe—'

Here he gave an ingenious impression of a plant opening its petals to the sun, but he quickly shrivelled. 'But no,' he said brokenly, 'it's all ze same ... persecution ... prison bars ...'

I was outraged. I told him angrily that I saw no connection between myself and a Gauleiter.

'Not you, dear friend—'

Nor did I think that any more ludicrous comparison could be made than one equating a dear, human, and profoundly religious creature like Edith Evans with Heinrich Himmler.

He nodded in a way which suggested that everyone is entitled to his own opinion, no one more so that he who has suffered a deprivation of liberty to play chess in an orchestra pit.

The next night Edith was brilliant. The only trouble was the almost entire absence of laughs. I made my entrance, and, inspired by the zest and brio of Edith Evans, I acted as well as I knew how, in complete and utter silence. It was acutely depressing. Not even the presence of three generals in the front row could justify the extraordinary dullness of the audience.

When I had a free moment, I rushed to the back of the auditorium in order to unravel the mystery. I did not have far to seek. The musicians had now reversed their positions, and sat facing the audience, their heads just visible above the rail of the orchestra pit. Lit from beneath, like mournful skittles waiting for the usual knocks of fate, they dampened the spirits of the onlookers.

Edith was very upset by the deterioration in the audience's quality, and left the stage with the unspoken conviction that she was face to face with *force-majeure*. I found no words to express my horror at such diabolical ingenuity. I just shook a negative head at Professor Strietzel, who smiled imperceptibly and shrugged a fatalistic shoulder.

The rest of the run was most successful, and for the record, I must add that the chess-games on the miniature board were resumed, and Edith never seemed to notice them any more. By the last performance, the Austrians were leading the Germans by twenty-four matches to twenty-one, with nineteen matches drawn.

SOURCE
Peter Ustinov, *Dear Me* (1977)

192

In his memoirs, Derek Salberg, for many years the manager of the 'Alex', the Alexandra Theatre, Birmingham, recalled a memorable opening night.

The most notable event in 1956 was the British premiere of *The Chalk Garden* with an all star cast including Edith Evans, Peggy Ashcroft and Felix Aylmer, produced by John Gielgud. The first night was the most glittering I can remember at the Alex, with an audience which included Laurence Olivier, 'Binkie' Beaumont, under whose management it was presented, Robert Helpman and many other notables. Our rather elderly stage doorkeeper who, after the performance, was simultaneously trying to control autograph hunters, deal with requests for taxis, give advice on restaurants and attend to his normal duties, answered a telephone call. By now distraught, and afraid to leave his stage door unattended, he shouted up the stairs, 'Is there an Edith Evans in the theatre? If so, she's wanted on the 'phone!'

SOURCE
Derek Salberg, *My Love Affair with a Theatre* (1978)

193

The following three anecdotes appear in Bryan Forbes's biography of Dame Edith.

Edith left little to chance. I particularly like the story of the young actor who once went up to her before the red light flashed for transmission time on a BBC drama broadcast. 'Good luck, Dame Edith,' he said. 'With some of us,' Edith replied, 'it isn't *luck*.'

SOURCE
Bryan Forbes, *Ned's Girl* (1977)

194

During the run of *Coriolanus* she was involved in a car crash; she was thrown out of the front passenger seat and broke her wrist, cracked some ribs and was very badly bruised. She was out of the company for three weeks as a result, returning before she had completely recovered with her arm in plaster. It so happened that on the matinée of the day she resumed her role the young Albert Finney, understudying Sir Laurence, was called upon to deputise for him. They had a rehearsal for Finney on the morning of the matinée. 'The set had a lot of steps in it,' Finney recalled. 'We all had to do a lot of going up and down, I remember, and there were a couple of occasions with Dame Edith where, as her son, I had to hold her and guide her and go up the stairs with her. When we broke at the end of the rehearsal, I said 'Dame Edith, is there anything I'm not doing right, anything that worries you or throws you?' She said, 'Just be careful when you hold me because my ribs are a little bruised. So don't hold me, because it'll make me want to wince. I'll become aware that I'm bruised. Just put your arm within an inch or so, so that I'll know it's there if I need it, but don't grip me.' I said, 'Okay, yes, but is there anything, any move I'm making that's not the way Larry does it, that's sort of, you know, wrong?' 'Albert,' she said, 'move where you like, dear. I'll get my face in somewhere.'

SOURCE
Bryan Forbes, *Ned's Girl* (1977)

195

Edith's views on full frontal nudity when that fad hit the West End hardly coincided with those of the perpetrator of *Oh, Calcutta!* 'I can't think what they're all after, what they're *at*, what they're trying to find out. What does it mean? One woman's just like another. I see myself every morning in the bath and it doesn't interest me to stay any longer than I have to. Even when I was young and considered to have quite a good figure... I'm not interested. I can't be bothered with it, really. Mystery, that's what the theatre's all about and there's no mystery in a lot of goose-pimples.'*

* *Sybil Thorndike's reaction was similar. 'My dear, I am a mother, a grandmother, and a great-grandmother. There is nothing I haven't seen.'*

SOURCE
Bryan Forbes, *Ned's Girl* (1977)

196

In 1936, at the New Theatre in London, Alec Guinness appeared with Edith Evans and John Gielgud in a celebrated production of Chekhov's The Seagull, *directed by Theodore Komisarjevsky, known as 'Komis'.*

A moment came when it was Edith's cue to speak. Gielgud was sitting next to her and, after a moment's pause, he whispered, 'Edith, it's you.' From where I was standing in the wings I could see she hadn't dried up; she just had no intention of speaking. The stage manager gave a prompt, which was firmly ignored. Komis, in the stalls, sat still; a deep silence fell on the stage and no one moved. I glanced at my watch. After four minutes Edith gave a slight shiver with her shoulders, as if touched by a chill breeze, and then quietly said her line, 'Let's go in,' with infinite sadness and yet somehow callously. And that's the way it stayed, through the remainder of the rehearsals and the run; a four-minute pause, an unheard-of length of time in the theatre, in which actors and audience seemed to hold their breath. It came of Edith's supreme daring, confidence and imagination.

SOURCE
Alec Guinness, *Blessings in Disguise* (1985)

197

I remember standing in the wings with a group of other students while we were doing *Trelawny of the Wells*, and talking to Edith Evans just before she went on. One of the girls had asked her some question about deportment or technique, and she replied: 'My dear, always try to think that you are the most wonderful creature that ever lived when you are on the stage, and the audience will believe it too'. Her cue came, and with head held high she glided on to the stage, her irregular features illuminated by a sort of ethereal radiance. Huddled together down in the O.P. corner, we watched her move about the stage—surely she was the most beautiful woman in the theatre!

SOURCE
Esmond Knight, *Seeking the Bubble* (1942)

198

Michael Redgrave played Orlando to Edith Evans' Rosalind at Stratford-upon-Avon in 1936. Redgrave never forgot the experience.

He always came back to Edith Evans. 'If you are going to play Orlando, you must love your Rosalind! You know, I made love to Edith on the night Vanessa was born.' Acting with Edith, he said, 'was like being in your mother's arms, like knowing how to swim, like riding a bicycle. You're safe... For the first time in my acting life, I felt completely unselfconscious. Acting with her made me feel, oh, it's so easy. You don't start acting, she told me, until you stop trying to act. It doesn't leave the ground until you don't have to think about it... For the first time, on stage or off, I felt completely free.'

SOURCE
Gyles Brandreth, *Brief Encounters* (2001)

CATHLEEN NESBITT
(1888–1982)

199

Cathleen Nesbitt was an elegant British actress, of Irish and Welsh descent, whose long career took her from the West End in 1910 (in a revival of Pinero's The Cabinet Minister*) to Broadway in 1981 (when she reprised her role as Mrs Higgins in a revival of* My Fair Lady *starring Rex Harrison and directed by Patrick Garland). She told Garland of her first atlantic crossing many years before.*

'The first time I went across the Atlantic was in the old Queen Mary. I was in a play by Lady Gregory and travelled with the Abbey Theatre Company from Dublin. It was my first job and I went over as an understudy. The leading lady was a marvellous woman, *tres grande dame*, but for all that she got dreadfully seasick, and I heard her say: "Captain, make the ship stop this minute and let me off."' It turned out that the dear leading actor, a distinguished Irish player, who was green, grey and white, alternately, as the ship lurched up and down, spread all his press notices in front of him on the floor, and was praying loudly: 'Oh dear God, now don't drown a great actor.' And to reassure himself he read aloud his notices: 'Now, God, listen to this. You can't possibly kill me, a famous actor, with press notices like that.'

SOURCE
Patrick Garland, *The Incomparable Rex* (1998)

ROBERTSON HARE
(1891–1979)

200

Robertson Hale was a delightful English character actor known as 'Bunny' to his friends and particularly associated with the Aldwych farces of the 1920s. Here Sir John Mills describes the production of Aren't Men Beasts *in which the young Mills appeared with Hare and Alfred Drayton in 1936.*

On two occasions, however, things happened that strained control to breaking point. During one scene with the three of us on stage Bunny Hare had to say, 'Indubitably' (a word he made famous), and then in excitement jump up in the air. On one momentous occasion at a matinée, after I can only suppose a large helping of baked beans for lunch, 'Indubitably' Bunny jumped as usual into the air and a foot from the stage produced one of the loudest and most spectacular farts it has even been my pleasure to hear. There was no question this time of it being an 'in' joke—the audience heard it. There was no need to go through the agony of suppressing the laughter; the house went up in smoke and we went up with it.

The next happening, however, was much more difficult to cope with. At one point Alfred had to shout at the top of his considerable voice, 'Shut up.' During one performance we were all in a line facing front, obeying Leslie's instructions and barking it into the abyss. As Alfie shouted the words the top plate of his false teeth flew out of his mouth making a bee-line for the stalls. With a miraculously quick reaction he shot out his right hand and caught them in mid-flight. The whole thing was so fast that the audience didn't see it, but unfortunately Bunny and I did. The rest of the scene was torture for us, Alfie turned up-stage and returned his high-flying choppers to their rightful home, while we struggled with the agony of suppressing the laughter that threatened to overwhelm us. Somehow we managed to get through it. But Alfie himself was livid. We were in disgrace. The audience didn't pay to see that sort of behaviour. It was two days before he forgave us.

SOURCE
John Mills, *Up in the Clouds, Gentlemen Please* (1980)

201

Tall, handsome, with a splendid profile topped by dark wavy hair, Leslie Faber was quite the opposite of a young actor by the name of Robertson (Bunny) Hare who was very short. Bunny hero-worshipped the magnificent Faber who was everything that Bunny was not or ever could be. An incongruous friendship sprang up between them. One day as they entered The Volunteer, a public house in Baker Street, a youngish, ill-kempt man with pale face and hollow cheeks, and wearing a crumpled raincoat was leaning on the bar;

his eyes suddenly glazed and uttering a strangulated cry he collapsed to the ground. In complete control of the situation, Faber said, 'Stand back' and, demanding a glass of water from the barmaid, he filled his mouth and 'squirted' it into the man's face. With a shudder the man revived, and Faber, taking his lapels in one hand, lifted him to his feet. With the other hand Faber extracted his wallet, peeled off a pound note and gave it to the unsteady man saying, 'There you are—if you have any sense you'll eat with it. If you haven't you'll drink with it. Get out into the fresh air!'

Bunny stood gaping with admiration at his hero—the aplomb, the wisdom, the sheer strength of this man. He never forgot it.

On holiday in Budleigh Salterton many years later, Bunny had just reached the bottom of a zig-zag staircase that led from the top of the cliffs to the beach below, when his wife said that she would like a box of chocolates. 'Very well, my dear—I'll get you some', and he started back up the steps. Halfway up a panting Bunny arrived at a small landing, to find an ill-kempt man with a pale face and hollow cheeks wearing a crumpled raincoat, leaning on the balustrade. As he passed, the man uttered a strangulated cry and with glazed eyes collapsed to the ground... Bunny's experience of his youth leaped to his mind—this would be his moment of triumph. He had to stop three passers-by before one agreed to search for water. Eventually some arrived and Bunny echoed Faber's command: 'Stand back.' Taking a mouthful of water, he 'squirted' it in the man's face. But even using two hands he failed to lift him without assistance. He fumbled for his wallet, remembering the pound note and the advice that went with it, but the man had already revived—shaking the water from his face, he glowered at Bunny and his eyes widened. 'You dirty rotten bastard,' he said and chased poor Bunny up the steps.

SOURCE
Donald Sinden, *Memoirs* (1982)

ALFRED LUNT (1892–1977) and LYNN FONTANNE (1887–1983)

202

Alfred Lunt and Lynn Fontanne, who married in 1922, became the pre-eminent couple of the American stage. When asked why they didn't bill themselves as 'Fontanne and Lunt', Alfred Lunt replied, 'This is theatre, dear boy, not a god-damned lifeboat.' Known as 'the fabulous Lunts', they were both fine comedians as well as straight actors. They played on both sides of the Atlantic with style and success: S. N. Behrman's version of Giraudoux's Amphitryon 38 *was a particular triumph in New York in 1937.*

During the early rehearsals for *Amphitryon 38*, Alfred arrived at the theatre in a great tizzy, the stage manager recalls, and called the company together for a talk. 'Ladies and gentlemen, it is impossible for me to play this role, so we can not go on with this play. Please consider the production cancelled. Speak to the company manager and pick up your cheques. I can't go on. I can't find the green umbrella.' He turned and left the theatre.

Lynn sat quietly down near the footlights and watched the perturbed actors who stood transfixed with dismay. Then she spoke, 'Don't worry, we'll go on, and he will find it.'

The rehearsal began and half an hour later, completely re-inspired by his respite, Alfred returned and raised his arm, announcing, 'Don't worry. I've found it. We'll start again at the beginning of the act.'

The exact origin of the green umbrella, meaning the inspiration for a role, seems shrouded in mystery. Noël Coward told Raymond Mander and Joe Mitchenson in June 1957 that the term dates from rehearsals for the repertory tour in 1927 which included *Pygmalion*, when Lynn suggested that he should use a green umbrella as Higgins, as he was depressed over his interpretation of the part.

George Greenberg, many times their stage manager, was sure his first knowledge came at the time of the above incident in connection with *Amphitryon 38*. All members or former members of the Lunts' companies know the umbrella well.

SOURCE
George Freedley, *The Lunts* (1958)

203

The Lunts specialized in 'daring' love scenes and physical intimacies that would be considered tame today. For example, during a scene in which Alfred stretched out on a sofa and Lynn took off his shoes, he stroked her face with his feet—in socks of course, but still a caress that might not have been quite so acceptable night after night from just any leading man to the puritanical American public. Once when the curtain fell on the scene, an old lady in the audience remarked with relief to her elderly friend, 'How nice to know they're married.'

SOURCE
Lilli Palmer, *Change Lobsters and Dance* (1976)

HENRY BAYNTON
(1892–1951)

204

Henry Baynton was an English actor-manager, born in Warwick, who devoted his life to playing Shakespeare. He began his career in 1910 in Oscar Asche's company and, in 1915, joined Frank Benson's company to play Hamlet. He formed his own company in 1917 and toured the British Isles for many years playing all the leading Shakespeare roles—not always to critical acclaim.

Baynton was one of the tribe of actors who endlessly toured the provinces in tatty productions of Shakespeare, catering for the most part to bewildered children. (He was inclined to slip out of the theatre, in full costume and make-up, to have a quick pint at the local and, on one notorious occasion, misjudged the length of Lady Macbeth's sleep walking scene. At the end of Lady M's effort no Macbeth could be found, so the lady stage-manager stepped forward and had the temerity to announce to the assembled scholars, who were studying the play for exams, 'That is where the plays ends. You can go home now.' As they huddled against the rain, trotting down the pier, who should come lurching up but Macbeth himself, in Viking helmet, somewhat awry, and plaited red wig flying in the wind. Astonished to see his audience leaving he called out, 'Surely not going home so soon?' He got no reply as they were hustled on their way by terrified tutors.

SOURCE
Alec Guinness, *Blessings in Disguise* (1985)

KATHARINE CORNELL
(1893–1974)

205

In the years following the Second World War Katharine Cornell contended with Helen Hayes for the title of 'First Lady' of Broadway. She worked hard to achieve her success and never tired of trying to perfect her technique.

By breathing, you can raise the tension and excitement in you so that you can come in on top of a scene, where you've got to come in high. The old actors used to call it 'shaking the ladder'. They used to have the old string ladders, rope ladders, that came down from the flies. And the old actors, for the big, big scenes, you know—the tremendous scenes—they'd go and take this ladder and shake it. And they'd shake it so hard. And I can do it in a minute; you can do it in a minute. You can get your circulation up in one second. Then you get so you don't have to shake that ladder, you can do it by breathing. And often I do it with my breathing. That's nothing I've learned from anybody outside. And I've often done it with my hands on my knees. And I did it when I came in in *The Green Hat* at the end, where—no, I didn't do it, Leslie Howard did it—when after I killed myself... I showed Leslie how to put his hands on his knees, and he'd come in like that. Because your whole flow of blood is very high. It's just a mechanical thing, to get your circulation up. I don't have to live through anything in a cellar; I don't have to see somebody dead down there. I can do it myself, mechanically, and with the help of my imagination.

SOURCE
Lewis Funke and John E. Booth, *Actors Talk about Acting* (1961)

CICELY COURTNEIDGE
(1893–1980)

206

Australian-born, Cicely Courtneidge enjoyed a long career as an actress and comic performer. Harold French appeared with her in The Little Revue *in 1923, directed by her husband Jack Hulbert, and described one memorable scene from it.*

The undertaker sketch opened with me alone on the stage, my back to the audience, polishing some sherry glasses. A second later, Cis made her entrance with a tray of rock-cakes, speaking in a 'refained' voice: 'I do hope as how the Whaite's aren't going to be lait.'

I had then to turn, see her for the first time, look at her admiringly and greet her with the line, 'You look a treat, Martha old girl, you reely do.'

On that first dress rehearsal, I polished my glasses, Cis made her entrance, said her first line. I turned, and that was as far as we got. The sight of Cis, in an obviously dyed red wig, hideous mauve dress, high-heeled bronze shoes, teetering across the stage with her rock-cakes was too much for me. I started to say my line, but couldn't get it out. I started to giggle. At that moment I saw Cis take in my sleazy frock-coat, my balding wig, my moustache. Then our eyes met, a deep gurgle rumbled in her throat. We tried, we tried desperately to behave, but it was no use, hysterical laughter took over.

'When you've quite finished behaving like children…' Jack's voice from the stalls, 'perhaps we can get on with the sketch.'

'I'm sorry, Jack', I blurted.

'Yes, I'm sorry, Jack', came from Cis, 'do you mind if we start again?'

'Please do.' The tone was icily polite.

Cis went off, and I started to polish my sherry glasses with one thought in my mind. Whatever happens, I must not catch Cis's eye. She teetered on, saying her line. I turned, looked somewhere in the direction of the dress circle, and said, 'You look a treat, Martha old girl, you reely do.' The fact that I hadn't looked, even vaguely, in her direction, was too much for Cis. The gurgle started again. Somehow or another we got through the lines leading to the entrance of Mai and Tommy. Cis had then to offer the rock-cakes to her guests. Suppressed laughter had made her hand unsteady, the rock-cakes left the plate and bounced about the stage. It was too much. All four of us collapsed, irretrievably, helplessly.

A roar came from the stalls. 'You're supposed to make *me* laugh, not yourselves. Get off-stage, the lot of you, we'll get on with the next number.'

I have to confess that never once did Cis or I go through that sketch without one or other of us 'drying up'. It was unprofessional, unforgivable, but there it was. There is nothing an audience dislikes more—and quite rightly—than actors enjoying their own private joke. Yet, curiously enough, the audience who came time and time again to the *Little Revue* not only forgave us, but anticipating our 'break-up', encouraged us, and heartily joined in. It is the only time in my long career I have ever known this to happen.

SOURCE
Harold French, *I Thought I Never Could* (1973)

CEDRIC HARDWICKE
(1893–1964)

207

The playwright George Bernard Shaw said that Cedric Hardwicke was his fifth favourite actor—'after the four Marx Brothers'. A distinguished Shavian and Shakespearean actor, Harwicke was also a noted raconteur.

It may have been the manager of this same company [at the Alhambra] who encountered an earnest student of the drama with a problem on his mind. The student, clearly a forerunner of the Method and its insistence on motivations wanted to know, 'Did Hamlet have an affair with Ophelia?' The manger did not have to rack his brains to answer that. 'In my company, always,' he replied.

Another scholar who thought perhaps too long and too hard about the same play was an old vaudevillian whom I knew very well in later years. He had saved all his money to fulfil his life's ambition of playing Hamlet. At his invitation, I went to see the production, and was startled to find that Hamlet's first appearance opened on the soliloquy 'To be or not to be...' In his dressing room after the performance I asked him why he had shuffled the tragedy in this way.

'Well,' said the old stager, pulling off his tights to change and go home, 'in that speech, Hamlet mentions "that bourne from which no traveller returns." Now, if you think about it, how could he say that *after* he's seen the bloody Ghost?'

The touring Shakespeareans always played *Richard III* on Saturday nights, after they had been handed their pay on Saturday afternoons so that they could settle up with their landladies before they moved on to the next town. One Saturday, the actor playing the Duke of Gloucester devoted his money to a more gratifying cause than paying for his lodgings. He made his entrance in *Richard* swaying like a ship at sea. The rowdies in the audience took only one look at him before they started yelling, 'Get off; you're drunk!'

Gloucester steadied himself and straightened out his assumed hump back. At full height and in a voice that reached the gallery, he intoned, 'What? Drunk? Me? Just wait 'til you see Buckingham.'

SOURCE
Sir Cedric Hardwicke, *A Victorian in Orbit* (1961)

208

I spent my evenings walking, and my daylight hours working at the Academy...Part of our training was in elocution, and I was glad to discover that I had not the problems in pronunciation encountered by one genteel young woman, who sorely harassed Tree. He pulled her up short one morning, during her reading of *Antony and Cleopatra*. 'You may have a "skay" in Kensington,' he observed ironically, but please understand that in Egypt it is only a "sky."'

My modest means saved me from another hazard, too, which a rich young American student stumbled over repeatedly in another early example of a typical Method problem—having to relate a playwright's line to your own experience. The line she balked at was, 'I lunch at the Berkeley and dine at the Savoy.' She attempted it time and again, but the words would not come right.

'For the love of Heaven, what's wrong with you today?' our instructor cried in despair.

'I'm sorry,' she said, 'but the line doesn't make sense to me. I always lunch at the Savoy and dine at the Berkeley.'

SOURCE
Sir Cedric Hardwicke, *A Victorian in Orbit* (1961)

209

On my way back from Italy, I was captured in London by Olivier, to play King Edward IV in his film production of *Richard III*; this performance in the theatre had been dazzling. With Sir John Gielgud, and Sir Ralph Richardson also in the cast, it was a veritable Birmingham Rep reunion, and I reminded them about the old actor seeing a playbill on which, as in this project of ours, four knights were featured. 'Imagine that,' exclaimed a friend of his, 'four knights in one cast.'

'That's what I give the play,' said the old actor, not in the least impressed.

SOURCE
Sir Cedric Hardwicke, *A Victorian in Orbit* (1961)

IVOR NOVELLO
(1893–1951)

210

Ivor Novello, born David Ivor Davies, was a Welsh composer and actor who became one of the most popular British entertainers of the first half of the twentieth century—and a friend, and in some ways rival, of the English composer, playwright, and actor Noël Coward. The playwright Ben Travers, famous for his Aldwych farces, visited the young Novello in his dressing room.

I called to see him in his dressing room after a matinée and he was as charming and co-operative as ever and asked me to sit down and write out the lyric of the song. While I was engaged in doing this the door opened and another very personable stripling of the theatrical world entered to salute his colleague.

I recognised him as the mature edition of a boy actor who had already blossomed forth as the author of a couple of promising light comedies. His name escaped me for the moment—then, as Ivor Novello introduced me, of course—I knew I hadn't really forgotten it; Noël Coward. They left me to my writing and went into a little huddle of candid and completely genuine mutual admiration.

'You're wonderful. Oh, I wish I were as wonderful as you are.'

'Oh, don't be so silly. You're much more wonderful than I am. You're marvellous.'

No matter which character spoke which line. They were both equally sincere and, ah, how right.

SOURCE
Ben Travers, *Vale of Laughter* (1957)

BEATRICE LILLIE
(1894–1989)

211

Beatrice Lillie was a Canadian-born British actress and revue artiste, known to all as 'Bea', who made her West End debut in 1914 and her Broadway debut in 1924. Married to a baronet, Sir Robert Peel, and noted for her wit, she enjoyed answering the telephone saying, 'C'est Lady Peel qui parle.' Here she tells a story from early in her career.

You'll *never* guess what happened next. Well, almost next, after an up and a down or three. I became a sort of paid, professional transvestite. I learned how to knot a bow tie, wear a top hat, wrestle with dress studs, swing a cane. I could toy with a cigarette like Gerald du Maurier and ogle a girl like Gilbert the Filbert, the King of the Knuts.

I was known, in fact, as the best-dressed man in London, and thereby hangs a tale that we'll get to in a minute. But beneath the starched shirt front there beat a heart emerald green in its innocence, I scarcely knew anything about *anything*, let alone the ways of the theaytah. After all, I was a *concert* artiste.

I was appearing in *A to Z* with Jack Buchanan, a tall, debonair Scot, who was making his London debut. He'd never had a singing or a dancing lesson, but with his smoky-grey eyes and dark brown wavy hair, with a look of wearing evening clothes as though he'd been poured into them, he went on to become a world-wide idol of the stage and cinema.

Backstage, I was still classified as a girl even if I hardly ever got into a skirt. We girls had dressing rooms on one side of the theatre—the Prince of Wales's—while the men were accommodated on the other.

Jack used to kid me about my being a girl hero, decked out in tails or flannel slacks (tennis anyone?) or whatever costume was called for. 'Tell me, Beattie,' he said one day, 'how do you dress, left or right?'

I hadn't a clue to what he was talking about, not the glimmer of an idea about the meaning of the twinkle in his eyes. I still thought *flies* were something you swatted.

'Come on, Beattie. Don't be shy. On which side do you *dress?*'

Suddenly, the light dawned, or so I thought.

'Oh, yes,' I answered. 'In Number Five. Stage left.'

Jack roared with laughter; thought I was brilliant.

SOURCE
Beatrice Lillie, *Every Other Inch a Lady* (1973)

ANEW McMASTER
(1894–1962)

212

Known as Mac, 'the last of the great Irish actor-managers', Anew McMaster founded a company in 1925 to present Shakespeare on tour, not only in Ireland and throughout the British Isles, but as far afield as Australia. As a young man, actor turned playwright Harold Pinter was in the company.

Joe Nolan, the business manager, came in one day and said: 'Mac, all the cinemas in Limerick are on strike. What shall I do?' 'Book Limerick!' Mac said. 'At once. We'll open on Monday.' There was no theatre in the town. We opened on the Monday in a two-thousand seater cinema, with *Othello*. There was no stage and no wingspace. It was St Patrick's night. The curtain was supposed to rise at nine o'clock. But the house wasn't full until eleven-thirty, so the play didn't begin until then. It was well past two in the morning before the curtain came down. Everyone of the two thousand people in the audience was drunk. Apart from that, they weren't accustomed to Shakespeare. For the first half of the play, up to 'I am your own for ever', we could not hear ourselves speak, could not hear the cues. The cast was alarmed. We expected the audience on stage at any moment. We kept our hands on our swords. I was playing Iago at the time. I came offstage with Mac at the interval and we gasped. 'Don't worry,' Mac said, 'don't worry.' After the interval he began to move. When we walked onto the stage for the 'Naked in bed, Iago, and not mean harm' scene (his great body hunched, his voice low with grit), they silenced. He tore into the fit. He made the play his and the place was his. By the time he had reached 'It is the very error of the moon; She comes more near the earth than she was won't, And makes men mad,' (the word 'mad' suddenly cauterized, ugly, shocking) the audience was quite still. And sober. I congratulated Mac. 'Not bad, was it? Not bad. Godfrey Tearle never did the fit, you know.'

SOURCE
Harold Pinter, *Mac* (1968)

213

In the trial scene in *The Merchant of Venice* one night I (as Bassanio) said to him instead of 'For thy three thousand ducats here is six,' quite involuntarily, 'For thy three thousand *buckets* here is six'. He replied quietly and with emphasis: 'If every *bucket* in six thousand *buckets* were in six parts, and every part a *bucket* I would not draw them—I would have my bond.' I could not continue. The other members of the court scene and I turned upstage. Some walked into the wings. But Mac stood, remorseless, grave, like an eagle, waiting for my reply.

SOURCE
Harold Pinter, *Mac* (1968)

RAYMOND MASSEY
(1896–1983)

214

Remembered as a film and television actor, Raymond Massey, Canadian-American by parentage, had a successful West End stage career in the 1920s and 1930s.

Like all actors, I had been called on for numerous charity shows. Charity leaned heavily on the theatre for support between the wars, but this would be my first time in one of the big so-called 'command' performances. King George [the Fifth] was not fond of the theatre. He paid his annual visit to his Actors Pension Fund Performance, grimly determined to do his duty in the best tradition of the senior service in which he had served with distinction. Queen Mary, on the other hand, was stage-struck in her regal way, genuinely enchanted by the theatre.

Command performances were at that time revivals of full-length plays produced for one occasion only and inevitably under-rehearsed. Gerald du Maurier did dozens of them both as actor and director. It must have been agony for him, the most meticulous of actors, to take part in such untidy operations. They were forced on him. Usually, the shows squeaked by without incident and were forgotten. But not this performance of *Bulldog Drummond* [in a version by A. E. W. Mason, who accompanied the King on this occasion].

Rehearsals had gone well. There were four of the original cast in the matinée production including Gilbert Hare, Alfred Drayton and Ronald Squire. Hare had retired from the theatre after the play had ended its long run and for five years he had been engaged in biochemical research at Cambridge. He now returned to the theatre to play his part of a wicked biochemist, Dr Lakington, in the command matinée. He seemed very nervous.

We were to play at the Adelphi, a huge theatre in the Strand. As the young American millionaire kidnapped by the bad guys, I made my first entrance in the second act supposedly drugged to the extent of semi-consciousness and with my arms pinioned, led by the arch-villain, Dr Lakington. I got myself trussed up by props and, a good five minutes before the cue, took my place by a scene door which opened onto the stage.

In the darkness I was relieved to see Mr Hare—his luxuriant wig identified him—standing near the door. I thought to myself, What a professional! All ready for our entrance! As our cue came closer, I whispered, 'Here I am, Mr. Hare.' The figure turned and to my horror it wasn't Gilbert Hare, but a stagehand waiting to hand some props to him.

I rushed to the prompt corner and told the stage manager. The stage wait was the time it took to bring Hare from his dressing-room on the second floor. I suppose it was only two or three minutes, but in stage time it seemed eternity.

Edith Evans and Alfred Drayton were on stage. They had been warned of a delay. Back at the door I heard our cue. I was helpless. I felt like a traitor. I could do nothing without Hare. Through a peephole I watched Edith Evans keep things going in one of the most astonishing improvisations I have ever seen. She was playing a fake Russian countess, and she started off with a stream of Russian double-talk which so bewildered Drayton that he panicked and left the stage. Alone, she proceeded to toy most seductively with a long cigarette holder while softly humming snatches of 'The Volga Boat Song.' The audience apparently was in her hand. All, that is, but the Royal Patron of the Pension Fund. Just as the breathless and shattered Gilbert Hare was about to make his belated entrance, the Monarch's quarterdeck tones were clearly heard—'Mason, is this one of your damned, dramatic pauses?'

SOURCE
Raymond Massey, *A Hundred Different Lives* (1979)

JOSEPH SCHILDKRAUT
(1896–1964)

215

Schildkraut was an Austrian-American actor, celebrated for his Peer Gynt and best remembered as Otto Frank in The Diary of Anne Frank.

Rodgers and Hammerstein often told the story that when Gertrude Lawrence died during the run of *The King and I*, Yul Brynner burst into tears, not because of Lawrence's death but because he would finally get top billing.

When *The Diary of Anne Frank* opened at the Cort Theatre, Joseph Schildkraut had sole billing above the title on the marquee. When Susan Strasberg received raves, it was decided to put her name alongside Schildkraut's. The star definitely didn't like the idea, but Merle Debuskey suggested to the actor that a photo be taken of him at the top of a ladder leaning on a marquee holding Strasberg's hand as if he was leading her up into stardom. He bought it since, in his mind, it was all about his generosity in sharing the space above the title.

SOURCE
Ken Bloom, *Show and Tell* (2016)

ALFRED JOHN (A.J.) BROWN
(1897–1978)

216

A. J. Brown was a much-loved English character actor whom the director Michael Rudman met at the very end of his career.

When we were on tour in Brighton, I was backstage and an announcement came over the tannoy. 'Ladies and Gentlemen, there is a problem with audibility in the balcony.' AJ replied, 'I'm not having any difficulty in hearing the balcony.'

Also in Brighton, there was a constant stream of ladies of a certain age asking to see AJ. They all had silver hair and a gleam in their eye. They wanted to see 'Jack' and they all said how fond they were of him. *Donkey's Years* had been on for well over a year when AJ's eightieth birthday came up. I took him to dinner at Odins. I asked him a question I had always wanted to ask.

ME: AJ, tell me why your shoelaces are undone at curtain call?

AJ: Because, dear boy, it helps me to get home quicker.

When we opened, the advance was only £500. Somehow Peter Barkworth knew that. We were all worried. AJ said, 'Don't worry, chaps, this play will run longer than I will.'

And it did. But only by one month. One Saturday, AJ did the matinée. He did the first act and then passed on, quietly, with his shoelaces still done up.

SOURCE
Michael Rudman, *I Joke Too Much* (2014)

GERTRUDE LAWRENCE
(1898–1952)

217

The English actress's career ranged from appearing with Noël Coward in his play Private Lives *in 1931 to starring with Yul Brynner in the original stage production of* The King and I *in 1951. After the Second World War Daphne du Maurier wrote her play* September Tide *for her. It opened in London in*

1948 and Queen Mary attended a matinée. After the performance when Her Majesty came round to meet the cast, she told them, 'You should all speak up.' 'You see,' said Gertrude Lawrence, turning to the rest of the cast, 'I told you.'

'You in particular,' said the Queen.

This recollection of the production comes from one of the younger members of the cast, Bryan Forbes.

I had an arrangement with Michael Gough whereby I partly shared the services of his dresser, an engaging and eccentric character named Herbert. Herbert's principal responsibility came during the second act when Micky had to dive from the balcony of the house into the harbour to rescue the drifting boat. He dived, of course, into a pile of mattresses strategically placed off-stage and out of sight of the audience. He then had to plunge into a bath of lukewarm water to simulate the real thing for his reappearance. Herbert had to be standing by to assist.

During one matinée when the Aldwych was packed with middle-aged matrons all balancing tea trays on their knees, one of the cleats securing Michael Relph's weighty set suddenly gave way. Ossie dashed in search of stage-hands to repair the damage before the set caved in. Now it so happened that this incident took place a few minutes before Micky was due to make his celebrated plunge into the harbour. Herbert was waiting in the wings and before he disappeared Ossie handed him a support rope and told him to hang on to it until help arrived.

Meanwhile on-stage Gertie and Micky continued with the scene, unaware of the drama being enacted in the wings. Micky leapt from the balcony and groped his way in the semi-darkness to the bath of water.

During his absence Gertie went to a cupboard in the supposedly totally deserted house and took some towels out in readiness for Micky's drenched return. It was a vital plot point and carefully established in the dialogue that she and her son-in-law were isolated and alone—the storm was raging and there was nobody for miles around.

Unbeknown to Gertie, Herbert was standing holding the rope on the other side of the cupboard door. It was a hot afternoon and he was curiously dressed in pin-stripe trousers, collarless shirt and white tennis shoes. I should also add that he had a small Hitler moustache. The total effect was startling.

Gertie opened the cupboard door as she had done for the last two hundred performances and revealed Herbert. She was too dumbfounded to close the door again, and for a few seconds she and Herbert stood transfixed like characters in a Disney cartoon. Herbert, being of the old school of theatrical dressers, was also a stickler for etiquette. He couldn't help himself. He gave a little bow and said, 'Good afternoon, Miss Lawrence.'

Up to this point the audience had been mystified but not unduly alarmed by this sudden plot twist. After all, since they hadn't seen the play before, it was conceivable that Miss du Maurier had intended that her central character be suddenly confronted with Hitler in tennis shoes inside a cupboard.

But when Herbert paid his respects to Miss Lawrence the game was up. Gertie managed to close the door and then started to collapse. She turned away up-stage in a futile attempt to conceal her mounting hysteria and, of course, minus towels, bumped straight into the wet and unsuspecting Micky. He had clambered back over the balcony and was greeted with a howl of laughter from the audience and a leading lady staggering around as though inexplicably drunk.

In such circumstances an actor's first instinct is to check his flies, which Micky did. Finding that everything was intact, he began his dialogue as per cue, but received no answering cue for by now Gertie—one of the world's great gigglers—was on the floor. Micky assumed that she had gone temporarily insane and carried on, giving her dialogue as well as his own and attempting to retrieve the situation. Needing a towel, he went back to the cupboard. Renewed hysteria, this time in anticipation, from the audience. Micky opened the cupboard door. The cupboard was bare. And so the second act staggered to its conclusion, Micky having to wait until curtain-fall for an explanation.

SOURCE
Bryan Forbes, *Notes for a Life* (1974)

PAUL ROBESON
(1898–1976)

218

The great American singer and actor appeared as Othello at Stratford-upon-Avon in 1960. The young Diana Rigg was in the company.

I was living in digs with an actress called Edna Landor. I thought she was a lesbian, but she went on to have an affair with Paul Robeson. He was living at a place called Shottery Lodge and Edna would say, 'Paul wants me to hear his lines. Will you come with me?' So I used to sit in the kitchen at Shottery Lodge, with Paul's secretary, truly believing that Edna was in the bedroom hearing his lines. It's a wonderful euphemism, isn't it? I was so naïve, so innocent.

SOURCE
Gyles Brandreth, *Brief Encounters* (2001)

CHARLES LAUGHTON
(1899–1962)

219

Yorkshire-born Charles Laughton, celebrated as a screen actor, was also a hugely successful stage actor, notably in the 1930s. He demonstrated his commitment to the American film world by becoming an American citizen in 1940. In 1929, he married the actress Elsa Lanchester.

The last night of the Old Vic season was memorable. The theatre was crowded to its utmost limit: the audience was in festive mood. Charles Laughton made the first speech, to hoarse calls from the gallery of 'Good old Nero!'—he had played that part in a recently shown film [*The Sign of the Cross*]. Then they called for Elsa Lanchester, who was in the audience. She had made a success in all her parts, and was a great favourite.

'Bring her up!' shouted some one in the gallery.

'Many people have tried to do that, my friend, but they have not succeeded,' swiftly answered Elsa's husband.

SOURCE
Janet Dunbar, *Flora Robson* (1960)

220

Charles went on tour in *On the Spot* when the London run finished. He was away for a few weeks and visited all the 'key' cities with the play. For the whole of the London run Charles had given the impression to audiences that he really played the organ in *On the Spot*—his rendering of Gounod's *Ave Maria* in particular was supposed to be an excellent interpretation. But one night in Manchester something went wrong. He was walking towards the instrument and it began to play before he got there... his off-stage accomplice had mistimed his cue and started too soon. The audience yelled with laughter and it was some time before Charles could pick up the broken threads of the play again and keep them quiet. At the end of the show Charles made a speech. He said: 'Ladies and Gentlemen of Manchester, you are the only people in the world who know that I cannot play the organ. Will you please keep my secret?'

SOURCE
Elsa Lanchester, *Charles Laughton and I* (1938)

MICHEAL MacLIAMMOIR
(1899–1978)

221

Micheal MacLiammoir, born Alfred Willmore, was a London-born child actor, from a Protestant family, who transformed himself into a Gaelic-speaking Irish actor-manager of Catholic descent. With his partner, Hilton Edwards, he founded the Gate Theatre in Dublin in 1928. He produced and appeared in his own plays, in Irish classics, and in Shakespeare.

11th May 1956: Special Matinée for school children of the *Merchant*. This, oddly enough, glorious: the best audience for Shakespeare, outside some remote country town in the West of Ireland, that one can imagine, for the canker of an academic half-misunderstanding of the Master has not yet corrupted their minds: they are so young they have no knowledge of him whatever, and they are the very people for whom he wrote.

When Bassanio guessed rightly about the leaden casket they frenziedly applauded: when Portia got Shylock into a hole about his pound of flesh they rose to their feet loudly screaming: when Salerio (or is it now Salerino?) came with the news about the wreck of Antonio's ships they listened in silence as stricken as though they were hearing the story of their own ruin. None of them seemed to know what fate was in store for any of the people on the stage, or what perils or triumphs were to be revealed, and this is the only way to enjoy the Merchant or any of those plays of his that are one degree less in stature than the greatest works. The pleasure of ignorance is not, perhaps, as complete as that of knowledge, which comes, it seems to me, as a subtle reward for the scholar, but ignorance has moments, as it had today, as lovely as young hair blown in a frolic wind straight from Parnassus.

SOURCE
Michael MacLiammoir, *Each Actor on His Ass* (1961)

222

The actor Simon Callow, while a student at Queen's University, Belfast, worked as the unpaid dresser for MacLiammoir, who was presenting his celebrated one-man show about Oscar Wilde, The Importance of Being Oscar.

I would arrive at the theatre somewhat before he did, to iron and arrange his clothes. I was a stranger to these arts and he showed them to me, as well as the arts of packing a suitcase and preparing his interval drink of gin and tea. He always arrived in the highest good humour, full of jest and profanity. He divested himself of his clothes to the accompaniment of a seamless patter of erotic speculation, literary quotation, character assassination ('of course when poor dear Cyril Cusack played Hamlet in a section of costumes purloined from sundry shows of the previous season, he became the Prince of Great Denmark Street') and self-revelation. As he stood in his underpants he gazed in a melancholy manner at his groin. 'My testicles' he said, moodily, 'have become distended'—the bulge did seem unusually substantial—'as a result of a virus contracted, I fear, from a seaman. Are you a virgin?' The unexpectedness of the question made me blush. 'No' I lied. 'Good, good. And to which are you more inclined, men or women?' 'Both' I lied again. '*Very* good,' he said, 'although I must confess the older I get, the less I am able to enjoy the company of women—except of course our own dear Enid who is so notorious a Sapphic as to be virtually *hors concours*. And now, my dear boy, the time of the performance must surely be approaching?' I was keeping a close watch on the clock. I had been firmly instructed that I was to announce when there was half an hour before the curtain rose, when there was a quarter of an hour, when five minutes, and finally, when it was time for us to go to the stage.

As the time approached, a change came over Micheal. The patter became a trickle and finally dried up. His make-up—which in fact only amounted to touching up his street make-up—was quickly effected; his costume consisted of nothing more than evening dress, and of course a green carnation. He sat in front of his mirror staring, haunted, at his face. He seemed barely to hear the calls. As the curtain got closer and closer, he started to tremble. Sweat trickled through his rouge. He grasped on to the table in front of him till his knuckles were white. The stage manager arrived to give him his call. He reached out for my hand. 'Lead me,' he said. 'I can't see, d'you see.' Down the pitch-dark corridor we went, his finger nails digging ruts into my palms, while with his free hand he crossed himself again and again. 'Jesus, Mary and Joseph. Jesus protect me. Jesus.' We reached the stage. I said: 'There are three stairs now.' 'Where? Where?' I helped him up, one, two, three. He fumbled with the black cotton drape, pushed it aside, and was on stage. In the pitch black, the light dazzled, but I heard big, solid, welcoming applause, and then Micheal's voice, rock-steady, as if he'd been on for hours: 'To drift with every passion till my soul…' I slipped round to the front and watched the ebullient unrecognizable figure juggle words and emotions, drawing his audience of largely middle-aged, middle-class Belfast burghers and their wives into his charmed circle, luring them into a world of sophistication and wit that they would under any other circumstances abhor, somehow making them feel that he and they shared a secret and a wisdom.

SOURCE
Simon Callow, *Being an Actor* (1984)

CHARLES GOLDNER
(1900–1955)

223

Charles Goldner was an Austrian-born English-speaking actor, whose work ranged from international film to a Broadway musical. Here he is in Lillian Hellman's play Watch on the Rhine.

Charles Goldner, as the villain, ran a sweepstake on the box office figures every night—most of the cast, being stars, were on a percentage and entitled to be given the figure. He always won for he made his first entrance from the French windows centre stage, came down to kiss Athene's hand and then straightened up, his bulging eyes sweeping the house from stalls to gallery, and counting any empty seats that might be visible in inconspicuous corners.

The only other time I saw that trick performed was during a production of *Two Gentlemen of Verona* when the dog that Michael Aldridge had bought from the Dog's Home in Bristol, and who had behaved perfectly during rehearsals, was so startled at seeing the auditorium full of people on his first entrance that he walked down to the footlights, stared straight out in front, surveyed the theatre from floor to ceiling as if counting the house and got the biggest round of the evening.

SOURCE
Kitty Black, *Upper Circle* (1984)

HELEN HAYES
(1900–1993)

224

Of the several actresses to be accorded the title of 'First Lady of the American Stage', probably none was held in greater affection than Helen Hayes. 'The accolade was embarrassing,' she said herself, 'because there were several other "first ladies" around—Katherine Cornell, Lynn Fontanne, and Ina Claire, to name three. But since the label stuck, I began to feel an obligation to live up to it. Poor little me.' It was in 1955 that Miss Hayes first 'became' a theatre.

There are probably no more than a dozen actresses in the whole history of world theatre who have had playhouses named after them; of those, only one has to my knowledge managed to outlive her own building, and she is Helen Hayes. When a couple of years ago, property-hungry Broadway developers tore down the New York theatre named in her honour, a number of actors led by Jason Robards and Colleen Dewhurst took to the streets in protest, and some even got arrested trying to halt the bulldozers. Miss Hayes viewed the inexorable march of time rather more tranquilly:

'People kept calling to commiserate with me but I thought, well, I've outlasted all that brick and stone and steel. My theatre may have gone but I'm still here, and I rather liked the feeling. But then they took another theatre just next door to Sardi's and named that after me instead, only now we have a little problem there too. The show that happens to be playing there at the moment is Harvey Fierstein's *Torch Song Trilogy*, about homosexuality, and on the neon sign they don't have room to explain about it just being the theatre that bears my name, so the neon lights read HELEN HAYES TORCH SONG TRILOGY. The other day two old ladies were standing outside and one of them said, "Well, dear, I really hadn't intended to pay 30 dollars just to see a lot of homosexuality, but if Helen Hayes is doing it then it must be all right." So at least I'm still good for something at the box-office.'

SOURCE
Interview with Sheridan Morley, *The Times* (19 December 1984)

225

Before they were even finished writing their new play *To the Ladies*, George S. Kaufman and Marc Connelly and their producer George Tyler approached Helen Hayes to star in it. Connelly said to Hayes, 'Of course you play the piano?' She responded, 'Why, certainly.' 'Good,' replied Connelly. 'We have an idea for one of the acts—and it will help immeasurably if you play the piano.'

And when the show opened, Hayes played the piano beautifully, as promised. Months later Connelly learned that Hayes started piano lessons the day after their conversation.

SOURCE
Ken Bloom, *Show and Tell* (2016)

226

Mr Gillette* once told me a story of a small boy who was a mathematical genius—a true prodigy, who awed everyone but his parents. They were petrified of him. His life was so totally involved with equations that his parents feared monomania. In an effort to help them, Mr Gillette suggested that they take the child to the theatre in order to divert him and stimulate his imagination. With this end in mind, he presented them with tickets to Maude Adams's *Peter Pan*.

The anxious mother and father now sat in the theatre watching their son with gratitude and relief. He was obviously and utterly engrossed.

When intermission came, they happily asked how he liked the play.

'Do you know?' the boy answered. 'There were 71,832 words in that act.'

* *William Gillette played Sherlock Holmes in the original dramatization of the Arthur Conan Doyle stories. The novelist and playwright Booth Tarkington once said to Gillette: 'I would rather see you play Sherlock Holmes than be a child again on Christmas morning.'*

SOURCE
Helen Hayes, *On Reflection* (1974)

ANTON WALBROOK
(1900–1967)

227

Born Adolf Wohlbruck, Anton Walbrook moved to England and became a distinguished stage and film actor. Here he is in the same production of Watch on the Rhine *mentioned earlier for Charles Goldner. Spoliansky is the German-born child actress Irmgard Spoliansky.*

The closing scene was so unbearably poignant that the stage managers maintained nobody had ever actually *seen* the printed page. Anton was in floods of tears himself and little Spoliansky became agitated.

'Tell me, Mr Walbrook,' she asked. 'Are you going to cry like this every night?'

'Certainly not,' snapped Anton. 'In rehearsal *I* cry, in performance it is the bastards in front who cry.'

And cry they did. One afternoon John Gielgud came to the matinée. Soon he was awash, his handkerchief clapped to his face, tears rolling into the sodden linen.

SOURCE
Kitty Black, *Upper Circle* (1984)

MILDRED DUNNOCK

(1901–1991)

228

One of the most respected supporting actresses of the American theatre, Mildred Dunnock made her debut in 1932 in Life Begins. *Arthur Miller here describes how she secured perhaps her most celebrated role as Linda Loman in his 1949 play* Death of a Salesman.

It is here that the still unsolved mystery begins, the mystery of what makes a stage performer. There are persons who, in an office, seem exciting candidates for a role, but as soon as they step onto a stage the observers out front—if they are experienced—know that the blessing was not given them. For myself, I know it when, regardless of how well the actor is reading, my eyes begin to wander up to the brick wall back of the stage. Conversely, there are many who make little impression in an office, but once on the stage it is impossible to take one's attention from them. It is a question neither of technique nor of ability, I think, but some quality of surprise inherent in the person.

For instance, when we were searching for a woman to play Linda, the mother in *Death of a Salesman,* a lady came in whom we all knew but could never imagine in the part. We needed a woman who looked as though she had lived in a house dress all her life, even somewhat coarse and certainly less than brilliant. Mildred Dunnock insisted she was that woman, but she was frail, delicate, not long ago a teacher in a girl's college, and a cultivated citizen who probably would not be out of place in a cabinet post. We told her this, in effect, and she understood, and left.

And the next day the line of women formed again in the wings, and suddenly there was Milly again. Now she had padded herself from neck to hem line to look a bit bigger, and for a moment none of us recognized her, and she read again. As soon as she spoke we started to laugh at her ruse; but we saw, too, that she *was* a little more worn now, and seemed less well-maintained, and while she was not quite ordinary, she reminded you of women who were. But we all agreed, when she was finished reading, that she was not right, and she left.

Next day she was there again in another group, and the next and the next, and each day she agreed with us that she was wrong; and to make a long story short when it came time to make the final selection it had to be Milly, and she turned out to be magnificent. But in this case we had known her work; there was no doubt that she was an excellent actress.

The number of talented applicants who are turned down because they are unknown is very large. Such is the crap-shooting chanciness of the business, its chaos, and part of its charm.

SOURCE
The Theatrical Essays of Arthur Miller, ed. R. A. Martin (1978)

MAURICE EVANS
(1901–1989)

229

Maurice Evans was a British-born actor-manager who made a particular success playing Shakespeare in America. From 1953 he appeared in more television productions of Shakespeare than any other actor—including Hamlet, Macbeth, Richard II, *and* The Tempest. *On stage, his* Richard II *ran for 170 consecutive performances in New York in 1937 and his* Hamlet, *the following year, was the first unabridged version to be seen there. The critic John Mason Brown took his nine-year-old son to a matinée of* Hamlet.

We lunched first. Not at home. At a restaurant. At Giovanni's, in feast-day style worthy of the event. While he sipped a preliminary coke downstairs and I an old-fashioned, I tried to explain what he would see. It took more explanation that I had thought it would. I noticed that his eyes brightened whenever the Ghost was mentioned. Or whenever, in my narration, a cadaver bit the dust.

'Why don't they use pistols?' he asked while I was outlining the duel scene with its multiple jobs for the court mortician. It was only when I had described the poisoned foil, the poisoned wine, and the fury of the duel that he appeared to forgive Shakespeare for not having anticipated the age of the machine.

When he demanded, 'They won't really be dead, will they?' I knew he was interested. For him, make-believe and reality were still blissfully, terrifyingly one—at least up to an uncertain point.

Traffic held us up so that we were a minute or so late in getting to the theatre. Hence we missed the first scene on the parapet. But a friendly Negro doorman did his bit for Shakespeare that afternoon.

'Yessuh,' the doorman said to him, 'the Ghost is walkin' now. It's too dark to go in there. You gotta wait. But never you fear—he'll walk again.'

While we were waiting for the first scene to be over, I assured him for the tenth time that the Ghost was not real, and tried to tell him how the illusion of his disappearance would be achieved.

The auditorium was dark when, with other stragglers, we pushed our way in. After we reached our seats, I could hardly persuade him to take off his coat and muffler. His eyes were glued on the stage. I was pleased to see how, even for the young, *Hamlet* sweeps forward on its own feet without having to rely on footnotes.

He listened to every word. He was never bored. He sat far back in his seat, relaxed only during the soliloquies. Whenever there was a threat of action, he pushed forward. Whenever the Ghost appeared, he stood up. Once, when an offstage cannon sounded in the darkness, he came close to turning a somersault into the lap of the woman who was sitting beyond him.

'Holy smokes, what's that?' he cried.

The intermission almost broke his heart. When I suggested that he go out with me while I had a cigarette, he was at first unwilling to leave. His was that nicest of nice fears. He was afraid they might start without waiting for the audience.

On the sidewalk we encountered the doorman for the second time. 'Did you see the Ghost?' he beamed. 'Well, you'll see him again. He ain't done walkin'.'

On the way back to our seats came, 'Is Mr. Maurice Evans married?'

'No,' I replied, 'I don't think so.'

'Why doesn't he marry Ophelia?' he suggested. 'She's a mighty pretty girl.'

He was standing bolt upright during the whole of the play-within-the-play scene. The death of Polonius grieved him. 'He's such a funny, nice old man; he made me laugh.' But he started laughing again when Hamlet reached behind the curtains for Polonius's body, to say, 'I'll lug the guts into the neighboring room'

He jumped as if dynamited at that moment when Laertes and his followers were storming the castle. And I almost had to hold him to prevent his crawling over the seat in front of him during the duel.

After Hamlet's body had been carried by the four captains up the stairs and the curtain had fallen, he stayed—taped to his seat—applauding. He applauded, and applauded, and applauded.

'How'd you like it?' I asked in the taxi, homewardbound.

'Gee, it was swell! I liked it better than *Oklahoma!*' Then a pause. 'I like it a little better than Donald Duck.' Another pause—a long, reflective one. '"A little more than kin, and less than kind."—Gee! That's pretty, isn't it?'

SOURCE
John Mason Brown, *Morning Faces* (1950)

TALLULAH BANKHEAD
(1902–1968)

230

'Watching Tallulah on stage is like watching someone skating on thin ice—everyone wants to be there when it breaks,' said Mrs Patrick Campbell. Famous for her husky voice, quick wit, and outrageous behaviour, Tallulah Bankhead seldom found roles that did justice to her potential. At fifteen she won a competition in a film magazine that included a trip to New York as part of its prize. It was in New York that she discovered drugs and the Algonquin Hotel. 'Cocaine isn't habit-forming,' she later remarked, 'and I know because I've been taking it for years.' Work did not come immediately and she returned home until she got her 'break' in 1919.

The holidays came and went, and still no word from New York that producers were clamouring for my services. Suspicion started to chew at me. Was I to be retired on the brink of a career? I started to toss on my cot. Grandmother kept the cold water tap turned on. Then came an incident that went far toward convincing me I was destiny's darling.

In late February *39 East* came to Washington for a week's engagement. Written by Rachel Crothers, it was produced by Lee and J.J. Shubert in association with Mary Kirkpatrick. Miss Kirkpatrick was from Alabama. Her brother had been a classmate of Daddy's in college. The Bankheads and the Kirkpatricks were friends of long standing.

Mary called up Grandmother: 'I know how stage-struck Tallulah is. Please bring her to the matinée tomorrow. I'm leaving two tickets for you at the box office.' Coming home in Grandmother's limousine after the performance I started to wail like a banshee. 'I can play that part as well as she can,' I keened. 'If I'm not permitted to return to the stage I'll kill myself.'

The 'she' whom I traduced was Constance Binney. My suicide threat impressed no one but because a smouldering Tallulah is far from an ideal companion, Daddy, my aunts, my grandparents, all agreed I should return to the Algonquin, job or no job. Their lives would be more peaceful. So, they hoped, would mine.

I idled through most of the summer. Through the kindness of Lyman Brown I played for two weeks in summer stock in Somerville, Mass., another two weeks in Baltimore. Two years had almost elapsed since I invaded Manhattan, and I had yet to speak a word on its stage. I dreaded every visit of the postman...

One day the awesome Jobyna Howland, then playing in Rachel Crothers' *The Little Journey,* tapped me in the lobby. 'They're casting a second company of *39 East,* and I've spoken to Miss Crothers. She's agreed to hear you read for the Constance Binney part. There will be fifteen other girls trying for the role, but I think you might get it. And please, Tallulah, don't make up like a tart. Wear a simple little dress. Look and act your age.'

Jobyna briefed me thoroughly on how to behave: 'Miss Crothers is a very opinionated person who knows exactly what she wants. Should she stop you after you've read only four or five lines, don't be disappointed. She may have made up her mind that quickly. Don't waste her time pleading for a second chance if she thumbs you down.'

The reading was on a cold, badly lit stage. I was paralysed with fright. I had never read or had sides in my hands before. Just before my ordeal I was upset when a fifteen-year-old girl read for one of the minor roles. She was accompanied by her father who in his fright started off with: 'Miss Carruthers...' '*Crothers* is the name,' the author replied in chilly fashion. I wanted to bawl in sympathy.

In those days I felt stark naked unless I had my hat and gloves on. Handed the part, I was unable to get my gloves off. The sides of the part were typed on flimsy paper. I had difficulty trying to turn the sheets with my gloves half on, half off. I had read only ten or twelve lines when Miss Crothers stopped me. Despite Jobyna's briefing, I felt I had failed. I was certain my fumbling, my quivering voice, had betrayed me. Without further ado I burst into tears. To my astonishment Miss Crothers spoke up: 'That's very good indeed. Come to my house Friday evening and you can go over the role with the young man who will play opposite you.' Believe it or not, I had started crying at the moment the lines indicated emotional upset.

SOURCE
Tallulah Bankhead, *Tallulah* (1952)

231

In 1923 Tallulah made her debut on the London stage and appeared in more than a dozen plays in London over the next eight years, earning a reputation for making the most out of inferior material. Here is her description of a play called Conchita, *in which, in the second act, she entered carrying a monkey:*

On opening night, the monkey went berserk . . . snatched my black wig from my head, leaped from my arms and scampered down to the footlights. There he paused, peered out at the audience, then waved my wig over his head . . . The audience had been giggling at the absurd plot even before this simian had at me. Now it became hysterical. What did Tallulah do in this crisis? I turned a cartwheel! The audience roared . . . After the monkey business I was afraid they might boo me. Instead I received an ovation.

SOURCE
Tallulah Bankhead, *Tallulah* (1952)

232

In 1963 Tony Richardson was directing Tennessee Williams' The Milk Train Doesn't Stop Here Anymore *and, after trying and failing to get Katharine*

Hepburn for the role, cast Tallulah Bankhead. Although she was addicted to pills and in precarious health, Williams believed she was up to it and saw her being revived by it in the same way that Laurette Taylor had been by appearing in his play The Glass Menagerie.

Even before they got into the rehearsal room, Bankhead and Richardson were at loggerheads. At a pre-rehearsal cast dinner, thrown by Bankhead at her Fifty-Seventh street apartment and served by her maid, whom Bankhead referred to as 'Cunty,' Richardson found himself blurting, 'Fuck you!' to his rebarbative leading lady. The relationship between director and actress was toxic. 'Tallulah was the most unpleasant person I've ever worked with,' Richardson said. He found the rehearsals—'though they really couldn't be called that'—'torture.'

'On the way to rehearsal I'd have a frantic inner dialogue: "I've got to find a way to like her, to like something—even to feel sorry for her, feel pity, feel compassion."' Richardson couldn't relate to Bankhead, or she to him. 'Loud or soft—how do you want it?' she'd say when he would try to give her a note. 'There wasn't any choice,' Richardson said. 'Tallulah was simply past it. She couldn't remember, she couldn't perform.'

SOURCE
John Lahr, *Tennessee Williams: Mad Pilgrimage of the Flesh* (2014)

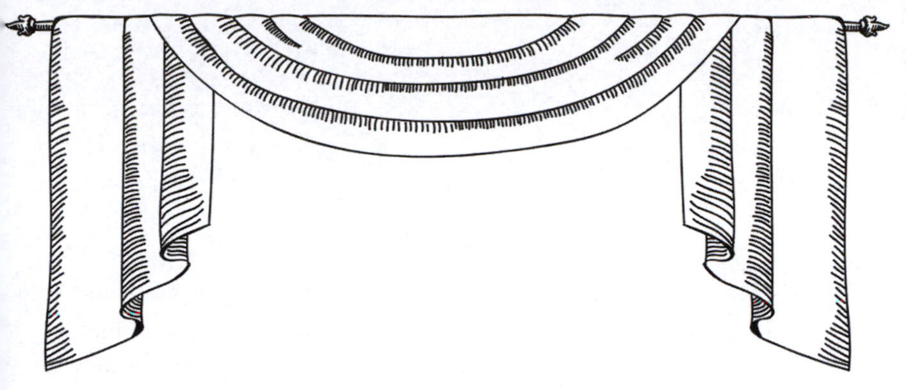

ACT THREE

PLAYERS FROM RALPH RICHARDSON TO NAEEM HYAT

'The players cannot keep counsel; they'll tell all'

HAMLET

RALPH RICHARDSON
(1902–1983)

233

Sir Ralph Richardson was one of the quintet of great British actor-knights of the mid-twentieth century, alongside Laurence Olivier, John Gielgud, Michael Redgrave, and Donald Wolfit. Richardson was certainly the most eccentric. His work ranged from Shakespeare (including a memorable Falstaff in 1945 for the Old Vic Company at the New Theatre) to Pinter (in whose No Man's Land *in 1975 he played alongside John Gielgud in London and New York).*

After an abortive period at the Brighton Art School, Richardson saw Frank Benson in *Hamlet*, and immediately decided to become an actor. In December, 1920, when he was seventeen—he was born at Cheltenham on December 19, 1902—he took himself off to a certain Frank Growcott, who ran a little theatre—the St. Nicholas Players—in a disused bacon factory at the back of Brighton station. Growcott received him with the lack of enthusiasm that managers show to all young men who wish to become actors. 'Don't be hasty', cried Richardson, determined to dazzle him with the force of his personality; 'I am a man of means. I will give you money: a pound a week for ten weeks. After that, if you like me, *you* can give *me* a pound a week.' A bargain was struck, and soon afterwards, in his own exuberant words to an interviewer in South Africa some years later, he 'burst on the English stage as a bombshell...I was employed primarily to imitate the bursting of bombs dropped in an air-raid scene in a war play. I did it with a petrol tin at the end of the scrap. I had a sheet of cues, which I read by the light of a candle under the stage. One night the candle went out. Bombs fell everywhere regardless of cues or courtesy.'

SOURCE
Harold Hobson, *Ralph Richardson* (1958)

'You,' he screamed, 'do you know the second grave-digger and the second player in *Hamlet?*' I said I was doubtful. 'Well, anyway, you play them tonight and tomorrow night. Reginald Jarman has been taken to hospital with diphtheria . . . On Friday you will play Biondello in *The Taming of the Shrew*, on Saturday afternoon Sylvius in *As You Like It*, and on Saturday evening Ross in *Macbeth*. Here are the books with the cuts. Rehearse now and go home and study.'

It is the kind of nightmare that young actors welcome with all their hearts. Every available moment of the day, Don studied the lines in an intense, feverish heat. As is usual in theatrical crises of this nature, his colleagues were more than helpful, and did all they could to encourage the young man who had found himself thrust into 'the glorious company of speaking actors in one fell swoop'. When the time came for the evening performance, willing hands helped him to make up, dress, adjust the wigs that did not fit him.

Despite the terror of the occasion, despite the feeling that his voice did not belong to him and that, unaccountably, the opening lines of *How They Brought the Good News from Ghent To Aix* were pounding ceaselessly through his brain, Don survived and did well. In that week, and the one that followed at the Theatre Royal, York, he played Second Player, Second Gravedigger, Biondello Sylvius, Ross, Sebastian, Octavius Caesar and Marullus. As a baptism of fire it was not unusual for those days; by contemporary standards it simply could not happen, for there are not the companies geared to so tightly-packed a repertoire.

Doran was pleased with his young apprentice, and sent for him to explain that the salary of the absent principal was to be halved and that Don would receive two pounds per week.

With what high hopes he now faced the future! Not only was he doing what he most wanted, but was also being paid for it. 'I was a Real Live Actor at last,' he wrote, 'and grew my hair very long'.

SOURCE
Ronald Harwood, *Sir Donald Wolfit* (1971)

251

The setting for this memorable performance was King William's School, Castletown, on the Isle of Man. Wolfit tells the story himself.

In those days a well-known firm of theatrical publishers used to purvey paper scenery. On strong lithograph paper was printed in large squares (about five feet) a woodland scene, an oak-chamber scene and a drawing-room scene. The proper method for mounting was to paste or glue the squares on to the canvas frames to the size required. The school had omitted to do this and had only tacked them on to the frames. It was, of course, the woodland scene that we used for *As You Like It*, reserving the oak-chamber scene for *Twelfth Night* in the evening.

After an excellent lunch in the masters' common-room we prepared ourselves for the play, crowded in the narrow space behind the wings. The play went smoothly, and the laughter from the crowded hall was continuous as the comedy unfolded. Many of the boys were seeing their first play. There was much doubling of small parts in the company and one actor had a very quick change from William, the country man, to Jaques de Boys, the second son of old Sir Rowland. He dashed off the stage, tore off his tunic and furry leggings, and as he dived to the washstand to clean his tanned face and body his tights fell about his knees. Suddenly we heard a veritable gale of laughter sweep the hall in the middle of what should have been a quiet scene. We gazed at one another in the wings in amazement as the laughter grew louder and louder. Nothing

Wilfrid and I became quite good friends. I often visited him in his dressing room.

One evening before he left I asked him if he had ever been to a drama academy. Wilfrid: 'Yes Moray. I did go to a drama academy. I learnt two things: one that I couldn't act and two—that it didn't matter!'

SOURCE
Moray Watson, *Looking Back and Dropping Names* (2016)

JOHN GIELGUD
(1904–2000)

261

John Gielgud first made his name in the 1930s, playing in Shakespeare at the Old Vic and, notably, the title role in Gordon Daviot's Richard of Bordeaux *at the New Theatre.*

Richard of Bordeaux being in its seventh month, its star was given two weeks' holiday, 'to make a break', took a suite in the Royal Crescent, Brighton, littered it with scripts, and asked me and Dick [Clowes] down for a couple of days.

He went for walks between us along the front, the ozone fertilizing his mind with ideas while his eyes spotted theatre faces with the excitement of a Gallery First-Nighter. 'I've got rather a good idea for *A Midsummer Night's Dream*—to do it nude, or as near as one could go—wouldn't it be superb?'

He made it sound just that, till he added, 'With everybody starkers we could just call it "Bottom",' and shrieked with nursery laughter...

One rainy afternoon he decided on a night out in London. By now I knew him well enough to guess that he would take us to a theatre, but not well enough to know which one.

After a fine early dinner at the Café Royal, Dick and I found ourselves sitting in the front of a stage box, with the holiday-maker lurking in the shadows. We were at the New Theatre, watching *Richard of Bordeaux*, 'I'm curious to see it from the front.'

As the theatre darkened Dick whispered to me, 'Would you call this "making a break"?'

Glen Byam Shaw was playing Richard as a rehearsal for his tour in the part, and playing well. At the end of one emotional scene between the king and his wife, I stole a look behind me: John G. was not just moved, he was weeping. I was in the company of a child playing with double mirrors.

When at the end we hurried through the pass-door, the stage-hands stacking scenery looked through the visitor without recognizing him. They had plainly never seen him in a suit.

Glen was staggered—'Thank God I didn't know'—and delighted by praise generous and sincere. Then John took Dick and me out to supper as if after a first night he had enjoyed.

Dick said, 'John dear, I know the play moved you, but I did once see you lean forward and count the house through your tears.'

'Dickie Clowes, that's a wicked thing to say. Actually it wasn't at all bad, I was surprised…'

SOURCE
Emlyn Williams, *Emlyn* (1973)

262

Laurence Olivier described Gielgud as 'always the poet, head upturned towards the stars'. He also had a keen sense of humour and a reputation for making gaffes.

Early in the Gielgud career, at the Ivy Restaurant, he was the luncheon guest of a prominent playwright of the time who was notoriously dull and garrulous company. Just as there came a pause for breath, a man passed the table. 'Thank God he didn't stop,' said John, 'he's a bigger bore than Eddie Knoblock,' and turned back to his host. Who was Eddie Knoblock...

...John was casting *The Laughing Woman*, a play about a brilliant young sculptor and his mistress. 'Bronnie is insisting on Stephen Haggard for the part. He's splendid but *much* too well-bred. It calls for an actor who would convey somebody savage, uncouth—Emlyn, *you* should be playing it!'

SOURCE
The Ages of Gielgud, ed. Ronald Harwood (1984)

263

To jump ahead. Years later, a friend told me of an example of John's absorption in the theatre, which cropped up quite unexpectedly. The two of them, playing in the same film, were sitting on the set in their canvas chairs, whiling away one of the long waits; John was reading. The other, wrestling with his *Times* crossword, leant over, 'Sorry, but is there a character in Shakespeare called the Earl of Westmoreland?'

'Yes,' John answered, without looking up, 'in *Henry IV Part Two*.' Then, to break the bad news, he turned to my friend. 'But it's a very poor part.' And went back to his book.

SOURCE
The Ages of Gielgud, ed. Ronald Harwood (1984)

264

One of Gielgud's most famous roles was Jack Worthing in Oscar Wilde's The Importance of Being Earnest, *the part played by George Alexander in*

1895. Many years later he reminisced about the part and the play with the director, Nicholas Hytner.

Sir John quoted Jack Worthing from memory. Every phrase was perfectly poised, every breath like music.

'John has just done an episode of *Inspector Morse,*' said Martin [Hensler, his Hungarian partner] to Maggie [Smith], 'We found out what John Thaw gets paid for playing Morse. I mean, it's unbelievable. John didn't get half as much. I was furious with his agent. What do they pay you for a film these days?'

Sir John seemed uninterested in money, so he left Martin to interrogate Maggie. He smiled at me benignly, and it suddenly occurred to me to ask him whether he'd known George Alexander.

'He died when I was quite young, maybe fourteen,' said Sir John, 'but I met him several times. My great-aunt Ellen Terry knew him well. We all thought poorly of him because of the disgraceful way he treated poor Wilde when he came out of jail. And I knew Lord Alfred Douglas. He came to see me in my dressing room after my opening night in 1939. He was an old man by then. I asked him about the first opening night in 1895. All he claimed to remember was that he'd written most of the best lines himself.'

SOURCE
Nicholas Hytner, *Balancing Acts* (2017)

265

At the beginning of February 1991, I was appearing in pantomime with Bonnie Langford, Barbara Windsor, and Brian Conley. The Gulf War had begun but it did not trouble us much, reminding me of a story the writer Beverley Nichols told about John Gielgud during the Second World War.

Hundreds of Iraqis have been killed in the first real land battle of the war. It's getting dawn-to-dusk coverage on radio and TV, and most nights I tune in briefly after the show. I didn't tonight, because I went with Bonnie and Barbara and Brian to an end-of-run celebration at Joe Allen's. We laughed a lot, gossiped, they talked about their plans. I got Barbara talking a bit about the Krays ('They only ever killed their own') but it was really showbiz-showbiz all the way. The war didn't get a look-in. War in a distant land (even when our boys are involved) is not a topic much touched upon by the Wimbledon Theatre panto players—though I did make Barbara laugh telling her the story Beverley Nichols told me years ago. It was during the darkest days of the Second World War. John Gielgud went to stay with Beverley in the country and, on Sunday morning, Beverley got up early to fetch the papers from the village shop. Gielgud had got there first and was sitting in the kitchen surrounded by all the newspapers, with headline after headline blaring doom and gloom, news of a setback and disaster on almost every front. Gielgud was ashen-faced, shaking his head in despair. 'John, what on earth has happened?' 'The worst,' wailed Gielgud, 'Gladys has got the most terrible notices!'

SOURCE
Gyles Brandreth, *Breaking the Code: Westminster Diaries 1990-2007* (2014)

266

This anecdote refers to Gielgud's 1942 production of Macbeth, *produced by Hugh 'Binkie' Beaumont, for whom Kitty Black, who tells the story, acted as a secretary.* Macbeth *is, by tradition, an unlucky play. In this production there were four fatalities: two witches, Duncan, and the set designer.*

For a long time John couldn't make up his mind about the Lady and finally announced that he would hold auditions in order to find a suitable new star. Among the letters was one application for the part of 'Lady McBeth' enclosing a photograph with the pathetic p.s. 'I do take my glasses off often.' Eventually he settled for Gwen

Ffrangcon-Davies who had been his exquisite partner in the romantic smash-hit *Richard of Bordeaux*, as well as in *Three Sisters* and *The Importance of being Earnest*.

From the first the disasters that seem to dog the Scottish play began to accumulate. First, William Walton disappeared. His agent had no idea where he was and as the music he had been commissioned to write had been conceived as an accompaniment to all the witches' scenes, which were to be spoken rhythmically against a recorded score, nobody could rehearse anything final until the composer had set down what had been agreed with the director. One day the office boy came into my room saying: 'There's a bloke outside who says he's supposed to be composing the music for *Macbeth*.'

'Mr Walton, Mr Walton,' I cried, hurrying out to meet him, 'where have you been? Where is the music?'

'I haven't written it yet,' he replied.

'Not written it!' I gasped. 'But we need it right away.'

'It won't take long,' he replied and proceeded to explain that composing the twenty-odd minutes of music required would barely take him a week, and he was as good as his word. He attended only one run-through of the play, made careful notes and when the score was delivered, every fanfare and musical bridge was correctly timed to the very last second. A piano version was made to enable the witches to rehearse their 'Double double' bits and eventually the whole thing was recorded by HMV on acetate one-sided 78s with thirty minutes of the London Philharmonic Orchestra conducted by Ernest Irving. They over-ran the recording session by an incredible amount of overtime and poor John had to produce a personal cheque as nobody would leave the studio until every last penny had been paid. Came the day when there was a run-through of the play with music, and in the empty theatre I felt like Ludwig of Bavaria listening to the final versions of *Tannhäuser* or *Lohengrin*.

John had put together a tremendously complicated effects score with wind howling at all the climaxes, bells ringing, doors being hammered on, etc. and the only way all this could be coordinated was for two operators—Mary and Viola—to manipulate the panatropes—gramophones with pick-up arms that could be spotted on to any given groove of the 78s—with the effects records on one machine and the Walton music on the other. John kept changing his mind and adding or subtracting effects with the result that finally there were one hundred and forty separate cues for effects, while the music was fed in to complement or underline the action. After the final matinée, John came to Viola and asked her to add another wind cue to the plot.

'But Mr Gielgud, there's only one more performance,' wailed the harassed stage manager.

'Yes, I know, but I *would* like to hear it just once,' said John, and who could resist him?

SOURCE
Kitty Black, *Upper Circle* (1984)

267

Peter Ustinov saw Gielgud being interviewed on American television and managing a gaffe to upset an entire country.

I once saw him on a local late-night television interview in Saint Louis, Missouri. He was busy playing *The Ages of Man*, his one-man show, in half a ball-park, and now he was being interviewed by a long-winded intellectual.

'One final question,' the interviewer said. 'Sir…Sir Gielgud…did you…oh, you must have had…we all did…at the start of your very wonderful…very wonderful and very meaningful…let me put it this way…did you have someone…a man…or…or indeed, a woman…at whom you could now point a finger and say… Yes!…This person helped me when I…'

By now John understood what was being asked of him, and he prepared to answer, disguising his dislike of all that is pretentious by a perfect courtesy.

'Yes, I think there was somebody who taught me a great deal at my dramatic school, and I certainly am grateful to him for his kindness and consideration toward me. His name was Claude Rains.'

And then, as an afterthought, he added—'I don't know what happened to him. I think he failed, and went to America.'

SOURCE
Peter Ustinov, *Dear Me* (1977)

268

The narrator is the playwright David Storey whose play Home *was first produced in London in 1970, with Gielgud and Richardson, directed by Lindsay Anderson.*

The beginning of rehearsals for *Home* was like watching two horses galloping along while, perched on a delicately fashioned carriage behind, a driver called out, 'Whoa! Stop!' finally turning to his fellow passenger and saying, wryly, 'Well, we'd better let them have a run...' If *The Contractor* [Storey's previous play] had seen the empirical method of directing at its most demanding, *Home* saw it as its most discreet:

'It isn't possible for an actor to sit on a stage without moving, Lindsay, for 25 minutes.'

'Is it 25 minutes?'

'It feels like 25.'

'Move, in that case, if you feel like it, John.'

Until a point had been reached:

'It's strange, but once sitting here, I don't feel I want to move again.'

'Don't, in that case.'

'I shan't.'

One critic observed:

'So perfect is the spell cast, indeed, that on the second night during one of the deeper silences, a mouse strolled on the stage, looked calmly round, and having satisfied its curiosity wandered off again . . . it would not surprise me that [he] too had been exhaustively rehearsed, his entrance and exit timed within the flick of a tail.'

SOURCE
At the Royal Court, ed. Richard Findlater (1981)

269

1953 was the year Sir John Gielgud was arrested and fined for importuning. He had been knighted in the Coronation Honours list, a citation many thought long overdue, and his name was outside the stately Haymarket Theatre as acting in and producing *A Day by the Sea* by N. C. Hunter. The play, written in an English Chekhovian style, was in rehearsal. I remember seeing the small mention in the Evening News that Mr John Gielgud, employed as a clerk, had been fined a tenner for soliciting. Clerk? The poor man with his reputation at stake must have been at his wits' end to have invented such a transparent porker. For the next week or so the posters outside the theatre were smeared with 'Dirty queer' graffiti and there was talk backstage that the knight-errant had been set up, with the policeman who arrested him positioned as a decoy. When he reported for rehearsal the following day, he was advised to enter via the front rather than through the stage door where there were reporters. The cast working on stage in his absence paused mid-sentence as he made his awkward way down the aisle. It was Sybil Thorndike who broke the tension, stepping forward and wagging her finger with a 'Who's been a naughty boy, then?'

SOURCE
Nigel Hawthorne, *Straight Face* (2002)

270

Touring with John was always delightful not only because the country flocked to see him, but he thought up such marvellous outings for the company on afternoons we were not working. He arranged a fleet of cars to take everyone to Fountain Abbey, for instance, or a vast lunch in an hotel in York, because he wanted us all to fall in love with the Minster. It was at the lunch in York, I remember, that a waitress asked him to sign the tablecloth. 'I'm sure she doesn't know me from Adam,' he said. 'She'll be terribly disappointed if I put my own name.' So he signed 'Jack Buchanan' and the waitress was thrilled.

SOURCE
Alec Guinness, *Blessings in Disguise* (1985)

271

In 1994, when Sir John Gielgud celebrated his ninetieth birthday and I was an MP, I invited him to lunch at the House of Commons.

Tuesday 12 April 1994
I invited John Gielgud to lunch to celebrate his ninetieth birthday. There was just the four of us: Sir John, Michele [Brandreth], me and Glenda [Jackson]. (Glenda was Michele's idea—and inspired. She looks so sour, but she was sweet and gossipy and exactly right for the occasion.) He arrived in Central Lobby at one, on the dot, twinkling and cherubic, amazingly upright and steady.

'It's a great honour that you should join us, Sir John,' I said.

'Oh, I'm delighted to have been asked. All my real friends are dead, you know.'

The stories just poured out of him. 'Marlene [Dietrich] invited me to hear her new record. We were in New York. We all went and gathered round the gramophone, and when we were settled the record was put on. It was simply an audience applauding her! We sat through the entire first side and then we listened to the other side: more of the same!'

He asked after Simon [Cadell] and said he remembered his grandmother, Jean Cadell, 'so well. She was a fine actress: she did *what she did* so well. She played Prism with me in New York, when Margaret moved up to play Lady Bracknell instead of Edith.'*

'Why didn't Dame Edith play the part in America?'

'She was introduced to a blind devotee of the theatre who heard her speak and said to her, "You are much too beautiful to play Lady Bracknell", and that was that. Edith was very much concerned about her beauty, you know. Margaret agreed to move up from Miss Prism to play Lady Bracknell on condition she could model her performance entirely on Edith's. It was typically modest of her.' (Pause. Sip of wine. Twinkle) 'Of course, Margaret's Lady Bracknell was very much the Lady Mayoress to Edith's Queen Mary.'

That prompted Queen Mary stories. 'Queen Mary herself enjoyed the theatre. King George enjoyed his play-going at the back of the box, chatting about racing with Sir Edward Elgar. They went to a matinée of Hamlet at the Haymarket and the Queen enquired at what time the performance was due to end. "You see, the King always has to have his tea punctually, and he is so anxious not to miss the girl with straws in her hair." '

The conversational cast list included Orson Welles, Micheal MacLiammoir (was it MacLiammoir or Orson who kept a flashlight up his sleeve so he could illuminate his face on the darkened stage?), Sir Ralph ('dear Ralph'), Mrs Pat, Kenneth Branagh ('so clever and so delightful'), Peter Brook ('so very clever—but oh dear...'), Binkie, Donald Wolfit ('He hated me, hated me. The feeling was entirely mutual').

He was extraordinary—and he's ninety. I said, 'After lunch, would you like to come to Prime Minister's Questions? I know the Prime Minister is hoping to pay a small tribute to you.'

'Oh, no, no,' he looked quite alarmed. 'I think I might find that a little embarrassing. So kind of him. He is so nice. I think I'll just slip away quietly, if you don't mind.' As we were walking him across Central Lobby back to the St Stephen's entrance, he paused and smiled and fluted gently, 'This has been great fun. You know, the last time I was here Mr Bonar Law was answering the questions.'

**In Gielgud's celebrated war-time production of Oscar Wilde's* The Importance of Being Earnest, *in which he played John Worthing, and in London, Edith Evans played Lady Bracknell and Margaret Rutherford played Miss Prism.*

SOURCE

Gyles Brandreth, *Breaking the Code: Westminster Diaries 1990–2007* (2014)

ESMOND KNIGHT
(1906–1987)

272

Knight played Rosencrantz in Gielgud's 1930 production of Hamlet, *among many other distiguished roles in a long career. Serving in the navy during the Second World War, he was injured in an attack on HMS* Prince of Wales, *but despite losing one eye and the other being damaged, he continued his acting career. In 1943, he received treatment which restored much of his sight, and went on to play Fluellen in Olivier's 1944 film of* Henry V.

Actors today are continually reminded by their elders of how inferior they are to those of Irving's day. Nevertheless, many of the 'laddies of the old school' whom I knew seemed only to concern themselves with how many of their street clothes they could retain while on the stage, or how soon they could get out of the theatre and go home. This attitude seems quite incomprehensible to the

her. He congratulated her especially upon the comedy which she had managed to put across. He said the humour would have pleased his grandfather because he always wanted audiences to be amused by his characters, who were essentially ordinary people.

SOURCE
Eric Johns, *Dames of the Theatre* (1974)

276

When I told her that she was a potato in Leicester—that the theatre bar there had a 'Spud Ashcroft' stuffed with prawns, she took both hands off the wheel and waved them about with pleasure and amazement. We nearly hit a lorry.

SOURCE
Peter Hall's Diaries, ed. John Goodwin (1983), 21 April 1974

KATHARINE HEPBURN
(1907–2003)

277

Hepburn is best remembered as an Oscar-winning screen actress, but she began her acting career in the theatre and, in 1969, made her only appearance in a stage musical in Coco. *She was famous for her no-nonsense manner and independent spirit.*

During the tour of *Coco* in Cleveland, suddenly a flashbulb went off near the stage. Katharine Hepburn stopped in the middle of her scene and peered out into the audience:

'Who the hell did that?' she wanted to know.

A young girl nervously confessed.

'If you had any guts, you would leave,' Miss Hepburn raged, then added: 'If we don't have regard for each other, it will be the end of us.'

Then she apologized to the audience and went back to the scene.

SOURCE
Peter Hay, *Broadway Anecdotes* (1989)

LAURENCE OLIVIER
(1907–1989)

278

According to his son Tarquin, 'Acting for him was as religion still is in the Middle East, the very air he breathed, the faith of which he had written to Jill [Esmond] in 1929: "It is my only hope of being of use to God and the world and I think everybody should try to be that." '

The director Peter Wood (1925–2016) compared Olivier with a racing driver: 'You did not direct him. You made room for him. You could unlock the garage door and give him the key to the car, but you interfered at your peril when he started driving on the right or the wrong side of the road.'

Olivier was the leading actor of his generation and the undisputed head of the profession. The first director of Britain's National Theatre, in 1970 he became the first actor to be made a life peer. Here he describes his entry onto the professional stage.

We were in the Brighton Hippodrome on a Sunday evening in the autumn of 1925.

I passed through the stage door and the stage doorkeeper said sharply, 'Name, please? Oh yes, you're new, aren't you? Well now, I've been told to warn you: be careful the way you make your entrance. This is the old type set. The doors in the set are framed right out—the same width all the way round, top, both sides *and bottom*. That means across the bottom of the doorway there is a sill—ooh—four and a half to five inches high. It's quite difficult not to trip over this, see?' The stage doorkeeper turned away to his books again. Taking my small suitcase containing my ready-made dinner jacket, shirt, shoes, studs, etc., and a tin with a few sticks of Leichner greasepaint in it, a tin of Cremine, a towel and a piece of soap, I went up to the topmost floor to dressing-room No. 12; here were quite a few old actors, already at their make-up. After a while one said, 'Listen, laddie' (no, *honestly*) 'it's possible you may not have come across this,' and told me about the sill. I said it was kind of him but I did know about it. Dressed, made-up and ready (rather too much black under the eyes), I sat and waited for the first time for my call, praying that my name would be pronounced correctly. Eventually, the sharp knock and the boy's voice, 'Mister Oliver, please.' I sighed in disappointment and realized I was probably in for quite a battle with this problem... The call-boy was on the lowest rung of the theatrical ladder, though advancement was quite possible; I imagine that Claude Rains must be the most spectacular example of one who started life as a call-boy. I followed the one who had called me 'Mr Oliver' down the back-stage stairs of the Brighton Hippodrome. On the way he said, 'Oh, you have to be careful, the entrance is a bit awkward. 'I know, thanks,' I said. This was getting tedious.

Some of my generation may remember an ancient ghost of a habit that still haunted *les grandes dames* of our theatre in our early days. It was a device, we assumed, deliberately cultivated to lend dignity, grandeur, hauteur, not to say majesty to their image as leading ladies, which was accomplished by raising their beautiful skirts and seemingly sailing across the threshold on their entrance. It was born of forgotten years' early training in how to cope with *that sill* somehow, without looking undignified.

I stepped on to the stage, which as I had guessed was pretty sizeable. Several yards away the stage manager was beckoning me from the traditional left-hand prompt corner. (Stage-right prompt corners were unusual, except for odd places like the Birmingham Rep.) I came up to him and said, 'I know, you're going to tell me about that old sill, aren't you?' He waved me impatiently round the back of the set to the upstage right entrance at the end of the back wall of the set, which of course flapped about like a becalmed sail; I waited two or three yards up right of it for my cue from the stage. There was a friendly stagehand standing near me. My cue came and I started forward, the stagehand just touched me on the sleeve and pointed to the bottom of the door; it was my turn to wave someone impatiently away. I gave the canvas door a push and strode manfully through it.

Of course I did a shattering trip over the sill, sailed through the air, and before I knew what was happening to me I found my front teeth wedged firmly between a pink bulb and a blue one in the middle of the footlights. I was appearing before a very ample house, which means that an audience reaction of any kind makes a thunderously loud noise to one on the stage facing it. The particular reaction stunned me for a second or two by its volume. I scrambled to my feet dusting myself off, and stood a while blinking at the audience; then turned and blinked at Ruby Miller, who was pro enough not to have turned a hair. I looked back once pleadingly to the audience, but they were not to be robbed as easily as that of their biggest laugh for ages.

SOURCE
Laurence Olivier, *Confessions of an Actor* (1982)

279

His Birmingham debut was in a new one-act comedy by Eden Phillpott, *Something to Talk About*, put on as a curtain-raiser. Olivier—Hitlerish in hair style and moustache—played a monocled aristocrat at a manor house party that is interrupted by the arrival of a burglar. 'Who are you?' the intruder asks. 'We are Conservatives,' was Olivier's haughty reply. But he didn't think this quite funny enough, and on the last night he changed it and said, 'We're Freemasons, froth-blowers and gugnuncs.' He thought that a marked improvement on the script and the audience reaction confirmed him in his opinion. But producer W. G. Fay did not share it. A matter of principle and discipline was at stake, and for once this small and gentle-natured Irishman displayed anger. Olivier has since acknowledged that he was 'a stupid little idiot' and that he might very easily have been fired but for Jackson* having mercy on him…Recalling those early days at Birmingham, Sir Cedric Hardwicke remembered Olivier as being noisy and lacking in subtlety, 'but I knew instinctively that he'd be a great actor'. Eileen Beldon, who worked many times with him, also noted a certain lack of subtlety. Half a century later she still vividly recalled their dialogue as members of the company were parting at the end of a production. 'He said to me in a very grand manner, "Thank you for a wonderful performance, Miss Beldon, I *do* hope we'll be working together again." And I snapped back, "I *do* hope we don't."'

* *Sir Barry Jackson (1879–1961) founded the Birmingham Repertory Theatre in 1913.*

SOURCE
John Cottrell, *Laurence Olivier* (1977 edition)

280

[Jill Esmond] and Larry had much in their backgrounds they were able to share. There were many of their generation orphaned by the Great War, and once this was accepted they had also the universal gaiety of that time. They had house parties and even imposed on them their eternal live readings of plays, often at Larry's insistence. When Jill asked him to do something else for a change he would whisper fiercely: 'Don't you realise...I want to be the greatest actor in the world!'

SOURCE
Tarquin Olivier, *My Father Laurence Olivier* (1992)

281

In Tyrone Guthrie's Old Vic production of Othello, *with a perplexed Ralph Richardson in the title role, Olivier decided to give Iago a homosexual edge.*

There was, I am bound to say, a dichotomy of purpose between Ralph's Othello and my Iago. Tony Guthrie and I were swept away by Professor Jones's contention that Iago was subconsciously in love with Othello and had to destroy him. Unfortunately there was not the slightest chance of Ralph entertaining this idea. I was, however, determined upon my wicked intentions, in cahoots with Tony; we constantly watched for occasions when our diagnosis might be made apparent to the discriminating among an audience, though I must say I have never yet discovered any means of divulging something that is definitely *subconscious* to any audience, no matter how discerning they may be. In a reckless moment during rehearsals I threw my arms round Ralph and kissed him full on the lips. He coolly disengaged himself from my embrace, patted me gently on the back of the neck and, more in sorrow than in anger, murmured, 'There, there now; dear boy; *good* boy...' Tony and I dropped all secret connivance after that.

I had one more trick up my sleeve; Ralph had to fall to the ground when Othello, frenzied by Iago's goading, is helpless in the clutches of a paroxysm. I would fall beside him and simulate an orgasm—terrifically daring, wasn't it? But when the wonderful Athene Seyler came round after a matinée she said, 'I'm sure I have *no* idea what you were up to when you threw yourself on the ground beside Ralph.' So that was the end of that stroke of genius and out it came.

SOURCE
Laurence Olivier, *Confessions of an Actor* (1982)

282

The first night of Richard III *at the New Theatre, 1944.*

One of his truly great, if not the greatest, performances began on the opening night of *Richard III* at the New Theatre in London in 1944, when he limped slowly downstage to begin the soliloquy:

'Now is the winter of our discontent
Made glorious summer by this sun of York...'

Yet during rehearsals he had been full of self-doubts and for the first time in his career he had found it difficult to learn his lines. In his well-documented biography, *The Oliviers*, Felix Barker reports: 'On the night before the opening Olivier was up until 4 a.m. in a room at Claridge's going over and over his part while Vivien Leigh and an old friend Garson Kanin, the American producer, gave him the cues.'

Another old friend, John Mills, has a story which illustrates that Olivier's fears and forebodings had reached a neurotic pitch just before the curtain went up. When Mills was getting ready to go to the first night he received a phone call from Olivier asking him to come round to the dressing-room before the performance.

Mills arrived to find Olivier pacing up and down the dressing-room in costume and fully made-up as Richard. He stared down the long, dagger-like, nose at Mills, fixed him with a piercing eye and opened the thin slit of a mouth to say: 'You are about to see the worst performance I've ever given. I haven't even been able to learn the bloody lines. I'll be terrible, terrible. I want you to know as one of my old friends. You can tell any of my other friends who're out there to expect the worst. If you're all warned in advance you won't be too disappointed.'

Mills, who had never seen him so deeply sunk in despondency tried to humour him, but it was useless. Now, full of foreboding himself, he went to the front of the house to await disaster. Then, as we know now, the curtain rose on a performance of such transcendent quality it will never be forgotten by those who were privileged to see it.

The pre-curtain moments of self-laceration were never again mentioned by Olivier to Mills. However, there can be no doubt that the fears were very real and much in excess of the usual first-night nerves. They may have been related to an instinctive assumption of the tortured, sado-masochistic character of Richard. Whatever the cause it is interesting to speculate as to whether the heights of achievement he reached that night were in inverse ratio to the depths of self-doubt he touched before the performance.

His attitude was very different on another occasion involving John Mills. After a long spell in the film studios Mills was apprehensively preparing for a return to the stage in *Ross*, the Terence Rattigan play about T. E. Lawrence. Mills had been persuaded to do it by Olivier who had warned him of the dangers of staying off the stage for too long a period, and it was to Olivier that he turned for help, especially about the conquering of first-night nerves. Olivier told him, 'There's a trick I've used on occasions and I find it works. Try it. Go to the theatre early on the first night, and get made up well in advance of the curtain. Then walk on to the stage and imagine that the curtain is already up and that you are facing the audience. Look out at them and shout, 'You are about to see the greatest fucking performance of your entire theatre-going lives. And I will be giving it. You lucky people.'

'Tell them that once or twice. Then go back to your dressing room and relax, and you'll find that when the curtain does go up you'll have the necessary confidence.'

SOURCE
Olivier, ed. Logan Gourlay (1973)

283

In 1951 Olivier played Caesar in Shaw's Caesar and Cleopatra *and Mark Antony in Shakespeare's* Antony and Cleopatra *on alternate nights.*

When they were settled in to a monumental success with the two plays more or less alternating, I went to his dressing room and watched him in vest and pants, making up as Caesar. He sat before the mirror, naked bulbs blazing all round it, a bust of Caesar to one side. In front of him were trays of powder, puffs, nail scissors, clippers, pots of various creams, rows of pencils and sticks of greasepaint on either side, and a couple of stands with wigs. He placed his cigarette in the ash-tray, leaned towards the mirror and examined his face: the moment between one entire personality and the creation of another.

He picked up a tiny concave of rubber, rubbed adhesive in with his little finger and placed it on the end of his nose, and then again with another in the middle. He added false eyelashes. As they dried he wiped his hands on a khaki towel. He squashed a sponge into a bowl of olive green suspension and daubed it all over his face. He stood and applied it to his forearms, and his dresser Pat sponged his legs.

Comparing him to the bust of Caesar's head I could see the shape of the nose was perfect, but the rest was still Larry, the colour of the Incredible Hulk.

We had chatted, he had puffed a cigarette between long periods of concentration. He studied himself archly in the mirror, now Julius Caesar entirely.

'What day is it?'

Pat's reply horrified him.

'But that's Antony!'

She corrected herself: 'No, it's Thursday.'

'Thank Christ. Otherwise someone would have to go out front and announce'—he put on a sergeant-major's voice and a toff's accent—

' "Laydees and gentlemen, either wait an hour and a hoff, or else hev the other pley" '

The eyes were Larry's smiling through Caesar's features. He had cast a spell on his face, knew it was good, and could open up his own again as if under an umbrella.

I once watched his Caesar from the wings. At the end of his first scene with Cleopatra as he declaimed 'Incorrigible, incorrigible, away!' and the revolving stage sped him in my direction he saw me from centre stage and the eyes reverted to his own, as easily as turning a page.

SOURCE
Tarquin Olivier, *My Father Laurence Olivier* (1992)

284

Tarquin was staying with Olivier and Vivien Leigh at their country house, Notley Abbey, and joined them for a country walk one Sunday afternoon.

There was a pasture and he explained that one of the best voice exercises was to bellow at the cows. If you shout or even raise your voice above normal speaking strength the tone too easily becomes metallic. His Macbeth had been notorious for that. It flays the vocal cords. Imitating the mooing of a cow caused the voice to gain resonance, so that great volume became rich and not rasping. He configured his throat and voice and bellowed. He loosened his collar and tie and brought his full diaphragm to bear. It was a glorious warm sound, not a snarl, more like the roar of a lion to let the pride know he was king. The cows were surprised.

SOURCE
Tarquin Olivier, *My Father Laurence Olivier* (1992)

285

Nigel Hawthorne appeared in West of Suez *by John Osborne at the Royal Court with Sir Ralph Richardson.*

At the final preview, I was on my way down the stairs to catch my train when I bumped straight into Laurence Olivier. He had auditioned me at the Old Vic not very long before and greeted me like an old friend, clasping my hand in a vice-like grip which he didn't release. Other members of the company squeezed by on their way home, calling out their greetings and their goodnights. He waited until all was quiet—almost deliberately, it seemed to me—then whispered, though there was no need, 'Where's Ralphie?' I took him to Sir Ralph's dressing room and left the two war horses together.

The following evening being the opening night, each dressing room was festooned with greetings cards and bouquets of flowers for which there were never enough vases. I went along to Sir Ralph to wish him luck. He sat, surrounded by unopened gifts and cards, his head buried in his hands. Hal, his dresser, looked despairing. I thought he was feeling unwell and asked whether I could do anything to help. The words came out in a rush. 'Larry didn't like it,' he said 'Told me I should never have done it.' At that moment, Penelope Wilton who played one of his daughters, tapped at the door. Between us, we tried everything to get Sir Ralph back on course. I remember telling him that Olivier was just a jealous old man and had said it only because he wished he'd played the part himself. It gave Sir Ralph scant comfort. His confidence had been damaged and that performance at least would be played with his old friend's disapproval running through his mind and sapping his concentration.

SOURCE
Nigel Hawthorne, *Straight Face* (2002)

286

David Weston, who understudied Ian McKellen in King Lear *in 2007, recalls meeting up with Australian actor Lewis Fiander.*

Lewis is a great raconteur and tells some great stories:

On the opening night of Olivier's acclaimed *Othello*, Lewis, who was not in the play went backstage to congratulate his friend, John Stride, who was playing Cassio. At the stage door he was met by a distraught stage manager.

'Who are you going to see?'

'John Stride'

'Forget John Stride. Larry's sitting up there all alone. Go up and congratulate him.'

He went up to find Olivier waiting very nervously in his dressing room. He looked up anxiously and enquired in a faltering voice: 'Ah, dear boy! Did you enjoy the play?'

All the great actors, Ian [McKellen] included, are chronically insecure.

SOURCE
David Weston, *Covering McKellen: An Understudy's Tale* (2011)

287

Lewis Fiander shared another Olivier anecdote with David Weston.

At the first Christmas at the Old Vic, Lewis was put in charge of organising the actors' children's party. He realised they had nobody to play Father Christmas.

He knocked at Olivier's door as he was making up for Othello.

'Come in! Dear boy, what can I do for you?'

'Well, Sir Laurence, I am organising the Christmas party...'

'Of course dear boy, shall I write you a cheque?'

'No Sir Laurence. We have enough money, but there is a role that must be filled.'

He paused whilst powdering his brow. 'A role? What role?'

'Father Christmas'

'Saint Nicholas? The role demands a beard?'

'Yes, Sir Laurence.'

'And a robe? A red robe?'

'Yes, Sir Laurence'

'And boots? I suppose I could wear my Vanya boots?'

'Yes, Sir Laurence.'

'And a nose? Saint Nicholas would have a prominent, red nose.'

'I suppose so, Sir Laurence.'

'Very well, I will accept.'

A few days later, Lewis met Joan Plowright in the corridor. 'What have you done? He wakes up in the middle of the night, crying 'Ho! Ho! Ho!' On the day of the party, a grotesque, bent figure arrived with a hugely deformed red nose, crying 'Ho! Ho! Ho!' in the voice of Richard III. The children were too terrified to go up for their presents.

SOURCE
David Weston, *Covering McKellen: An Understudy's Tale* (2011)

288

Sometimes he used his old age as a disguise. At the Garrick Club the members might pass him in the corridor, or even stand next to him in the loo and not recognize him. Occasionally he enjoyed his worn-out appearance as a kind of make-up. Once, when at the club's main table after a very late lunch, there were a number of other members stretching down each side of him. Just then the porter showed in some Americans by appointment to see the portraits and said: 'Here we have the Zoffany collection'.

Larry wiped his mouth with a napkin, became the old Italian from the Eduardo de Felipe play he was in (*Saturday, Sunday, Monday*) and all hunched up, struggled to his feet.

'I am Papa Zoffany,' he bowed. He indicated the others at table. 'And these are my sons Rocco, Luigi, Paulo...'

SOURCE
Tarquin Olivier, *My Father Laurence Olivier* (1992)

BETTE DAVIS
(1908–1989)

289

Before moving to Hollywood in 1930, Bette Davis was a successful New York stage actress. Thirty years later, she returned to Broadway, having secured two Oscars as one of the leading film actresses of her generation. Tennessee Williams' The Night of the Iguana *opened at the Royale Theater on 28 December 1961 and ran for 316 performances. It starred Patrick O'Neal and Margaret Leighton as well as Bette Davis. During the pre-Broadway run, Frank Corsaro called a secret cast meeting to discuss replacing Bette. Margaret*

Leighton said, 'I'm sorry to have to agree with that, but I don't think she's doing any service to the play.'

However, the one service that Davis provided—advance ticket sales—made it impossible to confront her, let alone fire her. She was the star—an economic fact of life that Davis would periodically underline to the company by refusing to perform a matinée while one of her assistants stood inside the box office to tally the number of people asking for their money back.

SOURCE
John Lahr, *Tennessee Williams: Mad Pilgrimage of the Flesh* (2014)

290

Patrick O'Neal's performance was suffering because of Bette Davis's behaviour: he began drinking and went incommunicado to escape from her, not letting anyone know his phone number to contact him. Davis had demanded that he be fired, claiming that his constant improvisation was a deliberate attempt to undermine her performance. Tennesse Williams disagreed.

News of Davis's demand somehow got back to O'Neal in his dressing room. He slipped into the theater. Davis saw him coming up the aisle. 'Where have you been?' she said. O'Neal charged up the stairs onto the stage. He lunged at Davis, knocking her to the ground and grabbing her by the throat. 'Patrick almost killed her,' Corsaro recalled. 'We had to run up and pull him off her. The thing that was amazing was, as he was doing it, she was smiling.' O'Neal ranted at her—'You filthy cunt!'—threw a table across the stage and stormed out of the theater.

O'Neal wasn't fired; but the next day, at Davis's command, Corsaro was. 'I can feel vibrations between he and I,' she said, quoting a line from the play. Williams didn't defend him. 'He was a frazzled man,' Corsaro said. 'You couldn't depend on him. He didn't want to get involved. Bowden, who was a wriggly guy, saw his chance to take over the production. Tennessee just sort of fell in with him.' Corsaro fought for two days to keep control of his production, 'hiding down in the back of the theater until the curtain went up and then taking notes.' He was discovered by one of Davis's factotums and banished to New York. 'We now have no director and our producer has just today gone into hospital for a three-day check up,' Maxtone-Graham said in the last entry of his backstage chronicle. 'I asked him before he left who was in charge, he said gaily, "Oh, Mr. Williams." And if that sodden relic who sits in the back row of the orchestra every night's in charge, I think it's time that I packed up my tapes. Good night, and to all a merry Christmas.'

SOURCE
John Lahr, *Tennessee Williams: Mad Pilgrimage of the Flesh* (2014)

REX HARRISON
(1908–1990)

291

For 'the incomparable Rex', who played in light comedy, Shaw, and Chekhov, but will always be remembered as the original and definitive Henry Higgins in My Fair Lady, *the love of theatre began when he was very young.*

What is worth mentioning about that period of his life, and is reported without dispute, is that from his fairly early years, Rex was very keen on putting on his own one-man productions. In fact the very first performance he gave was around the age of eight or nine, intoxicated from the result of seeing pantomime in the Hippodrome in Liverpool, when he returned home and in front of the audience of his parents and sisters placed a couple of chairs between the curtains of a bay window and presented his performance. With an originality, and it has to be admitted, a confidence that informed his entire life, this first performance consisted of no performance at all other than the repeated taking of bows to the adulation and applause of his family. It can be fairly said that the taste Rex acquired for star billing began at an early age.

SOURCE
Patrick Garland, *The Incomparable Rex* (1998)

292

Rex Harrison told Patrick Garland, who directed the revival of My Fair Lady, *and later became his biographer, about his first job in the theatre working for William Armstrong, who ran the Liverpool Playhouse.*

'The company went up to London, and they had a little success at the Everyman Theatre, came back slightly depleted; so rather reluctantly, William Armstrong took me on in the company. Three pounds a week I got then and he took me on as a sort of, not student exactly but a minor member of the company, and I got my first decent speaking part. I had one other bit part in a play called *Abraham Lincoln* by John Drinkwater.' This is a play of modest ambition, but very famous in its day, whose chief distinction was that the last line—'He's with the angels now'—is so peculiarly stressed that it can be pronounced any of five ways.

'I played the messenger who ran on, absolutely exhausted and out of breath. I came on, incredibly out of breath, and a voice from the stalls, William Armstrong said: "You all right, Harrison?" I said: "Yes, Mr Armstrong, yes. I'm acting."

' "Oh," he said, "I thought you were having a heart attack."

'You can see how bad I was, and so at the end Armstrong said to me: "Oh, please, Harrison," almost on his knees, "oh, give it up," he said, "please, give it up. Go into your father's business, please. Do anything, but for God's sake, don't try the theatre." '

SOURCE
Patrick Garland, *The Incomparable Rex* (1998)

293

According to Patrick Garland, Rex Harrison was obsessed with the difference between 'high' comedy and 'light' comedy.

'When I was first up in London from Huyton, I used to go to the gallery night after night. I was a great lover of the matinée idols of the time. I looked for work during the day, and I watched these actors at night. Ronnie Squire, Gerald du Maurier, Charles Hawtrey, Seymour Hicks. My goodness,' he said, 'I was lucky to have the chance to see them in full flight, all at their peak, working with all their talents, and this extraordinary elegance—elegance of dress, elegance of gesture—and highly wrought fabric of art, and this extraordinary *concealment* of art. To me, and my fellow-actors, we were utterly unable to emulate them. What they *didn't* do, what they didn't display, was so remote to everything we thought acting was, and what we had been taught in repertory. They didn't look a) as if they were acting, and b) they were trying to be funny, ever. They played their comedy, I can only say, on the balls of their feet. I remember to this day, their alert posture, well-balanced, but pitched slightly forward, attentive and yet relaxed. Producing gold cigarette cases out of inside pockets, with a kind of magicians sleight of hand, removing, opening, closing, concealing the case again, and then flicking up the cigarette from finger into mouth with the same effortless dexterity, and then lighting it as if from a hidden flame, and jigging, perhaps, the silver lighter for a few seconds from hand to hand, before mysteriously trousering it, without pausing in the conversation. They were marvellous! And what it was, I think, really what it was, was a great inner energy. You see, by definition, an actor can't get up on the stage and do nothing. That isn't acting. But equally, he shouldn't be seen to be acting. I can only compare their quality, their technique—if you have ever seen film of him, and if not, I urge you to do so—to the great pre-war Spanish bullfighter, Manolete. Everything he does is imbued with a kind of silence, and choreography and a sense of grace. The true comedian, like the true bullfighter, should affect to do nothing.'

SOURCE
Patrick Garland, *The Incomparable Rex* (1998)

294

When Jack Minster, long dead now but an urbane director of social comedies said of his first job in *French Without Tears*, that he wondered—as he stood on the balcony of the Liverpool Playhouse after the dazzling first night in 1936—whether life would ever be as sweet again, there was some truth in it. 'Mind you,' he went on 'it was a pretty sensational cast. The up and coming Trevor Howard, Roly Culver as the juvenile, the young Katy Hammond, the emerging Jessica Tandy, and of course not forgetting a spotty-faced butcher's son from Liverpool, who was a high comedian of genius called Reginald Harrison.'

Rex liked to correct this impression by making it clear he came from Huyton, not Liverpool; this substantial genteel suburb, which is to the big seaport what Edgbaston is to Birmingham. And this was long before Harold Wilson put Huyton on the political map, by choosing to represent it as his constituency in Parliament in the 1950s. According to Rex, and more significantly, his sister Sylvia, Countess de la Warr, his antecedents were virtually aristocratic. A romantic mist obscured the origins of the family fortune in the late eighteenth and early nineteenth century, hinting darkly at the Liverpool slave trade, but by his grandfather's time the family lived in some provincial style. Then, probably in the twenties the fortune foundered, and the money declined during the gradual laying off of merchant fleets. But it was always established that Rex's grandfather did fall on hard times and that his father, William, somehow or other lost hold of the family fortune, and was declared bankrupt. It was even rumoured that Belle Vale was turned into a jam factory and finally knocked down to make way for a housing estate.

William, his father, possessed the traditional family charm which Rex in later years inherited, perhaps from birth, and drifted through life with a singular nonchalance, a certain arrogance, combined with an indifference to work. Not unlike the curious father of Beatrix Potter at almost the same period, who trained as a barrister, but through a similar indifference to any form of industry, never practised the law, and spent his life mainly in his clubs or visiting friends. For William Harrison perhaps it may be said, life to him was always associated with play. Later Rex informed me he was brought up with his two sisters at Derry House, Tarbock Road, Huyton, a characteristic suburban house with a large front lawn and laburnum tree shading the front gate. So where therefore did this rumour about Rex being the son of a butcher in Liverpool spring from? It's difficult to tell. Which is fiction?

SOURCE
Patrick Garland, *The Incomparable Rex* (1998)

295

Rex Harrison was in London to finalize his costume for the American tour of My Fair Lady.

I remember vividly the day, and it *was* an entire day, we spent in Jermyn Street at Hawes and Curtis for his suits, and shirts, all of which were to be tailored for the show. The original cutter had been flown out to Cap Ferrat, to wait on him personally, had then returned to London, and we were now to try on the first set of clothes. When we arrived breezily in the morning, a sense of anticipation and delight was in the air and we were greeted by an effusive tailor, and the original cutter who had visited the south of France. I can only conclude, however, that by the time we ended there were in attendance the managing director, a member of the board, one master tailor, three junior cutters, a designer, the stage designer, and countless assistants exhausted and virtually on their knees. At one time Rex had regarded himself in the mirror looking with mischievous horror at the apparition which confronted him in the glass, and gesturing to it exclaimed to the heavens: 'For God's sake! This is fucking ridiculous!' And on a second occasion went so far as to rip from top to bottom all the stitches out of an entire suit of tails. The master tailor had tears in his eyes, but Rex was relentless. 'Well, this won't do at all, you'll simply have to start from scratch!' Tea, coffee, smoked salmon sandwiches, wine all came and went through out the day but Rex was indefatigable in his pursuit of perfection for his sartorial appearance, and it must be said that he could be sometimes as complimentary towards something he liked as he could be destructive towards something he hated.

He sailed out of the shop I remember, briskly in to Jermyn Street and the car where his chauffeur waited, leaving behind his carnage of tailors and cutters, weak-kneed and exhausted on the floor; Rex turned and with debonair charm exclaimed to the room: 'Thank you very much gentleman, not a bad day at all—now I'm going back to the Ritz to freshen myself up with a little champagne and a new set of togs, then the theatre and then I'm going to take Memsahib dancing at Annabels—so I look forward to seeing you all tomorrow morning at 9 a.m.,' breaking off with a triumphant cry, 'FOR THE HATS.'

SOURCE
Patrick Garland, *The Incomparable Rex* (1998)

296

During the revival of My Fair Lady.

The only way Rex could be remotely persuaded—many months later, on tour in Boston—to agree to a change of cast from the ailing English Eliza, was for him to see the American understudy, Nancy Ringham, during a matinée, and that meant, formally, for Rex to be 'off'. He was always, what is virtually a theatrical cliché, 'a consummate professional', and missed very few performances for a man of his age considering the demands of the role and his seventy-five years. The contemporary comedian who dashes off-stage from fright, unhappy notices, and other whey-faced timidities, was not in Mr Harrison's calendar. But, after many blandishments and guileful plaudits on our part, with great reluctance, Rex did finally agree to watch from the auditorium one matinée performance. And, it was made a stern condition, only if he was so thoroughly disguised 'the customers' (as he called the public) could not possibly recognize him. This was agreed, and once accepted, became something of a schoolboy charade, and hence rather fun. Rex took the disguise as seriously as he took everything else, and was determined to make a professional job of things; needless to say, at great expense, an entire suit of tailor-made clothes was hired from Brooks Brothers in New York, and there was the usual business of the handmade shirts. Even more elaborate was the make-up, the hairpiece, and the beard. By this time, Rex was intrigued by the idea of this extra-mural performance as a simple member of the audience, or General Public, and a great deal of preparation was devoted to it. Should he wear a full wig, and beard, should he have sideburns, should it be a moustache, white or brown, to match his hair? Should he wear make-up, or should he, as he said, 'aim for a Royal Court effect and not wear make-up at all?' Mistakenly, I proposed a flattering five-and-nine with blue eye-shadow, in the style of one of his spectacular bêtes noires, and the threatening forefinger lifted in my direction: 'I don't want to look a c**t, Patrick.'

Finally, he decided on a full wavy, white wig, which gave him some of the distinction of Paul Scofield as Salieri, and a white waxed moustache, and ministerial beard. He rejected the moustache pure and simple, as he felt 'it makes me look like that terrible Kentucky Fried Chicken arsehole…', and a generous spade-white beaver made him look like Clemenceau. We attempted the Edward VII look, which was almost too much 'the loveable old buffer' (not a role he craved), and our other efforts resulted in him complaining he looked like 'one of those low-comedy men from the RSC', which was possibly his most ferocious term of abuse. But when we stood away from him at his mirror—in attendance, his valet Walter, the wig-lady, two producers, the director, the dance-captain, the conductor, his lawyer, and I imagine the press-officer, Rex announced that he was highly delighted with the result. I fear that not one of us had paid anywhere near the same attention to the nervous understudy, just about to play Eliza, trembling no doubt in the Number Two dressing-room. But, that would have been the way Rex wanted it. In Number One, however, all was confident, relieved, even gratified. Standing his full six foot two or three, wearing a curiously old-fangled suit of traditional Brooks Brothers herringbone tweeds, almost like a caricature of an elderly senator in a Lubitsch comedy, or even more, like any scene with Sir Cedric Hardwicke in it, Rex surveyed himself in the cheval-glass, as we admiringly hovered around:

'I look like one of those wonderfully well-preserved old-fashioned Savannah queens!' he announced delightedly. Certainly he was unrecognizable as Professor Henry Higgins.

The plan was for all of us, as a protective shield to surround Rex on his circuitous way backstage, up and over galleries, fly bridges, corridors, side-exits, and pass doors, with the surreptitious shuffling of presidential assassins. We slipped, as unostentatiously as possible, into a cosy corner of the balcony stalls, three stories up—even a side-box would be too conspicuous it was felt—and it was pre-arranged none of the party would take their seats before the orchestra was well into the overture, and the audience's attention focused firmly in the direction of the stage. The usherette, at our signal, pulled back the curtain—we slunk in as a furtive group, and shovelled Rex into his seat in the midst of us. As we did so—it was an afternoon performance, you must remember—an outer door, beyond the curtain which led into the auditorium, opened at the same time, and one simple shaft of clear white light, momentarily, no longer than the opening and shutting of a door, fell comfortingly on Rex, in all his Colonel Saunders finery: 'Oh, look honey,' said one of the customers, right behind us in a loud stage-whisper, 'there's Rex Harrison!'

SOURCE
Patrick Garland, *The Incomparable Rex* (1998)

297

It had been John Standing who told me that when Rex was wooed by Sir Peter Hall to go to the National Theatre, the experience was not a happy one. Rex had no resistance to some of the plays that were mentioned but he did object violently to the policy of egalitarianism which prevailed at the National Theatre then, and he was particularly put out that there were no star dressing-rooms and everything to do with the billing was based on alphabetical order. However, he did propose an interesting solution, and told John that he had suggested to Peter Hall that if he dropped the 'H' at the beginning of his name he would be able to kill two birds with one stone: 'I told Hall, my name's Arrison, and I'll take top billing and dressing-room number One, please.'

SOURCE
Patrick Garland, *The Incomparable Rex* (1998)

ETHEL MERMAN
(1908–1984)

298

Ethel Merman (born Ethel Agnes Zimmermann) was the undisputed 'First Lady of the American musical comedy stage'.

Merman, when asked if she was ever nervous onstage would reply, 'If any of them out there could do what I'm doing, they'd be up here doing it.'

SOURCE
Ken Bloom, *Show and Tell* (2016)

MICHAEL REDGRAVE
(1908–1985)

299

Michael Redgrave was one of the great English classical actors of the twentieth century. I met him first in 1968. I remember him for his flawless portrayal of the unbending, scholarly schoolmaster in The Browning Version *and for his Uncle Vanya, the best performance by any actor I ever saw. Harold Hobson called the production at Chichester in 1962 'the admitted master achievement in British twentieth century theatre.' The company included Olivier, Joan Plowright, Rosemary Harris, Max Adrian, Fay Compton, Sybil Thorndike, and Lewis Casson. 'But the greatest of these,' wrote Bernard Levin, 'is Sir Michael Redgrave…I do not think he has ever done anything better—not even his Prospero. Foolish and laughing at one moment, tragic and pitiable at the next, and both together at the one after, Sir Michael dominates the play without—it is his greatest achievement—ever unbalancing it.'*

I first met Michael Redgrave a little over thirty years ago, when I was twenty and an undergraduate at Oxford, and he was sixty and a major star of stage and screen. I found his address in *Who's Who* and wrote to him out of the blue, telling him he was 'my kind of hero' (well, I was only twenty) and inviting him to come to Oxford to perform the prologue to the student pantomime I was producing at the Oxford Playhouse. Forty-eight hours later I received a telegram: WHAT FUN. ACCEPT WITH GREAT PLEASURE. REDGRAVE.

When the great day came, I went to Oxford Station to meet him. His train was late and crowded. The passengers poured out of the carriages and surged past the ticket barrier where I was waiting. There was no sign of my hero. The last passenger handed in his ticket and the platform was bare. The Playhouse curtain was going up within the hour and where was my star? I peered down the platform and there I saw him, in the far distance, a huge frame in a dishevelled raincoat, carrying a little battered suitcase and looking about him with a puzzled, vacant air. I ran towards him. He shuffled towards me.

'Sir Michael?'

'Yes?'

'Sir Michael!'

'Yes. Are you, er—'

'Yes'

'Oh good,' and his large, old face broke into a sweet smile. He had a wonderful smile.

'How are you, Sir Michael?'

'Not well,' he sighed, 'Not at all well.'

Slowly, painfully slowly, we made our way to the waiting taxi. Sir Michael explained that he felt unsteady, 'strange', and that his voice had gone, 'completely gone'. At the stage door, he said he thought a glass of port might help. Michèle, my girlfriend, ran into the

Gloucester Arms and bought a bottle. He wouldn't use a dressing room. He preferred to stand in the wings.

He took a glass of port, gargled with it and swallowed it down. He took another. And another. And one more. The orchestra had finished the overture. An expectanct hush had fallen over the auditorium.

'You're on now, Sir Michael,' I whispered.

'I don't think I can do it,' he said.

'You're on!'

And the stooped, shambling figure stepped from the wings onto the stage, and into the spotlight, and was *transformed*. Tall, erect, formidable. 'Ladies and gentlemen, good evening!' the voice boomed, the audience cheered, the magic happened.

That night he found the energy. Over the next fifteen years, as Parkinson's Disease took a firmer grip of him, finding the energy became increasingly difficult. At first no one realised what was wrong. One day (a year or so later) we were having lunch at the old Empress Restaurant in Grosvenor Square and his head simply fell forward onto the table. He seemed drunk, but he wasn't. He invited me and my girlfriend to lunch at his new house in Lower Belgrave Street and, showing us around, flopped down onto the stairs. He was bewildered. 'What is happening?'

He had long had a dread of first nights. In 1971, at the Mermaid Theatre, we witnessed the worst of them. It was a play by William Trevor, *The Old Boys*, with Michael in the lead, and because, by the dress rehearsal, he still didn't have a grasp of his lines, for the first night the management equipped him with a hearing aid through which he could be prompted. Unhappily, in the audience we could hear the prompter better than Michael could. We reckoned we could also hear the local minicab service. We certainly heard a cacophony of electric squawks and squeals and burrs and, when, suddenly, the apparatus fell from Michael's ear and disintegrated and scattered in pieces around him, it seemed to symbolise the heartrending end of a glorious career.

It wasn't the end, but the beginning of the end, and at least it got him to the Hospital for Nervous Diseases and a correct diagnosis. At last he knew what was wrong, even if he didn't like it. He described this period of his life as 'a grey expanse, with intermittent shafts of light'.

SOURCE
Gyles Brandreth, *Brief Encounters* (2001)

JEAN-LOUIS BARRAULT
(1910–1994)

300

France's leading actor-director of the mid-twentieth century (who first became internationally known through Marcel Carné's 1945 film Les Enfants du Paradis*) made a rare appearance at the Barbican Theatre in London on 30 October 1983. I was there and made a note of what happened in my diary.*

France's greatest actor—France's Olivier—came to the London home of the Royal Shakespeare Company and was put through an evening of humiliation. It was truly horrible. He had been booked (by our friend Patricia MacNaughton) to present an evening entitled *Le Langage du Corps*. We had booked not knowing quite what to expect, but excited at the prospect of simply seeing the great man. In the event, *Le Langage du Corps* turned out to be a lecture in French on the history of mime—and the audience didn't like it. They were wanting a *show*. They felt they'd paid for a show. They were going to have a show! As the hapless Barrault stood at his lectern chuntering on in French about the importance of the actor's body, the bulk of his audience was getting restless. At first they fidgeted, then they coughed, then they began to leave, some of them barracking as they went. 'Boring!' shouted one man. 'We can't understand you!' Eventually, poor Barrault, getting the message, left the stage, mumbling, *'Je suis désolé, messieurs-dames, désolé.'* The audience was now divided: half were angry (those that spoke no French), the other half (us) appalled that this great Frenchman was being treated in such a way. We sat, confused, not knowing what was going to happen next. Trevor Nunn was there, sitting on his hands. He is the director of the RSC. He should have been on stage apologising for the fiasco. Patricia MacNaughton was there, slumped in her seat. She speaks French. She could have been on stage, translating. In the event, someone emerged from the wings to tell us that Monsieur Barrault was greatly distressed by the misunderstanding. He had come to deliver a lecture in French. Clearly the audience was expecting something different. There would now be a short intermission. Those who wished to leave could do so. Monsieur Barrault would then resume his lecture for those that wished to hear him. We stayed and were rewarded. Poor Barrault, having lost confidence in his written lecture, returned to the stage and, apologising further in halting English, said he would now do his best to entertain us with a piece of mime. And then the 73-year-old literally *threw himself* into a frantic recreation of the celebrated sequence from *Les Enfants du Paradis* (made when he was 24!) where the mime impersonates a horse. He snorted, he whinnied, he ran in circles around the stage, he pawed the ground, he threw his head in the air—it was wonderful to watch in its way, but agony, also. He should never have been put in such a position. Those responsible should be deeply ashamed.

SOURCE
Gyles Brandreth, *Something Sensational to Read in the Train* (2009)

DAVID NIVEN
(1910–1983)

301

David Niven was a much-loved Oscar-winning English actor, known for his long film career and for two entertaining volumes of memoirs. He was not noted as a stage actor.

When I asked him if he had ever acted on stage, he positively lit up. I had obviously pressed the right button. Yes, he had even acted on Broadway—but only once. He had played Gloria Swanson's lover in an ill-fated French comedy. Unfortunately, she had designed her own costumes and on the opening night, in the first scene, he embraced her too energetically. Somewhere in the structure of her off-the-shoulder dress, a whalebone twanged, came loose and flew up his nostril. Niven froze and forgot his lines. He demonstrated all this brilliantly, ending with a cocktail stick up his nostril. He quoted a line from Walter Kerr's review in the Herald Tribune: 'Like the play, Miss Swanson's clothes fell apart in the first act'. Niven never acted on stage again. Miss Swanson did, but gave up designing clothes.

SOURCE
Stanley Price, *The Oldie* (November 2014)

CORAL BROWNE
(1913–1991)

302

'No one I know, darling,' said Coral Browne on seeing the 10-foot-high golden phallus designed for the National Theatre production of Oedipus *in 1968. Coral*

Browne was a beautiful Australian-born actress, married first to actor-turned-agent Philip Pearman and later to Vincent Price, and famous for her acerbic wit. She said of working with one player, 'It was like acting with half a ton of condemned veal.' She said of the affair between the mature Sir Godfrey Tearle and the young Jill Bennett: 'I could never understand what he saw in her until I saw her eating corn on the cob at the Caprice.' The stories about her are many and some, inevitably, are aprocryphal. Peter Bowles graduated from RADA *in 1956 and was taken on by the agent Philip Pearman who got him his first job as a spear carrier at the Old Vic.*

Coral Browne, who incidentally was married to Philip Pearman, played Lady Macbeth and I was actually sitting in the stalls when she came on for the costume parade and Michael Benthall asked her if she was happy with her wig. 'No dear, I'm not,' replied Coral forcefully in her cutting Australian drawl. 'I feel as though I'm looking out of a yak's arse.' This is a famous 'Coralism' and it's true. I was there.

SOURCE
Peter Bowles, *Ask Me If I'm Happy* (2010)

303

In 1962, Peter Bowles was in Bonne Soupe, *starring Coral Browne, who sat on a barstool commenting on her life as the other actors 'enacted her amours'.*

Coral spoke jokes, some scripted, some not. The ones that were not were quite often at my expense. The show was a huge hit. We had been running several months by now and the rather bored Coral Browne, who was and is still remembered by all the profession for being outrageous, generous and altogether quite wonderful, began to step up her jokes at my expense.

They were said out of the side of her mouth in that deadly Australian drawl. Quite often they were deliberately meant to be heard by the audience. After all she was watching the past being enacted, it was her life. 'You missed your laugh there, dear.' 'I think you should get on with it now dear.' That didn't sound too good, dear.' That sort of thing. Rather off-putting for a young actor who took himself and his acting very, very seriously indeed. I was becoming very unhappy and dreaded going on stage. My actress companion, who was quite full frontal in every way by now, didn't seem to notice. Then one night as I was about to rush on stage with my young Coral (we made our entrance together), she held me back, blocked my entrance, plucking my sleeve. With a sharp whisper of 'What are you doing, darling?' I managed to get on stage. Coral was ready and waiting. She belted out to the audience, 'he's missed his entrance again,' getting a huge laugh. Then there was no stopping her!

I managed to get through the scene and as soon as we were off stage I said to Erica, who seemed rather amused by what had happened, 'What were you doing? Why did you stop me from going on, on cue?'

'Oh, it was Coral,' she replied, giggling. 'She put me up to it. She wanted you to be late on.'

Loveable legendary character, or not, married to my agent or not, I 'who took my acting very, very seriously indeed', knocked on Coral's Number One dressing-room door in the interval. 'Come in'. I entered. She sat there in all her considerable sexual glory. High heels glinting, skirt gaping, stocking tops darkening and suspenders beckoning. 'Oh how lovely, dear,' she said, pulling on her cigarette. 'Sit down, have a gin.' She seemed to have no idea in the world that I had been upset, or indeed that I was upset. She was genuinely pleased to see me. After all, we had toured America together when I was nineteen and her lovely husband was my agent.

'Coral,' I said not sitting certainly not 'ginning', 'I understand you put Erica up to it—my late entrance, I mean.'

'Yes dear,' she said. 'It was fun, wasn't it? Got me the biggest laugh I've had in ages. We should keep it in.'

'Coral' I replied, 'that was a terrible thing to do to me. It made me look a complete prat. I warn you, Coral, if you do anything like that again, in fact if you make any more side-mouthed comments on my performance, I shall walk off'.

Coral immediately broke down sobbing and said, quite obviously deeply hurt, 'You wouldn't talk like that to me if I was Dame Edith Evans.'

SOURCE
Peter Bowles, *Ask Me If I'm Happy* (2010)

304

This story was told to the English actor David Weston by his friend the Australian actor Lewis Fiander.

When Coral Browne, the grand dame of Australian theatre came to do a play at the Vic her dressing room was adjacent to Larry's [Olivier]. One evening as he was applying his make-up, terrified screams emanated from Miss Browne's dressing room. Larry charged in to find out what was the matter.

'RATS! You've got fucking rats in your fucking old theatre!' (They were, in all probability, mice.)

'Don't worry, Coral, darling. I'll have traps put down.'

'Traps! What fucking use are traps? With what you pay 'em, the actors will eat all the cheese!'

SOURCE
David Weston, *Covering McKellen: An Understudy's Tale* (2011)

305

Rex Harrison told me about Coral Browne, whom he had seen not long before, *tres grande dame* in Los Angeles with up-swept and stylish grey hair. He told me he remembered her in earlier days, and of one glorious occasion when he was on stage, and casually looking into the wings—Coral was probably in her early twenties at that time—and to his astonishment she caught his eye from the wings, lifted up her pullover to reveal the most glorious pair of breasts he thought he had ever seen, and without a smile, or a wink, or the merest gesture, delicately restored her pullover to its rightful place. Rex admitted to me that it was with great difficulty he continued the rest of the scene.

SOURCE
Patrick Garland, *The Incomparable Rex* (1998)

TREVOR HOWARD
(1913–1988)

306

Trevor Howard, the film actor best remembered for the 1945 film Brief Encounter, *appeared on stage opposite Coral Browne in* The Waltz of the Toreadors *by Jean Anouilh. Ian Ogilvy played Gaston the Secretary to General St Pe in the play.*

We opened *The Waltz of the Toreadors* at the beautiful Theatre Royal Haymarket in 1974 and all went well for several weeks. The reviews were mostly favourable. The audiences were large and respectful. Trevor remembered his lines and Coral didn't try to seduce anybody. Then one night the management came round to our dressing rooms while we were getting ready for that evening's performance. 'We think Trevor's been drinking. He's got these Schweppes ginger ale bottles in his coat pockets and we've checked and they're full of neat whisky. Well, actually, right now they're half full. Well, actually some of them are empty. Also, he's having difficulty putting on his shoes. He's trying to stuff his left foot into his right shoe and vice versa. There might be a problem.'

That evening, for the first time since opening night, the entire cast was clustered in the wings to watch the opening of the play. Moments before the curtain rose, Trevor sat quiet and alone behind his desk on the darkened stage, looking fine in his general's uniform. He seemed composed and steady. Then, on cue, the curtain went up and the lights flooded the stage. Trevor frowned and leaned forward and stared out at the audience.

'FUCK OFF!' he roared.

Several members of the audience guessed correctly that, even in the freest of translations from its original French, this was probably not the opening line of Jean Anouilh's *The Waltz of the Toreadors* and those who were sufficiently offended took Trevor's instruction to heart and fucked off. We heard the banging of many seats as the affronted ones hurried from the auditorium. Satisfied at having winnowed away all the people he wouldn't care to have watching him act, Trevor settled down to do the play—but only in the vaguest way and almost entirely in his own words—or mine come to that. As his secretary, nearly all my scenes were with him—just the two of us on stage, with the General having the lion's share of the lines. But not on this night. This night I said most of Trevor's lines for him. It was lucky that I'd spent time with him helping him learn his part, because I knew it better than Trevor did, so the moment Trevor looked blank when it was his turn to speak—which was often—I would jump in and say his entire speech for him, transposing the subject and object pronouns as I went through it, and changing tenses—from past and present to *subjunctive* past and present and then back again—according to what would make sense if I was telling the story on his behalf, which of course I was. At the end of a speech—and as often as not—Trevor would blink owlishly up at me and say, loudly enough for the audience to hear, 'That was bloody good. Do that one again.' And I would jump to his next speech and say, 'Ah, yes indeed, General—what you mean to say is...' and off we'd go again.

The next day Trevor came into the theatre beaming with general joie de vivre. 'Went quite well last night, didn't it?' he said, entirely without irony.

SOURCE
Ian Ogilvy, *Once a Saint* (2016)

VIVIEN LEIGH
(1913–1967)

307

'By Jove, she's a clinker!' said Winston Churchill of Vivien Leigh. Leigh, the beautiful English actress, star of Gone With the Wind, *wife of Laurence Olivier, is just one of the remarkable characters featuring in this extract from the playwright John Osborne's memoirs. The others include his mother, Nellie Beatrice, the American singer and actor Paul Robeson, who was playing Othello at Stratford in 1959, the directors Tony Richardson and George Devine, the producer Binkie Beaumont, and Olivier himself, who had left Vivien Leigh to marry Joan Plowright, who had played his daughter in Osborne's play* The Entertainer.

I took Nellie Beatrice to see *Othello*. Afterwards Robeson joined the three of us upstairs for supper. Perhaps it was as well that my mother was not wearing her favourite outfit, what she might have described to him as her coral and nigger-brown rig-out. We waited apprehensively for his appearance, a handsome but exhausted giant. Nellie Beatrice was genuinely admiring in awe of this massive, Blakean figure, possibly wondering why he wasn't clad in one of Lord Sandy's left-over leopard skins.

She hardly spoke until we came to the main course, when she piped up in her most ingratiating-the-head-waiter voice, 'Oh, Mr Robinson,' she said, 'it's such an honour for us to meet you.' Mr Robinson acknowledged this sweetly. 'Especially for my son. He's such an admirer of yours. You see…' She looked around the restaurant, graciously drawing her audience, then said with deferential confidence: 'You see, Mr Robinson, he's always been very sorry for you *darkies*.' A large, gentle smile spread over his face. In those days, innocent of racial policing, cheerfulness did have a way of breaking in on simple prejudice.

After *Othello* Tony was to direct Vivien Leigh in Noël Coward's translation of the Feydeau farce, *Occupe-toi d'Amélie*, retitled *Look After Lulu*. The combined force of Vivien, Noël, Binkie Beaumont and Citizens Devine and Richardson was prickly and suspicious from the outset, as doomed an attempt to contradict the enmity of history as an allegiance between France and Albion.

Tony rang me from Nottingham, where *Lulu* had opened in an atmosphere of divisive conspiracy and recrimination. 'You've *got* to come up.' I was accustomed to this kind of urgent pleading when he was merely bored with his present company or wanted another hand at bridge. But I was curious to be an observer of the whole explosive enterprise. It also provided me with an acceptable excuse to get away from Stratford and the aimless defeated days Mary and I were spending together. As usual she was unconvinced and possibly relieved, and cheerfully waved me off without any pressure on when I should return.

I picked up Jocelyn and we set out north to watch the progress of the faltering Grand Alliance. We booked into the Turk's Head where Tony was waiting, enjoying every moment of intrigue and sub-plot. 'Thank God you've come. I think I'm going mad. Vivien's gone to pieces because of Joan, George is in a state, and Noël insists on being fucking witty all the time.'

A supper had been arranged after the performance and Tony insisted that we must be present. Binkie presided over the table that included Vivien, George, Meriel Forbes (Lady Richardson), who was also in the cast, Noël and a posse of Vivien's reinforcements, among them the preposterous agony-journalist, Godfrey Winn, who had been hearing her lines and comforting her as she sat by the telephone waiting for Olivier to call from Stratford, where he was about to open in *Coriolanus*. There was common anxiety about her health and state of mind. She had been in an almost unbroken condition of shock ever since Larry had peeled off his Archie Rice eyebrows in the Palace dressing-room and, addressing her image in the mirror said, in a reversion to Coward-like delivery, 'Of course, you know I'm in love with Joan Plowright, don't you?'

Coward himself, though increasingly impatient with what he considered to be a vulgar circus of tedious procrastination, was possibly more helpful than anyone. His cold eye saw quite correctly that Vivien must somehow reconcile herself to the divorce Olivier was set upon. His anxiety was prompted by fears for his leading lady's endurance, but also by his loyalty and affection for them both. Unlike most of the spectators to the whole miserable indignity of their situation, including Larry's forced hole-in-corner dalliance with Plowright, he appeared not to stoop to the silliness of 'taking sides'.

SOURCE
John Osborne, *Almost a Gentleman* (1991)

KENNETH MORE

(1914–1982)

308

Kenneth More left school with no idea of what he wanted to do with his life. On the spur of the moment while in London he phoned an old acquaintance of his fathers—Vivien Van Damm, the General Manager of the Windmill Theatre in Soho, who agreed to see him and immediately offered him a job.

Everyone was extremely friendly to me as a new arrival. I was told to report to Rudolph the stage manager, an oldish man, known as 'Old Rudy'. He had started his career as a stage carpenter, and so knew exactly how scenery should be made and how 'flats'—the large sections of background scenery, such as painted trees or castle walls—should be held when being moved so they would not be damaged.

'What am I to do?' I asked him. 'Move scenery?'

'No,' he said. 'That takes skill to learn. Your job now is to get the girls off stage quickly. When they come to the end of a tableau, the lights all go out—what we call a black-out. As soon as this happens, you dash on stage with their dressing-gowns, because they are not allowed to be seen moving without their clothes. You must get them off-stage fast, so we can get the next scene set.'

'But they are almost naked,' I pointed out.

'You'll soon get used to that,' he assured me. I felt less certain.

The first time I had to do this, three girls were standing in a giant papier mache oyster. They were supposed to be pearls, and to emphasise this they each wore a pearl necklace and not much else. They each held one hand in front of their fannies, and bits of seaweed dangled in odd places.

A tenor, dressed as a deep-sea fisherman, strolled down in front of the footlights and sang: 'When I'm beneath the ocean, all my cares are gone', an awful shanty someone had specially composed for him.

Of course, the audience didn't care a damn about the tenor or what he sang, or whether he could even sing (which was a pity, because Geoffrey Denton sang very well). Their eyes were on the girls. As the singer reached his final top note, Rudy gave me a nod. The lights snapped out and down came the curtain.

One tiny pilot light lit the stage sufficiently for me to see my way across it. I ran on, holding three dressing-gowns, and pushed them over the girls' shoulders, blushing scarlet as I did so. When they followed me into the wings, they were all laughing at my embarrassment.

'Don't worry love,' one told me. 'You'll get used to it. And we promise we won't get you into any trouble.'

And I thought, I hope they don't—or do I hope they do?

That was how I began my career in the theatre.

SOURCE
Kenneth More, *More or Less* (1978)

309

As assistant stage manager at the Windmill Theatre, Kenneth More had to understudy all the 'acting' roles, including that of a Beefeater at the Tower of London played by Eric Woodburn, who sang while a pageant of Henry VIII's semi-naked wives passed by.

This particular night was fairly slack for me, and I was doing a crossword puzzle in my room when Rudy ran up to me in a state of agitation.

'You're on!' he announced breathlessly.

'On? Doing what?'

'Eric's part.'

'No,' I cried. 'That's impossible. I can't sing a bloody note. And anyway, Eric's twice my size. His clothes won't fit.'

'You're on! You're on! In three minutes!' Rudy kept repeating, as though he had not heard me.

'What's happened to Eric, then?' I asked him. Even as I spoke, I saw Eric being carried past in full costume by two stagehands. He had twisted his ankle.

'Hurry! You've only got two minutes,' said Rudy.

Others were already tearing Eric's costume off him as he was carried away, and feeling that I was taking part in an incredible nightmare, I began to put on his ludicrous gear. The legs of the vast red trousers crinkled around my calves like another skin. My feet had inches to spare in his huge shoes, and his Beefeater's cap came down over my eyes. I could only hold it up sufficiently to see by packing a rolled-up page of a newspaper inside. The ruffle at the throat of the jacket covered my shin. I looked like a Womble or the Incredible Shrunken Man.

Someone stuck a halberd in my hand. Rudy said soothingly, as he propelled me on stage: 'Don't you worry, now, Kenny. I'll read the lines to you from the side.'

Then I was on my own. The stage was pitch dark. I could dimly see girls giggling at my appearance in the wings waiting to cross the battlements. The orchestra played the introduction to the sketch, and then the music faded as the curtain rose for me to begin Eric's monologue. I said nothing, for I did not know what to say. Eric's was the one part I had not learned because by no means of imagination could I double for him physically or as a singer.

The conductor took the musicians through the music for a second time, and now from the wings I heard a faint hissing, and then Rudy's voice reading from the script. He was not a man who found reading easy.

'Great Tower of London,' he said hoarsely.

I repeated in a very small, thin voice: 'Great Tower of London' and stopped. Then I heard him read the next line very slowly, as though he had difficulty in making out the words.

'...How little knew the mind.'

'How little knew the mind,' I repeated.

'...Who thee created...'

Line after laborious line had to be whispered and repeated in this way. The audience were, of course, seeing the sketch for the first time and had no idea whether it was meant to be serious or comic. They forced to assume the latter, and began to laugh.

As the lights went up, I knew that the girls were walking behind me and it was my cue to sing. I could see Alan D'Albert, the musical director, looking up at me from the orchestra pit with an appalled expression I shall not easily forget. I plunged into my song, as usual a line behind Rudy's prompting. I knew nothing of musical keys. The orchestra realised this and changed theirs to help me, I changed mine to help me.

Somehow the humiliation ended and I staggered thankfully off the stage, a grotesque parody of a Beefeater. Stagehands were holding their sides with laughter, and, luckily, so were the audience. Van Damm, who had heard of Eric's accident, was waiting for me. I expected the chop for my miserable performance, but instead he congratulated me.

'The funniest thing I have seen for months,' he said—and meant it.

SOURCE
Kenneth More, *More or Less* (1978)

310

The young Kenneth More secured a job at the Grand Theatre, Byker, near Newcastle run by E. Hamilton Jordan. His first role was playing Prince Rupert in The Prince and the Beggar Maid.

Somehow the first three days passed with their six performances. Then came *Son of the Sheikh* which we had been busily rehearsing each morning. This involved a big scene around an oasis in the Sahara Desert. We were all tearing around with turbans on, and

I was playing a Lancashire businessman who was on holiday there with his wife. Don't ask me why. Anyhow, he was very rich and very common. I had to talk Lancashire, to annoy the leading lady, my wife, who was very posh. To show I was rich, I had a big fat belly—a cushion stuffed under my shirt. Charlie Denville explained the background of the play to all of us.

'This is an eastern play, of course,' he said. 'Tons of atmosphere. It's an oasis, so we've got to have animals and sawdust. Animals for colour and effect.'

'What sort of animals have you in mind, Charlie?' I asked him.

'A camel, for one. The ship of the desert.'

'But where are you going to find a camel in Byker?'

'It's all been taken care of, dear boy. I've been to the local zoo, and they'll let me have one'

'Do you know what to feed a camel on?'

'No, but it's going to eat anything I give it. We'll also have a few chickens and ducks.'

'But you don't have chickens and ducks in the middle of the Sahara.'

'*I* do,' Charlie replied with finality. 'Anything that moves and flies is good value. The whole stage is going to be covered in sawdust, and the scene will be set for the three nights, so the animals can stay on the stage when the theatre's closed.'

Beryl protested, 'But, Charlie, the chickens and all those other animals will make an awful mess in the sawdust. The smell will be terrible.'

I felt especially unhappy about this because in one of my scenes I had to be knocked down by bandits.

'What about the chicken shit?' I asked Charlie. 'That's going to go all over me.'

Charlie Denville laid one hand gently on my shoulder.

'You're an actor,' he declared pontifically. 'That's all part of the fun. If you get a bit of chicken shit hanging out of your hair, they'll laugh.'

This play proved a terrible experience for us all. By the third night, the stage was covered with animal droppings. We had chickens, ducks, two goats and two donkeys, all contributing. The birds fluttered into the orchestra pit and had to be driven out by musicians wielding flutes and cornets like clubs. The whole theatre stank to high heaven. Stagehands, who were playing the bandits, would trip me up and roll my face in the mess, having the time of their lives. And to cap it all, there was no room for the camel to get on the stage properly.

It was essential that he was seen, to prove that a camel was actually in the cast, and ideally the brute should have come loping across the desert with the hero on his back to rescue my wife and me from the villains. But so much other livestock was crowding the stage that there simply wasn't room for him.

So the camel came in, just as far as the base of his neck, with the rest of his body outside in the wings. This semi-entrance at least proved he existed. On this last night, with a fight going on around the stage oasis, the camel suddenly decided he had had enough and started to pee. The sight was as yet unseen, but the sound was unmistakable. Immediately, the audience forgot our fight and shouted: 'Look at that camel! Eeeeh! It's pissing, man!'

The man who had hired the camel was supposed to see that his charge performed this function before each performance, but he'd been in the pub and had somehow forgotten to do so.

Water just poured from the beast. It trickled out of the wings and on to the stage. At first, the leading lady tried to ignore his, but finally, realising that the audience knew what was happening, she called at the top of her voice: 'Put a bucket under it!'

One of the stagehands did so and now the water flooded like the Niagara Falls into the bucket, the metal base and sides magnifying the noise. At the same time, someone else had the idea that if he could give the camel a drink, it would stop peeing. So we had the curious sight of one person (an actor!) holding a bucket for the camel to drink from, and another holding a bucket at the other end to catch water coming out—and all the time we on stage were supposed to be playing heavy drama. The audience went wild.

SOURCE
Kenneth More, *More or Less* (1978)

ORSON WELLES
(1915–1985)

311

'He is too big for the boots of any part,' wrote Kenneth Tynan of Welles as Captain Ahab in the 1955 London production of Moby Dick*. A huge talent—with a huge appetite for work and food and drink—Welles is remembered most as a film-maker, but he was also a stage actor and director of note.*

This anecdote is recalled by Micheal MacLiammoir who founded the Gate Theatre in Dublin with his partner, Hilton Edwards.

28th May, 1950: Came home yesterday to Dublin from Paris where I left Hilton with Orson. I'm feeling worried about Hilton whose face, usually of a cheerful (though not insistent) pink, has a pasty and exhausted appearance. This due to Orson's inexplicable dedication to Night Life which increases daily—or rather nightly—and thought strikes me that, in spite of all sorts of manifestations to the contrary, I am, in fact, much more difficult to coax than the much misjudged Hilton, also far less good-natured. Orson's first acting job was with us in our Dublin theatre, and Hilton was his first director, and maybe that is why, now that O. is to return for a period to the living stage, he requires the presence of dear old first Maestro from morn till midnight. Not only indeed has O. decided to return as Actor but also as Dramatist, and has reappeared in our lives as author of two brand new plays. Rehearsals never begin until two or three (or thereabouts) in the afternoon: they then work on till past midnight, frequently till two or three (or thereabouts) in the morning, and then Orson triumphantly gazes on the actors now stretched motionless on the floor, says: 'Gosh! They look tired! Come on, Hilton!' And then the Night Life begins.

Did this myself for two nights and then went on strike. Champagne was endlessly guzzled among inane inferno of noise in one dimly glittering haunt after another, and the sun rode high in the heavens as we staggered back to our hotel on the Boulevard Montparnasse with hours of work to face on the following day: no, this, for me, could not go on: So I told old Fly-By-Night Welles that I was too Delicate too Sensitive too Fragile to stand it, and I see no reason to record his ill-bred laughter or his crude middle-west comments on this plain statement of fact.

SOURCE
Micheal MacLiammoir, *Each Actor on His Ass* (1961)

INGRID BERGMAN
(1917–1982)

312

Ingrid Bergman was a Swedish actress best remembered as a film star who won three Oscars. In November 1946, she forsook the screen for a New York run of Joan of Lorraine *by Maxwell Anderson.*

I learned so much about an audience during that run. The public comes to the theatre not because they want to heckle and see things go wrong. They come because they hope it's going to be wonderful, and they're going to join in that one special occasion, that special night. The night things *did* go wrong, I was dressed in my armour, I was talking to my heavenly voices. I had to sit down on a narrow wooden bench with four small legs. Well, either I miscalculated or the bench wasn't in its proper place. Anyway, instead of sitting in the middle, I sat on the end. The bench tipped up, and bang, I sat down on my behind with a clash of armour. I sat there waiting for the laugh that was going to lift the roof off. But no. All I heard was one great breath of dismay...'Oooohh'...a marvellous sound of pity. Then complete silence. I learned at that moment that the audience doesn't want anything to happen to you—they're sorry for you; they're on your side; they don't laugh at you; they weep for you. Yes, they laugh when it's funny—when you ask them to laugh—but when it's serious they hold their breath waiting for you to take hold again.

SOURCE
Ingrid Bergman, *My Story* (1980)

313

Then nearly thirty years later she set off to tour America with The Constant Wife *by Somerset Maugham. The company manager, Griffith James, recounts an accident that befell her.*

We were playing in the Schubert Theatre in Century City and we'd been there two or three weeks. And one day one of the actors told us about a French restaurant about a ten minutes' walk away. So after the Saturday matinée and before the evening performance we decided to pay it a visit. Ingrid stumbled, twisted her ankle on a stone and we had to half-carry her back.

It was Saturday night and we couldn't find a doctor; when we finally did, he told us she'd broken a bone in her foot and began to put her leg in a plaster cast. I asked, 'How is she going to go on stage with that great thing?' He said, 'I'm the doctor. It's got to go on.' I called the theatre manager and said, 'She'll never be able to play tonight.' He panicked. 'But she must. We're sold out! We haven't got enough money in the box office to refund everybody. It's all gone to the bank!'

So Ingrid said, 'I'm going on!' I said, 'How can you? We can't even get a wheelchair.' She insisted: 'I'm going on!' Then we got all the cast in and had a long discussion. Now, if so-and-so does this, and so-and-so does that, we can work out this scene and that scene. In the meantime, the manager went out and made the announcement. 'Unfortunately Miss Bergman has broken a bone in her foot and it will be at least an hour before we can start the show. If anybody wants their money back they can have it.'

They all went into the bar, but not one soul left. And we were *an hour and a half late.* It took that long for the plaster cast to dry. Fortunately we had a butler in the play, so Ingrid sat in one of those swivel office chairs on casters and the butler pushed her on. She sat in the middle of the stage, swiveled around and spoke to each actor in turn. But of course this ruined their planned stage moves and they started bumping into each other. Ingrid had a whale of a time laughing at all the collisions. So the audience got a sort of play within a play and adored the whole thing.

Then for the last act we managed to find a wheelchair, and we put her in that. The finale was just the two of them, the husband and Ingrid on the stage, with Ingrid saying, 'I have to leave now,' and going off. And I was saying to myself, 'Now just stay there like a good girl and we'll bring the curtain down.' But not likely. She spun the chair around, headed for the door, missed the door completely, nearly knocked the whole set down—all the books fell off the shelves—and the audience roared. They'd never had such a good time. Then the actors came on and she propelled herself back, and they roared and cheered some more. It was quite remarkable. We moved across the United States pushing Ingrid in her wheelchair. And she played it like that for five weeks.

We found a bone specialist—the man who fixed up the bones of the New York Yankee baseball team—and he chiseled off the plaster cast and bandaged her. Then eventually a doctor said, 'I think you'll be able to walk now,' but by now Ingrid so loved being pushed around and playing it in a wheelchair—it was a new theatrical experience for her—that she said, 'Oh now, I think I should play it the way I am.' And it was the second week in Washington before she decided she'd play it on her two feet again.

Of course it was public knowledge now that she had played in a wheelchair and so, though the show went all right, it was really not as big a success as when she was in her chair. So she took her curtain call in the wheelchair and that brought the house down. Because that is what they'd come to see—Ingrid Bergman in a wheelchair. But she really is a very game girl. I couldn't think of any star I've ever worked with who would have gone on in such a situation.

SOURCE
Ingrid Bergman, *My Story* (1980)

FRANKIE HOWERD
(1917–1992)

314

Frankie Howerd is best remembered as a comedian, but he was also a comic actor whose roles ranged from Buttons in Cinderella *to Bottom in* A Midsummer Night's Dream. *This story is told by the actor Nigel Hawthorne.*

I didn't want another spell of touring, nor could I face twice nightly weekly rep after the luxury of once nightly. I wrote masses of letters, though seldom had a reply. Eventually, the director at Bromley Rep, which was weekly, agreed to see me. 'Yes,' he decided. 'You do look like Frankie Howerd.' Seeing that I was uncertain whether or not to take it as an insult, he hastily explained that Mr Howerd had agreed to take part in a farce called *Tons of Money* and a look-a-like was required. Frank, as he preferred to be called, was a slumped, lugubrious man who turned up for rehearsal in a chauffeur-driven car. He had a slender grasp of his lines by opening night, though that didn't seem to impede him. The play began with a breakfast scene. As he made his first entrance down the stairs, Frank would pause for the applause to die away, bend down and peck Sheila Hancock, who was playing his wife, on the cheek—'Morning, wife. Good morning, mother-in-law. Good morning, toast. Good morning, marmalade....'—then go straight down to the footlights to address the audience. 'Now I expect you're wondering what all this is about.' He would then proceed to tell them the entire plot of the play. When he had reached the end, he would hold up his hand—'Quiet for the actors, please'—and go back to more or less what the author had in mind when he wrote it.

SOURCE
Nigel Hawthorne, *Straight Face* (2002)

YUL BRYNNER
(1920–1985)

315

Rex Harrison had auditioned for the stage musical The King and I, *having already starred in the film* Anna and the King of Siam. *He told Patrick Garland:*

'Well, thank God, of course, I never heard a word, because if by any mischance they had liked what I did, which they obviously didn't, and offered me *The King and I*, I might have been tempted to do it, and what a mess that would have been. I mean, I might have missed an even greater opportunity, and a much more suitable triumph, of Higgins in *My Fair Lady* than ever an Oriental potentate could be.'

Yul Brynner, who did win the part of King Mongkut, and made it his own in much the same way Rex did with Professor Higgins, played it virtually up until his death. One evening in New York, in 1980, Rex and I went along to see him play it. Yul was having trouble with the top notes too, but had hit on an excellent way of dealing with it. Boiling up to the top C of 'Shall we Dance', as the band hit the note flat out, Yul Brynner opened his mouth, and lifted his right hand high above his head, finger outstretched giving the illusion he was hitting the top C. Rex and I were not, but two and a half thousand customers that night were entirely convinced. We were filled with genuine admiration. Rex said, 'That's the way to deal with that infernal top G in "Danced All Night".'

SOURCE
Patrick Garland, *The Incomparable Rex* (1998)

DIRK BOGARDE
(1921–1999)

316

Film actor and author Dirk Bogarde began his career in the theatre. The play he is describing is Cornelius *by J. B. Priestley.*

If Ann Wilton taught me two of the most important lessons in the Theatre, devotion and dedication, Max Adrian, who was also in the play, taught me quite another. But not less essential or timely. Humility. Overimpressed with my modest notices in the Daily Press, and well aware that the audiences not only liked me but thought I was funny, I started, within a very few performances to attempt to take over the play from the Principals. I mugged about, invented bits of, I thought, irresistible business, extended my laughs and behaved as if I was a one-man show at the Palladium. One matinée, unable to bear my behaviour any longer, Max, who played a humbled, timid little clerk, took up a great leather ledger and brought it crashing down on my totally unsuspecting head with an infuriated cry of 'Never do that again, I say!' Bewildered with the suddenness of the blow, the stars literally reeling about my head, I slammed into a wall and slid, winded and stunned, to the stage amidst the largest roar of delighted laughter I had ever heard in a theatre in my life. At my own expense. A salutary and necessary lesson for which I was ever grateful.

SOURCE
Dirk Bogarde, *A Postillion Struck by Lightning* (1977)

'I was booed tonight,' he growled.

'Really?' said Liz, her violet eyes still glued to the gogglebox.

'Oh, turn that bloody thing off,' said Richard, sulkily seeking an audience.

'Shush! I can't hear.'

'Don't you understand,' he went on. 'I was actually booed. On the stage.'

'Yes, dear,' said Liz. 'Never mind.'

Richard stalked out of the room and changed into his pyjamas. When he returned and found he was still eclipsed by television, he stormed across the room and kicked the set over with a bare foot. It crashed against a wall and one of the knobs fell to the floor. He kicked it again. This time his foot struck the bared metal screw, and as the screw cut deep between his first two toes he let out an almighty yell of anguish. Blood gushed from the wound. Four-letter expletives sliced the air. Elizabeth, remembering his tendency towards haemophilia, automatically fetched the bandage and iodine, but at the same time she dissolved into fits of laughter and that literally made Richard hopping mad. Next day he went on stage with a pronounced limp and grumbled: 'Some critics have said I play Hamlet like Richard the Third anyway. So what the hell is the difference?'

SOURCE
Fergus Cashin, *Richard Burton* (1971)

330

Though Burton says he could never be dedicated to the theatre in the way Olivier and Gielgud and Scofield are, he does genuinely enjoy acting. His handicap is his extremely low boredom boiling-point. 'I did many of those Shakespearean roles as a kind of duty,' he explained. 'I enjoyed them sometimes, but I found the stage a bit of drudgery for the most part; the terrifying thing of playing the same part eight times a week for, say a year, is enervating.' As a consequence of his restless disposition, he lacks a certain discipline as a stage actor, and during the course of a long run he can become somewhat unorthodox and cavalier. During his New York *Hamlet*, for example, when he knew that German adoption officials were visiting the theatre, he began his 'To be or not to be' soliloquy in German. And brother Graham recalls the night he went to see *Camelot*. 'There was the heaviest snowfall I have ever seen, and towards the end of the performance many people were slipping out to grab the first taxis. Richard came to the front of the stage and called out, "Hey, book a cab for me too, will you?"'

SOURCE
Fergus Cashin, *Richard Burton* (1971)

331

Richard Burton hadn't been married for a very long time to his fourth and (as it turned out) penultimate wife Susan, and Don Gregory told me that all had gone quite well at the previews until the moment came when he and his wife were sitting next to his partner Mike Merrick, and his wife, Annie, with Suzy Burton in the middle. They were all talking animatedly together, having been the best of friends through the difficult technical rehearsals and try-out period, and as they leafed through their souvenir programmes, Don's wife Kaye noticed something which made her blood freeze. In the souvenir programme among the many illustrations, there was a reproduction of a newspaper photograph of Richard Burton and Elizabeth Taylor shortly after they were married. Kaye had noticed Suzy Burton's eye fall on to the same offending photograph, and from that moment on the laughter and good cheer vanished and she remained ominously silent. At the interval instead of joining them for drinks in the bar she muttered some mild excuse and disappeared. All of them feared the worst. It was not long in arriving. The next morning Richard Burton's agent telephoned to insist that they would have to reprint the souvenir programmes for the run at the O-Keefe Centre. He was very sorry about it, but the photograph had deeply offended the new Mrs Burton, and the star of the show was insisting that changes had to be made. Don Gregory had only one course of action before him, and he took it, even though in his heart he felt certain it was a battle he would lose. The next day he went round to see Richard Burton in his dressing-room. 'I suppose you've seen the souvenir programme, Richard?'

'Yes.'

'Do we really have to destroy all those programmes just for that photograph of you and Liz Taylor?'

Richard Burton looked uncomfortable, and sympathetic, but explained there was really nothing he could do about it. It was not his will, but his wife was absolutely insistent. Don tried hopefully to appeal to his decent side.

'But Richard, leaving musicals and show business and everything out of it, don't you agree that it is quite justifiable that the management should print a picture of you and Elizabeth Taylor. Don't you think that's reasonable?'

Richard said, 'I'm sure that it's entirely reasonable, Don, but there is nothing I can do about it. I'm afraid you're going to have to reprint the programmes.'

'But Richard,' pleaded Don, 'don't you realise there are 79,000 programmes printed for the entire run?'

'Yes'

'Richard, that means we would have to reprint 79,000 souvenir programmes.'

'Yes'

'But why? I appeal to you—not as producer to star—but as a friend, man to man....'

Richard Burton turned thoughtfully and morosely on his dressing-room chair and stared gently at his producer. They had always got on very well together, and they understood one another at this moment.

'Don, you have to understand that I'm deeply uxorious.'

'What does that mean Richard?'

'It means Don, that I'm totally dominated by women. Completely in awe of my wife. I have been all my life. Submissive to every woman I've ever been married to. And I'm afraid to tell you that the result of my being uxorious is that you are going to have to pulp 79,000 souvenir programmes.'

And so it happened. The very next day the two producers, and the managers of the O-Keefe Centre hired additional extra staff, who may not have had to pulp and reprint all the programmes, but one by one, day and night for the next forty-eight hours before the play's opening premiere, they ripped out 79,000 copies of the photograph of Elizabeth Taylor and Richard Burton.

SOURCE
Patrick Garland, *The Incomparable Rex* (1998)

332

The 2007 King Lear *with the Royal Shakespeare Company is on tour and has reached Melbourne, Australia.*

Geoffrey Rush is in the audience. He would make a great Lear, but then so would Sam Neill and so many other mature actors—is that one of the reasons it is a great part—the universality of the role? But what makes a great actor? I remember Richard Burton saying to me as we watched Peter O'Toole loping onto the set of *Becket* after a very heavy lunch: 'See that old praying mantis? He's a great actor—he can play a king. Only great actors can play kings. I can

'Letters, my Lord, from Hamlet,' I gasped. And withdrew from my doublet a wadge of lavatory paper. In my panic I'd snatched it from the dunny floor instead of Hamlet's letters!

Wild ribald laughter from the audience encouraged me to tear off a sheet from the crumpled roll and hand it to the King.

'This to your Majesty!' I declaimed.

Claudius, gobsmacked, grasped the proffered sheet with his fingertips.

'This…From Hamlet?'

We were no longer in a play. This was vaudeville. Johnny Craig, now well in his stride, let his inspiration flow.

My Lord, these strange events take not amiss,
For when your bladder's full you've got to piss.
And if you, too, need urgently to go,
Volcania's throne awaits you down below!

That was it. Down came the curtain. Johnny and I were sacked on the spot.

SOURCE
Trader Faulkner, *Inside Trader* (2012)

334

Having moved to England in the 1950s, Trader Faulkner was besotted by his friend Dorothy Tutin but his passion was unrequited. He suspected Laurence Olivier of having more than a professional interest in the young actress.

The afternoon before our opening of *Macbeth* at the Stratford Theatre I was in the actors' pub, the Dirty Duck. A man asked if he might join me. We began to chat. He said he was on his way to the stage door to drop a note for Sir Laurence Olivier. I told him I was an actor in the company and could save him the trouble. He gave me the note. It was on a plain card. The handwriting was Dorothy's.

The man had met her at the Edinburgh Festival and mentioned he was going to Stratford the next day, and she'd asked him to deliver the note.

Saying I'd see Olivier got the card at once, I raced across the road to the comparative privacy of the Bancroft Gardens where I read it. It was a warm and loving message of good luck. No more. But, like Iago, I knew: *Trifles light as air are to the jealous confirmations strong as proof of holy writ.*

Inflamed by having had no word from Dorothy myself, my imagination ran riot. Olivier, my hero—to whom I'd once confided my love for Dorothy—was now my rival. You bastard, I thought. I ran to the theatre and up the stairs to the star dressing room.

Knock, knock…

'Larry?'

'Yes?'

'Could I disturb you for a moment?'

'Baby! A moment and no more. We're on in forty minutes.'

'I've got a message for you,' I told him 'A man in the Duck asked me to give you this.'

Olivier needed glasses to read. He put them on, glanced quickly at the card, then stared at me in the mirror.

There was a long pause.

'Little Tutin is a great actress,' he said finally, sitting back 'but it's time you stopped waving a banner for her, Cully, and concentrated on your own career—because you *are* talented, and for those who procrastinate it's always later than you think. For a start, you're wasting your time with all this flamenco dancing. Believe me, baby, British actors don't dance.'

I bit my tongue. This was not the time for a confrontation about my dancing. He took off his glasses and rubbed his eyes.

'Can I give you a piece of advice?'

I nodded.

'Malcolm. The way you're playing Malcolm.'

'What about it?'

'Having played it myself twenty-eight years ago, I know that it's one of Shakespeare's dreariest characters. But you do have a nice little speech at the end. And you're clowning it. Why, baby?'

'Clowning it?'

'Go on, say those last five lines.'

I did as he asked.

'This and what needful else, That calls upon us, by the grace of Grace, We will perform in measure, time and place: So, thanks to all at once and to each one, whom we invite to see us crowned at Scooone!'

My operatic 'scooone' was like Olivier's 'God for Harry, England and St Geeoooorge!' in his film of Henry V.

'Baby,' he said, 'you sound exactly like an air-raid siren. If you do it that way tonight the customers will piss themselves laughing. Is that what you want?'

'How would you do it?'

'To *see us* crowned *at Scone.*'

He sat me down beside him and from his make-up tray scooped out a blob of undertaker's wax, a tiny ball of which he put on the tip of my nose and reshaped it.

'Now, baby, you begin to look like Vivien's twin.'

He had switched to another of my roles that season—Sebastian, twin-brother to Vivien's Viola in *Twelfth Night*. He'd moulded my nose with a little wooden spatula to make a perfect retroussé identical to hers.

'That's the spatula I used for the very first performance of *Richard III* at the New Theatre in London.' He handed it to me. 'Here, baby, keep it. And learn how to do a proper nose.' Then, 'Christ! Out, quick! We're on in five minutes!'

I was halfway to my dressing room clutching the historic spatula—treasured still, like a fragment of the True Cross—before I realised how brilliantly he'd switched my mind away from Dorothy.

SOURCE
Trader Faulkner, *Inside Trader* (2012)

FENELLA FIELDING
(1927–2018)

335

The flamboyant and husky-voiced actress was engaged by the director Michael Rudman to appear at the Traverse Theatre in Edinburgh in 1972.

Once we did a version of *The Relapse* by Vanburgh; Fenella Fielding agreed to play Berinthia. All went smoothly until the opening night, and even until the interval of the opening night. We had all been to the bar for a drink and a chat and now we were settled into our cushioned seats for the second act. So far the play, which we had edited severely but fairly, was working. We had cut all the Lord Foppington scenes, normally the most successful, and kept all that was to do with Loveless, Amanda, Berinthia and Worthy. We had dressed it à la 1930's and played it as a contemporary comedy of manners, rather like a Noël Coward play.

After the interval, as I sat in the dark auditorium, I was feeling pleased. I was wrong.

We waited two minutes. Then three. Three minutes is a long time to be in the dark with one hundred strangers, some of them critics. Then we waited four minutes. And five. Everyone was restless. No one could see his watch. I rely on my timings on the stage management reports.

The thing was, Fenella hadn't finished her costume change. With a twenty minute interval and another five minutes of us being in the pitch dark, you imagined it was long enough, but apparently not. I knew that she was nervous, although she was excellent in the play that night and every night, but I realised after a little while that she was the reason for the delay. The doors were shut. The lights were out. It was hot. You could smell panic. Then it was eight minutes. I was breathing heavily. I didn't know what to do. I was desperate. Then I felt a sharp pain in my scalp. Then another. What the hell could that be? Then I realized what I was doing. I was tearing at my hair. Eventually, the second act began and the play was a success.

SOURCE
Michael Rudman, *I Joke Too Much* (2014)

RICHARD JOHNSON
(1927–2015)

336

Richard Johnson was a stage and film actor whose first job was a small part in John Gielgud's Hamlet *of 1944. He was an Associate Artist of the Royal Shakespeare Company from the 1960s until his death, with decided views on how Shakespeare should be played.*

Father Joe McCullough, chaplain at the Royal Marsden Hospital where Johnson was treated for his final illness, told how he had T-shirts made with EWMBH (Every Word Must Be Heard) on the front and GTFOWI (Get The Fuck On With It) on the back. These were available at the back of the church.

SOURCE
Account of Richard Johnson's memorial service, *The Oldie* (January 2016)

SIDNEY POITIER
(1927–)

337

Best known for his screen performances, Poitier began his acting career with the American Negro Theater. His description of playing A Raisin in the Sun *provides a revealing glimpse of a Method actor at work.*

I received the script almost a year before we went into production, right? And I read it, naturally, many, many, many times and I knew, generally, after ten or twenty readings, what the circumstances of the play were. I knew what the individual characters were like, generally. I understood my character kind of generally. Now I needed time to make my understanding of my character specific. In so doing I must understand all of the contributing elements that go to making up this character. First I must understand what are the driving forces in the man. In order to understand that, you must find out what are his political, social, economic, religious milieus, and how they contribute to the personality idiosyncrasies or whatever. And in so examining, I find that this, first, is a Negro man thirty-six years old, living in Chicago on the South Side—which of itself is quite significant in the building of a character, because only a particular kind of Negro lives on the South Side in this particular kind of circumstances, see? So that narrows the field already. And then we take: Why is this man living here? Is he here by choice? What is his relation to his community? What is his relation to his religion, if he has one? What is his relation to his economic disposition? Is it one in which he finds enough elasticity to function and maintain his manhood or is it a constant badge or remembrance of his inadequacies—you follow?—and all these things can be found in the script, or at least if they're not there they can be made compatible with what is in the script at one point or another. So that—after

and decided to see if I could make Nigel laugh. There was a moment in the play when he asked me where I'd been, and my line was, 'I went downstairs for a sandwich.' On this particular night, I thought I'd insert a little extra something.

Nigel: Where have you been?
Me: I went downstairs.... For a peanut butter sandwich

(There was a nasty pause, while Nigel gazed at me dispassionately—and without a flicker of the hoped-for smile. Then—)

Nigel: For a what?

(This wasn't Nigel's next line. I felt a twinge of panic. Had I bitten off more than I could chew?)

Me: Um—a peanut butter sandwich?
Nigel: (slowly, and with horrible emphasis on each word) A. Peanut. Butter. Sandwich. Really? So, this peanut butter—was it smooth or crunchy?

(Oh God. I'd made a terrible mistake)

Me: Er... smooth.
Nigel: Smooth, huh? Funny, when you were a kid you always used to like it crunch. So when did you change?
Me: Um... Oh, a while back.
Nigel: Yeah? A while back, huh?
Me: Yup. Look, do you think we could move on—
Nigel: No. Does Mom know?
Me: What?
Nigel: Never mind, I'll tell her. She won't like it. So—this sandwich—where did you get it? This oh-so-smooth-peanut-butter sandwich—;where did you get it huh?

(OK, please stop Nigel, I swear I'll never do this again)

Me: Um—at Jack's place.

Nigel: Jack's place? *Jack's place*? Don't lie to me kid—Jack's place has been closed for over a year…

I don't remember any more of this agonising cross talk act we were doing, so perhaps it was about now Nigel decided to let this poor, inexperienced sap of an actor off the hook. I've been grateful to him ever since—not for being let off the hook, although when he did it was a relief—but for the lesson he taught me. It was a lesson I needed to learn—don't ever try to mess with your fellow actors on stage, the chances are they're better at messing with you.

SOURCE
Ian Ogilvy, *Once a Saint* (2016)

RICHARD HARRIS
(1930–2002)

343

Richard Harris was an Irish-born actor, singer, and film star, with, in his heyday, a reputation as a hell-raiser. In later life, he gave up drinking and appeared on stage in 1989 in Pirandello's Henry IV, *produced by Thelma Holt, on tour and in the West End. Holt's assistant, Sweetpea Slight, recalls the experience.*

Richard Harris was high-maintenance. Thelma loved him for his brilliance as an actor—she found his work on stage very exciting—but also because he was Irish and ate porridge, as she herself did. Richard no longer drank, and appeared to *live on* porridge; this was certainly what he ate most nights in his dressing room before going on stage. The porridge settled his stomach, which was often upset by nerves, and he ate it with a silver spoon with his initials on, a present from Thelma.

Richard was tall and still looked strong, but his face was always pasty, and creased with the years. Thelma told him one evening that he looked like 'a half-baked apple strudel'. They had a robust, playful relationship and he became considerably reliant on her regular dressing room visits. I was usually with her, and he trusted me by the time we opened in the West End.

I had been around on that fateful night in Cardiff when he had locked himself in his dressing room, refusing to come out or to go on stage for that evening's performance. Duncan Welson [the co-producer], having been unable to reason with him, eventually summoned Thelma. She knocked on the door and pleaded with Richard to let her in, at which the door opened a fraction and an arm came out and pulled her in. I waited outside. Richard wanted the understudy to go on that night and he would go on the following night. 'No, you won't,' said Thelma. 'If you don't go on tonight you will not go on for the rest of the tour and by the time we get to London we will have found someone who won't be a tenth of you, but we *will* replace you.' It was at this point that she gave him her most treasured rosary beads. Then the door opened and I was allowed into the inner sanctum. After the performance, Duncan Weldon took us all to dinner where Richard announced he wanted Director Number Three fired....

Only once during the run in London did I have to visit Richard's dressing room alone. Despite Thelma having warned him of her impending absence, by the time I knocked on his dressing room door he had clearly forgotten and seeing me alone bellowed, 'Where's that fucking Irish red-headed bitch!'...

I couldn't tell if he was joking or not, but before I could explain where she was he had picked me up and thrown me across the dressing room on to a divan in front of the wall, which I narrowly missed smashing my head against. This was his idea of being friendly. I composed myself, then had to sit chatting to Richard, who sat cross-legged on the divan opposite, oblivious to the fact that he had no pants on.

Thelma never got her rosary back.

SOURCE
Sweetpea Slight, *Get Me the Urgent Biscuits* (2018)

DOROTHY TUTIN
(1931–2001)

344

Dorothy Tutin was an English actress whose work ranged from light comedy to Shakespeare. In a television interview with Derek Hart she recalled her times with the Royal Shakespeare in Company in 1961/2.

DH: I remember seeing you in a play by John Whiting called *The Devils,* in which you played a prioress possessed by the evil spirit of the prelate, Grandier. There was a scene where the witch-hunting priest tries to extract the evidence from you and you actually became possessed. Now, that is a situation which must be wildly outside your own experience. When you're doing something of that kind, is it a particularly difficult thing for you to do?

DT: That part was impossible really, impossible. It was a marvellous play, absolutely marvellous. But when I read it I said to Peter Hall who was producing it, 'The play is so wonderful—it would be too awful if I played it and couldn't do it at all; I must audition for it.' I had done another play of John Whiting's before and he said it would be all right and I wasn't to be nervous about it and just do it. The awful thing was whenever we came at rehearsals to the possession scene, I kept on saying, 'Well do you mind if I don't do that today? You know, I'll do it tomorrow, can we skip that bit?' I was terrified of doing it, I was balking it. Then one of the nuns came up to me and said, 'Dotty, aren't you going to do that scene, because until you do it, we can't get started either?' I was appalled to think that I had been stopping them from acting. And so that day at rehearsal, when we came to the possession scene, instead of saying, 'Sorry I can't, I'll do it later,' I did it and we started off. I didn't know what would happen, I just made my mind a blank and tried to imagine possession. The extraordinary thing was that the other nuns picked it up and in fact we had the experience that happened in the actual play in that nunnery, a sort of catching hysteria. We all got it; we never did it again like that. The problem about hysteria of that kind is that you can't portray it in any manner that is acceptable. The audience can imagine it for themselves far better than you could ever show it. In fact, it was best when it wasn't seen, when it was either talked about or when you only saw a little bit of it.

SOURCE
From *Acting in the Sixties*, ed. Hal Burton (1970)

GERALDINE McEWAN

(1932–2015)

345

The director John Counsell recalled 'discovering' the unique talent of Geraldine McEwan.

Exceptional histrionic talent in its various stages of development almost always stands out for all to see. There is therefore nothing very clever about spotting it.

Yet there are a handful, besides Mary, with whose early careers I have been sufficiently concerned to justify a claim that I have discovered them. One in particular, whose story reads like a fairytale.

It begins when I was preparing our first production of *A Midsummer Night's Dream* in 1946. Our assistant snack-bar attendant, hearing we needed some walkers-on to swell the numbers of Theseus's court, asked if her very handsome and well developed fourteen-year-old daughter could be one. As she was a dark Levantine type, I readily agreed, but rejected a further suggestion that she should bring along her bosom school friend, a fair-haired funny little creature with a turned-up nose who didn't look a day over twelve. However, after further earnest pleadings and to keep everybody happy I eventually agreed. After all, she was so small that, placed at the back, she wouldn't be seen. There I was wrong. Wherever there was a gap in the front rank of the rather solid-looking chiton-clad group, a small eager little face could be seen peering through, acting like mad. I was delighted—at least the child had personality. And so, whenever during the next couple of years we needed walkers-on she was included.

On one such occasion I had just given notice to an A.S.M. Crossing the stage during a performance, I was confronted by a very determined little figure.

(In a vehement whisper) 'Can I please come as A.S.M. instead of So-and-so?'

It was the little blonde with the turned up nose whose Irish-spelt surname I had difficulty in remembering. I was in a hurry and sought a quick end to the matter by asking a loaded question.

'How old are you?'

'Sixteen, but I'm nearly seventeen.'

'Sorry, I'm afraid you're too young.'

'Do you mean I can't?'

'I'm awfully sorry.'

'Oh…'

The gasp of disappointment was heart-rending. A large tear ran down the turned-up nose. I felt terrible and, for the first time giving the matter any thought, asked her to come and see me in my office after the performance. A glimmer of hope shone through the tears.

I had a word with Hugh Cruttwell, the stage director.

'We shall be needing a maid for *Life with Father* in three weeks' time. It's a tiny part, and little Thingummy McWhat's-it would look perfect. She can take So-and-so's place for the time being.'

Hugh seldom swore, but to this suggestion he reacted with a violent blasphemous obscenity that annoyed me. He explained later that he had been hoping for someone with experience and had been completely taken aback by being offered instead a raw schoolgirl. Had he said so at the time I would have probably changed my mind. As it was, after ticking him off for what amounted to insolence, I told him that the girl would quite definitely come for a month on approval.

That is how Geraldne McKeown (later to become McEwan) began her professional career. I told the story a few years later when proposing the toast at Geraldine and Hugh's wedding.

SOURCE
John Counsell, *Counsell's Opinion* (1963)

PETER O'TOOLE
(1932–2013)

346

O'Toole, stage actor and film star, is reminiscing on television about his friendship with Richard Burton with whom he appeared on screen in the film Becket. *At the time of the anecdote, Burton was married to Elizabeth Taylor and sometimes sought refuge from her demands in O'Toole's company.*

One day we were hiding in a pub at lunch and he said, 'Let's do *Hamlet*.'

I said 'No! Never! I've done that, so have you.'

He said. 'Let's do it again. Just to be perverse.'

I said, 'Oh no, no. It's the worst play in the world. I won't do it.'

He said 'Go on!'

So, I don't know, I'd had rather too much of the red ink or whatever. We tossed coins; we decided what we'd do. We'd have Olivier and John Gielgud to direct. And we tossed up to see who'd get John Gielgud and who would get Larry Olivier. And we tossed up to see who'd get New York and who'd get London. I got Larry Olivier in London and he got Gielgud in New York. And we DID it!

There is an amusing sequel to the story which O'Toole recounted during the same interview. O'Toole had been playing Hamlet for several weeks for the National Theatre at the Old Vic in London and was beginning to feel confident in the part.

I came up to do 'To be or not to be' from the bowels one night. And I was 'To being or not to being...' I could hear slight titters... It was an afternoon performance and I thought, 'What are they laughing at?' And of course when you do that soliloquy everybody knows it, so they could all join in anyway. It's a song. They should lower a song sheet. But I'm not used to too many titters. By this time I was feeling much better with the way things were going and, I don't know, I did some fine gesture [*he puts his hand up to his face*] and found I was wearing my bloody glasses! Because I'd been down below with the stage hands—picking out winners!

And I just sort of trudged through as far as I could and I thought, 'How can I get rid of these glasses?' I was wearing horn rims. And the only thing I could do was to sling 'em at Ophelia.

SOURCE
Michael Parkinson Show, BBC1, 24 June 1972 (Season 2, episode 4)

347

In a magazine interview, the American actor Kevin Spacey was asked, 'Who is the coolest person you have ever met?'

Peter O'Toole. I met him when he came backstage during *The Iceman Cometh* [at the Almeida Theatre, London, in 1999]. He surprised me and grabbed my head like it was a little football, with both of his hands around the back of it, and then began to say the most wonderful series of adjectives that I've heard—funny, brilliant, hilarious, quick, fast, clever. But as he was doing that, he was banging the back of my head with his hand, and I literally thought I was going to be knocked out because it was so hard. But I didn't care at this point. Peter O'Toole was bashing my head in with compliments, and it was fine by me. I thought, 'That's a way to die.'

SOURCE
Maxim Fashion (Fall/Winter 2001/2)

JAMES VILLIERS
(1933–1998)

348

Villiers was a plummy-voiced British actor of great style and authority.

James Villiers has left the world of acting with a strange legacy: the expression and the word 'luvvie'. James always, from 1955, when I first met him, called everyone 'lovey', and he was famous in the profession for using the expression and when actors imitated him, as they often did, they always used his word 'lovey'. It is an unfair legacy because James was not in any way a 'luvvie' in the sense the word is used today. He never ever spoke of acting, never ever spoke about himself; he was camp, yes, theatrical, yes, but definitely and absolutely not a 'luvvie'. James died before the derogatory meaning came into modern journalistic vogue.

SOURCE
Peter Bowles, *Ask Me If I'm Happy* (2010)

EILEEN ATKINS
(1934–)

349

In 1991 Dame Eileen Atkins was cast in The Night of the Iguana, *by Tennesse Williams, directed by Richard Eyre at the National Theatre. As was customary, the rehearsal period started with a read-through of the script for the full company.*

After the read-through Eileen [Atkins] said: 'It's such a relief to get that over. It doesn't get easier. It's a relief too not to have to look round the room and think who you're going to have an affair with on tour.'

SOURCE
Richard Eyre, *National Service* (2003)

RICHARD BRIERS
(1934–2013)

350

In 2010 Nicholas Hytner put on Dion Boucicault's comedy London Assurance *at the National Theatre with Simon Russell Beale as Sir Harcourt Courtly, Fiona Shaw as Lady Gay Spanker, and Richard Briers as Lady Gay's decrepit husband, Mr Adolphus Spanker.*

As the rest of the audience rolls in the aisles, who hasn't sat alone and sullen, seething at how unfunny a play is and how grotesquely it's overplayed? So you try to establish where the top is, and urge the actors not to go over it.

Simon's first entrance as Sir Harcourt, to the sound of Tibetan bells, in a huge brocaded dressing gown and plump dyed-brown kiss curls, pitched the base camp quite close to the summit. Half an hour later, Fiona made her first entrance as Lady Gay, beside herself with the thrill of the chase, invisible hounds baying at her feet, and climbed closer to it, only to find Richard Briers already there as her ancient husband, Mr Adolphus Spanker. There was plenty that an aspiring comic actor could have learned from Simon's vowels, as full as his waist; from the affected precision of his diction; from the imperceptible lift he gave his best lines. She could have learned from Fiona's 'pell-mell, helter-skelter' speed of thought, her unabashed brio: 'Horse, man, hound, earth, heaven. All, all, one piece of glowing ecstasy.' But whatever it was that brought the house down when Richard Briers wobbled unsteadily onto the stage cannot be taught.

SOURCE
Nicholas Hytner, *Balancing Acts* (2017)

JUDI DENCH
(1934–)

351

Dame Judi Dench CH first came to note playing Ophelia and Juliet at the Old Vic in 1957 and 1960. She went on to become one of the best-loved and most honoured British actresses, winning multiple awards for her work on stage, television, and film.

When I was young, my eldest brother Peter was in a school production of *Macbeth*. He played Duncan, so his first line was 'What bloody man is that?' And I thought 'Christ—this is for me! Not only Shakespeare but swearing!'

SOURCE
Judi Dench, interviewed in *The Radio Times* (30 September 2016)

352

In 1974 Judi Dench played Miss Trant in a musical version of J. B. Priestley's The Good Companions, *which tells of the trials and tribulations of a small travelling theatre company between the First and Second World Wars. Among her co-stars was Sir John Mills.*

He and his wife Mary used to invite Michael [Judi's husband, Michael Williams] and me to dinner with them after the show, and because our curtain came down quite late we had to tell the restaurant beforehand what we wanted to eat. So when Johnny came on with a clipboard in one scene, calling 'Miss Trant, Miss Trant,' he would come up to me with the whole of the menu, and say, 'What do you think you'd like tonight?' We would go right down the menu and choose something and I would say that Michael would probably have the fishcakes.

Johnny was a man after my own heart. He and I organised a very elaborate practical joke to play on a member of the company who we didn't think was behaving very well. He kept going and looking down at the orchestra, and we were thinking, Oh come on, there is a show supposed to be going on here. We had a scene at Crewe Station with three big theatre companies all going off in different directions on other trains, with a huge amount of suitcases. So we put two stage weights in the case for this particular person, and John had to give them out. Everyone used to take their case and swing it up above their heads, but of course his case was so heavy that it swung away from him and threw him down on the floor. John and I laughed so much when we did the scene that afterwards we were helpless with laughter in the corridor, and Ann Way, who was also in that scene, came towards us and said to John, 'I have never seen anything in my life so amateur!' She was quite right of course, but oh gosh, it was an irresistible afternoon.

SOURCE
Judi Dench, as told to John Miller, *And Furthermore* (2010)

353

Judi and I first met doing a play for ITV television in 1968. A glorious four-hander by Frederick Lonsdale called *On Approval* starring Maggie Smith, Robert Stephens, Judi Dench and myself. Maggie and Robert, I think, were engaged at the time which meant that Judi and I were somewhat thrown together. This sealed a lifelong friendship. I remember once, during time off from rehearsals, we were walking near Shaftesbury Avenue together when Judi suddenly said to me 'There's a postbox! Can you post this letter for me?' Bemused as to why she didn't just pop it in herself, I obeyed.

Judi: There now. I've GOT to do it!
Me: Do what?
Judi: 'Cabaret'. They want me to play Sally Bowles! It's terrifying, I've never been in a musical before!

Needless to say she was sensational. This production set her on the path to becoming one of the leading actresses of our day.

SOURCE
Moray Watson, *Looking Back and Dropping Names* (2016)

354

In September 1982 The Importance of Being Ernest *with Judi Dench, Anna Massey, Nigel Havers, and Martin Jarvis opened at the National Theatre, followed by an extended tour and then a return to the National.*

Back from the tour a week later, Nigel burst into my room at the National, crying, 'Do you know what *they're* doing?' He sounded like Bertie Wooster presenting Jeeves with a problem. '*They're* doing another play!'

I calmed him down and asked what he meant. He told me he had just been looking at the noticeboard and had seen that Judi Dench and Anna Massey were starting rehearsals for a two-handed play called *The Crew,* which would receive performances on certain nights in the National's 'Platform' series. 'How can they do this to us?' he yelped, 'they're taking on too much.' I knew what he meant. We were already short of rehearsal time for *Other Places.* He and

Anna had substantial parts in the first of the Pinter plays, *Family Voices,* and he was concerned that she would now have even less time to rehearse. We confronted Anna and Judi. They told us *The Crew* was by a young writer called Nick Harrad and dealt with the lives of two lesbian truck-drivers. It was well worth doing, they felt, and somehow they would fit it in. Nick was an important new find and it was only right his first play should be given a chance.

Fair enough. The days went by. Call sheets with rehearsal times for *The Crew* continued to appear on the board. Then one evening Nigel burst into the room again: 'It's all a wind-up. There's no such person as Nick Harrad. They're not doing a play at all. The whole thing's a hoax!'

It was. On further investigation, we found that all the notices had been fabricated by Judi and Anna. Despite this discovery we could never get them to own up. Judi in particular spoke warmly in praise of Nick Harrad and how much they were looking forward to performing his play.

Next day, Nigel and I were due to appear on a BBC Radio arts programme about life at the National. It was recorded in the studio in the late afternoon, to be transmitted a couple of hours later. When the interviewer asked how we enjoyed working with Miss Dench, Nigel and I exchanged glances. I heard myself begin: 'Terrific. Not only is she doing the Wilde and the Pinter but she somehow finds time to encourage new writers.'

Nigel seamlessly took over the baton: 'In fact, she and Anna Massey are rehearsing a play by a brilliant new writer, Nick Harrad…'

The interviewer nodded appreciatively as we gave him details of the two tough truckers and Nick's graphic account of their life on the road. We made it up as we went along. The interviewer concluded by thanking us for providing insight into the hard-working life of two of Britain's best-loved actresses.

Two hours later we strolled into Judi's dressing room as she prepared for Lady Bracknell. Anna was there. I switched on the portable radio we had brought in. The programme was just beginning: 'And now we hear how Judi Dench and Anna Massey are encouraging new talent at the National Theatre in a play about female truck-drivers, by newcomer Nick Harrad.' Judi didn't bat an eyelid. Anna's mouth twitched momentarily, then was still. They both listened, along with half a million others, as Nigel and I talked earnestly about *The Crew*. All Judi said as the programme finished was, 'You might have got the plot right. It's clear you haven't read the play at all.'

SOURCE
Martin Jarvis, *Acting Strangely* (1999)

355

In 1994 Judi Dench was playing Arkadina in The Seagull, *a role she found particularly challenging. The actor John Moffatt (1922–2012) was a close friend of both Judi and her husband, Michael Williams.*

If there was ever the slightest risk of taking myself, or a particular part, too seriously, I can always rely on my friends to send me up, and I still treasure a poem I received from John Moffatt during the rehearsals for this play:

Dame Judi Dench . . . known as Jude
Was excessively vulgar and lewd.
If she got no applause
She would shout 'Up Yours!'
To the audience. Dreadfully Rude!
From the first act right through to the last
She'd insult the rest of the cast.
She would sometimes yell 'Balls!'

To the orchestra stalls
And leave *ev'ryone* simply aghast.
The director said sadly 'Oh, dear,
Dame Judi's too vulgar I fear.
For the lead in *The Seagull*
I'd have liked Anna Neagle,
What a pity she's no longer here.'

SOURCE
Judi Dench, as told to John Miller, *And Furthermore* (2010)

MAGGIE SMITH
(1934–)

356

Dame Maggie Smith CH is a multi-award-winning British actress who began her career on stage at the Oxford Playhouse in 1952 and made her Broadway debut in the revue New Faces of '56. *Celebrated for her caustic wit, when she was playing Desdemona to Laurence Olivier's* Othello *for the National Theatre in 1964, she responded to his criticism of her diction by putting her head around his dressing room door while he was blacking up for his part, intoning: 'How now, brown cow?' During the run of* Othello, *at one performance Olivier, frustrated with her because she couldn't be persuaded to appear in a revival of* The Skin of Our Teeth, *slapped her as rehearsed but with unexpected force. She was knocked out and had to be carried off the stage by Iago and Lodovico. As she came to in the wings, she murmured: 'First time I've seen stars at the National.' A few years later, when she appeared in Ronald Harwood's* The Interpreters *the play was not an out-and-out success. After it had been running for a few weeks, the playwright called on her in her dressing room. To make conversation, Maggie Smith asked him what he was doing now. 'Struggling with a new play,' said Harwood. 'Aren't we all?' she replied.*

Back in 1957 she was in a revue called Share My Lettuce *with Kenneth Williams. In his autobiography, he recalled the adroitness of her off-stage asides.*

Share My Lettuce became very fashionable. On the night of the 7th of September Terence Rattigan came backstage and was very complimentary. That seemed to set the seal of approval on us as firmly as the Royal Warrant and two weeks later we transferred to the Comedy Theatre in the West End.

The dressing-room windows overlooked an open space across which I could talk to Maggie, and I remember one night she called out, 'What's in this bottle of stuff you've given me for my eyes?'

'It's a balm to soothe the pupils,' I told her. 'Some sort of alkaline solution. Why?'

'W-e-ll,' she called back, elongating the vowel disapprovingly, 'I just spilled a drop of it on the window sill and it's gone clean through the paint.' I can recall my involuntary alarm and the subsequent laughter as if it were yesterday.

Share My Lettuce flourished through the rest of the year, at Christmas there was talk of yet another transfer, and on the 29th of January 1958, with Maggie remarking 'This must be the longest tour in town', we had our third London opening at the Garrick Theatre.

It was here that I misbehaved in more ways than one and incurred Maggie's wrath. There was a sketch in the show where four men stood selling newspapers; one, two and three cried, 'Star,' 'News,' and 'Standard' respectively and I called out 'Figaro'; then we shouted the virtues of our papers, each of us attempting to drown the others till Maggie appeared. Dressed in a slinky black mackintosh, she walked sexily across the stage and as she passed the vendors one by one, they fell silent. When she was almost at the proscenium arch, the first man asked, 'Paper, lady?' and she exited saying, 'No thank you, dearie, I won't be needing any paper.' It always got a big laugh and there was an immediate stage black-out.

One night I didn't stay mute when she passed me, I sang 'Figaro' basso profundo and then continued with 'When you're a barber… Figaro, Figaro,' etc. Of course, Maggie couldn't say her line and after a momentary hesitation, she simply walked off stage, the electrics didn't get their cue, the blackout was late, and my choral efforts, while raising an initial titter, ruined the end of the scene.

During the interval, an irate Maggie came into my dressing room demanding an explanation. I was sitting at the make-up bench doing my face and she perched herself on it between me and the wash basin, flicking cigarette ash into the bowl while she talked.

'Why did you put in all that operatic stuff?'

'I thought it was a funny idea.'

'It ruined my tag line.'

'I had this urge to do something new.'

'You need to rehearse something new.'

'I know, but I just couldn't wait.'

Maggie suddenly leant over the sink and asked, 'Have you been peeing in here?'

I started a stammering denial, reddened and faltered.

'Hmm,' she said. 'I suppose you couldn't wait for that either?' Then we both started laughing, and a potential row over a foolish ad lib had an entirely happy ending.

SOURCE
Kenneth Williams, *Just Williams* (1985)

ALBERT FINNEY
(1936–2019)

357

Albert Finney was a British stage and film star, whose distinguished career began auspiciously when, in 1959, he was at Stratford-upon-Avon understudying the great Sir Laurence Olivier in Coriolanus. *This recollection comes from an interview with Clive Goodwin.*

Q. At Stratford you had the dream of every understudy come true. Laurence Olivier injured his leg and you took over the part of Coriolanus.

A. Yes, that was smashing. I don't know what was wrong with my work at Stratford. I mean it was more wrong then than it's ever been before or since, and I was aware of it being wrong. It was one of those times when you feel that everything you do—you know that kind of tunnel—and there's nothing you can do to get out of it. The more you try to get out of it, the more you're in it. My work was awful, just vile. Every time I went on the stage I felt, get off, get off, what are you doing? But when I went on for Sir Laurence in *Coriolanus,* all the difficulties I seemed to be going through left me. Because, first of all, the audience kind of expect you to come on in flannels with a book. Sir Laurence isn't playing—big groan. His part will be played by Al—Albert Finney. And then I came on, and I had the costume on, and so they immediately think I'm talented because I've actually got into the clothes. I've put the body make-up on and then I start and they can't see the book. And I actually got through it without drying, so they think I'm very good. If you're an understudy and you go on, the card you've actually got in your hand is that they think you might not be able to get through at all, and if you can get through with any degree of professionalism, they think you're very good. And I kind of felt, get in there. But it's terrible to hear that announcement—you know, you're in your dressing-room putting on the make-up—Sir Laurence won't be playing tonight; terrible groan through the auditorium. That's nice.

But I felt a kind of freedom doing *Coriolanus* because I had no responsibility; I was his understudy, it didn't matter what happened. It didn't matter if I dried; they'd expect it. If I fainted, well it's a lot of pressure on the lad, you know. So I didn't worry. All the clouds which were around the rest of my performances, all the rubbish, the tunnel I felt in with my work, all the difficulties blew out of the window. I just went on and did it. I felt very free. I don't think it was a good Coriolanus. When you hear Sir Laurence's tones ringing in your ears for the number of times he'd done the performances, it's very difficult for you not to be similar, because you're working on his blueprint. I learnt from that how a great actor can take the peaks and the valleys of a performance, the ups and downs of a character as written, and push them even further apart. He makes the climaxes higher and the depths of it lower than you feel is possible in the text. It was marvellous to go through it during a performance, kind of putting on his clothes and feeling well they don't touch me here at all, you know. Just feel your own way—how big you are on the graph, as it were. They you see he went right up there. I don't just mean vocally but emotionally and everything, and he went right down there. That was a very interesting realization. But I was glad when he was back actually. The theatre management gave me a steak between the matinée and evening show; I did it six times and it was always with a matinée and an evening show. So I quite enjoyed it.

SOURCE

From *Acting in the Sixties*, ed. Hal Burton (1970)

358

Eighteen-year-olds Peter Bowles and Albert Finney were flat-mates while studying at RADA.

Confidence is almost 80 per cent of what is needed for 'star quality', plus a bit of talent of course. My teacher was Albert Finney.

One night in our room we were discussing what part we would most like to play. We both had the same ambition, that when we left RADA and became professional actors we would play Macbeth. Albert asked me how I would approach the part. I went on about Scottish history, the possibility of playing it with a Scottish accent, probably in a kilt, and of course I would study all the great scholars, including Granville Barker.

'How would you approach it, Albert?' I asked.

'I'd learn the fucking lines and walk on,' said Albert.

SOURCE
Peter Bowles, *Ask Me If I'm Happy* (2010)

PETER BOWLES

(1936–)

359

Peter Bowles became a household name in Britain appearing with Penelope Keith in To the Manor Born *on television in the early 1980s. His long stage career has ranged from playing in Shakespeare at the Old Vic in the 1950s to playing the title role in* The Exorcist *in London in 2017.*

I'm reminded of the very first comedy role I played professionally. It was Algernon in *The Importance of Being Earnest*. It was part of a season of plays that included *The Diary of Anne Frank*—so not all comedy—and

room, then a stretcher. Michael is wheeled out, the oxygen mask over his face. One of the stage managers goes with him in the ambulance to St Thomas' Hospital. As he's carried into A&E she asks him if there is any message he'd like her to take back to the rehearsal room.

'Don't worry about those bastards,' he says. 'They're already on the phone to Simon Russell Beale.'

SOURCE
Nicholas Hytner, *Balancing Acts* (2017)

370

Peter Bowles was in the 1959–60 season at the Old Vic and his second part was in The Long and the Short and the Tall *by Willis Hall and Keith Waterhouse. The play had originally been a success in London, directed by Lindsay Anderson.*

Bryan Pringle, who was really my closest friend, was coming down to see the production to see me playing his part of Smudger. On St Pancras Station he bumped into Lindsay Anderson. After telling him where he was going and who he was going to see, Lindsay Anderson said, so Bryan told me, 'Peter Bowles in *The Long and the Short and the Tall?* There isn't a single part he could play.'

'Oh,' said Bryan. 'Why do you say that, Lindsay? Actually, he's playing Smudger.' 'That's even more ridiculous,' said Lindsay. 'Peter Bowles, in my opinion, can't act. I know because I've seen him wearing a suit.'

Now this left-wing snobbery has haunted me all my life, although I felt much better when years later Michael Gambon, who was playing Lear at Stratford, and is, in my and many other people's opinion, probably England's finest actor, apologized to me at a party. Michael, who is a bit of a 'dresser', had arrived in denims and was embarrassed.

'Don't be silly Michael,' I said. 'It doesn't matter what you wear.'

'Well, I'd have liked to have worn a suit but I've just driven up from Stratford and I've got no decent clothes down there because if you don't dress like a fucking petrol pump attendant they don't think you can act,' replied Michael.

SOURCE
Peter Bowles, *Ask Me If I'm Happy* (2010)

371

In 2000, I went to interview Sir Michael Gambon.

I tell Sir Michael I have done a ring-round to discover his faults and flaws. He starts giggling and pulling silly faces. 'Tee hee. What have they said?'

'Not much to worry you. They say that when you've been in a run for a while your interest goes, your concentration slips.'

'Oh God.' He pleads guilty. 'I get bored and then I muck about. Olivier would muck about too, you know. As Othello he'd walk on in the Senate scene and, under his breath, assume the voice of a West Indian bus conductor and hiss at us, 'Any more fares, please. No standing on the top deck.'

Why is he so cagey about his private life?

'The less people know about you the better. Ideally an actor should be a blank canvas. Otherwise you walk on as King Lear and the fellow in the front row whispers to his missus, "You know he collects antique guns, he's got hundreds of them." What does it matter what we get up to off stage, off screen?'

'I shouldn't do interviews because I don't believe in them and I can't be trusted. Years ago, when I did Oscar Wilde on the telly, a lad from the Birmingham Post asked me if I found it difficult playing the part of a homosexual. "No" I said, "it comes to me quite easily. I used to be one." The boy said, "Oh, really?" And I said, "Yes, but

I was forced to give it up." He didn't look at me. He just scribbled away. Eventually, he said, "May I ask why?" And I said, "Well, it made my eyes water." He didn't get the joke. He didn't know it was a joke.'

SOURCE
Gyles Brandreth, *Brief Encounters* (2001)

MARTIN JARVIS
(1941–)

372

Martin Jarvis had been cast as Lady Capulet in the (all boys) Whitgift School production of Romeo and Juliet.

A few days before the dress rehearsal, Mr Etherington beckoned me with his pipe to join him for a chat. 'Look,' he said, 'you're playing a woman and you're doing it jolly well too, but—' My heart galloped apace—oh lord, is he going to fire me? Is it the Forest Woodman scenario all over again? But, there's been no tap-tap-tap problems, and surely I've taken direction well? 'But,' he went on, 'we've got to make you *look* like a lady too.' He then told me the costumes had arrived from Nathan's, that they had been specially made for Stratford's last production of *Romeo* and that mine was a magnificent blue and pink number adorned with a hundred sparkling jewels. Apparently Lady Redgrave (Rachel Kempson) had looked magnificent in it. 'Now,' said Mr Etherington, 'contours. Got to give you a bit of a body-line. Thing to do,' he took his pipe from his mouth and cleared his throat, 'thing to do is borrow a bra from your mother or your girlfriend, stuff it with your rugby socks and er—Bob's your auntie. All right, Jarvis, run along.'

'Thank you, sir.'

The part was still mine but this was a problem I hadn't foreseen. Borrow a bra from my mother? I knew I would never be able to raise such a topic. Or my girlfriend? What? Except for vague yearnings after Beryl Ballard, whom I used to see on the 68 bus, school beret pinned precariously to the back of her Marilyn Monroe locks, I never went near girls. And certainly it would be impossible to obtain a girlfriend in time for the dress-rehearsal. Imagine sloping up to Beryl on the top-deck: 'Excuse me, Beryl, would you like to see *Kiss Me Kate* at the Essoldo on Saturday? Oh, and by the way, can I borrow your bra?' Imagine the cackling laughter of Beryl and her cronies, Barbara, Janet and Maureen. To say nothing of the conductor: ''Ere, I 'eard that—get back downstairs or I'll turn you off the bus.'

In the end I concocted something from my gym-shoe bag. Stuffing it with rugby socks, shorts and shirt to fill it out, I put my arms through the two looped drawstrings and, if I didn't bend too far forward, it worked pretty well. I had considered leaving the gym shoes in there too, but Lady Redgrave's stylish slip-ons didn't fit me, so I wore my own instead. They were black, and not dissimilar to the neat little boots that had peeped from beneath Tommy Trinder's skirts.

I had a modest success as Lady Capulet. My best moment was when, sweeping off-stage with a Twankeyish toss of head and swoop of voice, clasped hands resting on my bosom, I spoke the lines, 'Talk not to me, for I'll not speak a word. / Do as thou wilt, for I have done with thee.'

At the final performance I heard a peculiar and, for a moment, unidentifiable sound exploding behind me. It took me a moment to realise, as I skidded to a halt in the wings, that it was not a fart, but the sharp cupping sound of people putting their hands together in approval. An exit round.

SOURCE

Martin Jarvis, *Acting Strangely* (1999)

373

In 1982 Judi Dench went to the National Theatre to appear in The Importance of Being Earnest *as Lady Bracknell alongside Martin Jarvis as Jack Worthing and Nigel Havers as Algernon Moncrieff.*

When we went on tour with *The Importance,* Martin played a dreadful trick on Nigel in Glasgow. Between the matinée and the evening performance Martin changed all the clocks, and he had taped the sound of the audience arriving at the beginning of the show. Nigel was sitting in his dressing room with curlers in his hair, thinking he had got plenty of time to get ready, and Martin played the tape of the curtain going up. Nigel knew he had to get down the stairs, under the stage and up the other side, and he was screaming and throwing the curlers off. Any other man would have had a heart attack. He ran on the stage, and we were all standing there waiting for him, with the safety curtain down. He was completely shattered. Nigel told me later that it was because he used to pull a trick on Martin, who had said, 'I'll get back at you for this.'

SOURCE
Judi Dench, as told to John Miller, *And Furthermore* (2010)

MICHAEL CRAWFORD
(1942–)

374

Ian Ogilvy was cast in the film version of the stage hit No Sex Please: We're British.

No Sex Please: We're British had been a successful stage play in London starring, in the early part of its long run, Michael Crawford and my friend Simon Williams. Crawford was exceptionally funny as the bank clerk Brian Runnicles but he must have been a nightmare to work with because he would reduce the audience to hysterics with a piece of funny business, and would then prolong the business—and the laughter—well beyond the point when the plot stopped being the plot and became a personal playground for Crawford's flights of fancy. Meanwhile his fellow actors—professional to their fingertips—remained mired in the long-lost storyline. Their honest stage reactions to Runnicles' behaviour were soon exhausted by the sheer length of time Crawford took in his quest for laughter, so eventually they were reduced to simply standing mute and expressionless for as long as Crawford wanted the laughter prolonged, which on occasions went on for minutes at a time. I was told he didn't much like his fellow cast members getting any laughs at all and would do everything in his power to stop it happening. When the film of the play was first mooted, the role of Runnicles was naturally offered to Crawford; rumour had it that the offer was withdrawn by the producers because of Crawford's impossible and oddly insecure demands, which apparently included the instruction that all comedy moments not related directly to what Runnicles was either saying or doing were to be removed from the screenplay. This would have been both ridiculous and impossible, so the part was offered to, and accepted by, the ineffable and generous Ronnie Corbett who had spent a life-time in comedy, knew exactly how it was done and—unlike Michael Crawford—knew precisely when to stop doing it.

SOURCE
Ian Ogilvy, *Once a Saint* (2016)

VICTOR HENRY
(1943–1985)

375

Victor Henry was a fine actor who, following an accident, died tragically young. The narrator is Jack Shepherd.

The Royal Court Actors' Studio was still operating at this time. Junior members of the company, such as myself, were encouraged to attend. There were classes in basic skills, movement, method acting, clowning, comic masks, full masks, and so on. Bill Gaskill used to take improvisation classes in which he would set out to explore the world of the epic narrative. These sessions were often very baffling…'An old woman comes down to the river,' he said once. 'I want someone to act the narrative contained in that sentence.'

Everyone cringed. After a long silence an actor was picked out. A man.

'You want me to act out the sentence, "An old woman comes down to the river",' the actor repeated.

'Yes,' said Bill after another long silence.

The actor then tied a pullover round his head, hunched his shoulders, and started walking, as he hoped, towards the river.

'Start again,' said Bill, almost immediately. 'What you are showing me is…"The old woman comes down to the river." I want an old woman. Can you show me an old woman? Without using a headscarf, and without hunching your shoulders?'

The actor looked scared. 'I don't know,' he said.

'Try it again,' said Bill.

And so it went on.

I don't remember Victor Henry attending any of Bill's classes. He had theories of his own at this time. I remember him telling me that if you played a scene with your head on one side you could make middle-aged women cry. It had never occurred to me to want to do that but I showed interest, arguing that it seemed unlikely.

'Just watch me,' he replied. So I watched him one night, as Sparky in *Serjeant Musgrave's Dance,* playing a love scene with his right ear resting absurdly on his shoulder. I looked around the auditorium and, sure enough, middle-aged women were crying all over the place.

SOURCE
At the Royal Court, ed. Richard Findlater (1981)

376

Victor Henry played Rimbaud in Christopher Hampton's play Total Eclipse, *directed by Bill Gaskill at the Royal Court.*

One evening Bill Gaskill, on his routine tour of the dressing rooms, put his head round the door to say, 'Oh by the way, Victor's drunk.' It was thrown in so causally we asked if he was joking. 'Wait till you see him!' came the reply.

The curtain had risen only seconds before, and Kathleen Byron, who was playing my wife, nodded expectantly in my direction as the maid announced the arrival of M. Rimbaud. There was a very sticky pause and no sign whatever of Victor Henry. Finally, in desperation, we began to ad-lib—seldom a comfortable substitute for the real thing. Just as the audience were getting a bit fidgety, we were startled to hear a wail like a wild animal in distress coming from behind the couch on which we were sitting. Victor, puce of face and clearly not just drunk but legless, using all the strength he could muster, hauled himself to his feet and, clinging to the furniture for support, began to intone the dialogue, slurring it so badly it was impossible to understand. It is probably fair to say that, as the evening dragged by, clarity improved—though not by a great deal. That performance we managed to add an extra forty minutes to the running time, and customers missed their trains home. I was embarrassed, and indeed furious, particularly as I had friends watching the show. When they presented themselves backstage, I hardly knew where to begin, how to apologies, how to control my rage. Finally, in the most nonchalant voice I could muster, I managed to ask, 'What did you think of Victor Henry as Rimbaud?' There was no hesitation. 'Brilliant!' they enthused. 'Best thing in it!' There's no justice.

SOURCE
Nigel Hawthorne, *Straight Face* (2002)

377

The only other actor I knew at all was Victor Henry. Between them, they covered a lot of ground. Victor was the caricature of the self-destructive, demon-driven artist. He chewed whisky glasses till the blood ran down his cheeks. He picked fights, five foot four and weedy, as he was, with truck drivers. ('D'yer want me to take me glasses off? Is that what's holding yer back? OK, they're off. Now whatcha gonna do?') He thrust his hand up waitresses' skirts. Filth poured in torrents from his mouth. He destroyed other actors' performances if he didn't think they were good enough. He himself would appear on stage smashed out of his skull, giggling and making other actors laugh—and then suddenly he'd do something so extraordinarily pure and intense that your heart would stop beating. He was the most absolute actor I've ever seen. He alarmed me to the point of terror, but when he spoke about acting and the theatre, raging against the pusillanimity (he was playing Jimmy Porter at the time) of the entire theatre, except for himself and some—some—people at the Royal Court, insisting that the theatre's only job was to wage war on bourgeois mediocrity, I agreed with him, and wanted to be up there with him: me, as I felt, the embodiment of bourgeois mediocrity.

SOURCE
Simon Callow, *Being an Actor* (1984)

IAN OGILVY
(1943–)

378

Ian Ogilvy was on a UK tour of Dangerous Obsession *by N. J. Crisp and, during the Brighton week, the stage fright which had started to creep up on him for a couple of years finally overwhelmed him. Unable to remember his first line he recalls, 'I stumbled away out of sight of the audience sat down in the wings and started to sob in earnest.'*

The kind company manager found a kind Brighton doctor who was prepared to see me and the kind young paramedics put me in their ambulance and took me to him. By the time we arrived at his consulting rooms I was feeling a little better, because on this particular night the one thing I'd been dreading doing, I didn't have to do. I didn't have to do *Dangerous Obsession*. Somebody else—my unfortunate understudy—was at this very moment doing the play for me. The relief was enormous. It was as though a skilled surgeon had removed, painlessly, a ten-pound weight that had, for the last seven weeks, been lodged in my head. He'd also taken away another heavy lump of something or other that had been sitting in my chest cavity.

Everybody in Brighton that night seemed impossibly young. The doctor was a mere child, but a wise one all the same. After questioning me closely about what had been going on in my recent life, he said, 'Well, it's nothing terribly serious. You've been under a lot of strain and you've had a small nervous breakdown.'

I said was he sure it was a small one? Because it felt like quite a big one, actually.

'No, no. A bad one and you'd be baying at the moon. But you might like to give the stage-acting a bit of a rest for a while.'

'A rest? For how long?'

'Until you feel like doing it again. You'll know when. Or maybe you won't.'

'Won't what?'

'Maybe you'll never feel like you want to go back. And that's all right too.'

Oddly, it was the young doctor's *permission* that clinched it for me. Not *having* to go back. That was exactly how I felt—and how I've continued to feel ever since.

SOURCE
Ian Ogilvy, *Once a Saint* (2016)

ISLA BLAIR

(1944–)

379

Ian Ogilvy was acting opposite Isla Blair in Noël Coward's Hay Fever *in Hull.*

For some reason our director had thought it might be rather amusing to insert a funny, period car horn klaxon sound into the offstage effects—and not warn the cast that he'd done so.

When the unexpected BAAAARP! sound came, we actors suppressed our hysteria and forged on to the end of the play—all except Isla who, for some unaccountable reason, stopped talking entirely and stopped moving too, apart from a noticeable tremor in the area of her knees. She stood there, mute and immobile, in the middle of the stage and the rest of us had to improvise our way around her until the end. Once the curtain was down, we all clustered round Isla, demanding to know what had happened to her. Isla—with tears of either shame or laughter (or perhaps both) streaming down her face—stepped to one side and pointed at the floor. There was a large puddle on the spot where she'd been standing. So be warned—excessive laughter, if sufficiently stifled, can cause Isla Blair's bladder to throw in the towel.

SOURCE
Ian Ogilvy, *Once a Saint* (2016)

MARIA AITKEN
(1945–)

380

Maria Aitken's first speaking part in the theatre was in a provincial production of Tom Jones, *starring a television personality who remains nameless.*

I also took my assistant stage-management duties extremely seriously, and in those few minutes before curtain up, although my heart was full of my village wench role, my head was methodically checking the prop table. Six drinking-cups, wooden platters, shotgun, stuffed partridge... It was a litany I knew by heart; nevertheless I went through the motions of checking each object off on a list. The partridge was my particular concern, because it was the hub of the director's favourite joke. Tom Jones fired his twelve-bore stage right, and the partridge plopped out of the wings stage left. 'Don't argue, boyo—it's a classic,' said the director, and I was so bewildered by his sense of humour that I failed to get neurotic about his apparent sexual confusion.

My cue came, and I fled the sanctuary of the prop table for the wide unknown of the stage. I had evolved a sort of Loamshire sound for my comic village maiden, uneasily aware that regional accents were not my forte. My false hairpiece tumbled over my shoulders; my eyelashes were still tangentially attached; I had heaved and padded my unabundant bosom into a respectable cleavage, and every visible extremity was painted rustic nut-brown. They laughed. I only had eight lines and they laughed at five of them. I had the incredible disadvantages of an Oxford degree, a posh voice and the physique of an overbred setter, but the audience had believed in my common sexy wench enough to laugh at her.

'Quite the comedienne, boyo,' said the director in the interval. Rashly confident, I essayed some crack about his gender mix-ups, and was rewarded with the laugh accorded to my status as comic.

Act Two began, and I cavorted at the back of the stage with two other ASMs, busily representing a mob of three thousand. Tom Jones raised his gun. He fired. Nothing happened. Where was the partridge? Being a resourceful chap, the Star raised his gun again. 'Bang,' he said loudly. Suddenly I realized that I had hallucinated that bird on the prop table, that I had never set it there in the first place, absorbed in my own petty role, and that it was now up to me to Save the Play. Quick as a flash, I fell writhing to the ground, reasoning that as long as *something* died that Tom Jones wasn't aiming at, the director's favourite joke would remain intact. Unfortunately, a more practically minded member of our cavorting mob had simultaneously nipped off stage and thrown the partridge on. I never thought much of the original joke, but I can tell you with authority that when *two* things die that Tom Jones isn't aiming at, there is no joke at all. The entire episode was greeted with a bewildered silence.

I wept off my eyelashes as I swept the stage after curtain down, waiting for retribution. It arrived. 'Theatre is discipline, boyo. You can act your socks off, but it's no good if you're not reliable. Go back to your undergraduate amateurs where you can't spoil any more of my gags. You're fired.'

'But I bought three pairs of eyelashes for the run,' I sobbed, unable to believe that my career had ended the night it began. I trailed upstairs to pack up the barely used sticks of greasepaint, and wandered snuffling out of the stage-door. The Star was outside, engulfed in provincial pubescents waving autograph books. He took one look at my swollen face and led me to the nearest pub, heedless of the weeny-boppers' protestations. He extracted the story through my hiccups and gasps and towed me through a maze of carparks and alleys to another pub. I shied like a nervous horse when I saw the director propping up the bar, but the Star propelled me inexorably forward.

'Hallo,' he said pleasantly. 'I thought we'd find you here. I've brought Miss Initiative along for a drink.'

'She's fired,' said the director.

'No, I don't think so,' said the Star politely. 'I wouldn't feel the same about appearing here without her.'

I was dumbstruck. I'd never even spoken to him until that evening. By the time I re-focussed on what was happening, the Star and the director had their arms round each other's necks.

Later, much later, as they say in the women's magazines, I attempted to thank the Star.

'You've said thank you in the nicest possible way,' he said putting on his clothes. 'Now I have to go home to my wife.'

My heart was broken, but I got my job back. I've never been able to look at a partridge since.

SOURCE
Ronald Harwood, *A Night at the Theatre* (1984)

FRANCESCA ANNIS
(1945–)

381

In 1987, Ian Ogilvy was playing Vershinin in Three Sisters *directed by Elijah Moshinsky*

I played Vershinin, opposite the Masha of the exciting Joanne Whalley at Greenwich and then, in the West End, opposite the Masha of the equally exciting Francesca Annis.

In Greenwich, Joanne Whalley electrified the critics by creating a wonderful moment for herself and playing it to perfection. During the emotional parting from Vershinin, when he tries to push her way from him, Joanne made the rejection look violent by falling—and then somehow sliding—halfway across the stage. When Francesca took over, she decided to create her own moment of supreme drama—but not by any falling and sliding business; that belonged to another actress. Instead, she would scream—a dreadful, primal shriek that went on and on and was as theatrically effective in its way as Joanne's slide had been. What Francesca didn't know was the fun the rest of the cast, lurking close to the Tannoy speaker in the Green Room, had with her scream. The moment I left the stage I would run to the Green Room to hear the latest reason for Francesca's distress.

'Francesca Annis has just discovered that she hasn't got top billing.'

'Francesca Annis fails spectacularly during her audition for the role of Tosca.'

'Francesca Annis finds out that she's being paid ten quid a week less than anybody else.'

In fact she was being paid rather more, I later discovered. I didn't mind. Like so many of Francesca Annis's leading men, I was besotted with her.

SOURCE
Ian Ogilvy, *Once a Saint* (2016)

ANTONY SHER
(1949–)

382

The South African-born actor Antony Sher was appearing at the National Theatre in the 1992 production of Uncle Vanya, *directed by Sean Matts, at the same time as Ian McKellen was playing Richard III.*

Vanya was a success, a big success—you couldn't get a ticket—and all the acting was much praised, with special enthusiasm for the central quartet. My year at the National finally ended well. Yet with a little sting in its tail. Upsetting at the time, but comic too. Suitably Chekhovian.

The sequence of events began during a Vanya performance, just after Astrov's Act Two drunk scene. In the scene dock, I bumped into Karl Johnson (playing Waffles), who said, 'Have you heard?' Sean's been nominated for an Olivier for this.'

'No, I hadn't,' I said. 'How splendid.'

A little later, bumping into McKellen, I said excitedly, 'Did you know Sean's been nominated for an Olivier?'

'Yes,' he replied, looking uneasy, then quickly confessed, 'so have I.'

'Oh, that's terrific. Congratulations.'

Later still I bumped into Janet McTeer (Yelena) waiting for an entrance backstage and whispered, 'Sean and Ian have both been nominated for Oliviers,'

'I know,' she whispered back. 'I have too.'

'Wow, that's... that's wonderful. Great stuff.'

Now nearing the end of the performance, I bumped into Lesley Sharp (Sonya) on the stairs: 'Sean, Ian and Janet have all been nominated for Oliviers. Isn't that...?'

'And me,' she said. 'Me as well'.

'Goodness. But that's, I mean, that's...' Aware that my smile might be looking a bit numb, I said 'Well done' and hurried on.

After the show, in the bar, I saw our director. 'Sean!' I cried. 'You, Ian, Janet, Lesley, all nominated. How tremendous. Four nominations, that's really—'

'Five.'

'Five,' I repeated, my eyebrows raised in a last flicker of hope. 'Why, what's the... Uhm... fifth for?'

'Best revival.'

'Best revival, of course—congrats Mazeltov, what can I say?'

Dazed, I wandered over to where my guests for the evening were waiting. The Bermans: Myrtle and her husband, my trusty therapist, Monty.

'That was terrific,' he said. 'That was just the best thing we've seen in ages. I'm so glad you managed to get us in this evening.'

'So am I,' I answered, 'because I've got bad news for you. You're on duty.'

SOURCE
Antony Sher, *Beside Myself* (2001)

SIMON CALLOW

(1949–)

383

In 1967, aged eighteen, Simon Callow applied for work at the Old Vic before going to university. Laurence Olivier, then Director of the National Theatre, replied to Callow, suggesting he come to work in the Old Vic box office. Callow began to have 'mild megalomaniac delusions' of a glorious theatrical career.

The interview with the box office manager quickly knocked such nonsense out of my head. A grim, lizard-like man, Pat Layton, who prided himself on never having seen a single show at the National (he once blushingly admitted he'd seen 'half' of Othello), indicated that my duties would be largely confined to the mailing room. With time, I might eventually be allowed to man 'the window'—the advance window that is: the 'this evening's performance' window was his special preserve, and he used to sit at it like an iguana on a rock, eyes darting to left and right, doing what he liked best: refusing people tickets. He was at that time one of the most courted men in London, and it cannot be said that he wore his power lightly. Occasionally, one of the recipients of his favour would appear at the window, and would receive his smile: a terrifying sight, the glint on the blade of the guillotine.

SOURCE
Simon Callow, *Being an Actor* (1984)

384

I was peripheral to an all-star production of *The Doctor's Dilemma* at the Mermaid...The engagement was chiefly memorable for Bernard Miles thinking I was still in the box office and asking me to take some people round to the restaurant just before the curtain went up. And for my being off; that is, missing an entrance. It was a matinée, my dressing room was full of delightful people talking vivaciously and I didn't hear my cue. Eventually an increasingly insistent voice could be heard over the tannoy: 'Mr Callow, you are *off*!' I suddenly felt very ill indeed, rushed out of the dressing room, to run slap into Frank Thornton: 'Too late, old boy, too late.' And then James Villiers: 'Haha, haha, haha.' I foolishly stood in the wings, willing the play ten minutes back in time, then crawled away, a hollow feeling in my stomach, shame burning bright red on my brow. At the interval, I went to every member of the cast in turn. They were all very decent. 'Never mind, could happen to anyone, done it myself,' etcetera. Derek Godfrey was particularly magnanimous in view of the fact that Redpenny's non-appearance at a crucial moment had transformed him into the most heartless character on the English stage. Finally, I came to an actress of a certain age who had not, in fact, been on stage at the time, and was not personally affected by my absence. She received my apologies generously. 'Not at all, darling,' she said, in the cut-glass accent that was always a surprise after the charladies she was usually called upon to play, 'It must be so much worse for you than it is for us. Because, after all'—a pitying little smile—'when you come down to it, there can't be *any* excuse, *ever*, can there?'

SOURCE
Simon Callow, *Being an Actor* (1984)

385

In 1979, at the National Theatre, Simon Callow played Mozart to Paul Scofield's Salieri in the original production of Peter Shaffer's Amadeus.

Paul and I, very different acting animals, had found each other's wavelengths. I'd overcome my awe and was feasting hungrily off the extraordinary riches he was sending my way. One day, we were rehearsing the scene round the piano. Over our heads, there was a tiny flicker from a lighting fitting. We carried on acting. The flicker persisted, and so did we. A flame leapt out, and shot along the cable above us. We continued with the scene. By now the whole ceiling was ablaze. The stage management were dragging tables and sound equipment to the other side of the room. We kept on acting. Finally, the scene came to an end. Without moving, as bits of the ceiling fell about our ears, Paul turned to me and said: 'Are you really going to do it like that?' We bolted for the door. Somehow then I realized that we were a team. (As we got into the corridor and firemen rushed into the room from which smoke was now billowing, Michael Rudman sauntered past. 'Simon Callow overacting again, I suppose,' he said.)

SOURCE
Simon Callow, *Being an Actor* (1984)

DANIEL DAY-LEWIS
(1957–)

386

The Oscar-winning actor's early stage career included Romeo for the Royal Shakespeare Company and, in 1989, Hamlet at the National Theatre in London. Before starting rehearsals for the production, Day-Lewis sent the director, Richard Eyre, a postcard.

8th January. Card from Dan [Day-Lewis]: 'Each time it's an adventure working with you; each time the gradients gain severity. Each time we've worked with new plays and this seems like the newest, richest, most wonderful, most intriguing, most irresistible of them all. I wouldn't ever have considered doing this, had you not suggested it. It goes beyond thanks.' And on the other side: 'three o'clock Father's Funeral / five o'clock Mother's Wedding.'

SOURCE
Richard Eyre, *National Service* (2003)

387

Daniel Day-Lewis put paid to one of the most infamous stage anecdotes of all time, revealing that he didn't literally see his late father's ghost when playing Hamlet.

The double Oscar winner played the Dane at the National Theatre in 1989, but quit the production mid-performance and has not returned to the theatre since. He subsequently explained that he had seen his father, the poet Cecil Day-Lewis, who died when his son was 15, standing on the stage staring at him.

However, in an interview published last week, Day-Lewis insisted that he was speaking more metaphorically than literally. 'I may have said a lot of things in the immediate aftermath,' he told *Time Magazine*, 'and to some extent I probably saw my father's ghost every night, because of course if you're working in a play like Hamlet you explore everything through your own experience.'

He continued: 'That correspondence between father and son, or the son and the father who is no longer alive, played a huge part in that experience. So yes, of course, it was communication with my own dead father, but I don't remember seeing any ghosts of my father on that dreadful night!'

After leaving the theatre during Hamlet, Day-Lewis collapsed backstage. His understudy Jeremy Northam completed the run and Day-Lewis didn't act at all for several years afterwards.

The actor has often been asked about his experiences; in 2003, he told the *Guardian* that it was 'a very vivid, almost hallunicatory moment in which I was engaged in a dialogue with my father . . . but that wasn't the reason I had to leave the stage. I had to leave the stage because I was an empty vessel. I had nothing in me, nothing to say, nothing to give.'

SOURCE
The Guardian (29 October 2012)

KEVIN SPACEY
(1959–)

388

Before facing allegations of past sexual harassment in 2017, the American film and stage actor spent much of his life in London, notably as the artistic director at the Old Vic from 2004 to 2014, and in 1999 when he appeared in Eugene O'Neill's The Icecan Cometh *at the Almeida Theatre, alongside British actor Tim Pigott-Smith.*

Theatre came early in Kevin Spacey's life. On a trip to London at aged 10 he saw a production of Sherlock Holmes where the revolving scenery crashed down on Dr Watson's head; the actor extracted himself, strolled up-stage, lit a cigarette and declared, 'I knew I should never have moved to Kensington.' Spacey hoots. 'I thought it was incredible, the funniest thing I'd ever seen. That's what I wanted to do...And—oh, the circles of my life—I told that story in the dressing room at the Almeida, and Tim Pigott-Smith turned round and said, "Yes, Dr Watson was me."'

SOURCE
Marie Claire (UK) (April 2003)

NOMA DUMEZWENI
(1969–)

389

Now a winner of two Olivier Awards and perhaps best known for playing Hermione Granger on stage in the original production of Harry Potter and the Cursed Child, *it was not until Noma Dumezweni was called on to take over a leading part from Kim Cattrall (star of* Sex and the City*) at short notice that she realized the depths her own talents. The play* Linda, *by Penelope Skinner, was in its final days of rehearsal at the Royal Court in London, when Kim Cattrall, playing the huge leading part, was forced to drop out on medical advice.* The Guardian *newspaper took up the story and interviewed the new leading lady.*

When Kim Cattrall withdrew from *Linda* at the Royal Court last month, Noma Dumezweni had a week to prepare to replace her as the lead character. She appeared on stage at press night, script in hand, to audience cheers. 'If there were an Olivier award for courage and chutzpah in the line of duty then it's fair to say that Noma Dumezweni would be a shoo-in for this year's gong,' one critic observed....

Your performance has been called the rescue mission of the year. How did you pull it off?

I met the company on Friday afternoon, read with them and was blocked so I knew where to move. From the Monday it was technical rehearsals. We were on the set 10am–10pm. And then the first preview in front of an audience was on the Thursday. They said: 'Don't worry, just read it.' So I had my script on stage until the beginning of last week. What's been amazing is I haven't had time to think about it. And the company has been extraordinary. I'm from a South African background and there's this phrase—ubuntu—'I am because we are'. And that's what this is about... What I love about it is, Michael [Longhurst, the production's director] didn't go: 'You're a black woman.' He just went: 'I want you to do it because I know you can. I saw what you did at the reading.' These sort of parts don't come to me that often. I'm a great theatre actor and a great supporting actor—this is the year of finally acknowledging that—but here I am playing a role that was originally going to be a white woman, and that's what the set-up around the casting is. I'm very, very proud of it. Kudos everybody.

SOURCE
Interview by Liz Hoggard, 'I'm starting to believe in the universe right now', *The Guardian* (20 December 2015)

AUDRA McDONALD
(1970–)

390

Broadway star Audra McDonald has won six Tony Awards—more than any other actor. Here Nicholas Hytner, Artistic Director of the National Theatre, recalls seeing her auditioning, fresh out of training at Juilliard, when he was casting for the 1994 Broadway production of Rodgers and Hammerstein's Carousel.

[A] Juilliard graduate called Audra McDonald comes in to audition, and I know almost from the first note she sings that I'll never stop boasting about being in on the start of her career. Audra comes back to sing for Mary Rodgers and Jamie Hammerstein, takes a deep breath, and faints dead away. She recovers, and out pours a stream of golden sound, even more golden because she means it. Mary and Jamie are ecstatic.

SOURCE
Nicholas Hytner, *Balancing Acts* (2017)

BENEDICT CUMBERBATCH
(1976–)

391

In 2010, Nicholas Hytner was artistic director at the National Theatre, when it staged a production of Frankenstein, *directed by Danny Boyle with a script by Nick Dean. The twist would be to have the two lead actors alternate the roles of Frankenstein and the Creature he created. Benedict Cumberbatch, then appearing in a Terence Rattigan play at the National, asked to audition. Boyle was unsure if Cumberbatch could play the creature as effectively as he would play the educated Frankenstein.*

I very rarely sat in on other directors' auditions, but Danny wanted me to watch Benedict with him in case he needed a second opinion. I told him I was certain that Benedict could do anything he was asked to do, but I was happy to watch. Danny described the opening sequence to Benedict: the birth of a fully grown adult who learns first to see, then walk, then talk in a fierce fast-forward of infancy.

'So it would be great if you could do that for us now,' he said.

'Absolutely no problem,' said Benedict.

He lay on the floor of the rehearsal studio and shut his eyes. A few seconds later he opened them. They grew large in amazement, as he saw the world for the first time. He started slowly to twitch his limbs. Slowly and painfully, he tried to hoist himself to his feet. His legs buckled from under him: his limbs were like jelly. He collapsed painfully, and grunted in shock. He repeated the noise he'd just made, and realised he had a voice. He tried to stand again, grunting, mewling, bouncing off the walls. Locked in a room with him, it was impossible not to share his birth-pangs. I started to sweat hoping it would end soon, but Benedict had only just started, and out of the corner of my eye I saw Danny beaming with delight.

On and on went Benedict: the Creature's agonies weren't going to stop until somebody pulled the plug. After about twenty-five minutes Danny finally thanked Benedict very much, so Benedict thanked Danny very much, and returned to his dressing room to get ready for Rattigan.

'He'll be great,' said Danny.

SOURCE
Nicholas Hytner, *Balancing Acts* (2017)

BEN WISHAW
(1980–)

392

Ben Wishaw is now perhaps popularly known for parts on film, ranging from Q in the recent James Bond films to voicing Paddington Bear. In 2004, soon after completing his training at RADA, Trevor Nunn cast him as Hamlet for a production at the Old Vic—remarkable at his age: he was just 24 and looked even younger. He was nominated for an Olivier for his performance. Here Nicholas Hytner recalls him making his mark in the National's epic adaptation of Philip Pullman's His Dark Materials.

Meanwhile, everytime there was a break, the young actor playing Brother Jasper came quietly to the front of the stage to run through his long, sinister address to the Magisterium. He was straight out of RADA, and there was nothing I hadn't thrown at him: he was a stolen child, a gyptian, an armoured bear, a deamon goose, a witch in a long black wig and silk skirt. Brother Jasper was his big moment, and I'd hardly had time to notice how good he was. 'This kid is mesmerizing.' I whispered to Aletta [Collins, Associate Director], who

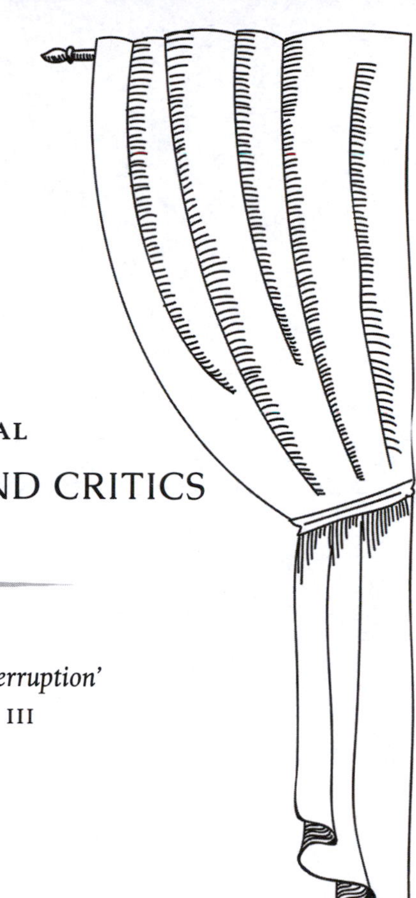

INTERVAL

AUDIENCES AND CRITICS

'Pardon us the interruption'

RICHARD III

AUDIENCES

Long experience has taught me that in England nobody goes to the theatre unless he or she has bronchitis.
JAMES AGATE, *Ego 8* (1947)

The best audience is intelligent, well-educated and a little drunk.
ALBEN W. BARKLEY

Audiences, no the plural is impossible. Whether it is in Butte, Montana or Broadway it's an audience. The same great, hulking monster with four thousand eyes and forty thousand teeth.
JOHN BARRYMORE, quoted in R. May, *The Wit of the Theatre* (1969)

How many idiots go to make up a public?
PIERRE BEAUMARCHAIS, quoted in A. Houssaye, *Behind the Scenes of the Comédie Française* (1889)

In the theatre the audience wants to be surprised—but by things they expect.
TRISTAN BERNARD, *Contes, Repliques et Bon Mots* (1964)

The Marquess and Marchioness of Empty are in front again.
MRS PATRICK CAMPBELL, usual remark when faced with a thin house

Just say the lines as written. There will be some in the audience who won't understand yet will deeply admire them.
CORNEILLE, admitting to an actor that he did not always know the meaning of what he had written; T. Revesz, *Bolcsek Mosolya* (1960), quoted in P. Hay, *Theatrical Anecdotes* (1987)

The audience was tremendously fashionable, and for the first part of the play [*Bitter Sweet*], almost as responsive as so many cornflour blancmanges.
NOËL COWARD

Now the common haunters [of the theatre] are for the most part, the lewdest persons in the land, apt for pilfery, perjury, forgery, or any rogueries; the very scum, rascality, and baggage of the people, thieves, cut-purses, shifters—briefly an unclean generation, and spawn of vipers.... For a play is like a sincke in a Towne, whereunto all the filth doth runne: or a boyle in the body, that draweth all the ill humours to it.
HENRY CROSSE (1603)

By sitting on the stage, if you be a Knight, you may happily get yourself a Mistresse: if a mere Fleet Street Gentleman, a wife.
THOMAS DEKKER, *The Gull's Handbook* (1609)

It is extraordinary how an audience as a whole is sharper than any single member of it.
PETER HALL, *Diaries* (19 October 1977)

The author seeks to keep from me
The murderer's identity
And you are not a friend of his
If you keep shouting who it is...

A. P. HERBERT, from the poem 'At the Theatre: To the Lady behind Me'

I would produce *Noah's Ark* in modern dress. The curtain will not rise until the last straggler is in his seat. Then Noah will appear and announce 'Now it's going to rain for forty days.' At this point the ceiling in the theatre will open and drench the entire audience. If they try to escape, I will be standing by the exit with a hose to catch them.
GEORGE S. KAUFMAN, planning his revenge on habitual latecomers

The critic says: this is an extremely bad play—why is that? The audience says: this is an extremely bad play—why was I born?
JEAN KERR

It is well understood by every dramatist that a late-dining audience needs several minutes of dialogue before it recovers from its bewilderment at finding itself in a theatre.
A. A. MILNE

Besides this perpetual pelting (with rotten oranges) from the gallery, which renders an English playhouse so uncomfortable, there is no end to their calling out and knocking with their sticks 'til the curtain is drawn up.
DR MORITZ, on 18th-century English audiences,
The Era Almanack (1872)

Adulterers, whore-masters, panders, whores and such like effeminate, idle, unchaste, lascivious, graceless persons were the most assiduous play-hunters in their time.
OVID, *Ars Amatoria* (1 BC)

There still remains to mortify a wit,
The many-headed monster of the pit.
ALEXANDER POPE, *Imitations of Horace*, Book II, Epistle I (1737)

I don't think actors really love their audience; they are more in the nature of a lion-tamer.
RALPH RICHARDSON, quoted in *Great Acting*, ed. H. Burton (1967)

Persistent coughers should be removed, placed side by side in the road, and treated by gently passing a warm steam-roller over their chests.
GEORGE BERNARD SHAW

It is extraordinary how the sibilation of a single hiss will win through a tempest of cheers!
BRAM STOKER

Some nights they're porridge; some nights—electricity!
SYBIL THORNDIKE

The audience strummed their catarrhs.
ALEXANDER WOOLLCOTT

AUDIENCE MEMBERS OVERHEARD

Thank goodness I have at last found a place where I can see and hear comfortably.
Anonymous woman who had just fallen from the overcrowded gallery into the pit, *The Era Almanack* (1872); quoted in G. Snell, *The Book of Theatre Quotes* (1982)

How different, how very different, from the home-life of our own dear Queen!
Victorian theatre-goer after watching Sarah Bernhardt's frenzied performance as the Queen of Egypt in Shakespeare's *Antony and Cleopatra*

How different, how very different from the home life of our own dear queens.
Member of the audience at Wyndham's Theatre after a performance of the American homosexual comedy *The Boys in the Band*

Rather an unpleasant family those Lears.
Comment during a performance of *King Lear*; quoted in W. Pett Ridge, *A Story Teller: Forty Years in London* (1924)

And the funny thing is (*pause*)—exactly the same thing happened to Dorothy.
Comment after a performance of *Vivat Vivat Regina* (1970), in which Mary Queen of Scots is beheaded; recalled by the leading lady in the play, Eileen Atkins

Well Mildred, that was the worst play I've seen since *King Lear*.
Overheard by director John Fernald after a Saturday matinée of his production of *The Cherry Orchard*, Liverpool Playhouse (1948); recalled by Noel Davis

Look, here comes old Ginger again!
Reaction to the carrot-red wig sported by Olivier for Hotspur in *Henry IV, Part I* (1945); overheard by John Mills and quoted in Anthony Holden, *Olivier* (1988)

One friend still recalls playing King Lear, the pinnacle of any actor's dramatic ambitions, and the reaction that followed one of his most harrowing speeches—a rustling of sweet wrappers from the stalls, followed by: 'Who's pinched the Raspberry Ripple?'
MICHAEL SIMKINS, actor and author

But perhaps my favourite story is when a mobile phone rang during a performance of Anton Chekhov's *Uncle Vanya*. Eventually, it was answered by the miscreant in the audience, who announced in a loud stage whisper: 'I can't talk now, I'm watching a play.' After a pause, clearly being asked about the performance, she replied: 'No, not very . . .'
MICHAEL SIMKINS

CRITICS

When a play is crashingly dull the critic has only two resources. One is sleep, in justification whereof I shall quote William Archer's dictum that the first qualification for a dramatic critic is the capacity to sleep while sitting bolt upright.
JAMES AGATE (1932)

If Attila the Hun were alive today, he'd be a dramatic critic.
EDWARD ALBEE (1983)

The dramatic critic is like the clergyman—he stands in a favoured position, and however hard he may hit, the recipient of his blows is, for the most part, unable to strike back.
JOHN AYE, *Humour in the Theatre* (1932)

Critics are like eunuchs in a harem. They're there every night, they see it done every night, they see how it should be done every night, but they can't do it themselves.
BRENDAN BEHAN

Critics should be searched for certain adjectives at the door of the theatre. Irreverent, probing and, (above all) satirical. I would have all such adjectives left with their coats in the foyer, only to be redeemed when their notices are written.
ALAN BENNETT

The critic cannot do his work without hurting; he resembles the dentist.
ERIC BENTLEY, *What is Theatre?* (1956)

When *The Rink* opened, *The New York Times* critic Frank Rich was not kind. Liza Minnelli was distraught. "He dismissed me in two sentences," she cried. Librettist Terrence McNally replied, "You're lucky. He dismissed me in two very long paragraphs."
KEN BLOOM, *Show and Tell* (2016)

At any London first night you'll see the critics creeping off to the pub halfway through Act III. Of course they pretend they have to catch the early editions.
BASIL BOOTHROYD

There are nowadays a sort of persons they call critics that, egad, have no more wit in them than so many hobby horses.
GEORGE VILLIERS, 2nd Duke of Buckingham, *The Rehearsal* (1671)

Critics never worry me unless they are right—but that does not often occur.
NOËL COWARD

There are very few critics who when given an egg of talent in their hands can resist crushing it.
PETER HALL, *Diaries* (14 July 1974)

My performance in *The Sport of Kings* continued to improve, though the local critic wrote that I was too inexperienced for the role. I found out later that *she* was still at school.
NIGEL HAWTHORNE, while at the Royal Theatre, Northampton (1954)

The critic is often an unsuccessful author, almost always an inferior one.
LEIGH HUNT

The dramatic critic who is without prejudice is on the same plane with the General who does not believe in taking life.
GEORGE JEAN NATHAN, *Comedians All* (1919)

The better and more honest a critic you are, the fewer friends will eventually send flowers up to the funeral parlour.
GEORGE JEAN NATHAN

Critics: those who would send Hedda Gabler to the Marriage Guidance Council.
JOHN OSBORNE, *A Better Class of Person* (1981)

A critic is a legless man who teaches running.
CHANNING POLLOCK

A drama critic is a man who leaves no turn unstoned.
GEORGE BERNARD SHAW, *New York Times* (1950)

As for the little puny critics, who scatter their peevish strictures in private circles, and scribble at every author who has the eminence of being un-connected with them, as they are usually spleen-swoln from a vain idea of increasing their consequence, there will always be found a petulance and illiberality in their remarks which should place them as far beneath the notice of a gentleman, as their original dullness had sunk them from the level of the most unsuccessful author.
RICHARD BRINSLEY SHERIDAN, preface to *The Rivals* (1775)

A man who knows the way but can't drive the car.
KENNETH TYNAN, definition of a critic, quoted in *New York Times Magazine* (9 January 1966)

A good drama critic is one who perceives what is happening in the theatre of his time. A great drama critic is one who perceives what is not happening.
KENNETH TYNAN

They search for ages for the wrong word which, to give them credit, they eventually find.
PETER USTINOV

The critic leaves at curtain fall
To find, in starting to review it,
He scarcely saw the play at all
For starting to review it.

E. B. WHITE, 'The Critic', *The New Yorker* (17 October 1925)

Has anybody seen a dramatic critic in the daytime? Of course not. They come out after dark, up to no good.

P. G. WODEHOUSE, *New York Mirror* (1955)

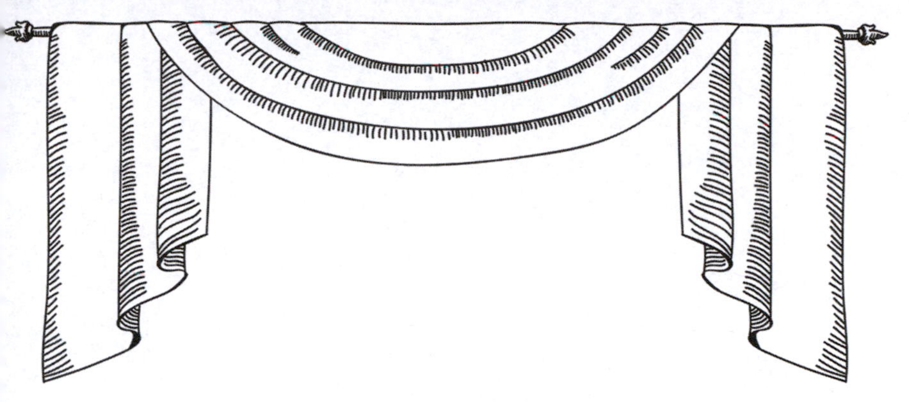

ACT FOUR

PLAYWRIGHTS, PRODUCERS, AND DIRECTORS

'The play's the thing'

HAMLET

CHRISTOPHER MARLOWE
(1564–1593)

396

After Shakespeare, in his day, Marlowe was the best-known Elizabethan playwright. His Dr Faustus *was once the occasion of some considerable alarm for 'certaine players at Exeter'.*

Certaine Players at Exeter acting *upon* the stage the tragicall storie of Dr. Faustus the Conjurer; as a certain number of Devels kept everie one his circle there, and as Faustus was busie in his magicall invocations, on a sudden they wer all dasht, every one harkning other in the eare, for they were all perswaded there was one devell too many amongst them; and so after a little pause desired the people to pardon them, they could go no further with this matter: the people also understanding the thing as it was, every man hastened to be first out of dores. The players (as I heard it) contrarye to their custome spending the night in reading and in prayer got them out of the towne the next morning.

SOURCE
Gentleman's Magazine (new series), vol 34

WILLIAM SHAKESPEARE
(1564–1616)

397

The Globe Theatre caught fire on 29 June 1613, during a performance of Shakespeare's Henry VIII. *A few days later the diplomat and poet Sir Henry Wotton wrote to his nephew Sir Edmund Bacon.*

Now I will entertain you at the present with what hath happened this Week at the Banks side.* The King's Players had a new Play, called *All is true*, representing some principal pieces of the Reign of Henry the 8th which was set forth with many extraordinary circumstances of Pomp and Majesty, even to the matting of the Stage; the Knights of the Order, with their Georges and Garter, the Guards with their embroidered Coats, and the like: sufficient in truth within a while to make Greatness very familiar, if not ridiculous. Now King Henry making a Masque at the Cardinal Wolsey's House, and certain Cannons being shot off at his entry, some of the Paper, or other stuff, wherewith one of them was stopped, did light on the Thatch, where being thought at first but an idle smoak, and their Eyes more attentive to the show, it kindled inwardly, and ran round like a train, consuming within less than an hour the whole House to the ground.

This was the fatal period of that virtuous Fabrique wherein yet nothing did perish, but Wood and Straw and a few forsaken Cloaks; only one Man had his Breeches set on fire, that would perhaps have broiled him, if he had not by the benefit of a provident wit put it out with Bottle-Ale.

**Bankside, the southern side of the Thames, between Southwark and Blackfriars Bridge, was the principal brothel district of London, but noted, too, for its theatres such as the Globe, the Rose, the Swan, and the Fortune.*

SOURCE
Sir Henry Wotton, *Reliquiae Wottonianae*, 4th edition (1685)

BEN JONSON
(1572–1637)

398

Ben Jonson, whose great plays include Volpone *and* The Alchemist, *had an unusual upbringing, if John Aubrey's account is to be believed.*

His mother, after his father's death, married a Bricklayer; and 'tis generally said that he wrought sometime with his father-in-lawe (and particularly on the Garden-wall of Lincoln's Inne next to Chancery Lane) and that a Knight, a Bencher, walking thro', and hearing his repeate some Greeke verses out of Homer, discoursing with him and finding him to have a Witt extraordinary, gave him some Exhibition to maintaine him at Trinity College in Cambridge.

Then he went into the Lowe-countreys, and spent some time (not very long) in the armie, not to disgrace, as you may find in his *Epigrammes.*

Then he came over into England, and acted and wrote, but both ill, at the Green Curtaine, a kind of Nursery or obscure Play-house, somewhere in the Suburbes (I thinke towards Shoreditch or Clarkenwell).

Then he undertook again to write a Playe, and did hitt it admirably well, viz. *Every Man…* [*in His Humour*], which was his first good one […]

He was (or rather had been) of a clear and faire skin; his habit was very plaine. I have heard Mr Lacy, the Player, say that he was wont to weare a coate like a coachman's coate, with slitts under the armepitts. He would many times exceed in drinke (Canarie was his beloved liquor) then he would tumble home to bed, and, when he had thoroughly perspired, then to studie.

SOURCE
Aubrey's Brief Lives, ed. Oliver Lawson Dick, 3rd edition (1971)

399

Eastward Ho, *by Jonson, Chapman, and Marston, made fun of King James I's Scottish courtiers.*

He was dilated by Sir James Murray to the King, for writing something against the Scots, in a play Eastward Hoe, and voluntarily imprisoned himself with Chapman and Marston, who had written it amonst them. The report was, that they should then have had their ears cut and noses. After their delivery, he banqueted all his friends; there was Camden, Selden, and others; at the midst of the feast his old Mother dranke to him, and shew him a paper which she had (if the sentence had taken execution) to have mixed in the prisson among his drinke, which was full of lustie strong poison, and that she was no churle, she told, she minded first to have drunk of it herself.

SOURCE
Note of Ben Jonson's Conversations with William Drummond of Hawthornden, ed. David Laing (1842)

ROGER BOYLE, FIRST EARL OF ORRERY (1621–1679)

400

Samuel Pepys records the first performance of Orrery's play, The Black Prince, *on 19 October 1667.*

Full of my desire of seeing my Lord Orrery's new play this afternoon at the King's House, 'The Black Prince', the first time it is acted; where, though we came by two o'clock, yet there was no room in the pit, but were forced to go into one of the upper boxes, at 4*s*. apiece, which is the first time I ever sat in a box in my life. And in the same box came, by and by, behind me, my Lord Berkeley and his lady, but I did not turn my face to them to be known, so that I was excused from giving them my seat. And this pleasure I had, that from this place the scenes do appear very fine indeed, and much better than in the pit. The house infinite full, and the King and Duke of York there. By and by the play begun, and in it nothing particular but a very fine dance for variety of figures, but a little too long... the whole house was mightily pleased all along till the reading of a letter, which was so long and so unnecessary that they frequently began to laugh, and to hiss twenty times, that had it not been for the King's being there, they had certainly hissed it off the stage. But I must confess that, as my Lord Berkeley said behind me, the having of that long letter was a thing so absurd, that he could not imagine how a man of his parts could possibly fall into it; or if he did, if he had but let any friend read it, the friend would have told him of it; and, I must confess, it is one of the most remarkable instances of a wise man's not being wise at all times... After the play done, and nothing pleasing them from the time of the letter to the end of the play, people being put into a bad humour of disliking, I home by coach, and could not forbear laughing almost all the way, and all the evening to my going to bed, at the ridiculousness of the letter, and the more because my wife was angry with me and the world for laughing, because the King was there.

SOURCE
Diary of Samuel Pepys (1667)

JOHN DRYDEN
(1631–1700)

401

The first Poet Laureate, Dryden was an influential critic in such works as his Essays on Dramatic Poesy, *as well as a major poet and playwright. His 'rival' in this passage, John Crowne, was the author of a number of successful comedies.*

Even Dryden was very suspicious of rivals. He would compliment Crowne when a play of his failed, but was cold to him if he met with success.

He sometimes used to own that Crowne had some genius, but then he always added that 'his father and Crowne's mother were very well acquainted.'

SOURCE
Joseph Spence, *Observations, Anecdotes, and Characters of Books and Men*, ed. James M. Osborn (1966)

JOHN CROWNE
(?1640–?1703)

402

A tale of the dashing of an author's hopes of royal preferment.

It was at the very latter End of King Charles's Reign, that Mr Crown being tyr'd with the Fatigue of Writing, and shock'd by the Uncertainty of Theatrical Success, and desirous to shelter himself from the Resentments of those numerous Enemies which he had made by his City Politicks, made his Application immediately to the King himself, and desir'd his Majesty to establish him in some Office, that might be a Security to him for Life. The King had the Goodness to assure him he should have an Office, but added that he would first see another Comedy. Mr Crown endeavouring to excuse himself, by telling the King that he plotted slowly and awkwardly; the King replyed, that he would help him to a Plot, and so put into his Hands the Spanish comedy called *Non pued Esser*. Mr Crown was oblig'd immediately to go to work upon it; but, after he had writ three Acts of it, found to his Surprise, that the Spanish Play had some time before been translated, and acted, and damn'd, under the Title of *Tango's Wiles, or the Coffee-house*. Yet, supported by the King's Command, he went boldly on and finish'd it; and here see the Influence of a Royal Encouragement...

...The Play was now just ready to appear to the World; and as every one that had seen it rehears'd was highly pleas'd with it; every one who had heard of it was big with the Expectation of it; and Mr Crown was delighted with the flattering Hope of being made happy for the rest of his Life, by the Performance of the King's Promise; when, upon the very last Day of the Rehearsal, he met Cave Underhill coming from the Play-House as he himself was going towards it: Upon which the Poet reprimanding the Player for neglecting so considerable a Part as he had in the Comedy, and neglecting it on a Day of so much Consequence, as the very last Day of Rehearsal: Oh Lord, Sir, sayd Underhill, we are all undone. Wherefore, says Mr Crown, is the Play-House on Fire? The whole Nation, replys the Player, will quickly be so, for the King is dead. At the hearing which dismal Words, the Author was little better; for he who but the Moment before was ravish'd with the Thought of the Pleasure, which he was about to give to his King, and of the Favours which he was afterwards to receive from him, this Moment found, to his unspeakable Sorrow, that his Royal Patron was gone for ever, and with him all his Hopes. The King indeed reviv'd from his Apoplectick Fit, but three Days after dyed, and Mr Crown by his Death was replung'd in the deepest Melancholy.

SOURCE
John Dennis, *The Critical Works*, ed. E. Hooker (1943)

WILLIAM WYCHERLEY
(1641–1716)

403

William Wycherley, the personification of the Restoration gentleman, and author of The Country Wife, *wrote: 'A mistress should be like a little country retreat near the town, not to dwell in constantly, but only for a night and away.' Here 'one of King Charles's Mistresses' was the Duchess of Cleveland.*

Upon the writing his first Play, which was *St. James's Park*, he became acquainted with several of the most celebrated Wits both of the Court and Town. The writing of that Play was likewise the Occasion of his becoming acquainted with one of King Charles's Mistresses after a very particular manner. As Mr Wycherley was going thro' Pall-mall towards St. James's in his Chariot, he met the foresaid Lady in hers, who, thrusting half her Body out of the Chariot, cry'd out aloud to him, *You,* Wycherley, *you are a Son of a Whore,* at the same time laughing aloud and heartily. Perhaps, Sir, if you never heard of this Passage before, you may be surpris'd at so strange a Greeting from one of the most beautiful and best-bred Ladies in the World. Mr Wycherley was certainly very much surpris'd at it, yet not so much but he soon apprehended it was spoke with Allusion to the latter End of a Song in the forementioned'd Play.

When Parents are Slaves
Their Brats cannot be any other,
Great Wits and great Braves
Have always a Punk to their Mother.

As, during Mr Wycherley's Surprise, the Chariots drove different ways, they were soon at a considerable Distance from each other, when Mr Wycherley recovering from his Surprise, ordered his Coachman to drive back, and to overtake the Lady. As soon as he got over-against her, he said to her, *Madam, you have been pleased to bestow a Title on me which generally belongs to the Fortunate. Will your Ladyship be at the Play to Night?* Well, she reply'd, *what if I am there? Why then I will be there to wait on your Ladyship, tho' I disappoint a very fine Woman who has made me an Assignation.* So, said she, *you are sure to disappoint a Woman who has favour'd you for one who has not.* Yes, he reply'd, *if she who has not favour'd me is the finer Woman of the two. But he who will be constant to your Ladyship, till he can find a finer Woman, is sure to die your Captive.* The Lady blush'd, and bade her Coachman drive away. As she was then in all her Bloom, and the most celebrated Beauty that was then in England, or perhaps that has been in England since, she was touch'd with the Gallantry of that Compliment. In short, she was that Night in the first Row of the King's Box in Drury Lane and Mr Wycherley in the Pit under her, where he entertained her during the whole Play. And this, Sir, was the beginning of a Correspondence between these two Persons, which afterwards made a great Noise in the Town.

SOURCE
John Dennis, *The Critical Works*, ed. E. Hooker (1943)

CHRISTOPHER RICH
(1657–1714)

404

Sir John Gielgud was celebrated in his time for dropping theatrical 'bricks'. The tradition is an old one, illustrated here by Christopher Rich, manager of London's Drury Lane Theare at the end of the seventeenth century. 'Mich' was the comic actor Michael Stoppelaer.

It was Mich's faculty to utter absurd speeches and disagreeable truths, without any design to give offence. I shall quote one anecdote, which will give the reader an idea of his character. Rich was talking to some of the actors, when Stoppelaer was present, concerning the disproportioned agreement he had made with Hallam, who acted Aumerle. Stoppelaer shook his head and said, *Upon my soul, Sir, he got on the blind side of you there.* Rich, apprehensive of hearing something more offensive, left the company: somebody present observed that Stoppelaer's speech was exceedingly improper, and really affronting, because every body knew that Mr Rich had a great blemish in one of his eyes.—'*Upon my word*', said Mich, '*I never heard of it before, and will go immediately and ask his pardon.*'

SOURCE
Thomas Davies, *Dramatic Miscellanies* (1785)

JOHN RICH
(?1692–1761)

405

The son of Christopher Rich, John Rich was a theatrical manager himself, and probably the greatest Harlequin and pantomime performer of his day. Foote is Samuel Foote, the actor and dramatist.

The education of Mr Rich had been grossly neglected; for though his understanding was good, his language was vulgar and ungrammatical: he was a perfect male Slip-slop.* However, he had much entertainment in his conversation, and loved a private party where he could unbend himself. From an habitual inattention, he had contracted a strange and perverse custom of calling every body Mister; and this gave occasion to an unmannerly bon mot of Foote. After

Mr Rich had called him Mister several times, Foote grew warm, and asked him the reason of his not calling him by his name. 'Don't be angry,' said Mr Rich; 'for I sometimes forget my own name.'—'That's extraordinary indeed,' replied Foote; 'I knew you could not write your own name, but I did not suppose you could forget it.'

A character in Henry Fielding's novel Joseph Andrews.

SOURCE
Thomas Davies, *Memoirs of David Garrick*, ed. Stephen Jones (2 vols, 1808)

MR KING
(*fl.* 1680s)

406

By prudent management of their salaries, theatre staff could sometimes become wealthier than their employers. Booth and Wilks were the actors Barton Booth and Robert Wilks.

Box-keepers, whatever they may be now, by the managers' keeping an eye over their conduct, were formerly richer than their masters. A remarkable instance of it I heard many years since. Colley Cibber had, in a prologue, or some part of a play, given such offence to a certain great man in power, that the playhouse, by order of the Lord-chamberlain, was shut up for some time; Cibber was arrested, and the damages laid at ten thousand pounds. Of this misfortune Booth and Wilks were talking very seriously, at the playhouse, in the presence of a Mr King, the box-keeper; who asked if he could be of any service, by offering to bail Cibber.—'Why, you blockhead,' says Wilks, 'it is for ten thousand pounds.'—'I should be very sorry' said the box-keeper, 'if I could not be answerable for twice that sum.' The managers stared at each other; and Booth said, with some emotion, to Wilks, 'What have you and I been doing, Bob, all this time?'

SOURCE
Thomas Davies, *Dramatic Miscellanies* (1785)

CHARLES MACKLIN
(?1699–1797)

407

Irish-born, Macklin was a dramatist as well as one of those actors that seems to arrive in every other generation and be acclaimed for bringing a new 'naturalism' to their acting. Macklin's play The Man of the World *was an undisguised attack on the influence of the Scottish Lord Bute at the court of King George III. Its performance in England was officially delayed for seventeen years. It left Macklin with a lasting hatred of the Scots.*

After he had left the stage, which the utter loss of memory compelled him to do, my father paid him a visit in London, and his account of it gave curious evidence of an inveterate prejudice surviving the decay of physical and intellectual Power. The old man, with lack-lustre eye, was sitting in his arm-chair unconscious of any one being present, till Mrs Macklin addressed him. 'My dear, here is Mr. Macready come to see you.' 'Who?' said Macklin. 'Mr. Macready, my dear.' 'Ha! Who is he?' 'Mr. Macready, you know, who went to Dublin to act for your benefit.' 'Ha! My benefit? What was it? What did he act?' 'I acted Egerton, sir,' said my father, 'in your own play.' 'Ha! My play? What was it?' ' "The Man of the World," sir.' 'Ha, "Man of the World!" Devilish good title! Who wrote it?' 'You did, sir.' 'Did I? Well! What was it about?' 'Why, sir, there was a Scotchman'—'Ah d—n them!' My father finding it useless to prolong this last interview with his old preceptor, took his leave.

SOURCE
Macready's Reminiscences, ed. Sir F. Pollock (1876)

JAMES THOMSON
(1700–1748)

408

As well as being a poet and playwright, Thomson was the author of 'Rule Britannia'. His play Agamemnon *was written in 1738.*

Thomson, in reading his play of Agamemnon to the actors, in the green-room,* pronounced every line with such a broad Scotch accent, that they could not restrain themselves from a loud laugh. Upon this, the author good-naturedly said to the manager, 'Do you, Sir, take my play, and go on with it; for, though I can write a tragedy, I find I cannot read one.'

**The origin of the green-room is disputed, but Sir Donald Sinden, actor and theatre historian, would brook no argument. He told me: 'For performances the stage was covered with a green cloth which simulated grass for exterior scenes or a green carpet for interior. The stage is still known to actors as "the green" and the room where they await their entrances is "the green-room".'*

SOURCE
Thomas Davies, *Dramatic Miscellanies* (1785)

409

Agamemnon, though well acted, was not written agreeably to the taste of the critics, who very justly observed that he had not entirely preserved ancient manners and characters; Clytemnestra did not resemble the portrait drawn of her by Aeschylus, which is more consistent and agreeable to history. The displeasure of the audience shown to certain scenes produced a whimsical effect upon the author; he had promised to meet some friends at a tavern as soon as the play was ended, but he was obliged to defer his attending them to a very late hour. When he came, they asked him the reason of his stay; he told them that the critics had sweated him so terribly by their severe treatment of certain parts of his tragedy, that the perspiration was so violent as to render his wig unfit to wear; and that he had spent a great deal of time among the peruke-makers in procuring a proper cover for his head.

SOURCE
Thomas Davies, *Memoirs of David Garrick*, ed. Stephen Jones (2 vols, 1808)

SAMUEL JOHNSON
(1709–1784)

410

Johnson was only eight years older than his pupil, David Garrick. Both were born in Lichfield and travelled together, sharing a horse, on their first foray to London. Johnson's achievements as poet, critic, essayist, and lexicographer are not in doubt. As a dramatist, however, he was not so successful: his tragedy, Irene, *staged by Garrick, was short-lived. Although the two men often argued with and criticized one another, they remained friends for the rest of Garrick's life. On being told of his demise, Johnson remarked, 'I am disappointed in that death which has eclipsed the gaiety of nations and impoverished the public stock of harmless pleasure.'*

Johnson thought the opportunity fair to think of his tragedy of *Irene*, which was his whole stock on his first arrival in town, in the year 1737. That play was accordingly put into rehearsal in January 1749. As a precursor to prepare the way, and awaken the public attention, *The Vanity of Human Wishes,* a Poem in Imitation of the Tenth Satire of Juvenal, by the Author of *London,* was published in the same month. In the Gentleman's Magazine, for February, 1749, we find that the tragedy of *Irene* was acted at Drury-lane, on Monday, February the 6th, and from that time, without interruption, to Monday, February the 20th, being in all thirteen nights. Since that time it has not been exhibited on any stage. *Irene* may be added to some other plays in our language, which have lost their place in the theatre, but continue to please in the closet. During the representation of this piece, Johnson attended every night behind the scenes. Conceiving that his character, as an author, required some ornament for his person, he chose, upon that occasion, to decorate himself with a handsome waistcoat, and a gold-laced hat. The late Mr Topham Beauclerc, who had had a great deal of that humour which pleases the more for seeming undesigned, used to give a pleasant description of this Green-room finery, as related by the author himself; 'But,' said Johnson, with great gravity, 'I soon laid aside my gold-laced hat, lest it should make me proud.' The amount of the three benefit nights for the tragedy of *Irene,* it is to be feared, was not very considerable, as the profit, that stimulating motive, never invited the author to another dramatic attempt. Some years afterwards, when the present writer was intimate with Garrick, and knew Johnson to be in distress, he asked the manager why he did not produce another tragedy for his Lichfield friend? Garrick's answer was remarkable. 'When Johnson writes tragedy, declamation roars, and passion sleeps: when Shakespeare wrote, he dipped his pen in his own heart.'

SOURCE

Johnsonian Miscellanies, ed. George Birkbeck Hill (2 vols, 1897)

411

The Shakespearean commentator George Stevens is talking to Dr Johnson. Goldsmith's play was She Stoops to Conquer.

'Though you brought a Tragedy, Sir, to Drury-Lane, and at one time were so intimate with Garrick, you never appeared to have much theatrical acquaintance.'—'Sir, while I had, in common with other dramatic authors, the liberty of the scenes, without considering my admission behind them as a favour, I was frequently at the theatre. At that period all the wenches knew me, and dropped me a curtsey as they passed on to the stage. But since poor Goldsmith's last Comedy, I scarce recollect having seen the inside of a playhouse. To speak the truth, there is small encouragement there for a man whose sight and hearing are become so imperfect as mine. I may add that, Garrick and Henderson* excepted, I never met with a performer who had studied his art, or could give an intelligible reason for what he did.'

**This is John Henderson, often called 'the Bath Roscius'.*

SOURCE
Johnsonian Miscellanies, ed. George Birkbeck Hill (2 vols, 1897)

412

Mrs B. having recently desired Johnson to look over her new play of the *Siege of Sinope* before it was acted, he always found means to evade it; at last she pressed him so closely that he actually refused to do it and told her that she herself, by carefully looking it over, would be able to see if there was anything amiss as well as he could. 'But, sir,' said she, 'I have no time. I have already so many irons in the fire.' 'Why then, madam,' he said (quite out of patience), 'the best thing I can advise you to do is, to put your tragedy along with your irons.'

SOURCE
Johnsonian Miscellanies, ed. George Birkbeck Hill (2 vols, 1897)

WILLIAM HAVARD

(1710–1778)

413

Havard was a British actor and dramatist who appeared at Goodman's Fields Theatre and at Drury Lane, usually in secondary roles, between 1730 and his retirement in 1769. He also appeared in his own plays, King Charles I *at Lincoln Inn Fields, in 1737, and* The Elopement *at Drury Lane in 1763.*

Havard undertook the tragedy of 'Charles I' at the desire of the manager of the company of Lincoln's Inn Fields, to which he then belonged, in 1737. The manager had probably read of the salutary effects produced on the genius of Euripides by seclusion in his cave, and he was determined to give Havard the same advantage in a garret during the composition of his task. He invited him to his house, took him up to one of its airiest apartments, and there locked him up for so many hours every day, well knowing his desultory habits; nor released him till the unfortunate bard had repeated through the keyhole a certain number of new speeches in the progressive tragedy.

SOURCE
Thomas Campbell, *Life of Mrs Siddons* (1834)

OLIVER GOLDSMITH

(1728–1774)

414

Both these anecdotes concern Goldsmith's most famous play, She Stoops to Conquer.

It has been said that Goldsmith's comedy of *She Stoops to Conquer,* originated in the following adventure of the author. Some friend had given the young poet a guinea, when he left his mother's residence at Ballymahon, for a school in Edgworth's Town, where, it appears he finished his education. He had diverted himself by viewing the gentlemen's seats on the road, until night-fall, when he found himself a mile or two out of the direct road, in the middle of the streets of Ardagh. Here he inquired for the best house in the place, meaning an inn; but a fencing-master, named Kelly, wilfully misunderstanding him, directed him to the large, old-fashioned residence of Sir Ralph Featherstone, as the landlord of the town. There he was shown into the parlour, and found the hospitable master of the house sitting by a good fire. His mistake was immediately perceived by Sir Ralph, who being a man of humour, and well acquainted with the poet's family, encouraged him in the deception. Goldsmith ordered a good supper, invited his host and the family to partake of it, treated them to a bottle or two of wine, and, on going to bed, ordered a hot cake for his breakfast; nor was it until his departure, when he called for his bill, that he discovered that, while he imagined he was at an inn, he had been hospitably entertained at a private family of the first respectability in the country.

SOURCE
J. H. Leigh Hunt, *Readings for Railways* (1849)

415

Richard Cumberland recalls the first night of She Stoops to Conquer *in 1773.*

We were not over-sanguine of success, but perfectly determined to struggle hard for our author: we accordingly assembled our strength at the Shakespeare Tavern in a considerable body for an early dinner, where Samuel Johnson took the chair at the head of a long table, and was the life and soul of the corps... Our illustrious president was in inimitable glee, and poor Goldsmith that day took all his raillery as patiently and complacently as my friend Boswell would have done any day, or every day of his life. In the mean time we did not forget our duty, and betook ourselves in good time to our separate and allotted posts, and waited the awful drawing up of the curtain. As our stations were pre-concerted, so were our signals for plaudits arranged and determined upon in a manner, that gave every one his cue where to look for them, and how to follow them up.

We had amongst us a very worthy and efficient member, long since lost to his friends and the world at large, Adam Drummond, of amiable memory, who was gifted by nature with the most sonorous, and at the same time the most contagious, laugh, that ever echoed from the human lungs. The neighing of the horse of the son of Hystaspes was a whisper to it; the whole thunder of the theatre could not drown it. This kind and ingenuous friend fairly forewarned us that he knew no more when to give his fire than the cannon did, that was planted on a battery. He desired therefore to have a flapper at his elbow, and I had the honour to be deputed to that office. I planted him in an upper box, pretty nearly over the stage, in full view of the pit and galleries, and perfectly well situated to give the echo all its play through the hollows and recesses of the theatre. The success of our manoeuvres was complete. All eyes were upon Johnson, who sat in a front row of a side box, and when he laughed every body thought themselves warranted to roar. In the mean time my friend followed signals with a rattle so irresistibly comic, that, when he had repeated it several times, the attention of the spectators was so engrossed by his person and performances that the progress of the play seemed likely to become a secondary object, and I found it prudent to insinuate to him that he might halt his music without any prejudice to the author; but alas, it was now too late to rein him in; he had laughed upon my signal where he found no joke, and now unluckily he fancied that he found a joke in almost every thing that was said; so that nothing in nature could be more mal-a-propos than some of his bursts every now and then were. These were dangerous moments, for the pit began to take umbrage; but we carried our play through, and triumphed.

SOURCE
Richard Cumberland, *Memoirs* (1806)

RICHARD BRINSLEY SHERIDAN (1751–1816)

416

The Rivals, The School for Scandal, *and* The Critic *are the three plays for which Sheridan is most highly regarded. He was also owner of Drury Lane Theatre, in succession to Garrick, besides being in the House of Commons from 1780 to 1812. This famous anecdote has been recounted ever since the fire of 1809 destroyed Drury Lane and bankrupted Sheridan.*

Such was the state of this luckless property,—and it would have been difficult to imagine any change for the worse that could befall it—when, early in the present year, an event occurred, that seemed to fill up at once the measure of its ruin. On the night of the 24th of February, while the House of Commons was occupied with Mr Ponsonby's motion on the Conduct of the War in Spain, and Mr Sheridan was in attendance, with the intention, no doubt, of speaking, the House was suddenly illuminated by a blaze of light; and, the Debate being interrupted, it was ascertained that the Theatre of Drury Lane was on fire. A motion was made to adjourn; but Mr Sheridan said, with much calmness, that, 'whatever might be the extent of the private calamity, he hoped it would not interfere with the public business of the country.' He then left the House; and, proceeding to Drury Lane, witnessed, with a fortitude which strongly interested all who observed him, the entire destruction of his property.

It is said that, as he sat at the Piazza Coffee-house, during the fire, taking some refreshment, a friend of his having remarked on the philosophic calmness with which he bore his misfortune, Sheridan answered, 'A man may surely be allowed to take a glass of wine by his own fire-side.'

SOURCE
Thomas Moore, *Memoirs of R. B. Sheridan* (1826)

417

He had a particular difficulty with actresses. A year before taking over from Garrick, he wrote what must be the most hostile private account ever penned on the subject. It was in a letter intended to prevent his sister-in-law Mary from accepting an offer of work from Garrick, whom he accused of being a liar and corrupter of innocence. He said Mary would be forced 'to play the Coquet, the Wanton, to retail loose innuendoes in Comedy, or glow with warm Descriptions in Tragedy; and in bother to be haul'd about, squeez'd and kiss'd by beastly pimping Actors!... everything around them is unchaste—their Studies are Lessons of Vice and Passion.—Like Wretches who work in unwholesome Mines, Their senses are corrupted in the operation of their Trade.'

Sheridan himself was never averse to illicit squeezing and kissing; it was the idea of it happening in the theatre to a woman in his own family that he disliked so much. He claimed that he himself 'had always an Instinctive Abhorrence' to the theatre as 'the greatest Nursery of Vice and Misery on the Face of the Earth'; said he was convinced that most actresses were unhappy in their work, and that none could hope to marry decent men.

SOURCE
Claire Tomalin, *Mrs Jordan's Profession*, (1994)

418

He could not make enemies. If anyone came to request the repayment of a loan from him, he borrowed more. A cordial shake of his hand was a receipt in full for all demands. He could 'coin his smile with drachmas', cancelled bonds with *bons mots,* and gave jokes in discharge of a bill.

SOURCE
William Hazlitt, 'On the Spirit of Obligations', *New Monthly Magazine* (24 January 1824)

FANNY BURNEY
(1752–1840)

419

Fanny Burney was successful as a novelist, but less so as a dramatist. Her play Edwyn and Elgiva*—in spite of John Philip Kemble and Mrs Siddons being in the cast—lasted just one night.*

On the 21st of March, 1795, a tragedy, called 'Edwyn and Elgiva', written by Miss Burney, afterwards Madam D'Arblay, was produced at Drury Lane. 'We are sorry,' says the *London Chronicle,* the following day, 'that we cannot congratulate the fair authoress on the success of her first dramatic essay: for even the benedictions of the three bishops, whom she chose for her heroes, were not able to procure the salvation of it;—a circumstance which will probably induce her hereafter to employ something more than spiritual aid in support of a temporal cause.'

Miss Burney was peculiarly unfortunate in bringing bishops into her tragedy. At that time there was a liquor much in popular use, called Bishop: it was a sort of negus or punch, I believe, though the origin of its name I must leave more learned antiquaries to determine. But, be that as it may, when jolly fellows met at a tavern, the first order to the waiter was, *to bring in the Bishop.* Unacquainted with the language of taverns, Miss Burney made her King exclaim, in an early scene, '*Bring in the Bishop!*' and the summons filled the audience with as much hilarity as if they had drank of the exhilirating liquor. They continued in the best possible humour throughout the piece.

SOURCE
Thomas Campbell, *Life of Mrs Siddons* (1834)

ROBERT ELLISTON
(1774–1831)

420

Robert Elliston, judged a reasonable actor, was also a successful theatre manager, running numerous theatres throughout England, including Drury Lane from 1819 to 1827.

Elliston had become proprietor of the Olympic Pavilion, as it was then called, in Wych Street, built originally by old Astley for equestrian performances. At his suggestion I wrote a speaking harlequinade, with songs for the *Columbine*, the subject being 'Little Red Riding Hood'. On the first night of its representation (December 21, 1818) every trick failed, not a scene could be induced to close or to open properly, and the curtain fell at length amidst a storm of disapprobation.

I was with Mr Elliston and his family in a private box. He sent round an order to the prompter that not one of the carpenters, scene-shifters, or property-men was to leave the theatre till he had spoken to them. As soon as the house was cleared, the curtain was raised, and all the culprits assembled on the stage in front of one of the scenes in the piece representing the interior of a cottage, having a door in one half and a latticed window in the other. Elliston led me forward, and standing in the centre, with his back to the footlights, harangued them in the most grandiloquent language—expatiated on the enormity of their offence, their ingratitude to the man whose bread they were eating, the disgrace they had brought upon the theatre, the cruel injury they had inflicted on the young and promising author by his side; then, pointing in the most tragical attitude to his wife and daughters, who remained in the box, bade them look upon the family they had ruined, and burying his face in his handkerchief to stifle his sobs, passed slowly through the door in the scene, leaving his auditors silent, abashed, and somewhat affected, yet rather relieved by being let off with a lecture. The next minute the casement in the other flat was thrown violently open, and thrusting in his head, his face scarlet with fury, he roared out 'I discharge you all!'

I feel my utter incapacity to convey an idea of this ludicrous scene, and I question whether any one unacquainted with the man, his voice, action, and wonderful facial expression, could thoroughly realize the glorious absurdity of it from verbal description.

SOURCE
George Raymond, *The Life and Enterprises of R. W. Elliston* (1857)

421

Under the various phases of Elliston's character, we must here exhibit an instance of forbearance and good nature. Amongst the persons employed at the Olympic was a scene-painter, who had the misfortune of not being highly popular with his fellow-labourers in the establishment—in fact, a most disagreeable fellow. One of the carpenters projected a trick to mortify him, and this was placing a vessel nearly full of red paint on the upper edge of his working-room door, as it stood ajar, which, on any one entering, would consequently be capsized, like 'Prone-descending rain', right over his person. The vessel being all ready, the next purpose was to induce the said artist to make his way to the room in question.

But by some mismanagement, at the moment, Elliston himself came by, and having business to transact in the scenic department, with his usual dignity of action, threw open the charged door, when the vermilion shower fell with a precision over his head and shoulders, which almost threatened suffocation. Consternation filled the minds of the skulking conspirators—and well it might. As soon as Elliston could recover his breath, in terrific accents he commanded that the whole establishment should be summoned before him; this was instantly obeyed. Red and fiery, he yet sat down with imperturbed dignity, when, shaking his gory locks, or rather the cardinal's hat, with which he had just been invested, he demanded instant explanation of the event, and the surrender of the offender.

The real culprit now stood forward, and at once confessed himself both the adviser and perpetrator of the plot, but thoroughly explaining for whom the revenge was intended.

'Ay!' said Elliston—'for Mr. —, say you?'

'Upon my honour!' was the reply.

'Then I forgive you!' rejoined the manager, and off he marched to incarnadine the Olympic pump with the evidence of his dishonour.

SOURCE
George Raymond, *The Life and Enterprises of R. W. Elliston* (1857)

eluding detection in buying seats at the box-office to sell at a hundred per cent profit on the streets, that Augustin devised the following plan. The purchaser of seats for a particular night received simply a slip of paper with a number on it, exchangeable at night for the actual ticket purchased. As speculators could not sell slips, containing merely a numeral, and no indication of the number or location of seats, they retired from the field.

SOURCE
Joseph Francis Daly, *The Life of Augustin Daly* (1917)

HENRY IRVING
(1838–1905)

431

The acknowledged giant of the theatre of the Victorian age, Irving was as much a theatre manager and producer as he was an actor.

The Lady of Lyons was produced on April 17, 1879. It kept in the bill for a portion of each week for the remainder of the first and the whole of the second season; in all forty-five times—no inconsiderable run of such an old and hackneyed play.

The production was a very beautiful one. There was a specially attractive feature in it: the French army. At the end of the fourth act Claude, all his hopes shattered and he being consumed with remorse, accepts Colonel Damas' offer to go with him to the war in that fine melodramatic outburst:

'Place me wherever a foe is most dreaded—wherever France most needs a life!'

As Irving stage-managed it the army, already on its way, was tramping along the road outside. Through window and open door the endless columns were seen, officers and men in due order and the flags in proper place. It seemed as if the line would stretch out till the crack of doom! A very large number of soldiers had been employed as supers, and were of course especially suitable for the work. In those days the supers of London theatres were largely supplied from the Brigade of Guards. The men liked it, for it provided easy beer-money, and the officers liked them to have the opportunity as it kept them out of mischief. We had always on our staff as an additional super-master a Sergeant of Guards who used to provide the men, and was of course in a position to keep them in order.

The men entered thoroughly into the spirit of the thing, and it was really wonderful how, availing themselves of their professional training they were able to seemingly multiply their forces. Often have I admired the dexterity, ease and rapidity with which that moving army was kept going with a hundred and fifty men.

SOURCE
Bram Stoker, *Personal Reminiscences of Henry Irving* (1906)

432

One more funny matter there was in the doing of the play [*The Corsican Brothers* staged by Irving in 1880]. The supper-party at Baron Montgiron's house was supposed to be a very 'toney' affair, the male guests being the *crême de la crême* of Parisian society, the ladies being of the *demi-monde;* all of both classes being persons to whom a 'square' meal was no rarity. As, however, the majority of the guests were 'extras' or 'supers' it was hard to curb their zeal in matters of alimentation. When the servants used to throw open the doors of the supper-room and announce '*Monsieur est servi!*' they would make one wild rush and surround the table like hyenas.

For their delectation bread and sponge-cake—media which lend themselves to sculptural efforts—and *gâteaux* of alluring aspect were provided. The champagne flowed in profusion—indeed in such profusion and of so realistic an appearance that all over the house the opera-glasses used to be levelled and speculations as to the brand and *cuvée* arose. Indeed a rumour went round the press that the nightly wine bill was of colossal dimensions. In reality, the champagne provided was lemonade put up specially in champagne bottles and foiled with exactness. It certainly *looked* like champagne and foamed out as the corks popped. The orgy grew nightly in violence till at the end of a couple of weeks the nobles of France manifested a hunger and thirst libellous to the Faubourg St. Germain. Irving pondered over the matter, and one day gave orders that special food should be provided, wrought partly of plaster-o'-Paris and partly of *papier-mâché.* He told the Property Master to keep the matter secret. There was hardly any need for the admonition. In a theatre a joke is a very sacred thing, and there is no one from highest to lowest that will not go out of his way to further it. That night when the emaciated nobles of France dashed at their quarry, one and all received a sudden check. There were many unintentional ejaculations of surprise and disappointment from the guests, and much suppressed laughter from the stage hands who were by this time all in the secret and watching from the wings.

After that night there was a notable improvement in the table manners of the guests. One and all they took their food leisurely and examined it critically. And so the succulent sponge-cake in due time reappeared; there was no need for a second lesson against greed.

SOURCE

Bram Stoker, *Personal Reminiscences of Henry Irving* (1906)

MASTER ARNOTT

(*fl.* 1870)

433

Master Arnott was Irving's property master and worked for him on his celebrated production of The Bells. *The play by Leopold Lewis opened on 25 November 1871 at the Lyceum Theatre in London and ran initially for 151 performances. Irving staged the play repeatedly throughout his career, playing the role of Mathias for the last time the night before his death in 1905.*

One of these men, Arnott, the Property Master and a fine workman, had had an odd experience during the Bristol week. Something had gone wrong with the travelling 'property' horse used in the vision scene of *The Bells*, and he had come up to town to bring the real one from the storage. In touring it was usual to bring a 'profile' representation of the gallant steed. 'Profile' has in theatrical parlance a special meaning other than its dictionary meaning of an 'outline'. It is thin wood covered on both sides with rough canvas carefully glued down. It is very strong and can be cut in safety to any shape. The profile horse was of course an outline, but the art of the scene-painter had rounded it out to seemingly natural dimensions. Now the 'real' horse, though a lifeless 'property', had in fact been originally alive. It was formed of the skin of a moderately sized pony; and being embellished with picturesque attachments in the shape of mane and tail was a really creditable object. But it was expensive to carry as it took up much space. Arnott and two of his men ran up to fetch this down as there was not time to make a new profile horse. When they got to Paddington he found that the [railway] authorities refused to carry the goods by weight on account of its bulk, and asked him something like £4 for the journey. He expressed his feelings freely, as men occasionally do under irritating circumstances, and said he would go somewhere else.

The clerk in the office smiled and Arnott went away; he was a clever man who did not like to be beaten, and railways were his natural enemies. He thought the matter over. Having looked over the time-table and found that the cost of a horse-box to Bristol was only £1 13s., he went to the department in charge of such matters and ordered one, paying for it at once and arranging that it should go on the next fast train. By some manoeuvring he so managed that he and his men took Koveski's horse into the box and closed the doors.

When the train arrived at Bristol there had to be some shunting to and fro so as to place the horse-box in the siding arranged for such matters. The officials in charge threw open the door for the horse to walk out. But he would yield to no blandishment, nor even to the violence of chastisement usual at such times. A little time passed and the officials got anxious, for the siding was required for other purposes. The station at Bristol is not roomy and more than one line has to use it. The official in charge told him to take out his damned horse!

'Not me!' said he, for he was now seeing his way to 'get back' at the railway company. 'I've paid for the carriage of the horse and I want him delivered out of your premises. The rate I paid includes the services of the necessary officials.'

The porters tried again, but the horse would not stir. Now it is a dangerous matter to go into a horse-box in case the horse should prove restive. One after another the porters declined, till at last one plucky lad volunteered to go in by the little window close to the horse's head. Those on the platform waited in apprehension, till he suddenly ran out from the box laughing and crying out:

'Why you blamed fools. He ain't a 'orse at all. He's a stuffed 'un!'

SOURCE
Bram Stoker, *Personal Reminiscences of Henry Irving* (1906)

JIMMY ALLEN
(*fl.* 1890)

434

Poor Jimmy Allen deserves a niche in the Chronicle of the Lyceum. He was an old Indian Mutiny N.C.O. How he drifted on to the stage I never heard, but he was, all through my time under Irving, his prompter. It was Allen's pride to make out elaborate prompt-books of all the Lyceum plays. He was a very faithful servant. He used to take the rehearsals of supers, minor people, and under-studies. His only difficulty was in selecting the correct moments to introduce or to eliminate the aspirate... There was a scene in *Louis XI* in which certain Burgundian Lords (local) were required to breathe defiance at the old and crafty monarch. 'Look 'ere, boys, you swagger on, see? Stare at the old King, as much as to say "Oo are *you?*" with a look of 'ate, see?' 'Please, Sir,' objected a certain waggish super, 'there are only seven of us.'

'Now then, you ladies,' he shouted, as he was rehearsing the witches in the Brocken scene in *Faust*, 'don't let me see any grinnin' faces, you're not on 'Ampstead 'Eath, remember, you're in 'Ell.'

By dint of rigid economy exercised over a wilderness of years, he scraped together enough upon which to retire. He had taken for a wife a woman much younger than himself who entirely consumed his hard-gained substance. There was nothing before him but the workhouse. One night he came down to the theatre when I was playing *The Only Way*, handed over to me his precious, careful prompt-books, went home and shot himself.

SOURCE
Sir John Martin-Harvey, *Autobiography* (1933)

SQUIRE BANCROFT
(1841–1926)

435

As the next two passages show, the actor-manager Squire Bancroft was always prepared to challenge theatrical traditions.

It may be curious to mention here the first morning performance we ever gave at the Prince of Wales's Theatre, which was on March 6th [1869], in the height of the run of *School*, when all the seats were booked every night long in advance. The experiment, however, was so novel, that it only attracted a moderate house in the daytime, and it was not for some years that *matinées* became popular.

SOURCE
Sir Squire and Lady Bancroft, *On and Off the Stage*

436

To take the events of that opening night [at the Haymarket, Saturday, 31 January 1880] in proper sequence, I must begin with the Pit question, and the riot that occurred when the curtain rose. Anonymous reports had reached me that there would most likely be a disturbance. I was sanguine enough, however, to hope that the following advertisement issued beforehand, and the nature of the accommodation offered in place of the old pit, would have prevented anything of the kind. Those hopes were vain:

> 'As some disappointment may be felt at the abolition of the pit, Mr. and Mrs. Bancroft deem it necessary to explain the alteration. With the present expenses of a first-class theatre, it is impossible to give up the floor of the house—its most remunerative portion—to low-priced seats, and the management, being unwilling to place any part of the audience in close and

> confined space under the balcony, the only alternative was to allot to the frequenters of the pit the tier usually devoted to the upper boxes, and now called the second circle. In carrying out the structural alterations of the theatre, Mr. and Mrs. Bancroft have, they hope, specially attended to the comfort of visitors to these seats by raising the ceiling, building a new stone staircase, a refreshment-room, and by removing all obstacles to a clear view of the stage.'

Naturally enough, I think it may be expected that I should here express some views on this then important subject, and tell what led me to the bold measure of daring to abolish the pit, more especially from the Haymarket Theatre, which had been long known to boast, and truly enough, the possession of the best and most comfortable pit ever to be found in a playhouse, from the reason that it did not go under the dress circle.

To begin, it is perhaps necessary to remind young play-goers that the pit in the old days occupied the entire floor of the theatre, extending to the orchestra, and as the charge for admission in the leading houses was three shillings and sixpence, the pit quite earned its title of being 'the backbone of the theatre'. The dress circle and private boxes were the resort of the better classes, the wealthy, or the fastidious. The modern stall was then unknown. Gradually this luxury was introduced. Row by row, very insidiously, the cushioned chairs encroached upon the narrow benches, which, year after year, were removed further and further from the stage, until at last, in many theatres, all that was left of the old-fashioned pit was a dark, low-ceilinged place hidden away under the dress circle, which, by contrast with its former proud state, seemed but a kind of cellar, or reminder of the black-hole of Calcutta.

That thousands of earnest play-goers would far rather sit there in heat and discomfort than go up aloft to better accommodation

I don't doubt for a moment, nor do I for another moment deny that I should very likely find myself of the party under their circumstances; but that seems to me outside the question. Matters had entirely changed. The pit had long lost, in most West End theatres, the possibility of being the support it used to prove, owing to the managers of them having, row by row, robbed it of its power, and made the stalls instead their 'backbone'. This grew to be eminently the case with our management, which could not have endured without high-priced admission.

I don't think anything I might add to these remarks would advance the argument, I will return to the hooting and howling which greeted the raising of the curtain, mingled with noisy cries of 'Where's the pit?' At the great disadvantage of being dressed for Sir Frederick Blount,* in which I wore a flaxen foppish wig and pink complexion, I walked upon the stage and faced the anger of the few who made the noise, which quite drowned the friendly greeting of the many. Utterly unprepared what to say, for I had disregarded the anonymous warnings, I believe I owed something to the manner in which I spoke the few broken sentences I was allowed, through the tumult, to utter, and to never showing during that *mauvais quart d'heure* (to be exact, more than twenty minutes) the least sign of temper. What I said was not of much moment, and very likely my attempts to speak were neither soothing nor judicious; but I am not of a 'knuckling-under' disposition, and, at least, I thought myself justified in claiming the respect of the audience. Unfortunately the diversion tended largely to disconcert the actors, and to add greatly to the nervousness due to the position of all concerned.

* *Character in* Money, *by Lord Lytton (1840).*

SOURCE
Sir Squire and Lady Bancroft, *On and Off the Stage*

JOHNSTON FORBES-ROBERTSON
(1853–1937)

437

A successful actor whose Hamlet at the Lyceum in 1897 was especially admired for the beauty of his voice, Johnston Forbes-Robertson worked under Henry Irving before becoming a manager in his own right.

Once when I was bemoaning to Clayton the trouble I had in wording with sufficient tact letters to authors whose plays I could not accept for production—'My dear fellow,' said Clayton, 'I solved the question only yesterday. I wrote to a man who had sent me an abominable play, and said, "My dear Sir, I have read your play. Oh—my very dear Sir! Yours truly, John Clayton."' I told this story on many occasions with great success. At last I told it to one who did not laugh. He was my secretary. It seemed to me hard, indeed, that one's own secretary should not laugh at one's funny stories. It appeared to me that he had mistaken his vocation, and I said in a tone of some irritation, 'You don't seem to think that funny.' Said he, 'No, I don't. It was to me Mr. Clayton wrote that letter!'

SOURCE
Sir Johnston Forbes-Robertson, *A Player under Three Reigns* (1925)

438

But to return to the Lyceum. Loveday [H. J. Loveday, Irving's stage manager] was always much concerned at Irving's lavish expenditure on the furnishing of the stage, who would discard at once any property or scene, no matter what it cost, if it did not quite satisfy him. I remember on one occasion I was sitting in Irving's dressing-room while he was making up, when Loveday came in with a very beautiful sceptre he had had made for *Richard III*. He drew it from its case and showed it to Irving with much pride. Irving handled it for a moment, and said sharply, 'No good, too heavy.' Poor Loveday appealed to me silently from behind Irving's chair, with a most eloquent look as who should say, 'What is to be done with this man?' Upon this I seized the sceptre and waved it about, walking up and down saying, 'Too heavy? Oh, no! It's got to be heavy. It is not a fairy's wand, it's an imposing sceptre. Please stand up and try it properly.' Irving said meekly, 'Is it? Well, let's see.' He got up and paced the room, trying it this way and that; then turning to Loveday said very humbly, 'Thank you, Loveday. Yes, it's a nice sceptre. I'll use it.' Loveday was all beams, and his look of gratitude to me I shall never forget.

SOURCE
Sir Johnston Forbes-Robertson, *A Player under Three Reigns* (1925)

DAVID BELASCO
(1853–1931)

439

During his career on Broadway he directed or produced more than 300 plays and was accepted as the master of naturalism. This made him the prime target when a reaction against this form of theatrical realism set in. The critic, George Jean Nathan, claimed derisively that he had seen a signed photograph of Dante on Belasco's inlaid onyx commode. But during Belasco's heyday plays such as his Civil War drama, The Heart of Maryland, *set him in the forefront of American dramatic art.*

Although Belasco was often sued for plagiarism, he was never convicted. He could prove that the Belasco stamp was unique. Once he contributed a series of learned articles about acting to *The Booklovers*

Magazine. It turned out that they had originally appeared in England under the signature of George Henry Lewes, an eminent British critic. Belasco explained that his name on the article was a clerical mistake made by a subordinate who had since disappeared. Just a regrettable oversight in Belasco's opinion.

He measurably improved the standards of stage décor by his ingenious use of lighting and his meticulous attention to the details of scenery. He was the first manager to conceal footlights in the interest of reality. He was one of the few men in that time to understand the importance of direction. He rehearsed his companies remorselessly. He did not so much interpret as invent and mold performances. He tortured his actors. He stuck a pin in Frances Starr's beguiling behind to make her scream dramatically. In the heat of a rehearsal, he sometimes threw his watch on the floor and stamped on it. It was a dollar watch that he kept in stock for the purpose, but the gesture was sobering.

All the actors whom he took in charge were gratified. He expected to take charge of them in every part of their lives. When Mrs Leslie Carter married for the second time without telling him, Belasco excommunicated her and never saw her again, although she kept on writing to him and hoping for a reconciliation. He was a tyrant and an artist manqué.

SOURCE
Brooks Atkinson, *Broadway* (1970)

440

If an actor made Belasco angry, he'd deal with him harshly. He'd scream at the performer, his anger rising until he was practically apoplectic. He was so angry that he'd pull out his pocket watch and throw it to the floor. That got the actor's attention. Little did they know that he had boxes of cheap watches in his office just to achieve this effect.

In one show, he became so incensed that he took a fire axe and attacked the scenery. He was crazed. How dare an actor be so stupid! The axe flew through the air and took another chunk out of the set. The actors were frozen. The axe continued to swing until the set was a pile of kindling. He definitely got their attention. What they didn't know was that Belasco had never liked the set and had already ordered a new one that was in the process of being built.

SOURCE
Ken Bloom, *Show and Tell* (2016)

OSCAR WILDE
(1854–1900)

441

Oscar Wilde's plays include Vera, or The Nihilists *(1880),* The Duchess of Padua *(1881), and* Salome *(1891), but his reputation as a playwright rests on the four social comedies he wrote in the 1890s before his arrest and imprisonment during the run of* The Importance of Being Earnest *in the early summer of 1895.*

A *Woman of No Importance* first appeared at the Theatre Royal, Haymarket, on April 19th 1893, and repeated the success of *Lady Windermere's Fan*. The critics had complained that in the earlier comedy the action of the play had been held up while the characters delivered themselves of epigrams. But 'English critics always confuse the action of a play with the incidents of a melodrama', said Wilde. 'I wrote the first act of *A Woman of No Importance* in answer to the critics who said that *Lady Windermere's Fan* lacked action. In the act in question there was absolutely no action at all. It was a perfect act.' The critics were duly irritated, and the audience were thoroughly exhilarated. They could have gone on listening for ever to the absent-minded 'Lady Hunstanton', who says of 'Lord Illingworth': 'I was in hopes he would have married Lady Kelso. But I believe he said her family was too large. Or was it her feet? I forget which.' And the interchanges between 'Lord Illingworth' and 'Mrs. Allonby' kept the house in a state of animation:

> *Lord Illingworth (not wishing to follow the rest of the party indoors)*: Yes, let us stay here. The Book of Life begins with a man and a woman in a garden.
> *Mrs. Allonby*: It ends with Revelations.

Thunderous applause and cries of 'author' at the close of the play brought a large man, who was sitting in a box in full view of the audience, to his feet. In clear tones, which were heard in every part of the theatre, he announced: 'Ladies and Gentlemen: I regret to inform you that Mr. Oscar Wilde is not in the house.' As the speaker was Mr Oscar Wilde, he was in a position to know. Much felicitation was in progress behind the scenes, and when Wilde joined the happy throng in Tree's dressing-room such words as 'marvellous', 'unique', 'wonderful' and 'great' were being bandied about. Author and actor congratulated each other. Then:

'I shall always regard you as the best critic of my plays', said Wilde fervently.

'But I have never criticised your plays,' said Tree reproachfully.

'That's why', said Wilde complacently.

SOURCE
Hesketh Pearson, *The Life of Oscar Wilde* (1946)

442

The Importance of Being Earnest was originally in four acts. Alexander [the actor-manager Sir George Alexander] said that it should be in three. Wilde did not like to scrap any of his lines, which, after all, however easily conceived, had been indited with some effort. In telling me that Wilde had fought for nearly an hour to retain a scene, Alexander could only remember the end of their bout:

'Do you realise, Alec, what you are asking me to sacrifice?'

'You will be able to use it in another play.'

'It may not fit into another play.'

'What does that matter? You are clever enough to think of a hundred things just as good.'

'Of course I am... a thousand if need be... but that is not the point. This scene that you feel is superfluous cost me terrible exhausting labour and heart-rending nerve-racking strain. You may not believe me, but I assure you on my honour that it must have taken fully five minutes to write.'

SOURCE
Hesketh Pearson, *The Life of Oscar Wilde* (1946)

GEORGE BERNARD SHAW
(1856–1950)

443

Dublin-born, Bernard Shaw was the leading playwright of his time and his many plays include Man and Superman *(1902),* Pygmalion *(1912),* Heartbreak House *(1920), and* Saint Joan *(1923). He was awarded the Nobel Prize for Literature in 1925.*

Shaw found fault at rehearsal with the last-act explosion in Barry Jackson's production of *Heartbreak House* and demanded a bigger bang. The stage manager assured him that on opening night there would be a bang to remember and accordingly warned the cast to that effect. When the cue came up, Edith Evans spoke the line, then prudently covered her face with her hands. Nothing happened. The audience was halfway out of the theatre when a sudden, thunderous crash brought the ceiling down and sent two playgoers to the hospital. Shaw for once, seemed satisfied.

SOURCE
Sir Cedric Hardwicke, *A Victorian in Orbit* (1961)

444

Arnold Daly was an actor who sprang into prominence in New York as the producer of Shaw's plays. He came to London in 1911 both to play Bluntschli in Arms and the Man *and, he hoped, to secure the American rights to Shaw's subsequent plays. However, when Shaw saw him act he was appalled.*

My Dear Daly

It is no use our squabbling. I am within my rights; and defiance of them, however earnestly you may believe it to be justifiable, is not possible, because you cannot do it single handed, and no-one would join you in the enterprise. I quite understand that it is very hard on an artist to be unable to use the material for his art which he feels to be the right material, and sees lying ready to his hand if only it belonged to him. I have suffered a good deal in that way myself. I have had to look on at actors and actresses who could have made my plays successes for themselves and for me, wasting their time and money and reputations on stuff which they were injudicious enough to prefer to mine. But I could not help that. Their talent was at their own disposal; and they did not choose to place it at mine. Well, the same thing is happening to you. You want my stuff; and I choose to dispose of it otherwise. I may be wrong; but I must follow my own judgment. And just as I found other actors who did believe in me, so you must find other authors who believe in you—not that I disbelieve in you for *all* stage purposes, you understand. I mean that, in my opinion, you are not as good for my purposes as other actors who are at my disposal.

The fact that Arms and the Man has been a failure will not stop you in other directions, as it is not known to the public, and your notices have been very good. It would be waste of time for me to explain the failure to you: if you could see the play as I see it, the failure would not have occurred. As to what you say about drugging and so forth, let me say that I can give you a good character as to your physical training for the work. I have made no complaint of that, because I have none to make. On the contrary I was struck with the way in which you got into trim and kept in it. You behaved badly in other ways. You neglected your own work and claimed for yourself the position of manager, producer and author, with the result that all that part of your business which required minute study and swift, brilliant work: that is, the whole part except the last half of the First Act (which you did very well) was hopelessly bad, and let the performance down, in spite of all the others could do, to a point at which the play was hardly recognizable by anyone who had seen it played before. But though I blame you strongly for not having been so good as you might have been if you had stuck to your work and minded your own business as the others were minding theirs, I do not think you could have saved the situation even if you had done your best. I will not tell you why: you would not believe me.

Whether you believe me or not, I will now tell you exactly how you stand at present. In your own theatre, with your own company under your own management, you are worth what you can make. In an engagement, you are worth in London £15 a week in a certain line of parts. As a juvenile leading man you are worth absolutely nothing at all: any management can lay his hand on half a dozen young ambitioners who can beat you at that for half the money. If you stayed in London for five years and worked hard and made yourself agreeable enough to be welcome as a member of a company, you would improve a good deal; but you are not built that way, and would not do it. Your best plan is to induce Whitney to back you for an American campaign in a new play or plays, and give you another chance on the strength of your London notices. But in selecting the plays, DO face your age and limitations frankly. You are all right for comic and character juveniles; but for staid sympathetic ones in realistic modern tailoring you are out of the question. Your day for Eugenes and Valentines and Apjohns is gone by: you must bow to the clock and the calendar as other men have to do. You are not, for stage purposes, an English gentleman. You are a bit of a genius, and a bit of a blackguard, and a bit of a spoilt child; and you are quite unable to shake any of these bits off on the stage. You have never been hammered by others into the hard-beaten professionalism that makes the capable and biddable actor; and you have been too fond of yourself to hammer yourself hard enough. You must try to get parts in which your qualities and your faults contribute equally to a likeable effect. In addition to your cleverness, you have a sort of Irish Emigrant pathos about you that will always secure you more indulgence than you deserve. With that stock in trade, there is a chance for you yet; and you have my friendliest wishes that you may have luck.

And so farewell, as far as professional relations are concerned. I have done my best for you; and you have done your worst for me; but I bear no malice, and quite recognize that you want to make my plays a success, and honestly believe you could if I would let you. Only I won't, for which you must forgive me as cordially as you can.

Yours sincerely
G. Bernard Shaw

SOURCE
G. B. Shaw, *Collected Letters 1911-25*, ed. Dan Laurence (1985)

445

Having failed to make a pre-arranged visit to Shaw, the American actress Helen Hayes recalled her eventual meeting with him some years afterwards.

I was, however, given a second chance with Bernard Shaw some years later, when we met at Lady Throckmorton's at Coughton Court, Warwickshire. The stately home was built for Lord Francis Throckmorton by Elizabeth I. He had been her ambassador to Mary Stuart. Since the Gunpowder Plot was hatched there, the ensuing explosion resulted in a cloud over the family. The Crown reduced the family title to a simple baronetcy.

The Dowager Lady Throckmorton, whose charming but drowsy son Sir Robert was dubbed The Sleepy Baronet by Charlie [Chaplin], had a pleasant exchange with the then 80-year-old playwright, who was not in the best of moods. For the first time in his life, he was about to have a tooth pulled and he was furious.

Shaw was a testy Irish terrier—spirited and spry—a grizzled, ancient puppy of a man with a complexion so beautiful that it was remarkable. Mary Anderson, herself an octogenarian, who, I believe, had been painted as Juliet by Rossetti, remarked about it with an envy all the ladies present shared.

'Now, Bernard,' she teased, 'I don't want to hear any canard about splashing your face with icewater and rubbing it off with the sleeve of your Norfolk jacket. You don't have a line or a wrinkle. What is the secret?'

'Comfortable boots and open bowels,' he snapped, putting an end to her.

As for me, he had remembered the unfortunate incident that took place years before. Perhaps too well. We were all to suffer that day from his fear of dentistry, and consequently not to be spared his bite.

'You're appearing in Housman's *Victoria*, aren't you?' he asked amiably enough.

'Yes, Mr. Shaw,' I replied. Laurence Housman had told me that G.B.S. was mad about his play.

'Silly little part, isn't it?' Shaw now observed, dispensing with the zenith of both the British Empire and my career in one fell swoop.

SOURCE
Helen Hayes, *On Reflection* (1974)

446

Mrs Shaw received us in a kindly, reassuring way and pointed out with pride the quite hideous pictures and bronze statuettes in the drawing-room; explained that G.B.S. would join us as soon as he had finished a piece of work in his study, and kept up a general chicken-like clucking which meant we hardly had to utter a word. As the clock struck one a big mahogany door was thrown open by a flunkey in braided uniform and white gloves who announced as if at an embassy reception, 'Mr Shaw'. I was standing nearest to the door and nearly caught the old gentleman as he hurtled into the room in his purple woollen suit and green knitted tie. He was unexpectedly tall and rather beautiful; his fluffy blanco-white beard and pale baby-smooth skin were particularly striking. He entered smiling and full of greeting, with a hand extended to be shaken, but I hadn't been told how poor his sight was: I put out my hand to take his and he missed me by a yard, scampering past but calling out joyously, 'I have just put the finishing touches to the play.' 'Oh, well done!'

cried Mrs Shaw, clapping her hands. Sydney gave me a nodding, smiling, satisfied look, as if to say, 'Young man, you are witnessing history in the making.' The footman announced luncheon and we trooped out of the drawing-room to the rather dingy dining room, furnished with a long table and high-backed Windsor chairs which were pulled out and pushed in by two further flunkeys as Shavian bottoms were settled. Before our arrival Merula and I had speculated, depressingly on the likelihood of dewberry soup and nut cutlets, but we were totally wrong. For Cockerell, the niece and ourselves it was roast chicken and white wine; the Shaws pushed little bits of greenery around their plates and sipped water. There wasn't much conversation to speak of as G.B.S. talked continuously, mostly recounting the jokes to be found in *In Good King Charles*, etc. and falling about with laughter in his slatted wooden chair. Sydney attempted to get him on to heavier things such as the likelihood of war but he dismissed everything as 'bally-hoo' except what he had given Newton or the King to say in his comedy.

Back in the drawing-room Mrs Shaw gathered her niece, Merula and me at a bronze bust of Shaw, standing on a pedestal, while we had our coffee. 'This side', she said 'shows Shaw the philosopher. Now come round here!' We shifted a few paces and were joined by the great man who stood listening smiling and approving. 'From this angle', Mrs Shaw explained, 'you see Bernard the humourist. You will notice the mouth turns up at the corner; while from this side'—we all shuffled back to our first position—'the corner of the mouth turns down: The Philosopher!' We inclined our heads gravely; Shaw looked serious so we took our leave and Sydney shepherded us away. I knew I had met an undoubted man of genius but what had impressed me most, in spite of the overriding garrulousness and the evident self-satisfaction, was the exquisite, almost eighteenth-century courtesy. Shaw's manners were a delightful mixture of formality, ease and charm, of a sort rarely encountered nowadays, except in the very old and very distinguished.

SOURCE
Alec Guinness, *Blessings in Disguise* (1985)

447

You invite Shaw down to your place because you think he will entertain your friends with brilliant conversation. But before you know where you are he has chosen a school for your son, made your will for you, regulated your diet and assumed all the privileges of your family solicitor, your housekeeper, your clergyman, your doctor and your dressmaker. When he has finished with everyone else he incites the children to rebellion. And when he can find nothing more to do he goes away and forgets all about you.

SOURCE
Anonymous hostess. B. Cerf, *Shake Well before Using* (1948); quoted in F. S. Pepper, *Dictionary of Biographical Quotations* (1985)

PHILIP BEN GREET
(1857–1936)

448

One of the great Victorian and Edwardian 'characters' of the theatre, Greet helped Lilian Baylis to run the Old Vic Theatre when she took over its management in 1912.

When he came to the Vic in 1914, Greet was already fifty-six with thirty-five years experience of many kinds of stages. Although an ardent playgoer from boyhood, he had been forbidden to attend the

Vic by an otherwise broad-minded father; and he obeyed the veto (with, no doubt, little temptation to break it) until the night that he approached Miss Baylis. Trained in the old stock companies—he claimed that he had to play nineteen roles in his first week as an actor—he became a touring manager who at one time had twenty-five companies on the road, playing small provincial dates. He worked with William Poel on experiments in near Elizabethan productions,* and in presenting *Everyman*; he ran a school of acting in Bedford Street; he was a pioneer of professional open-air theatre, and (in 1886) inaugurated the Open Air Theatre in Regents Park; for two years he had presented Shakespeare to audiences of LCC schoolchildren at the invitation of the Board of Education; and he had toured with a Shakespearian company throughout America.

The spiritual qualifications of B.G.—as he was usually called—were, for Miss Baylis, more impressive. Like her, he was a devoted Anglican. He was a pillar of the Actors' Church Union, and of the Church and Stage Guild. B.G. viewed Shakespeare as a moral oracle who helps us all to achieve 'serenity of mind' and 'the way of gentleness and mercy' and whose works must therefore be brought to the widest possible audience. In Dame Sybil's [Thorndike] words, Shakespeare was 'the nearest approach to Almighty God that B.G. knew'. (In the nursing home where he died, many years later, he asked the doctor to change his nurse, because the one in attendance didn't know a line of the Bard.) But if he revered Shakespeare, it was not as someone supernatural and remote. As Margaret Webster put it, 'Shakespeare, to him, was bread, breathing and a cup of tea.' He believed in simplicity—and that suited Lilian Baylis's budget very well.

B.G. was tall and sturdy, with a shock of white hair, deep blue eyes, and a cherubic face, which frequently went scarlet with violent rages. He got angry when he couldn't remember his lines, which happened frequently; he would stuff them up his sleeves, or into his hat, or pin them behind a property tree, but he would still drop sections of speeches, and rhubarb his way through the gap. He got angry when he saw (or imagined) that a property had been moved. In the middle of a speech he would say, quite audibly to the audience: '*That* bloody thing should be *there*'—transferring it to the place in which he expected to see it—or 'I'll bloody *kill* him (meaning the ASM) when I get off. As I was saying . . .' He was a belligerent, explosive man; and it was not long before he was at war with Lilian. They had terrible rows, forgave each other and then did battle royal again. Both were shrewd enough to realize that they couldn't do without each other, at that time. His value to her is plain. He knew about Shakespeare—as much as, if not more than, anybody in the theatre. He knew about actors: he had trained scores of them, and he brought a number to the Vic. He knew about management and production on the cheap, having to survive one disaster after another and come up smiling—or fighting. He knew about opera—enough, at least, to help in productions. He knew about audiences. As he never demanded—indeed, never encouraged—novel readings or original business, and as most of the actors were used to working together, the plays could be staged in rapid succession with little rehearsal—a necessity at the Vic. And he did it all free—for the first year, at least. Later he took 'expenses'.

* *Poel (1852–1934) was committed to staging Shakespeare in a proper 'Elizabethan manner of presentation', believing that the nearer a production is to the text, the more theatrically effective the result.*

SOURCE
Richard Findlater, *Lilian Baylis* (1975)

CHARLES FROHMAN
(1860–1915)

449

When the Lusitania *was torpedoed in 1915 she claimed among her victims Charles Frohman, the fifty-five-year-old American impresario. As a manager he started out by organizing touring companies.*

The Northern Pacific Railroad had just been opened to the coast, and Charles followed the new route. A series of tragic, dramatic, and comic experiences began. The tour was through the heart of the old cow country. One night, when the train was stalled by the wrecking of a bridge near Miles City, Montana, a group of cowboys started to 'shoot up' the train. Frohman, with ready resource, singled out the leader and said:

'We've got a theatrical company here and we will give you a performance.'

He got Rowland Buckstone to stand out on the prairie and recite 'The Smuggler's Life', 'The Execution', and 'The Sanguinary Pirate' by the light of a big bonfire which was built while the show was going on. This tickled the cowboys and brought salvos of shots and shouts of laughter.

At Miles City occurred what might have been a serious episode. When the company reached the hotel at about eleven in the morning Charles Wheatleigh, the 'first old man', asked the hotel-keeper what time breakfast was served. When he replied 'Eight-thirty o'clock' Wheatleigh pounded the desk and said:

'That is for farmers. When do artists eat?'

The clerk was a typical Westerner, and thought this was an insult. He made a lunge for Wheatleigh, when Frohman stepped in and settled the difficulty in his usual suave and smiling way.

Now began a return journey from Portland that was even more precarious than the trip out. Baggage had to be sacrificed; there was scarcely any scenery. One 'back drop' showing the interior of a cathedral was used for every kind of scene, from a gambling-house to a ball-room. To the financial hardship of the homeward trip was added real physical trial. Frohman showed in towns wherever there was the least prospect of any kind of a house. The company therefore played in skating-rinks, school-houses, even barns. In some places the members of the company had to take the oil-lamps that served as footlights back in the make-shift dressing-rooms while they dressed.

At Bozeman, Montana, occurred an incident which showed both the humour and the precariousness of the situation. Frohman assembled the company in the waiting-room of the station and, stepping up to the ticket-office, laid down one hundred and thirty dollars in cash.

'Where do you want to go?' asked the agent.

Shoving the money at him, Frohman said, 'How far will this take us?'

The agent looked out of the window, counted up the company, and said, 'To Billings.'

Turning to the company, Frohman said, with a smile, 'Ladies and gentlemen, we play Billings next.'

Just then he received a telegram from Alf Hayman, who was on ahead of the company:

> *What town shall I bill?*

Frohman wired back:

> *Bill Billings.*

Hayman again wired:

> *Have no printing and can get no credit. What shall I do?*

Frohman's resource came into stead, for he telegraphed:

Notify theaters that we are a high-class company from Wallack's Theater in New York and use no ordinary printing.
We employ only newspapers and dodgers.

At Bismarck, North Dakota, the company gave 'Moths'. In this play the spurned hero, a singer, has a line which reads, 'There are many marquises, but very few *tenors.*'

Money had been so scarce for months that this remark was the last straw, so the company burst into laughter, and the performance was nearly broken up. Frohman, who stood in the back of the house, enjoyed it as much as the rest.

Through all these hardships Frohman remained serene and smiling. His unfailing optimism tided over the dark days. The end came at Winona, Minnesota. The company had sacrificed everything it could possibly sacrifice. Frohman borrowed a considerable sum from the railroad agent to go to Chicago, where he obtained six hundred dollars from Frank Sanger. With this he paid the friendly agent and brought the company back to New York.

Even the last lap of this disastrous journey was not without its humor. The men were all assembled in the smoking-car on the way from Albany to New York. Frohman for once sat silent. When somebody asked him why he looked so glum, he said, 'I'm thinking of what I have got to face to-morrow.'

Up spoke Wheatleigh, whose marital troubles were well known. He slapped Frohman on the back and said:

'Charley, your troubles are slight. Think of me. I've got to face my wife to-morrow.'

It was characteristic of Frohman's high sense of integrity that he gave his personal note to each member of the company for back salary in full, and before five years passed had discharged every debt.

SOURCE
Isaac F. Marcosson and Daniel Frohman, *Charles Frohman: Manager and Man* (1916)

450

Peter Pan, *by J. M. Barrie, was probably Frohman's most celebrated London production.*

The very beginning of 'Peter Pan', so far as the stage presentation was concerned, was full of romantic interest. Barrie had agreed to write a play for Frohman, and met him at dinner one night at the Garrick Club in London. Barrie seemed nervous and ill at ease.

'What's the matter?' said Charles.

'Simply this,' said Barrie. 'You know I have an agreement to deliver you the manuscript of a play?'

'Yes,' said Frohman.

'Well, I have it, all right,' said Barrie, 'but I am sure it will not be a commercial success. But it is a dream-child of mine, and I am so anxious to see it on the stage that I have written another play which I will be glad to give you and which will compensate you for any loss on the one I am so eager to see produced.'

'Don't bother about that,' said Frohman. 'I will produce both plays.'

Now the extraordinary thing about this episode is that the play about whose success Barrie was so doubtful was 'Peter Pan', which made several fortunes. The manuscript he offered Frohman to indemnify him from loss was 'Alice-Sit-By-The-Fire', which lasted only a season. Such is the estimate that the author often puts on his own work!

When Frohman first read 'Peter Pan' he was so entranced that he could not resist telling all his friends about it. He would stop them in the street and act out the scenes. Yet it required the most stupendous courage and confidence to put on a play that, from the manuscript, sounded like a combination of circus and extravaganza; a play in which children flew in and out of rooms, crocodiles swallowed alarm-clocks, a man exchanged places with his dog in its kennel, and various other seemingly absurd and ridiculous things happened.

But Charles believed in Barrie. He had gone to an extraordinary expense to produce 'Peter Pan' in England. He duplicated it in the United States.

No one will be surprised to know that in connection with 'Peter Pan' is one of the most sweetly gracious acts in Frohman's life. The original of *Peter* was sick in bed at his home when the play was produced in London. The little lad was heartsick because he could not see it. When Frohman came to London Barrie told him about it.

'If the boy can't come to the play, we will take the play to the boy,' he said.

Frohman sent his company out to the boy's home with as many 'props' as could be jammed into the sick-room. While the delighted and excited child sat propped up in bed the wonders of the fairy play were unfolded before him. It is probably the only instance where a play was done before a child in his home.

SOURCE
Isaac F. Marcosson and Daniel Frohman, *Charles Frohman: Manager and Man* (1916)

WILLIAM BUTLER YEATS
(1865–1939)

451

Yeats was an Irish poet and dramatist who, in 1923, was awarded the Nobel Prize for Literature. With Lady Gregory, he founded the Abbey Theatre in Dublin.

Where can we go from here? It seems to me that this is the end of the road for what is falsely labelled 'realism'. The theatre never was and never can be 'real'. Its rule of life is not 'let us *be*', but 'let's *pretend.*' The actor portraying a murderer cannot drum up a 'real' impulse or his performance would clap him in the electric chair. The stage lovers can only pretend their romantic ardour, or the play would be padlocked.

I am reminded that at the Abbey Theatre in Dublin one day, W.B. Yeats, the poet and playwright, was looking for realism in creating the lighting effects for a glorious sunset. Hour after hour, until evening came, he had the electricians try every conceivable combination of colours and rheostats. At last, he saw exactly the effect he wanted. 'That's it!' he cried. 'Hold it, hold it!'

'We can't hold it, sir,' came a stage hand's apologetic voice. 'The bloody theatre's on fire.'

SOURCE
Sir Cedric Hardwicke, *A Victorian in Orbit* (1961)

EDWARD GORDON CRAIG
(1872–1966)

452

Edward Gordon Craig was the son of Ellen Terry, and noted as a stage designer and theatre 'theorist'. Kenneth Tynan, the critic, dined with Craig and recalled their conversation in his book Curtains.

Far from being pent up in the past, Craig keeps in touch with every new development in theatre, cinema, and even television. He was soon urging me to see the new French underwater documentary, *Le Monde du Silence:* 'It's like nothing you've ever dreamed of. Or, rather, it's like *everything* you've ever dreamed of.' He showed a keen interest in 'this fellow Orson Well-ess' of whose films he had heard much. 'I'll tell you a thing about Well-ess,' he said. 'A Paris paper published an interview with him, in which he said that one day he was standing in the American Express in Paris when the door *flew* open to reveal a cloaked figure in a funny hat. *Me!* He threw himself to the ground in veneration. I gathered him up and took him to my studio and spent six months teaching him the art of the theatre.' Craig was now shaking with glee. 'Magnificent, isn't it? *Because I've never met the fellow in my life!*' He nudged me and we rocked.

SOURCE
Kenneth Tynan, *Curtains* (1961)

GEORGE CRAM ('JIG') COOK
(1873–1924)

453

Fired by a vision of a new society 'Jig' Cook founded, in 1915, the Provincetown Players, the most influential group in America's Little Theatre movement. Turning their backs on bourgeois materialism and the conventional realism of the theatre of the time, they set out to establish a new order of dramatic art which would concentrate on 'the relation of the modern writer's social feeling to his art'. Cook and his wife, Susan Glaspell, left the company in 1922, but not before they had discovered and established probably their most famous member, the playwright Eugene O'Neill.

Still another problem was the law. As a small, unlicenced theatre, the Provincetown was not allowed to sell tickets at the box office. Anyone interested in the burgeoning group had to subscribe, receiving seats by mail for all performances. As such a group, the Provincetown changed plays every two weeks and gave three performances a week, one on Sunday. Jig was eventually arrested and ordered by a judge to justify the Provincetown Players and their Sabbath performances. He rose magnificently to the occasion. Already conspicuous because of his leonine mop of blue-white hair, he jumped to his feet and told the judge: 'We are doing it for fun. Of course, profound fun. The fun of death, for instance—the profound amusement of imagined death, followed swiftly enough, Your Honour, by the real moment.' To this rather surprising explanation, the judge responded even more surprisingly. He whipped out his wallet and on the spot took a season subscription. The arresting policeman watched this in bafflement. 'What shall I do if they play again on Sunday?' he asked the judge. 'Oh, do something else,' the judge snapped.

SOURCE
Allen Churchill, *The Improper Bohemians* (1961)

LILIAN BAYLIS
(1874–1937)

454

During her management of the Old Vic Theatre Lilian Baylis presented every one of Shakespeare's plays between 1914 and 1923. She was also well known for what the actor Russell Thorndike here describes as her 'oddities'.

I once saw her receiving Queen Mary, and heard her address Her Majesty as 'dear' in a perfectly natural conversation. This was on the occasion of the Vic's Centenary Matinée [1918].

It was to be a long programme, strengthened with many West End Stars. Sybil and I had been asked to arrange a number of scenes played by different people, showing the history of the old theatre.

The first scene was between the Duke of Wellington and Grimaldi. It was due to ring up at two sharp, and at five to, a reception committee waited to receive the Queen at the Stage door, which led to the Royal Box.

Our Royal Family are noted for their punctuality, but on this occasion, the King was inspecting the Union Jack Club. The King's arrival there caused a congestion of traffic on the Bridge and in Waterloo Road, and the Queen's arrival at the Vic was therefore held up.

The minutes ticked on. Knowing that it would be a very long performance, Miss Baylis began to fear that her Early-doorites [i.e. the early arrivals] would be inconvenienced for the evening's opera. This she would not tolerate, and said that we must really start the show, and ring down directly the Queen arrived. It was pointed out that this would not be at all in order.

But 'I won't keep my Opera Patrons waiting,' was another slogan of Miss Baylis. At ten past two, while Henry Vibart as Wellington and myself as Grimaldi were waiting on the stage, to our horror the curtain suddenly rose without warning. Miss Baylis had taken it upon herself to push the curtain bell, as she called out quite loudly: 'Queen or no Queen, we really must make a start.'

In confusion we began our dialogue, and then half-way through the episode, Miss Baylis cried out from the wings: 'Ring down, She's here.'

She rushed on to the stage, and said: 'Come on, Mr. Vibart, you're dressed as a soldier, and she'll like that. Come on, Sybil, and Russell, bring your red-hot poker and hold it like a gun, so that she'll see you've been a soldier.'

We were pushed down the steps into the crowd of receptionists, just as Her Majesty and Princess Mary were being received by Mrs Randall Davidson.

Miss Baylis treated the Queen as just one of her Vic patrons. 'I'm glad you've turned up at last, dear,' she said, 'and I know it's not your fault being late, as I hear that your Dear Husband going to the Union Jack Club has held up the road. But we've got a long programme to get through, and had made a start, so let's get on with things. Here's John Booth, who has written a history of the Vic, price ninepence, post free tenpence. But we've had a special copy made for you, in a cover made near Stratford-on-Avon, where Shakespeare's wife lived. What's the name of the village?' Someone prompted her, Shottery.

Miss Baylis then asked the Queen not to look at it till later, and pointed to the steps leading to the Royal Box. The Queen, with a smile of appreciation, began to mount the steps, when Miss Baylis dashed at the Curtain leading to the stalls and called out towards the Orchestra well: 'Go on, Corrie. She's here. Play the King.'

The various people who were privileged to visit the Royal Box recounted the extraordinary things which Miss Baylis said. She pointed out the large picture of Emma Cons,* and told Her Majesty that she had hung it there on purpose, as she thought it would be interesting to the Queen.

'We have always had a photograph of the dear King in this Box, but I've hung him over there on the prompt side for to-day. You can see it in the box opposite.'

She went on to say how very fond her patrons were of the dear King and how the Vic Theatre throughout the War had not only had 'His song' (meaning the National Anthem) played by the Orchestra right through, but had insisted on the audience singing it too. She ended her conversation about the King by feeling sure that the Queen was very happy in her Family.

Certainly the oddities of Miss Baylis added to her personal attraction. People just loved her, because she was herself.

**Emma Cons, a social worker, bought the Old Vic after it had closed in 1880. She re-opened it as 'The Royal Victoria Hall and Coffee Tavern', offering a 'purified entertainment and no intoxicating drinks', but the Old Vic it would always be called, and in 1898 Emma Cons' niece, Lilian Baylis, joined her as manager.*

SOURCE
Russell and Sybil Thorndike, *Lilian Baylis* (1938)

455

Emma Cons died in 1912. Her portrait...used to hang in the vestibule...Nearby, hung a portrait of King George V. 'Not quite so large as Aunt Emma's', Lilian Baylis once explained to Queen Mary, 'because your dear husband has not done so much for the Old Vic.'

SOURCE
Ronald Harwood, *Sir Donald Wolfit* (1971)

456

The director Tyrone Guthrie describes his first interview with Lilian Baylis at the Old Vic.

I remember arriving at the stage door; I remember the doorkeeper; the stone steps up into a corridor and a woman cooking a whiting for Miss Baylis's lunch on a little gas ring behind a festoon of faded pink cotton, which was supposed to conceal the fact that the cooking area was in a public corridor.* The office was densely crowded: here a 'Hamlet' chair, there a rickety sofa, a pretty little marquetry chair—forlorn stray from some Edwardian drawing-room. As I wait, the sapphire plush cover of a side table is violently agitated and two dogs rush snarling out—Scamp and Sue. They were quite nasty little dogs, *spoiled* and bad-tempered. Miss Baylis, someone once said, came to dogs too late in life. She loved them not wisely but too well. Beneath that table Scamp and Sue had a home from home—basket, water, bones and so on. The top of the table was covered with portfolios, sketches for sets and dresses.

But the room was dominated by The Desk; a large affair in oak with a roll top. It was densely covered with papers; on the top were knick-knacks. Presents from Margate, Lucerne, the Trossachs, a bowl of Benares brass full of rusty paper clips and shrivelled rubber bands; a bunch of flowers, a tray of dirty tea things and three telephones. Tacked to the roll top was a postcard reproduction of Dürer's *Praying Hands.* All this I remember perfectly—and hearing Miss Baylis in the corridor, asking the person with the whiting what the dogs were getting for lunch. Of her entrance into the office, what she looked like, or said, I have no recollection whatever. Nothing was concluded at that interview. I gathered later that she had not liked me very much, and when eventually she did engage me it was with no feeling of pleasure or confidence. She did not, I'm afraid, regard me as one of those God-sent shining ones, those saviours upon whom she liked to believe her life and that of the old Vic depended. There was a vacancy; I was willing to fill it. The salary being what it was, I guess the queue of applicants did not stretch far.

**'She was mortal enough,' said Russell Thorndike, 'to require a little food during the day besides her cups of tea. Towards the end of a long matinée the salubrious fumes of sausage, bacon or kippers would float over the footlights and fill the stalls accompanied by the sound of fizzling and spitting.'*

SOURCE
Sir Tyrone Guthrie, *A Life in the Theatre* (1960)

457

There was a very old man in the company who had gained his position by reason of the scarcity of men owing to the War, so old was he that he used to say to the ancient chorus ladies of the Opera, 'Good luck, girls.' He had the right to this hilarity. He was a very old

Vic-ite, too, which first stabilised his position. He also claimed the privilege of old age by thinking and talking a good deal about his state of health. He put the best of his failing strength into such parts as he was called upon to play. As often as not his exertions brought him to the dressing-warren (I will not say room) in a state of nervous or temperamental breakdown. He had the greatest sympathy with me, because when I joined the company I was perhaps a sicker man than he. In fact Miss Baylis realised that I was not really fit enough to play such parts as I was cast for, but she, on the Doctor's advice, let me keep in the dressing-room a bottle of brandy which I was allowed to quaff at my own discretion. One night I noticed towards the end of a scene, in which this old gentleman had played an important part, that he was seriously distressed and faint. I gave him a drink of brandy, and told him to help himself whenever he felt he needed it.

A week or so later we had all run out of spirit gum, and as it was cheaper to buy it in large quantities one of the men volunteered to call in on Thomas the chemist in St. Martin's Lane, who sold the best spirit gum on the market. My brandy bottle being then empty, he took it with him to fill up with gum, for, like everything else, there was a scarcity of bottles. That night was a clean-shaven play, 'Julius Caesar', so the bottle remained in my cupboard. I came off from the quarrel scene to find the gentleman gasping in the dressing-room. He had come into the room while I was on the stage to have a nip of the brandy. Unfortunately he took a good gulp of strong gum, so that his tongue and uvula were literally cleaving to the roof of his mouth. Someone meaning to be helpful suggested that when mending a puncture of a tyre, one sprinkled powder to take away the stickiness of the gum, and so he peppered talcum into the unfortunate old gentleman's open mouth. Hearing that it was extremely unlikely that the old gentleman would be able to play his small part in the battle scene, Miss Baylis came out of her office in a panic. She entered the room and saw the old man sitting on the floor and choking. She caught sight of the brandy bottle and jumped to the conclusion that he was drunk. 'I won't have alcohol in the dressing-room,' she declared hotly. 'You must keep it locked up in the office.'

'But, Miss Baylis,' I said, 'he's ill—he's not drunk.'

She looked quickly at the sufferer and said: 'Put out your tongue.' He couldn't, but she saw the whiteness of the Talcum powder and said: 'Quite right, he's ill, poor fellow. I've never seen a whiter tongue in my life.' And she was very angry when we all began to laugh.

SOURCE
Russell and Sybil Thorndike, *Lilian Baylis* (1938)

458

Miss Baylis was very exercised in her mind about a proposed production of *Henry V* which Ben Greet had told her would draw all the First World War soldiers in London. The only thing she knew about the play was The Prayer. At our first meeting, she asked me if I would kneel. Thinking she was about to ask me to play Henry, I told her that at present I could neither kneel nor walk, but that I hoped to get better soon. She then knelt down by her roll-top desk, with one hand resting upon the base of the telephone. The prayer which followed was exactly like a business talk over the telephone. The 'Dear God' she addressed seemed to be on the other end of the line. She told Him who she was and what she was praying for, and hoped that in the presence of the soldier home from the front (me), He would listen. She asked Him if it was right to do *Henry V*? It was a long cast and would need more actors. And that meant spending more money. The last sentence of the prayer was that God should send her some good actors—and, as an afterthought—she added the word 'cheap'.

SOURCE
Russell and Sybil Thorndike, *Lilian Baylis* (1938)

459

Miss Baylis puts John Gielgud in his place.

I had an amusing encounter with Lilian Baylis about this time. The Vic was about to open again for a new season, and Lilian sent me one of her characteristic letters (neatly typed, with most of the typing crossed out and her own writing crowded in on top of it) asking me to come down to see her and discuss some of her plans. Delighted and flattered at being considered so important, I stepped into my car and drove to the Vic. I marched in to Lilian's office in my best West End style, with a new hat and yellow gloves held negligently in my hand. Lilian greeted me warmly, and we talked enthusiastically together for half an hour. As I got up to go I said grandly, 'I should simply love to come down some time and act and produce again at the Vic for you if you'd let me, but of course I'm awfully busy for the next month or two.' Lilian, looking steadily at my rapidly receding hair, said briskly, 'Oh no, dear, you play all the young parts you can while you're still able to!' I left the Vic in a distinctly chastened frame of mind, determined that I would never again attempt to impress so shrewd a judge of character as Lilian Baylis.

SOURCE
Sir John Gielgud, *Early Stages* (1939)

LEWIS CASSON
(1875–1969)

460

Sybil Thorndike, who tells this story, played Volumnia in the Old Vic production of Coriolanus *in 1938 (with Laurence Olivier in the title role), which was directed by her husband, Lewis Casson.*

Tragedy you have to drag out of yourself, and it hurts so frightfully that many actors dodge it. But Larry's Coriolanus was magnificent. He and Lewis worked all-out on it. I remember them having a breathing competition during the rehearsals. Lewis said, 'You've got to do this speech all in one breath', and Larry said, 'I bet you couldn't', but Lewis did. Larry has a longer breath than anybody I know. He could do the Matins exhortation 'Dearly Beloved Brethren' twice through in one breath. Lewis could do it in one and a half, and my father in one. All of which is pretty good. As children we used to listen fascinated in church to see if Father could get through the collect in one go.

SOURCE
Elizabeth Sprigge, *Sybil Thorndike Casson* (1971)

461

'Lewis' rehearsals were violent, storm-tossed affairs, during which he barked and growled and roared at his actors, while they seethed or yelled or quaked in their shoes, according to temperament. The loudest retaliation usually came from Sybil. Preparing to start a speech for perhaps the sixth time she would summon up the approximate emotion, draw breath, open her mouth and get as far as, for instance: 'Now I—' 'No!' shouts Lewis. 'But I haven't *started* yet,' expostulates Sybil. 'But you were doing it wrong.' 'Well how can I get it right if you don't let me *do* the speech. What I was trying to—' 'If you start the speech wrong it will be wrong all through—' 'But you didn't even *let* me start. How could it be wrong?' 'The way you took your breath.' 'Lewis! What does it matter how I take my breath? The important thing is for me to know what she *feels* like.' 'Rubbish! The important thing is that you say it so that the *audience* knows what she's feeling, and if you can't do that, we might as well pack up and go home!'

SOURCE
Jonathan Croall, *Sybil Thorndike: A Star of Life* (2008)

CHARLES DORAN
(1877–1964)

462

Charles Doran was an Irish actor and one of the last of the touring actor-managers in the tradition of Frank Benson and Ben Greet. Among those who joined his company at the start of their careers were Donald Wolfit and Ralph Richardson.

Charles Doran's Shakespearean Company was not exactly famous, but at any rate it was better known than the St. Nicholas Players. It was then appearing at the Devonshire Park Theatre in Eastbourne, and one afternoon in June 1921, [Ralph] Richardson cycled over from Brighton to try and get a rise in his profession. He interviewed Doran after a matinée of *The Merchant of Venice*, and was told to recite something. He began, 'Friends, Romans, countrymen.' 'Stop', said Doran. 'Am I no good?' cried Richardson, showing his first sign of disquietude. 'It isn't that. You're standing on my trousers. You're engaged.' 'Wait a minute,' said Richardson, who at that time prided himself on his financial acumen…'I am not, as you might suppose, a rich man. I shall want £2 a week.' Now, Doran, possibly recalling that the Actors' Association minimum was three, said, 'I will give you £3, but you must hand me ten shillings back.' So both of them made a profit.

SOURCE
Sir Harold Hobson, *Ralph Richardson* (1958)

JULIAN WYLIE
(1878–1934)

463

Julian Wylie was a British theatre manager and impresario, who, as a producer, became the 'Pantomime King' of his day.

I saw no signs of the temperamental storms and rages for which he was said to be famous among pantomime artists. Leslie Henson once told me of a rehearsal of *Dick Whittington,* in which he had appeared under Julian's direction. There was an unusually complicated change of set to be negotiated, from a 'Desert' scene to 'A Staircase in the Palace'. In the first there was a trap-door which had to be closed before the curtain went up on the second, in which a lady was discovered singing on the stairs. After a verse or two she was supposed to descend in stately fashion. But this she dared not do, fearing that the trap might still be open.

'For heaven's sake, come *forward*', Wylie yelled each time.

But the lady demurred, and the change had to be rehearsed all over again. At last Wylie could bear it no longer. He bounded on to the stage with a roar, and immediately vanished into the still open trap. There was a murmur of consternation. Then Julian's head suddenly popped up through the hole in the stage. 'I heard you laughing', he announced, though actually everyone had been too much alarmed to see the joke.

SOURCE
Sir John Gielgud, *Early Stages* (1939)

FREDERICK LONSDALE
(1881–1954)

464

A popular and prolific playwright, whose successes include Aren't We All?, On Approval, *and* The Last of Mrs Cheyney *(which opened in 1925 and ran for 514 performances), Lonsdale's greatest triumphs were behind him when the actor Kenneth More first encountered him.*

As I came to know Lonsdale better, I liked him a lot. He appeared even grander than Noël Coward, but I sensed he had not been born to wealth, and indeed his background was humble.

Like me, he had spent his childhood in Jersey, and money was generally short. One Friday afternoon, when he was a boy, his parents were so hard up that his mother told him they had no meat at all for the weekend. Freddie decided to remedy this in the only way he could—by nipping out to the local butcher's shop and pinching a leg of lamb when the butcher's back was turned.

Years later, in the 1930s, at the height of his fame, when he owned a yacht and two Bentleys, Freddie went back to that shop, because the theft had played on his nonconformist conscience. The butcher was alone behind the counter, cutting up a carcass.

'Good morning,' Lonsdale began. 'Do you know who I am?'

The butcher looked at him blankly.

'No,' he admitted. 'Who are you?'

'I happen to be Mr. Frederick Lonsdale. You may have heard of me? I write plays.'

'Oh, yes?'

'Yes. As a matter of fact I have two plays running in London now, at this very moment.'

'Really?' said the butcher, quite unimpressed. 'So what do you want here, Mr. Frederick Lonsdale? Some meat?'

'Actually, no,' Freddie went on. 'You won't remember, of course, but twenty-five years ago a small boy came into your shop one Friday afternoon and stole a leg of lamb. Well, I was that boy, I have come to pay for that meat and to apologise.'

'Ahhh!' shouted the butcher. He picked up his cleaver and swung it above his head. 'So *you're* the little bugger? I've waited all these years for this!'

And he chased him out of the shop and down the street.

SOURCE
Kenneth More, *More or Less* (1978)

THEODORE KOMISARJEVSKY
(1882–1954)

465

Fyodor Fyodorovich Komissarzhevsky, better known as Theodore Komisarjevsky, and known to friends and colleague as 'Komis', was a Russian, later British, director and designer, whose career began in Moscow, but who made his greatest impact directing Chekhov and Shakespeare in London and Stratford-upon-Avon.

In 1937 Komisarjevsky directed *Antony and Cleopatra* at the Memorial Theatre in Stratford. Komisarjevsky cast fellow Russian Eugenie Leontovich as Cleopatra. Unfortunately, her Russian accent was so thick Shakespeare's lines became incomprehensible prompting the respected critic James Agate to write a devastating review headlined:

ANTON AND CLEOPATROVA: A TRAGEDY BY KOMISPEARE

SOURCE
Ronald Harwood, *Sir Donald Wolfit* (1971)

GILBERT MILLER
(1884–1969)

466

The British actor Alec Guinness recalled his first encounter with the American producer Gilbert Miller. It was during the Second World War.

I received a frantic call from, of all people, Terence Rattigan. He was in New York, on leave from RAF bomber duties, and his play *Flare Path* was about to go into rehearsal for Gilbert Miller's production company. Peggy Webster was to direct it. There was no one available, he said, to play the juvenile; I *must* do it. When I pointed out that it would be impossible, because of naval duties, etc., Terry said that everything had been fixed already; Gilbert had approached the British Ambassador, who had contacted the Admiralty, informing them of the propaganda value of the play: the upshot was that I was to be given eight weeks' leave to do *Flare*

Path, if I was willing. Well, I was willing. It would be, in any case, just as useful a war effort as shifting beds while waiting for a ship to be built. Gilbert Miller summoned me to his New York office. 'How much do you want?' he asked. I had heard, in the past, that with Gilbert you should always fly high. Tony Quayle had once lost a job because he had only asked for twenty pounds a week and Gilbert had squealed, 'I never use actors who want less than sixty.' So, as casually as I could, I said I should consider something like five hundred dollars a week as appropriate. The highest salary I had received to date had been thirty pounds. I think even Gilbert was taken aback, but he didn't quibble and generously threw in all taxes and Equity dues.

SOURCE
Alec Guinness, *Blessings in Disguise* (1985)

ROBERT ATKINS
(1886–1972)

467

Actor and director, Atkins served his apprenticeship with Beerbohm Tree and Frank Benson. For many years he was associated with the Old Vic and the Open Air Theatre, Regent's Park, believing strongly in presenting plays as close to the Elizabethan model as possible.

And then there was Robert Atkins. What actor has not tried to imitate his voice—the essence is there but never that idiosyncratic timbre wherein all his bass vowel sounds came through a cavern and down his nose. He it was, at the Open Air Theatre at Regent's Park where the stage is of grass surrounded by real trees and bushes, who stopped a rehearsal and, advancing on an inept young actor, delivered himself of a resounding Johnsonian phrase: 'Scenery by God. The words by the greatest poet the world has ever known. A director—not bad, and then... YOU come on.'

I would love to have been present when he and the actor Ralph Truman were walking beside the docks in Bristol as they espied a four-masted schooner. 'Look at her,' mused Atkins. 'That beautiful barque has sailed the seven seas bringing us tea from Ceylon, jewels from India, silks from China, spices from Samarkand and there she lies about to depart at our behest.' He called to a deck-hand: 'Sailor! Whither sailest thou?' Hardly bothering to turn, the deck-hand replied, 'F— off.'

He was incredibly perceptive over theatrical matters. He could immediately put his finger on a fault. He attended the first night of Peter O'Toole's *Hamlet*. The settings by Sean Kenny, directed by Sir Laurence Olivier at the Old Vic Theatre, the first home of England's National Theatre Company. Expectation was in the air. The house lights lowered. In the stygian gloom of the battlements Francisco and Bernardo began the play...

'Have *you* had quiet guard?'

'Not a mouse stirring.'

Atkins turned to his companion and his hollow boom, ventured, 'That's a *very interesting* intonation—I don't think I'm going to like this.' Theatrically he was right. You cannot be so particular in the first ten or fifteen lines of a play.

Again when John Neville was playing Hamlet at the Old Vic during the Fifties, Atkins was asked later what he thought of him. 'Well, with a little more sex and a little less sanctity he'd make a very passable Laertes.'

At Stratford-upon-Avon it was always the custom for the leading actor to read the lesson in Holy Trinity Church on the Sunday nearest Shakespeare's birthday. In 1945 Atkins was not asked. Extremely annoyed, he cornered Canon Prentice in the High Street, 'Can you adduce any cogent reason why *I* should not be reading the f—ing lesson?' The Canon humbly tried to explain that someone else had been booked earlier, etc. 'Well,' grumbled Atkins. 'You can stuff yer church and you can stuff yer steeple!—except of course the bells which I understand are the most melodious in Warwickshire.'

SOURCE
Donald Sinden, *A Touch of the Memoirs* (1982)

468

Here the writer and actor Robert Speaight is given a piece of Atkins's mind.

I recall a rehearsal of *Othello* at which I slipped up over a trifling piece of business. Atkins advanced with menacing tread from the auditorium on to the stage and, after his characteristic gestatory pause, delivered himself of the following tirade:

'It's all this bloody education. Forget your Latin, forget your Greek, forget all the French and German that you've ever learnt…for God's sake, be *primitive.*'

SOURCE
Robert Speaight, *The Property Basket* (1970)

469

Everyone who has ever worked for Atkins has endless stories of his remarks, my own favourite being one of Michael Bentine's, dating from the time when that genius was a struggling juvenile and cast as Demetrius opposite the statuesque Helen Cherry. 'Put in some lifts, my boy' advised Robert, and Michael experienced his first uncomfortably high heels. Tottering uncertainly on to the stage he was greeted by a roar from the auditorium. 'You're supposed to come from Verona, my boy. Not bloody Pisa.'

SOURCE
Kitty Black, *Upper Circle* (1984)

470

I had heard of the legendary Robert Atkins, almost the last of the Shakespearean actor-managers. Over eighty years old by this time, he had been directing recently at the Regent's Park Open Air Theatre in London. Years before, he had been responsible for some of Stratford's most celebrated productions. Even in my short period on the outermost fringe of the profession, I had heard actors speak of Robert Atkins with equal amounts of affection and fear. They all mimicked his resonant articulation, raising a hand that quivered in beneficent tandem with the fruity throb of his voice. I had listened enthralled to all the stories: how he had remarked to a young actress playing Peaseblossom in *A Midsummer Night's Dream*, when she had failed to appear in one scene and he found her cast down on the ground in despair, head in her lap: 'It's no good looking up your entrance—you've missed it.' How he was passed over in favour of the young Michael Redgrave as the reader in Stratford Church's celebration of Shakespeare's birthday. As Redgrave approached the lectern, Robert's fruity bass echoed scornfully around the congregation: 'Give me one cogent reason why I should not read the fucking lesson.' And how, after glorious years as star director of the Stratford-upon-Avon Memorial Theatre Company, he was summoned to the office of Sir Fordham Flower, Chairman of the Board and founder of the famous Midlands brewery, there to be summarily dismissed from the post he loved. Bobby was silent while Sir Fordham spoke for several minutes, thanking him for his outstanding work and for the magnificence of his productions and performances. Sir Fordham finally ground to a halt. Robert said nothing. Then, taking his time, he walked to the door, opened it with a flourish, turned and remarked gravely, 'Flower's Ale is piss...'

SOURCE
Martin Jarvis, *Acting Strangely* (1999)

BEN TRAVERS
(1886–1980)

471

Ben Travers was the author of a string of hugely successful farces. His first was an adaptation of his own novel, The Dippers. *His first major success was* A Cuckoo in the Nest *presented at the Aldwych Theatre in 1925.*

In those days the theatre was governed by the feudal system. Certain actor-managers staked their claims to certain theatres and stayed there for years on end: Beerbohm Tree at his Majesty's, Cyril Maude at the Haymarket, George Alexander at the St. James's, Bourchier at the Garrick, Oscar Asche at the Adelphi, Seymour Hicks at the Vaudeville. Generally speaking they maintained the same supporting cast in each case, and at that time it was an accepted custom for an actor-manager's wife to be his leading lady; at any rate on the stage.

SOURCE
Ben Travers, *Vale of Laughter* (1957)

472

Charles Hawtrey, having originally had the option for the farce The Dippers, *had sold it to T. C. Dagnall as a vehicle for Cyril Maude, on the understanding that Hawtrey should produce it. He had already asked for various revisions from Ben Travers and yet on the first day of rehearsal Ben Travers arrived at the Criterion Theatre to discover Charles Hawtrey with a massive red pencil in his hand methodically scoring line after line of dialogue from the pages.*

The pencil duly hovered—struck. Out. A cry of anguish burst from my lips.

'Oh, Mr Hawtrey—'

He glanced up at me over his glasses. His countenance softened in a smile of welcome—'Oh, there you are.'

'Mr Hawtrey—that last line. Must that go? I'm sorry, but really I always thought it was—rather a good line.'

He gazed at me. He spoke in a tone of gentle incredulity.

'A good line? My dear boy, it is an *excellent line*. Don't on any account lose it. Put it in another play.'

SOURCE
Ben Travers, *Vale of Laughter* (1957)

GEORGE ABBOTT
(1887–1995)

473

George Abbott was an American producer and director whose extraordinary career spanned nine decades. Universally known as 'Mr Abbott' he brooked no argument. When an actor asked him, 'What's my motivation?' he replied. 'Your job.' In New York, while directing Say Who You Are, *he instructed the leading actor, Francis Matthews, to take an ashtray from the mantelpiece and place on a table downstage. Matthews enquired why he should do this, given neither he nor anyone else on stage was smoking. Mr Abbott replied: 'Because I ask you to, Mr Matthews.'*

After one try-out performance of a musical, Abbott said to the songwriters, 'This song is out, that song is out.' The songwriters got their hackles up and threatened to send for their lawyer. Abbott replied, 'Don't send for your lawyer unless he can write songs.'

SOURCE
Ken Bloom, *Show and Tell* (2016)

EUGENE O'NEILL
(1888–1953)

474

O'Neill won four Pulitzer Prizes for his plays and was awarded the 1936 Nobel Prize for Literature. His career was launched via the Provincetown Players, an influential collective of artists, writers, intellectuals, and amateur theatre enthusiasts who, under the leadership of the husband-and-wife team of George Cram 'Jig' Cook and Susan Glaspell, produced two seasons in Provincetown, Massachusetts (1915 and 1916) and six seasons in New York City between 1916 and 1923. After the departure of Jig Cook, O'Neill became one of the 'Triumvirate' that steered the group, until he too left in 1926, three years before the Provincetown closed for good. All God's Chillun Got Wings *was first produced by the Provincetown Players in 1924.*

Though the Triumvirate [O'Neill, Kenneth Macgowan, and Robert Edmond Jones] appeared to be heading up a far more formal Provincetown than the one under Jig Cook, it was still capable of arousing violent controversy—as a truly Bohemian theatre should. This happened first with *All God's Chillun Got Wings*, which dealt with the ever-touchy subject of marriage between a Negro and a white girl. At one point onstage, the girl kisses her husband's hand and this, together with the idea of miscegenation, produced a storm in the press. Even before the play opened a photograph of Mary Blair, who played the wife, was syndicated under the heading: WHITE ACTRESS KISSES NEGRO'S HAND. The Provincetown subscribed to a bureau which up to now had duly delivered small monthly batches of newspaper clippings. Now the clippings began to arrive in bales. Later, it was figured that the cost of the clippings on *All God's Chillun* exceeded the cost of scenery for the play.

the audience seated all around as in a circus. The phrase hadn't yet been invented, but this would be theatre in the round.

Larry conducted a lightning rehearsal with the company, improvising exits and entrances, and rearranging business; George Chamberlain and I, assisted by the critics of *Dagbladet,* the *Daily Telegraph* and *Paris-Soir,* arranged eight hundred and seventy basket chairs in circles round the ballroom. Miss Baylis put on her academic robes and kept things going with royalty and ambassadors till we were ready.

The audience thought it a gallant effort and were with us from the start; actors always thrive on emergency and the company did marvels. But *Hamlet* is a very long play. After two hours of improvisation the actors became exhausted and a little flustered. The finale was a shambles, but not quite in the way the author intended. Still it had been quite a good evening; royalty looked pleased, ambassadors clapped white-gloved hands and the press next morning acclaimed a 'sporting gesture' and a *Hamlet* of more than ordinary vitality.

The performance would have worked better if we had been permitted to use all the entrances to the hotel ballroom. But one—the most effective one, a double door at the head of a short flight of steps—was strictly forbidden. The head porter, six foot six, in frock coat and brass buttons, was obdurate. 'This door cannot, it must not, it will not open.' Ours not to reason why; besides, there was no time for argument. The reason emerged next morning. I asked the man, who seemed a reasonable and friendly person, why he had been so firm. 'I will show you,' he said, and tiptoed down a veranda towards the double door. In the architrave was the nest of a pair of blue-tits; the little hen, nervous but gallant, fluttered about our heads. 'If this door had been used, she would have deserted her eggs; you wouldn't have wanted that.'

SOURCE
Sir Tyrone Guthrie, *A Life in the Theatre* (1960)

488

He saw talent in unlikely places but sometimes refused to recognise it in the well-established. One day, cashing a cheque in a London bank, he spied a cherubic face behind the grille, a man quite unknown to him to whom he said, 'What are you doing in a cage? Come out and be an actor.' It was like a call from the Sea of Galilee. The young man left his money-changing and took up a career in the theatre, not perhaps a tremendously successful one but at least it was a happy life.

SOURCE
Alec Guinness, *Blessings in Disguise* (1985)

489

The idea of an open stage theatre must have been in his mind, however vaguely, for years before I knew him, but the determination and enthusiasm to put such an idea into practice came to him, I am sure, during a night of terrible storm in June 1937, in Denmark. It was the first night of Olivier's *Hamlet* at Elsinore, with the Old Vic Company, before a cluster of crowned heads gathered from all over Scandinavia. The performance was supposed to have taken place at Elsinore Castle, on a set similar to what we had used in London placed at one end of the large courtyard, facing serried ranks of slatted chairs. Weather conditions were so appalling by four in the afternoon that messages were sent to the royal parties cancelling the show, but they were already making their sedate ways and could not be turned back. It was decided to present the play in the ballroom of the Marienlist Hotel where the company was staying. It was a large cream, ochre and gilded room with a pocket-sized stage standing high at one end, on which there was sufficient room for an upright piano, a potted palm and a three-piece band. Tony quickly marked out a circle in the middle of the room, which would be the acting area, surrounded it (with everyone's help) with little gilt chairs, leaving two or three avenues for entrances and exits and access to the little stage, which could be mounted by a few steps. The company was given the briefest instructions: 'Suggest you use the platform for Claudius and Gertrude in the play scene. Get rid of the piano. I love the palm. Could leave it. As you will. Larry will be in charge. Use any entrance you can find. Be polite to Kings and Queens if they get in your way. Alec, make your entrance as Osric through the French window.' 'But, Tony, they give on to the beach. There's a roaring wind, heavy seas and lashing rain.' The telegraphese continued: 'Arrive wet. Very dramatic. Polonius, use the service door. When you are killed, wrap yourself up in those vulgar velvet curtains. Rather startling. No time for more. Larry will work out a few details. Enjoy yourselves. I'm going to explain to the old lady (Lilian Baylis) what we are up to. She's having a little lie-down. Must break it gently.' And he was gone taking the gleam in his eye with him. Larry arranged things swiftly and to the point but much had to be left to improvisation.

It was the most exciting theatrical experience most of us had ever had. There was an energy, company-spirit and sense of achievement, which were quite remarkable.

SOURCE
Alec Guinness, *Blessings in Disguise* (1985)

490

He often labelled a play in the Shakespeare canon with a single word, such as Spite (for *The Merchant of Venice*), Adolescence (*Romeo and Juliet*), Ambition (*Macbeth*), Spiritual Pride (for *Measure for Measure*), etc., to convey its essential element. He asked me to say in a word what *Hamlet* is about, and before I could give a floundering answer he said, with a frightening smile, 'Mummy!'

SOURCE
Alec Guinness, *Blessings in Disguise* (1985)

491

According to Laurence Olivier's son, Tarquin, it was Tyrone Guthrie who gave Olivier the most valuable piece of advice in his life.

My mother and I went to see Larry as Sergius in Shaw's 'Arms and the Man'. The story has frequently been told but it is an axiomatic turning point in his acting, at the hands of Tony Guthrie as was the previous one with 'Henry V'. Larry could not find any reality in the part, and Guthrie asked him why on earth not, didn't he *love* Sergius? Larry's reply, as they walked down the Manchester pavement, was vituperative.

'Well,' said Tony, 'if you don't love him you'll never be any good as him will you?'

This Larry described as the richest pearl of advice in his whole life, and he came to adore Sergius for his faults, his arrogance and absurdities. He invested him with all his imagination, invented a dreadful little jig for him to dance, each time tripping over his spurs.

SOURCE
Tarquin Olivier, *My Father Laurence Olivier* (1992)

LEE STRASBERG
(1901–1982)

492

Lee Strasberg must accept responsibility for Method acting, the style that characterized his work with the Group Theatre, of which he was a co-founder with Harold Clurman and Cheryl Crawford in 1931. They created outstanding productions including Paul Green's The House of Connelly *(their first, in 1931) and Clifford Odets's first play* Awake and Sing! *These extracts from*

LAURENCE OLIVIER
(1907–1989)

505

Laurence Olivier was a director, producer, and manager, as well as the pre-eminent actor of his generation. Michael Blakemore was invited to become an associate director of the National Theatre in 1970 by Olivier, the founder-director of the company. John Dexter was already in place as an associate director.

The engagement did not get off to a good start, and nearly ended before it had begun. The first hurdle was my contract. Terry Owen [Blakemore's agent] told me the National was offering a non-negotiable £75 a week. Remembering my conversation with John, I asked Terry to persist. He came back saying they wouldn't budge. I couldn't believe that Dexter would accept such a figure, so I asked Terry if he could find out more. The next day he informed me with some embarrassment that John was being paid £125 per week. I was stunned, and not solely about the size of the differential; it would mean starting my new job not as the equal of a colleague I had chosen but as his junior partner, and my salary would make this evident throughout the organisation. It was not the engagement I had been offered. I asked Terry to fight and there was a standoff of about a week. Then Olivier's secretary rang to tell me that Sir Laurence would like me to come and see him.

We met at four o'clock the following afternoon. He greeted me with ominous ease and I realised at once that the National's intractable position emanated from his office. What was the justification, I asked him, for paying such differing salaries? He cited the fact as if it was self-evident that John was much more experienced, had directed a film, and had had a production on Broadway. But then I'd had a production on Broadway, *Joe Egg*, and had received a Tony nomination to boot. Moreover, I was two things John certainly wasn't, a published novelist and someone with fifteen years of honourable service in Olivier's own profession. Did this count for nothing? In a constrained manner we argued back and forth. I began to get a little angry.

'But, Larry, you asked me to choose someone with whom I felt I could work as an equal, and as soon as I do so you promote him over my head! You can't have it both ways!'

He was listening to me as still as a predatory animal and with a smile on his lips that was razor-blade thin.

'I can have it any way I like!' he crooned. Richard the Third had just addressed me.

SOURCE
Michael Blakemore, *Stage Blood* (2013)

BERNARD MILES
(1907–1991)

506

Bernard Miles was an actor, writer, director, and theatre manager, who opened the Mermaid Theatre in 1959—the first theatre to be built in the city of London since the seventeenth century. In this anecdote, the young Nigel Hawthorne had turned down playing Cutler Walpole in Bernard Shaw's The Doctor's Dilemma *at the Mermaid.*

Bob Chetwyn, who was to direct, came on the line and asked me to pop over to the Mermaid Theatre office for tea, 'just to say hello' as we'd never met, swearing blind that he wouldn't talk me into changing my mind.

station. He was a stocky, bear-like man, thirty-nine years old, with curly hair already greying at the sides. He had a pugnacious chubby face, small piercing eyes and a pursed mouth that seemed permanently set in a wry half-smile, as if he were about to break into derisive laughter at the lunacy of the world. Or at the absurdities of the Arts Council, who consistently refused to recognise the value and importance of the work he was doing with young people.

As I entered the scruffy room, Croft was seated in the centre of a half-circle of rickety metal chairs, flanked by three or four Youth Theatre members. Clearly these were lads who had graduated from the playground. They all seemed to be dressed in black leather jackets and motorcycle boots. I stood there uncertainly in my school blazer and cavalry twills. A fair-haired boy of about my age whom I had seen playing Rosencrantz, flicked ash from his cigarette and nodded at me casually. This was Simon Ward who, along with Ian McShane, John Shrapnel, Hywell Bennett, Helen Mirren and Michael York, was to form the nucleus of the Youth Theatre company over the next few seasons.

Croft rose from his chair and greeted me with a hearty handshake. 'Well Martin' he said. There was a crisp northern edge to his voice. He could have been a fighting lord himself. He told me to sit down. I drew up one of the battered chairs. He asked me what I had been doing and I told him about my love of Shakespeare and acting and my hopes of getting into Rada. 'Ah, yes, Rada.' The sardonic mouth and slightly rolled 'r' made me wonder if he disapproved of that mainstream establishment. In fact, I discovered later, two of his leading actors, Jane Merrow and David Weston, were already at the Academy and Simon Ward and Hywell Bennett would soon be following them. I learned too that John Fernald, Rada's principal, regarded Croft's productions with some admiration—even if they contained rather more blood and guts than the supposed refinements of Rada's bona fide drama training. No Barkworth pencil-sharpeners here. I knew the next Youth Theatre production was to be a modern-dress *Julius Caesar* and I told Croft I had prepared a speech of Cassius. 'Ah yes, Cassius. Splendid, Martin...' he said in the same amused tone. Again, I wasn't sure of his attitude.

As I got up I noticed how many chunky concrete pillars there were in the room. They seemed to be holding up the entire building. I moved to a space near the centre. I had been practising in my bedroom for the last week and the combination of speech and movement that I had put together had seemed logical and fluid: cross over to the bed to try to persuade Brutus to join the conspiracy, swing up to the chest of drawers, stalk away with nostrils aquiver when Brutus won't listen, turning my back on him. Then swiftly cross over to look out of the window, where the washing was flapping on the line in next door's garden. Pretty good I thought.

It didn't work out quite like that in this subterranean echo chamber. I started off all right but, when I made my first pre-planned move, I found myself stuck directly behind one of the great concrete pillars. I was completely hidden from Croft's view; indeed, from all the others except Simon Ward who, by leaning slightly to his left, which he did, was the only one who was able to judge how my mysterious Cassius was shaping up so far. Not too well.

Nevertheless, I kept talking, speaking louder to compensate for the unfortunate masking problem. I just couldn't seem to move. I felt utterly rooted. All I could do was continue the speech, projecting madly, until my next 'bedroom' move. This got me out into the open for a couple of lines. Then, as if thrust by some unseen hand, I moved four places to the right, to be obscured once again by another floor to ceiling pillar. I heard my voice rising an octave and bouncing off the walls. I hammered away until my bedroom template allowed me to emerge, still talking, and (thanks to the memory of next-door's washing) fling myself upstage, before turning sharply, in plain sight of my audience.

There was suddenly silence in the room. I sat down coolly. Simon's face was inscrutable. He and the other black-jacketed boys looked at their motorcycle boots. They drew on their cigarettes. Nobody spoke. Croft tapped himself thoughtfully two or three times on his barrel chest, a gesture I was to see him make a hundred times in the future. Tap, tap, tap. Before the image of Miss Fisher and the Forest Woodman could fully materialise, Croft, accompanying his tapping with a slow nodding of the head, regarded me for some moments and said, 'Cassius, yes, well Martin, very good.' Tap, tap, tap again. Then—'Yes, very self-effacing.' Then, with a final double tap and a nod, he invited me to join the company.

SOURCE
Martin Jarvis, *Acting Strangely* (1999)

JACK LYNN
(1923–2012)

518

British actor and director Jack Lynn was also a teacher, at the Pasadena Playhouse in California and the Royal Academy of Dramatic Art in London. Ian Ogilvy was one of his students.

In my second year, Jack Lynn directed a RADA production for the Southwark Shakespeare festival. Our contribution that year was *Measure for Measure*. It starred Gemma Jones, who was already one of the great white hopes of the academy. I played the small part of Barnardine, 'a dissolute prisoner'. Once again Jack covered me in wig and beard and moustache probably in an attempt to rough me up a little—at least in my outward appearance. He then discovered that a fellow cast member called John Golightly had a strange talent. John had a double-jointed back and could bend himself backwards disconcertingly further than seemed possible. With that in mind, Jack devised a horribly violent scuffle in the jail where John Golightly and I were both prisoners. This entirely superfluous to the plot fight ended with me bending John slowly and sadistically over my knee. With him screaming in agony—and when it looked like his back could take no more stress with out breaking—John would suddenly let everything go, flopping into an impossibly tight upside down U-shape—and at the same moment a stage manager in the wings snapped a piece of wood with a horrible cracking sound. There were screams from the audience and there was a rumour that somebody had even fainted. Jack Lynn was delighted.

SOURCE
Ian Ogilvy, *Once a Saint* (2016)

519

It was in this production that *Measure for Measure* gained a new scene. A couple of actors couldn't make their costume changes in time, so Jack Lynn simply wrote a two-minute cod-Shakespeare scene to give them a little breathing space. A critic, writing in one of the better-class London newspapers, commented that it was '...so refreshing to see the full folio performed at last'.

SOURCE
Ian Ogilvy, *Once a Saint* (2016)

PETER BROOK

(1925–)

520

Some of Brook's productions were controversial, but when his existentialist King Lear *was taken to Europe it was received with rapture.**

Wherever they went in Europe, they were applauded. 'We must change our lives,' Iván Boldizsár, editor of the *New Hungarian Quarterly*, said in Budapest, a city famed for its Shakespearian scholarship and possessing in Miklós Gábor one of the majestic actors of his time. In Belgrade President Tito came to talk to the cast. On the last Rumanian night riots developed in the streets of Bucharest; students trying to break into the theatre, and every part of the house, except the President's box, packed to its distant crevices. Critics in Moscow praised a performance in depth, the emergence of 'psychological and philosophical realities'; at the opening Sviatoslav Richter, the Russian pianist, led twenty minutes' applause from the front row. I like especially a brief news story published in a Czech paper after the first performance in the great green and gold Smetanova Divadlo in Prague:

> Six minutes before *King Lear* was due to start, a man hailed a taxi far away in Strasnice. 'Can we get there in time?' The driver willingly gave it a try. One minute before the time the taxi stopped in front of the theatre. Neither the driver nor the passenger had small money. A banknote changed hands. 'I shall bring you the small change after the performance.' And he did. The name of the taxi-driver is Comrade Buldro, from the Trojická Street Garages. A truly exemplary service.

**Charles Marowitz, the assistant director, recorded an untoward incident during the original dress rehearsal in London. As Paul Scofield, in the title role, embarked on a long speech a photographer began taking shots. Scofield suddenly turned downstage, hurled his cloak at the man, growled, 'Get that thing away from here', and continued his speech as Lear. It happened so quickly, and was so electrifying, that one observer remarked, 'I felt like saying, keep it in!'*

SOURCE
J.C. Trewin, *Peter Brook* (1971)

521

John Kane, who played both Puck and Philostrate in Brook's production of A Midsummer Night's Dream *at Stratford-upon-Avon in 1970, related this anecdote to the author and critic J. C. Trewin. Brook had decided to invite children to the rehearsals as he thought their response might be instructive.*

Most of the children at the *Dream* rehearsal, though they enjoyed the experience, really could not understand what was going on half the time. Still, Kane relates a conversation with one little girl at the end of the performance:

He: Did you enjoy the play?
She: Oh yes, very much.
He: Did you understand what was happening?
She: Oh yes.
He: How did you like the fairies?
She: Very much.
He: Would you have liked them better if they had worn wings and things?
She: Oh no. I liked them best when they were wearing their ordinary clothes. Wings and things don't matter.
He: Have you been to the theatre before?
She: Oh yes. Lots of times.
He: Does your daddy work in the theatre?
She: Yes.

He: What does he do?
She: He's a director.
He: What's his name?
She: Peter Brook.

SOURCE
J. C. Trewin, *Peter Brook* (1971)

522

Peter Brook had been trying to set up a film with the actor Nigel Hawthorne about a Russian Jew with a phenomenal memory but both the money and the additional casting proved elusive.

One morning, I was working away in my office when the phone rang. It was Peter. Would I meet him at two o'clock at the Round House in Camden Town as there was something he wanted me to see? I was under the impression that the Round House had been out of commission for some time. Besides, I lived in the country so it was highly inconvenient for me to come into London at such short notice. But, because it was Peter, I went.

I was first there and waited outside where there were some Portakabins used, I think, as the box office and for various other administrative purposes. Peter arrived and, having introduced me to a young man he described as the director, led the way from the light into the dark [...] Occupying the entire central section of the Round House was a huge white plastic bouncy castle. The young director led us to the 'drawbridge' and we were invited to remove our shoes and, in our stockinged feet, Peter and I solemnly climbed the ramp. Music, quite loud music, filled the whole area. Peter Brook and I stood alone in our socks on the base of the bouncy castle. I watched him carefully as I wasn't sure what was expected of me. Suddenly, Peter started to jump, Well, it was more of a self-conscious spring than a jump. He was very stiff, arms by his side, his face betraying no emotion at all. Still watching him, I followed suit. Every so often, Peter threw himself with some caution and the minimum of abandon against the white plastic battlements and then back to base with a meticulous hop. Not a word was spoken. He just fastened his ice-blue eyes on mine as together we solemnly bounced up and down, I was fairly certain that he expected some kind of reaction from me but decided to play it safe by staring back, confidently radiating an inner assurance.

Finally, with the merest suggestion of an oriental bow, Peter indicated that he'd had enough. Together we returned down the ramp of the 'drawbridge' and replaced our shoes. As we left the Round House, our eyes screwed up against the bright light outside, Peter turned to me to say, 'That was interesting, wasn't it?' 'Yes' I replied. 'Very.' And I meant it. Then I made my way home to East Hertfordshire. To this day, no further reference to our experience on the white, plastic bouncy castle at the Round House has ever been made.

SOURCE
Nigel Hawthorne, *Straight Face*, (2002)

JOHN BARTON
(1928–2018)

523

John Barton, who has died aged 89, was a former don at King's College, Cambridge, who in 1960, became the cofounder with Peter (later Sir Peter) Hall, of the Royal Shakespeare Company; over the next 50 years he had a huge impact on the way Shakespeare is performed, and directed some of the company's most memorable productions.

Bearded, cardiganed, intense and demanding, Barton was a man around whom stories tended to accumulate. As a young director, he reportedly chewed razor blades during rehearsals, mesmerizing his actors as he slowly turned the blades over and over in his mouth until they drew blood. Once, he was so absorbed that he fell backwards off the stage into the orchestra-pit, whereupon he dusted himself down as if nothing had happened and resumed.

In *Directions by Indirections* (1985) his account of Barton's RSC work, Michael Greenwald recalled: 'He has been known to step into paint buckets on otherwise empty stages; while giving his cast notes, he has managed to insert his chair leg into a coffee cup; it is not uncommon to see him driving around Stratford with his car door wide open; he invariably has a half-dozen cigarettes lit at one time during rehearsal because he has forgotten where he has laid each one.'

SOURCE
Daily Telegraph obituary (20 January 2018)

524

Peter Hall overlapped at Cambridge with John Barton, who was already well established in student drama when Hall arrived at Cambridge.

John was already a fiercely professional director, expert at staging and lighting. He dominated the ADC and Marlowe committees with his rigorous demands and would have no truck with amateurism. He was completely obsessed by the theatre and would work round the clock, without thought for sleep or food. He smoked continuously, fell over things, dropped cups of coffee and, to ease the enthusiasm which threatened to possess him, would chew razor blades throughout rehearsals by gently flopping them over and over on his tongue. I have seen many actors and actresses, at Cambridge and, later, at Stratford, mesmerised by that revolving blade. Occasionally, a tell-tale trickle of blood would seep out of the corner of his mouth as John elucidated a particularly difficult textual point.

SOURCE
Peter Hall, *Making an Exhibition of Myself* (1993)

JOHN OSBORNE
(1929–1994)

525

John Osborne was an actor and playwright—and, at the beginning of his career, play-reader.

I became a play reader for £2 a week, taking home nightly some thirty or forty scripts. When I once complained of the burden to Tony, he said, his voice rising to its most imitable pitch, 'But you don't *read* them? Not all *through*?' I ventured some pious pretence about talent being missed through hasty scanning. He picked up a few scripts from my bag and went through half a dozen. Some took him twenty seconds, some half a minute, two minutes at most, a high-pitched, awesome Geiger counter. 'There, that's how you read a play.'

The plays sent in at the time could be divided into a few recognizable categories. A number of them were written by clergymen's wives. Almost every post brought a play about Mary Queen of Scots, the Virgin Queen, Queen Victoria and Lady Jane Grey. These were all regular runners, but Mary Queen of Scots was Red Rum to them all. Then there were the plays about literary figures like D. H. Lawrence or Henry James; Loamshire plays; plays set in the past and plays set in the future where lone survivors of the Atomic Holocaust addressed themselves but not each other. Schoolteachers were almost as prolific as clergymen's wives. I read what was probably Robert Bolt's first play, *A Critic on the Hearth*, and recommended it. Tony made it clear that for someone who had written the best play since the war I had a lamentable critical intelligence.

SOURCE
John Osborne, *Almost a Gentleman* (1991)

DOREEN CANNON
(1930–1995)

526

Doreen Cannon was a New York actress and pioneer of the Stanislavski technique of Method acting. She became head of acting at the Drama Centre in London in 1963. Simon Callow, one of her students, found himself unable to 'be' a character rather than 'acting'. For a long time he was unable to tackle his 'emotional inhibitions'.

It was Doreen Cannon who opened the floodgates. Scene: the classroom at the Drama Centre called the Church, the room in which my right leg had hammered its quarter-metal tattoo. Up there, on that same concrete stage, I was about to perform a 'Life-and-Death' exercise: an extreme situation calling for desperate measures. My scenario was to return home from work early and find my girl in bed with another man. I entered, surveyed the scene coldly, uttered withering phrases, shamed them by my sang-froid, and sulked after the man left. Altogether, I behaved much as people do in West End dramas about infidelity or indeed, for all I know, in life. The script, was, though I say it myself, rather fine, polished and accurate and economical. Mrs C thought otherwise. 'Don't believe it,' she almost yawned. 'Is that really what you'd do if you found your girl in bed with another man? Oh dear. I am sorry for you both.' Not me, lady, I nearly said, the CHARACTER. You know, him (except that in the Method, one never says him, only me). I bit my tongue, and thought: 'Pearls before swine, too bad you can't see it.' But then I thought, 'I'm sick of this, day in, day out, whine, whine it's never good enough for you, I'm always made to feel emotionally impotent, well I'm not.' Through these fumings I heard the New York accent wearily say, 'OK, let's try it again. Only this time, try to give yourself a chance.' Without replying, I turned on my heels, walked out of the room, and paced up and down outside waiting for the cue to begin the scene, gorging like a hungry dog on my hatred of the woman. 'OK, let's go,' the drawl drawled. I opened the door. I spied the adulterous couple. A noise like a lion's roar came from my throat. I seized the man, plucked him out of the bed and hurled him across the room. The girl came to me pleading and sobbing. I flung her back on to the bed. I rent her clothes into tiny shreds. The man, genuinely frightened said, 'Simon....' Another roar, and I picked up a three-seat settee and smashed it on the ground. It broke in half. Ann, the girl, by now really, as herself, terrified, started to cry. 'I've never seen you like this before, stop it, stop it.' 'GREAT!' came a cry from the room. 'Great. That's what it's all about! Do you see that, do you understand that?' she said to the class. 'That is a breakthrough.'

SOURCE
Simon Callow, *Being an Actor* (1984)

RADU PEN CIULESCU

(1930–)

527

The Romanian-born director Radu Pen Ciulescu was another advocate of the Stanislavski technique.

We were, most of us, involved in a production of *Woyzeck* staged by a gentle Romanian Radu Penciulescu whose limited English vocabulary qwas mostly translated directly and wrongly from the French. 'Be more disponible,' he would cry, agitatedly. 'Disponible?' people would mutter. 'What the fuck's disponible?' And then do what they thought it might be. He was generally quite pleased. But then he would scream, 'Don't pose!' The guilty actor, feeling himself accused of narcissism, would become very upset, and then struggle to be spontaneous. 'Don't pose,' the cry would come again. 'I'm *not* posing.' 'Yes, yes, between this word and that one, you are *posing*. You shall not.' Enlightenment. *Pausing* was the offence. Much less shaming.

SOURCE
Simon Callow, *Being an Actor* (1984)

WILLIAM GASKILL

(1930–2016)

528

As a director, Bill Gaskill was especially associated with the Royal Court Theatre in London's Sloane Square and the National Theatre at the Old Vic. In this anecdote, Nicholas Hytner recalls the show that marked the National's 50th anniversary in 2013.

Among the biggest regrets of my twelve years as the National's director is that I found nothing for Maggie Smith, who, like Joan Plowright, was part of Olivier's first company. She was aware of the irony when I asked her to be in the birthday show: irony is one of her special subjects. But she suggested a short enigmatic speech from George Farquhar's *The Beaux' Stratagem*. She said she remembered it because when she played Mrs Sullen, it took her so long to work out what it meant. I didn't believe this: in a rehearsal room, she's always several steps ahead of everyone else. At the party after the show, she spoke to William Gaskill, *The Beaux' Stratagem*'s director in 1970. He admired how still she'd been. 'You told me not to move my hands,' she said, pleased he'd noticed. More than forty years on, she still remembered his note, maybe because it was so practical and unpretentious, and a lesson in how a director should talk to an actor.

SOURCE
Nicholas Hytner, *Balancing Acts* (2017)

PETER HALL
(1930–2017)

529

Peter Hall's first claim to fame came in August 1955 when he was twenty-four and directed the world premiere in English of Samuel Beckett's play Waiting for Godot. *According to Hall, 'On the first night, very little went right.'*

When the performance finished, I met my new and extremely smooth international agent, a man who had promised great things for me in London and America. He was puce with rage and for the first time in our relationship expressed a strong opinion. 'Well, you've done it now,' he spluttered. 'We were just getting you going...and you go and do an awful thing like this.' I decided then and there that he was not for me. I've never been very good at hiding my feelings if my beliefs were threatened. By now, I believed passionately in Beckett and in *Waiting for Godot*. Nonetheless, I was suddenly frightened—which I had not been as the curtain fell.

SOURCE
Peter Hall, *Making an Exhibition of Myself* (1993)

530

When Peter Hall created the Royal Shakespeare Company in 1961, censorship of the theatre by the Lord Chamberlain was still in existence. Nonetheless, the new RSC was having success with controversial new plays such as Peter Weiss's Marat Sade.

The RSC was widely seen as progressive and daring—and the box office boomed.

Most important of all, the debate about the very existence of the Lord Chamberlain hotted up. It began to look more and more absurd that the theatre was gagged by an official of the Court (a practice two hundred years old) and that playwrights did not have the same freedoms as novelists, journalists or broadcasters whose only curb was, rightly, the law of the land.

I prepared an anthology of verse for one of our special poetry evenings at the Aldwych. It included a poem by e.e. cummings which had the word 'shit' in the last line. The Lord Chamberlain promptly banned it. So we printed it in the programme (which was not against the law). At the performance, the house-lights were raised when the poem should have been spoken, and the audience were asked to read it silently to themselves. The RSC made front-page news again.

SOURCE
Peter Hall, *Making an Exhibition of Myself* (1993)

531

Michael Blakemore had mixed feelings about his near-contemporary and fellow director, Peter Hall.

As for Peter Hall, after he left the National he continued to hurtle down the motorway of his formidable career, usually with a full load of passengers aboard, one studying the road map, another occasionally taking the wheel, another unwrapping the sandwiches, all assuming they were there for the journey. Occasionally one of them would find himself sitting stunned and abrased on the hard shoulder, and staring in disbelief as a carload of people vanished over the hill. One such was John Bury, who had been dropped from the production of *The Ring* at Bayreuth, which the two men had been planning for years.

What Peter had in common with Larry [Olivier] was a driven, almost heroic capacity for work, and the qualities I had deplored in him at the National I rather came to admire in his later career. Like all of us who work freelance he used his hits to bury the memory of his flops and to set up his next string of engagements. I enjoyed a number of his many productions, among which were his *Merchant of Venice* with Dustin Hoffman and his international success with Oscar Wilde's *An Ideal Husband*. He was cleverer than the producers he worked for, and devised contracts that ensured that he, if not they, was never out of pocket whether his shows succeeded or failed. When any one producer could no longer afford him he would move on and find another.

He was constantly flying back and forth across the Atlantic, pursuing more opportunities than a single director could possibly accommodate. This provoked my New York agent, Robby Lantz, who had also briefly represented Peter, to invent a conundrum. 'Why', Robby would enquire in his permanently amused Berliner accent, 'is Concorde a disaster for Anglo-American theatre?' 'Why?'

you would dutifully ask him, and he would answer, 'Because it reduces the preparation time of Peter Hall's productions from eight hours to three!'

SOURCE
Michael Blakemore, *Stage Blood* (2013)

HAROLD PINTER
(1930–2005)

532

Harold Pinter was a Nobel Prize-winning British playwright, screenwriter, actor and director, who first came to prominence with his play The Birthday Party *in 1957. When he was a young actor of twenty working in Scarborough, the future playwright Alan Ayckbourn was cast in a production of* The Birthday Party *which Pinter was set to direct.*

When he arrived in Scarborough he was in a very defensive, not to say depressed state. We had probably three weeks to rehearse. I remember asking Pinter about my character. Where does he come from? Where is he going to? What can you tell me about him that will give me more understanding? And Harold just said, 'Mind your own fucking business. Concentrate on what's there.'

SOURCE
Michael Billington, *The Life and Work of Harold Pinter* (1996)

533

Nicholas Hytner, director of Britain's National Theatre between 2003 and 2015, recalls two encounters with the playwright Harold Pinter.

Shortly before Harold Pinter won the Nobel Prize in 2005, I was having dinner with the designer Bob Crowley in a restaurant not unlike the one he lampooned in *Celebration*; three years earlier I'd chickened out of saying that I couldn't share his enthusiasm for reviving a thirty-minute play that had only recently been produced at the Almeida. We saw Harold having dinner in the opposite corner. Bob waved to him: they'd worked together often. Maybe I should have been on my guard when Harold's wife, Antonia Fraser, made a hasty exit about twenty minutes later, but suddenly Harold was bearing down on me.

'You're a fucking liar,' he shouted. The entire restaurant went silent. 'You're a fucking liar, and you're a fucking shit.' I had no idea what to say, so I said nothing.

'You told me you would revive *Celebration* at the National Theatre,' said Harold quieter now, but with Pinteresque menace. 'You told me you'd put it in a double bill with *The Room*. You're a liar and a shit.'

'I'm really sorry if I gave you that impression, Harold,' I said meekly. 'That wasn't my intention. I'm genuinely sorry.'

'Don't fucking apologise to me,' roared Harold, 'I'm not interested in your fucking apology. You're a shit and a liar, and now I've fucking told you.' And he left the restaurant.

Bob waited for all the other tables to stop looking at us. 'Rite of passage,' he said. 'You can't call yourself a director of the National Theatre until Harold Pinter has called you a shit.'

SOURCE
Nicholas Hytner, *Balancing Acts* (2017)

534

In 2007, I sent word to Harold that we'd like to do a new production of one of his early plays, *The Hothouse*. He couldn't have been more charming or enthusiastic. He was delighted we were doing it,

Gielgud was my idol in many ways, not necessarily as a director. So it came about, and he cast Michael Bryant as the German boy, and Brian Bedford as the son, and it was an extraordinary experience. I remember my first day, I suppose my first day in the English theatre. I went to the rehearsal, very much the new boy, incredibly nervous, and John directed a move, put in a move, a physical move, on every single line of the first, say, fifteen minutes. 'You can stand up there, you can sit down there, it would be amusing if you took the dishes out there,' and so on, but on every single line. And then, just as we were closing the rehearsal, he said: 'Oh well, let's just run it, it'll be fun.' Everything was either 'fun' or 'amusing'. So, they indeed ran the first ten minutes, and it was horrendous in the sense they all looked like a lot of mice on amphetamines, racing and running about. And John suddenly rose, one of those quasi-passionate excalmations of his, and said. 'This is a nightmare, stop it, what are you all doing?' and Brian Bedford fearlessly came down and said: 'We are doing, John, or trying to do, the moves you have given us.' And John looked genuinely puzzled and said: 'What on earth for? Everyone knows I can't direct.' That was my first day in the theatre.

SOURCE
Peter Shaffer, interviewed by Richard Eyre, *Talking Theatre: Interviews with Theatre People* (2009)

ALAN BENNETT
(1934–)

539

Alan Bennett is a playwright, actor, and national treasure.

I suppose I go to the theatre thinking anything may happen. I mean, quite apart from the play, somebody might collapse on stage. I know that seems frivolous, but I think that's an element in what an audience is there for—the possibility of disaster. And the possibility of triumph as well, but it's the uncertainty. Having performed, I know the sheer terror of it: it is quite a perilous proceeding. If you're in an audience and something goes wrong on stage—you know, somebody dries, say, or whatever—the audience is like a cat suddenly seeing a bird: it's on to it. There's a huge tension in the auditorium. Quite frightening. I do think of an audience as slightly like a wild beast.

SOURCE
Alan Bennett, interviewed by Richard Eyre, *Talking Theatre: Interviews with Theatre People* (2009)

EDWARD BOND
(1934–)

540

The actor Nigel Hawthorne had become friendly with the playwright Edward Bond while working at the Royal Court.

I was doing a season of plays at the old Playhouse Theatre in Sheffield when Colin George, who ran the place, asked whether

I would care to do a lunch-time production. Immediately, I thought of Edward and wrote asking his advice. The outcome was his permission to direct *Black Mass*, a short piece, ideal for the slot, and on an anti-apartheid theme, which he rightly thought might appeal to me because of my South African background.

It occurred to me that the audience might need a little help understanding the complexities of the apartheid system, so at the box office, without any explanation we issued two types of tickets, white and coloured—red, green, orange or magenta—whatever we had in stock. After the play had been going for three or four minutes, we slammed on the house lights and two actors dressed as South African policemen strolled on, one of them explaining in a South African accent that it would appear that there were some people sitting in the wrong seats, so would members of the audience kindly hold their tickets aloft for inspection? Students from Sheffield University then infiltrated the house armed with torches to inspect the tickets and finally a decision was made. 'It is against the law for holders of tickets other than those coloured white to be seated anywhere but the last two rows of the theatre. Before the play can continue, would those people in error take their lawful places?'

The audience cooperated like a dream and, after a lot of shunting around with couples being separated and families divided, we lowered the house lights and proceeded with the play. When it came to the interval, another couple of surprises were in store for members of the public. In order to get a drink, they had to present their ticket. If it was a white ticket, they were laughing. The surroundings were tastefully decorated with arrangements of South African flowers and travel posters adorning the bar but, on the other hand, if the tickets were not white but coloured, their holders discovered a partition dividing the bar, the 'coloured' side with old bits of paper scattered on the floor, baked bean tins for ashtrays and their drinks served in paper cups. The lavatories were similarly governed by 'separate development' essentials. No soap or towel or even toilet paper, just small sheets of newspaper held together with string and, when you sought privacy, there was no key, just a photograph of the chief architect of apartheid, Dr Verwoerd, adorning the back of the door and watching your every move. The audience took it all in good part and I think it added to the message of Edward's play rather than detracting from it.

SOURCE
Nigel Hawthorne, *Straight Face* (2002)

541

Simon Callow was back at the Royal Court playing in the revival of Edward Bond's Restoration. *Bond was also directing but Callow was not finding his notes helpful and asked Bond for some specific insights into his character Lord Are.*

'Um. He's like a piano being played with a stiletto knife.' Thanks a bunch, I thought. 'And another thing: he's like an eighteenth century carriage with a steam engine inside.' How could I explain to Edward that what I needed was something much simpler, something concrete, something, which would give me a *sensation*. 'I think I begin to see what you mean,' I lied. 'Let's try the speech again.' After two lines, Edward stopped me. 'It is a little bit better,' he said, 'but you're still making it too complicated. Don't you see, when he talks to the audience, he's talking to his friends. He expects them to agree with him. 'Aaarrgh,' I cried. I was on to something at last. I winged a couple of lines. Edward laughed—for the first time. I tried a few more—then the whole speech. I'd got it. It all came in a great rush. The essential sunniness of the man's temperament became clear. His whole life is played out in the confidence of his friends' approval; and what else matters to a gentleman? We packed up and went home. We both knew that the penny had dropped. The rest was easy—just doing it. The life of the character had been established, however, and it would flourish.

This sense of independent life in the character was not strange to Edward. It was he who had answered, when I asked why the man was called Lord Are (R), 'That's all he would tell me.' And he who had told me the wonderful story of his writing *The Bundle*. One of the characters had begun to take over every scene in which he appeared. The RSC phoned every day to find out how the play was progressing. 'Fine,' said Edward, 'but I have no idea how it'll end, because of this character.' Finally, they said 'We've got to have the play next week to start casting.' 'All right,' he said, 'I'll kill him.' He did, and the play was ready by the weekend.

SOURCE
Simon Callow, *Being an Actor* (1984)

PATRICK GARLAND
(1935–2013)

542

Patrick Garland was a noted British director who rose to the challenge of directing Rex Harrison in the revival of My Fair Lady *at the beginning of the 1980s and, later, wrote a biography of his leading man.*

Rex returned in the afternoon, and somewhat timidly I began to introduce the changes that I'd made in the morning, somewhat intimidated, and certainly apprehensive of his sudden rages, aware that Rex was always very conservative and disliked any form of change. However, as he began to perform the scene, and as I'd already observed, was in many ways ahead of all the others, and most secure on his lines, the moves which I had changed in the morning no longer seemed to be quite as essential as I had thought. In fact, Rex appeared positively jaunty, and bounced the lines back and forth with pleasure and with charm, and I found myself interrupting far less than I thought I was going to have to do; eventually it began to dawn on me that there was nothing wrong with the original blocking, as so long as Rex was on stage there was no need to alter anything because where he was, there the focus was. He could be behind the study chair, bent behind the globe crouching over a gramophone, in a weak barely lit (although that was unlikely!) far corner of the stage, wherever he was the eye would automatically fall. It is saddening to have to admit, but such is the power of Rex's physical presence, that he could be anywhere he liked on stage and people would look for him; remove him from the scene and put in, dare I say it, an inferior, or less charismatic actor, and the eye immediately became restless in its intuitive search for harmony. This to me was as vivid an illustration of what is meant by that mysterious word 'star quality' than almost anything that I can think of.

SOURCE
Patrick Garland, *The Incomparable Rex* (1998)

543

With three of the principals off on the afternoon that Rex was going to look at the understudy, Higgins, Eliza, and Doolittle, Rex murmured to me, as he saw Cathleen sitting in the wings in her wheelchair: 'All we need is for Cathleen to feel sick, and we might as well all go home. There won't be anybody in the house!' In fact, later that day, it was absolutely extraordinary. Obviously we had to tell the truth, and advertise the fact that Rex Harrison would not be performing that afternoon and there were queues around the block demanding their money back as long as there had been earlier for advance booking to buy their tickets to see him perform. Beyond the theatre were officials with bullhorns and loud hailers, and no less that four tough-looking Boston cops standing around the box-office window. Outside the foyer, keeping the queues in line, as they threatened to get out of control, were several other Boston cops on horseback wielding night-sticks. When people asked me, as from time to time they do, what is the definition of a star, I often think of that image outside the box-office of the Boston theatre. A star is when you are not appearing at the matinée, and the local police force has to send out uniformed cops on horseback to stop the crowds from rioting. Even in extremity, I confess I had to hand it to Rex.

SOURCE
Patrick Garland, *The Incomparable Rex* (1998)

SIMON GRAY
(1936–2008)

544

The English playwright described some of his experiences on Broadway.

There was a party at Sardi's to celebrate the opening of my first play on Broadway. The producer, whose only venture into the theatre this was to be, sat sobbing at the end of a long table in an upstairs room that had emptied with the arrival of the *New York Times* review (epoch of Clive Barnes).

GRAY. Oh, come on now, no need to cry now. Only a play! *(Little pause.)* Old chap?
PRODUCER. Only a play? When I invested all my wife's money in it? And I haven't told her yet?

Early the following morning, my wife and I stole with our luggage through the hotel lobby, to avoid the manager who had given us cheap rates, a high standard of service and mysteriously obsequious smiles because, as we'd also learnt at the Sardi's party, he too had invested money in us.

Back in New York some months later, with a new piece. Standing in a bar next to the theatre during the interval of the second preview, my third large whisky smouldering in my mitt. A friendly figure hovers beside me, orders himself a drink.

FRIENDLY. (*after a pause, turns*). Saw the same guy's last. That was crap too.
GRAY. (*shakes his head gloomily*). State of Broadway.
FRIENDLY. Somebody ought to give him the bum's rush. Got enough crap of our own. Don't need his.
GRAY. Yeah.

A smooth theatrical production, though, interrupted only by life itself. Our youngest actor mugged twice in his dressing-room during the first week of performance. One of the understudies raped in a car-park during rehearsals. Our leading lady held at knife-point for two hours behind the theatre. Flying home after a week of previews, I phoned from the airport.

STAGE-MANAGER. Hello.
GRAY. Hello, Simon here.
STAGE-MANAGER. Oh, hi, Simon, what can I do for you?
GRAY. Just wondering how it went this evening.
STAGE-MANAGER. The first act went pretty well, I thought.
GRAY. Good. (*Pause.*) And the second act?
STAGE-MANAGER. There wasn't a second act.
GRAY. Oh. (*Pause*) Any particular reason?
STAGE-MANAGER. The company went to see *Hello Dolly*.

GRAY. Instead of doing the second act, you mean?
STAGE-MANAGER. Right.
GRAY. Oh. (*After a pause.*) Any particular reason?
STAGE-MANAGER. Somebody reported a bomb in the theatre.
GRAY. Oh. (*Attempts lightness.*) Which?
STAGE-MANAGER. (*laughs politely*). Ours.

On my third visit to Broadway, all went well apart from the discovery of the wardrobe mistress's body in the wardrobe an hour before curtain up on the first night. Natural causes, however, which in New York, opening doors on to inexplicable mysteries, are more alarming that the run-of-the-mill foul-play.

SOURCE
Ronald Harwood, *A Night at the Theatre* (1984)

545

The casting itself turned out to be the usual exhausting process, only more so. Casting is *always* more exhausting in the States, and casting at the Matrix turned out to be more exhausting than anywhere else in the States, in my experience anyway, partly because a lot of the actors were involved in television series and so their schedules caused problems, and partly because Kristoffer Tabori, the director, and Joe Stern, the producer, were meticulously courteous with the actors. I'm all in favour of that, but sometimes they passed beyond courtesy into what seemed to me very like perversity, if not actual perversion—actors who were seen to be wrong for their parts within two minutes being kept long past their scheduled ten minutes, as if spinning out their ordeal (and ours) made it up to them for their being no-hopers. One chap came in for the part of Nick, who is meant to be a bright young Cambridge-educated middle-class English type on the make, and offered a boisterously anti-Semitic version of an East End Jew, complete with lisp and even a touch of a drool. Tabori and Stern kept him at it, not for the courteous ten minutes, not for an inexplicable twenty minutes, but for forty minutes—lisping, slobbering, whining, wheedling, wringing his hands. Furthermore he *looked* completely wrong, being short and bald, with a beard. (Actually, now I come to think of it, the chap who got the part—Bart Braddleman—is short, balding, with a bit of a beard and is apparently a Sephardic Jew. But he got everything else right. Or seemed to at the time.)

Every casting session ran two or three hours over. We weren't altogether helped by our casting lady, who would sometimes forget to notify us of cancellations, and then of substitutions, so that I would write down my impressions beside the wrong name, which would lead to endless muddles afterwards. 'No good,' I'd say of the actor I took to be—let's call him Sprinkleman. 'For one thing he's far too old. For another he obviously can't do English.' 'Too old!' Kris Tabori or Joe Stern would exclaim. 'He's twenty-six. And what do you mean he can't do English, he *is* English!' 'English! He's from the Bronx, from the sound of him. And at least forty.' And so it went, until the casting lady would suddenly remember that the one I'd got down on my list as Sprinkleman had in fact been replaced by Yorricks, or whatever, hadn't she mentioned it, sorry. Of course Joe Sterna and Kristoffer Tabori, being familiar with most of the actors around Los Angeles, could spot on sight the difference between a Yorricks and a Sprinkleman, and knew exactly who they were talking about. The result was that for long stretches of utterly worthless conversation I must have given the impression that I wasn't only highly unobservant, but positively out to lunch.

SOURCE
Simon Gray, *How's That for Telling 'Em, Fat Lady?* (1988)

546

The rehearsal had begun. Not for long. Act One Scene Two, the curse of *The Common Pursuit*, had been rewritten so completely during Sam's absence that the two actors involved—Kristoffer Tabori and Wayne Alexander (who'd put the new text on to the computer, and then collated it)—still hadn't had a chance to learn it properly. Nor had Sam had a chance to digest it properly. He turned to me and snarled out an intelligent question about the meaning of some new or changed lines, but in such a way as to suggest that he was snarling at Kristoffer Tabori for having failed to learn the new lines properly. Whereupon Tabori threw his script to the ground, stamped on it, screaming that the speech he was accused of failing to learn had never been in the script before, how had he possibly had time to learn it? Whereupon Sam snarled back, and Tabori screamed back, until they were snarling and screaming simultaneously. Both of them, of course, were in a sense right. Though the speech had never been in the script before (Tabori), a version of it had been (Weisman). Where Tabori was in the wrong was in thinking that *he* was being criticized for not knowing the speech, when in fact I was being interrogated about the purpose of the changes I'd made in it. Where Weisman was in the wrong was in giving such general offence so offensively that somebody in earshot was bound, sooner or later, to take it personally.

I don't know how genuine Tabori's tantrum was. His gesticulations and counter-screamings were so extravagant that they were more like an impersonated dementia than the genuine article. Weisman met whatever it was with a contemptuous disdain finally walking out of the auditorium, saying 'I don't know what's going on here but I'll wait. I'll go out and we'll have a break while you get yourself together, and when you're ready I'll come back in, yer know what I mean? Yer know what I mean?' Kristoffer Tabori and Wayne Alexander, who are old friends went slouching off, laughing angrily. I waited a few minutes, then shambled after Weisman a cigarette between my lips. I found him by himself, goating about with his beard in a corner of the lobby. Having reintroduced myself to him so to speak, I said, 'Those lines you were asking about, we'd better discuss them.' He said, 'Yeah. Right.' We got into the text for a time, cleared up the point he'd raised, then I said, 'Let's go back and tell the actors what we've decided,' and he said, 'Yeah, right, let's go talk to the actors.'

SOURCE
Simon Gray, *How's That for Telling 'Em, Fat Lady?* (1988)

547

According to Joe the word of mouth from the previews has been 'terrific, just terrific', which is not always to the advantage of a First Night, as the critics like to think that they generate the word of mouth, and certainly don't like to think that they're being usurped by it.

A New York producer, who knew his show was a bummer, was astonished to read rave reviews after the First Night. 'Now,' he is reported to have said, 'all we got to do is stop the word of mouth.'

SOURCE
Simon Gray, *How's That for Telling 'Em, Fat Lady?* (1988)

TOM STOPPARD
(1937–)

548

Sir Tom Stoppard is a Czech-born British playwright and screenwriter who first came to prominence with Rosencrantz and Guildenstern Are Dead *in 1966. Ideas, wit, and wordplay characterize his work. This anecdote springs from a profile of the playwright published in the* Guardian *in 2002 in which the paper said of Stoppard: 'Underpinning all his work and increasingly apparent in his later plays, however, is an attempt to come to terms with the characteristic Beckettian view that "I am a human nothingness".'*

Sir Tom may be modest, but not so modest as to consider himself 'a human nothing'. In a letter to yersterday's *Guardian*, he pointed out that this was 'a mistranscription from the tape of a talk I gave over thirty years ago, published at the time in the *Sunday Times*. As the paper explained a week later, the phrase should have read, "I am assuming nothing". Such are the pitfalls of the clippings library.'

SOURCE
Alexander Chancellor, *Daily Telegraph* (25 June 2002)

549

In August 1993 Antony Sher was rehearsing Tom Stoppard's play Travesties *directed by Adrian Noble and was keeping a diary.*

17/8/93

Stoppard back in rehearsals today. He was supposed to stay away for longer, but it seems he can't. He's thoroughly enjoying himself, bringing in more and more rewrites. Takes you aside to show them, with a mixture of pride and modesty. Sometimes there are alternatives—should the line be 'putting a spanner in Lenin's works' or 'putting a spanner in Lenin's Collected Works?' At other times he hands it over glumly: 'Well, it's not going to get into any anthology.' I thought he was joking till I glanced in a *Book of Modern Quotations* lying on the stage management desk and found several pages devoted to him. I've noticed all the other actors doing what I do: carefully hoarding the handwritten rewrites: Adrian caught me doing this today. Blushing, I said, 'There are American universities that'll pay the earth for these.' He replied; 'Sod American Universities—I'm taking mine to Christie's.'

SOURCE
Antony Sher, *Beside Myself* (2001)

550

16/9/93

Press night. Went wonderfully. Packed to the rafters and a dream audience for a comedy. I flew. Everyone very high afterwards. At Joe Allen's I presented Stoppard with the original drawing of my first-night card to the others: a cartoon of him as Wilde. He mentioned that he'd bought both my novels and asked which he should read first? I wanted to say, neither—I don't want that big brain levelled at any more of my work. He surprised me by reavealing that he hadn't been to university and, like me, wishes he had. (He wants to be brighter?) When the waiter came for our order, he ordered duck salad as a starter and Caesar salad as a main course. The waiter was momentarily confused. 'So that's two salads?' Tom replied 'Yes, sorry, I save my creativity for my work.'

SOURCE
Antony Sher, *Beside Myself* (2001)

YVONNE BREWSTER

(1938–)

551

Jamaican born director and writer Yvonne Brewster co-founded Talawa Theatre Company in the United Kingdom and The Barn in Jamaica—the country's first professional theatre company. Brewster first came to Britain in the mid-1950s to study at Rose Bruford College, where she was the first black female drama student in the country. While Artisitic Director of Talawa (1985–2003), Brewster did much to change the types of roles that were offered to black actors.

At Talawa Theatre Company, our policy was to give black actors work they weren't being offered—and nobody was offering them the chance to do Shakespeare. Norman Beaton was best known for the sitcom *Desmond's*, but he was an extraordinary actor. His *Krapp's Last Tape* was so moving—the best I've ever seen. We were in Pizza Hut when I agreed he should play Lear, and he almost fell off his stool. Norman thought of Lear as something like the head of a credit union. Black people tend to put their faith in credit unions rather than banks, so Lear would be king of the money.

Norman had learned all the lines, but just before rehearsal he got sick. I went home and locked myself away. We had to continue—we already had money from the Arts Council—but we couldn't do Norman's idea. I had to reconfigure the production in just two and a half weeks. It was imagist and futuristic—Ellen Cairns, our fantastic designer, created a stage like a disk, with black leather costumes and a perspex throne that looked like glass.

Ben Thomas was already in the cast. I told him, 'Donald Wolfit played Lear at 40. You're 39. You're going to do it!' He's a brave, excellent actor—but was also a tall, strapping man in his prime. To make sense of it, we gave the king a heart condition, always reaching for his pills. Black people are prone to heart conditions, and also worry about madness—the rates of schizophrenia are far higher in the black population. The psychiatrist Aggrey Burke often used King Lear in lectures to demonstrate aspects of society—I was humbled by that.

[...] David Harewood, who played Edmund, hadn't done any Shakespeare before—he was so scared. He would ride his bike up and down the pavement outside the rehearsal rooms to try and get the iambic rhythm.

Mona Hammond played the Fool as a schizophrenic—even her makeup was split down the middle. At a workshop at the National, Peter Brook asked me, 'When do you know you've succeeded?' I replied, 'When I forget I know the actor. Mona is a dear friend of mine—I used to look after her baby son. But I stood at the back one night, and forgot I knew her. I was just watching the Fool.' For me, that's a test of how you've allowed the play to belong to the actors.

People said things about the production that they'd never say today. People asked, how can you cast a black Edmund—he's a bad role model for all the naughty boys in Brixton! Some critics hated it—and when I was on *Desert Island Discs*, Sue Lawley asked me about casting these Shakespearean—read 'white'—roles and said, 'What gives you permission to do that?' I said, 'Darling, that question shows your lack of imagination.' They cut that part of the interview...

SOURCE
Yvonne Brewster, interviewed by David Jays for *The Guardian* (1 February 2016)

ALAN AYCKBOURN
(1939–)

552

Perhaps Britain's most prolific playwright, Ayckbourn has written more than 80 plays—many first performed at the Stephen Joseph Theatre in Scarborough where he was artistic director from 1972 to 2009. Here he is being interviewed in 2001 about his most recent work.

I've written a new play which they're doing at the National next year—*House and Garden*—which has an outrageous concept. It takes place in two theatres simultaneously—in this case the Olivier and the Lyttleton: the actors run between the two. There's absolutely no sense in doing this at all, except that when we did it in Scarborough—and I hope it will happen at the National—people got terribly excited by the idea. And they got excited by the curtain call, when the actors ran from both buildings in order to take two sets of bows; and then we carried the whole action out into the foyer. All you can do is strike matches; you can't ever light bonfires, but you can strike a match for a minute and make the theatre flare. I think if we all do that occasionally, all us writers and directors then it [theatre] still lives.

SOURCE
Alan Ayckbourn, interviewed by Richard Eyre in *Talking Theatre: Interviews with Theatre People* (2009)

MICHAEL RUDMAN
(1939–)

553

Michael Rudman is an American-born theatre director based in Britain, whose early career saw him as the artistic director of the Traverse Theatre in Edinburgh and the Hampstead Theatre in London.

For the rehearsals of this Strindberg piece, we would gather at St. James' Church Hall, a modern building attached to an old church in West Hampstead. The hall had an overhanging bit of roof, which makes an appearance in this story.

The rehearsals were highly charged. Some of the actors were distressed from early on.

Georgina Hale: Bullshit, Michael, I want to play it for real.
Peter Woodthorpe: I don't like the set. It will never work. I hate it.

And

Richard Moore: I don't want to be difficult, but…

Susan Hampshire was serene. She had learned the lines beforehand. She was mildly dyslexic and thought that she would never be able to learn them otherwise. It was a charming thing to do, but it did constrain her, until one day when something extraordinary happened.

In the second week of rehearsal, on a rainy Tuesday morning, between eleven o'clock and one, four actors did their nuts. Each one of them burst into tears and choked out an emotional speech about the obstacles that they were facing and the impossibility of overcoming them.

The set, the rehearsal room, the other actors, the director, all came under heavy fire. After each of these psychological cadenzas, the actor rushed from the room and into the rain.

But the actor did not stay for long in the rain. No, the actor managed to get under the little bit of roof that was protruding from St. James' Church hall. It was the director who stood in the rain begging the actor to reconsider, to return to the rehearsal, and to understand that it was all going to get much better and that the performances, once integrated, would be terrific.

I suppose that when you are crying, you don't notice the rain especially if you are under a bit of roof. But, if you are directing and not crying, you do and I did. I noticed that I was getting very wet.

Often a play will engender in the men and women who perform it, the very emotions that the characters live through. Any good actor takes on the thoughts, the language and the behaviour of his character in the game, just as children do. It is natural. Not that actors are children. Far from it. They are gifted adults capable of understanding and imitating other adults. That is why, contrary to popular belief, they are on the whole an intelligent and mentally healthy set of people.

If the play touches many nerves, as this one did, and if the actors are highly strung, as these were, then you can get these outbursts, especially at that time of rehearsals, the second week, when it is the moment to start giving a performance and to feel what help or hindrance you are going to get from the other actors, the director and the designer. On this rainy day, the actors could see and feel only the hindrances.

And so the speeches went on. First Peter, then Richard, then Susan, then Georgina. And each one ran from the room in tears after the speech. And each time the director went out to find his place in the wet, and then he would coax the actor back into the room. Then we had lunch and after lunch, a good afternoon's rehearsal and after that everything was fine. I can't remember another cross word being spoken.

That evening, Susan gave me a lift back to the theatre where I had left my car. We had been friends for a long time. There was a friendly pause as we drove down Abbey Road. Then I spoke.

'Wasn't that remarkable?'

'Yes' said Susan.

'I don't think I've ever seen anything like it. It must be the play. Or the rain.'

'I rehearsed mine,' said Susan.

'What?'

'My speech. I worked on it last night.'

'You knew that it was going to happen?'
'Oh, yes. Sooner or later. So I prepared a speech.'
'Well, Susan. It was a very good speech.'
'I know. I prepared it.'
'I hope you won't have to do another one.'
'I won't.'
And she didn't.

SOURCE
Michael Rudman, *I Joke Too Much* (2014)

TREVOR NUNN
(1940–)

554

In 1984/5, Kenneth Branagh was appearing with the Royal Shakespeare Company in productions of Henry V, Hamlet, *and* Love's Labours Lost. *The joint artistic director of the RSC was Trevor Nunn. Branagh, along with other members of the company, had been finding their leader frustratingly elusive.*

Hamlet opened to a divided press who ran the usual gamut of opinions about the production and performances. I had some good mentions and received further careers advice. 'Mr Branagh cannot speak the verse. He is a resolutely modern actor.' I rather liked the second bit. Traditional and contemporary, that's what I long to be.

Love's Labour's Lost started rehearsal before *Hamlet* had finished previewing—such was the increasingly frenetic pace of the Stratford season. The day began at 10, six days a week, and there would be rehearsal until 5.30, and at 7.30 most of the Company on any one night would have a show to do. At this stage my nights off—the nights *The Merchant of Venice* was playing—were increasingly rare. But not as rare as a visit from Trevor Nunn, with Terry Hands, the joint artistic director of the RSC.

The great day came in the middle of the season. The entire Company gathered in the Conference Hall. It was the first time I'd seen this man whose work I so admired, and I was desperate for him to see *Henry V*. Terry Hands had already made a visit and had been most kind and encouraging about the performance. I learnt a great deal from Trevor's performance that day. He is unquestionably a star. He sat leaning forward in his chair, speaking quietly in that warm, honeyed voice, and within five minutes the entire Company were leaning forward and straining to hear him. The impression was of a room of worshippers. Everyone was afraid to move in case they missed something in Trevor's address, which took on more and more the feel of a quiet religious chant.

He spoke of this as a 'confessional'. He was well aware of his absence from the Company and knew that many of us felt hurt. Things would change. The whole speech was completely beguiling. He seemed, as they say, a regular guy. He talked of his hopes for the Company, his plans for the new musical *Les Miserables*, which he hoped very much would include some of us, and as far as his failure to see the work at Stratford was concerned, he was determined to put that right. His triumphant finale was pitched to the mesmerised audience in a tone of quiet, Martin Luther King intensity. Trevor 'had a dream', and that dream appeared to be to see all the Stratford shows within a fortnight. I imagine that subsequently he woke and found other things to do. The next time I saw Trevor was twelve months later. Still dreaming, I presume.

SOURCE
Kenneth Branagh, *Beginning* (1989)

555

On performance 138 of *Henry V* at the Barbican the word went round: 'he' was in. I wondered who 'he' was? The Shah of Iran? Ronald Reagan? Donald Duck? No, Trevor. Trevor was in. I wasn't sure why. I knew that some of the Company had written to *Jim'll fix it* asking to meet him, and perhaps this was his response. Well, my time was nearly up at the RSC and he wasn't going to get away with catching the penultimate performance of a show that had opened the previous Stratford season. No, not without a piece of my mind. I wasn't going to be 'Trev'd', the famous charm would not work with yours truly. No way.

Dressing Room One, Barbican. Two minutes after curtain down. I'm just taking my shirt off when there's a knock at the door—right, here I go. I turned round to vent my spleen, but I could no longer see or hear. I had been enveloped in Trevor's hair and beard and deafeningly loud in my right ear was an enormous vowel sound which turned out to be, 'Huuuuuuuuuuuuugely enjoyable.'

I tried to speak but it was impossible. Eventually he let go of my hand, and stared intently at me as if I was a long lost brother. If it were possible he got more 'ooooo's in the next repetition: 'Really... huuuuuuuuuuuuuuuuuuugely enjoyable.'

I didn't dare speak. Despite the innocuous remark he looked as though he was going to cry. Oh. Hello. Here comes the big one. He was pumping my hand now as if he were leaving for the front, definitely on the edge of a breakdown. The subtext was 'I'm worthless. I'm no one, but I will just try and say these things to you, a genius.' The body language was pure Uriah Heep. Martin Luther King returned for the closing lines. 'May I just say (pause. I thought he was going to fall over.)... may I just say that it is my very great ambition to work... with you (he started to move backwards)... really...(one hand on the door)... I really mean that...(fingers

W. R. CHETWOOD
(d.1776)

581

W. R. Chetwood was the author of A General History of the Stage, *published in 1749.*

I remember, above twenty Years past, I was one of the Audience, at a new Play: Before me sat a Sea-Officer, with whom I had some Acquaintance; on each Hand of him a Couple of Sparks, both prepar'd with their offensive Instruments vulgarly term'd *Cat-calls,** which they were often tuning, before the Play began. The Officer did not take any Notice of them till the Curtain drew up; but when they continued their Sow-gelder's Music (as he unpolitely call'd it), he beg'd they would not prevent his hearing the Actors, tho' they might not care whether they heard, or no; but they took little Notice of his civil Request, which he repeated again and again, to no Purpose: But, at last, one of them condescended to tell him, *If he did not like it, he might let it alone. Why, really,* reply'd the Sailor, *I do not like it, and would have you let your Noise alone; I have paid my Money to see and hear the Play, and your ridiculous Noise not only hinders me, but a great many other People that are here, I believe, with the same Design: Now if you prevent us, you rob us of our Money, and our Time; therefore I intreat you, as you look like Gentlemen to behave as such.* One of them seem'd mollified, and put his Whistle in his Pocket; but the other was incorrigible. The blunt Tar made him one Speech more. *Sir,* said he, *I advise you, once more, to follow the Example of this Gentleman, and put up your Pipe.* But the Piper sneer'd in his Face, and clap'd his troublesome Instrument to his Mouth, with Cheeks swell'd out like a Trumpeter, to give it a redoubled, and louder Noise; but, like the broken Crow of a Cock in a Fright, the Squeak was stopt in the Middle by a Blow from the Officer, which he gave him with so strong a Will, that his

Child's Trumpet was struck thro' his Cheek, and his Companion led him out to a Surgeon; so that we had more Room, and less Noise; and not one that saw or heard the Affair, but what were well pleased with his Treatment; and, notwithstanding his great Blustering, he never thought it worth his while to call upon the Officer, tho' he knew where to find him.

**The 'cat-call', which today is a whistling noise, started life as the whistle itself.*

SOURCE
W. R. Chetwood, *A General History of the Stage* (1749)

CHARLES HOLLAND
(1733–1769)

582

Holland made his first appearance on the stage in the title role of Oroonoko at Drury Lane in 1755. He was much admired by David Garrick, who cast him as Florizel in The Winter's Tale. *He had a reputation as a ladies' man and died of the smallpox, aged only 36. He was one of the many players of his time who had to contend with the challenge of having audience members seated on the stage.*

The Stage was at 5s.—Pit and Boxes all joined together at 5s. There was only one entrance on each side the stage, which was always particularly crowded. First, they sported their own figures to gratify self consequence, and impede and interfere with the performers, who had to come on and go off the stage. Affronting the audience was another darling delight—particularly, offending the galleries, and thereby incurring the displeasure of the gods, who shewed their resentment by dispersing golden showers of oranges and half-eaten pippins, to the infinite terror of the ladies of fashion seeing me alone in a large room with a bumper of cooling wine at my grasp.'

SOURCE
John O'Keefe, *Recollections of the Life of John O'Keefe* (1826)

JOHN PHILIP KEMBLE
(1757–1823)

584

John Philip Kemble was an English actor-manager born into a theatrical family. His father, Roger Kemble, managed a touring company; with his elder sister, Sarah Siddons, he achieved considerable success at the Theatre Royal, Drury Lane; his other sisters, Ann Hatton and Elizabeth Whitlock, and his brothers, Charles Kemble and Stephen Kemble, were also noted players of the day.

On the 13th of April 1779, [Arthur] Murphy's tragedy of *Zenobia* was performed, and a Mrs Mason was the heroine of the evening. The stage-box was unfortunately occupied by a lady of some distinction, whose ill-nature vented itself in the form of criticism; and Mrs Mason became the object of her derision, which she expressed by loud and ill-bred laughter, to the annoyance of the poor victim, and of everybody but the persons in her immediate suite.

Mr Kemble too, because he perhaps could not shout like Cummins, or because he had a dark complexion; because he had the reputation of learning or because the lady cared not about a reason when she wanted to amuse herself, he also became a mark for this silly woman's annoyance.

I do not suppose that she was aware of Dr Johnson's opinion of *Zenobia*, that it had too much Tig. and Teri. in it (the names of two of the characters being Tigranes and Teribazus) but Mr Kemble performed the part of the latter, who is the lover of the piece, and shared with Mrs Mason the contempt and derision of Miss S. and her party. In the interesting scenes of the last act, she found full gratification for her spleen, as both her objects were together upon the stage, and she redoubled her efforts to cover them with disgrace. The actress had made little impression on anybody, but Kemble was shocked at the brutal treatment she received. As to the insults designed for himself during the evening, he had retorted them by looks of infinite disdain. His sensibility was noticed in the box by loud and repeated peals of laughter from the lady and her echoes. At this, Kemble suddenly stopped, and being called upon by the audience to proceed, with great gravity and a pointed bow to the stage-box, he said 'he was ready to proceed with the play as soon as THAT lady had finished her conversation, which he perceived the going on with the tragedy only interrupted.'

The audience received this rudeness of the stage-box as an insolent attempt to control their amusements, and with shouts, which could not be laughed down, ordered the lady and her party out of the theatre.

SOURCE
James Boaden, *Life of John Philip Kemble* (1825)

WASHINGTON IRVING
(1783–1859)

585

Washington Irving, noted American author and diplomat, was witness to some of the remarkable goings-on in the theatre of New York at the turn of the nineteenth century.

The Park Theatre opened in 1798 in New York, fronting on City Hall Park, was a great advance in theatre architecture. It was a large stone building, in contrast to the old John Street Theatre, which had been of wood, and its three tiers of boxes, a gallery, and a pit gave it seating capacity of about 2,000. The gallery was set aside for Negroes and the third tier of boxes was reserved for prostitutes! The doors opened at half-past six and at seven the programme began. It usually consisted of two pieces, a tragedy and comedy, and sometimes even three, with a comic song or dance in between. The atmosphere in the theatre, and the behaviour of the audience is described (as of 1802) by Washington Irving in his Jonathan Oldstyle Letters:

> I was much amused with the waggery and humour of the gallery which, by the way, is kept in excellent order by the constables who are stationed there. The noise in this part of the house is somewhat similar to that which prevailed in Noah's Ark; for we have an imitation of the whistles and yells of every kind of animal. This, in some measure, compensates for the want of music, as the gentlemen of our orchestra are very economic of their favours. Somehow or other, the anger of the gods seemed to be aroused all of a sudden, and they commenced a discharge of apples, nuts and gingerbread on the heads of the honest folks in the pit, who had no possibility of retreating from this new kind of thunderbolts. I can't say but I was a little irritated at being saluted aside of my head with a rotten pippin; and was going to shake my cane at them, but was prevented by a decent-looking man behind me, who informed me that it was useless to threaten or expostulate.
>
> "They are only amusing themselves a little at our expense," said he; "sit down quietly and bend your back to it."

SOURCE

Herbert Marshall and Mildred Stock, *Ira Aldridge: The Negro Tragedian* (1958)

JOHN JOHNSTONE (LESTER) WALLACK (1820–1888)

586

The Wallack family, of English origin, were instrumental in the development of the theatre in New York. James Wallack bought the New York Lyceum in 1852, renaming it Wallack's. During the 1860s his nephew John Johnstone, who took the stage name of Lester, maintained the tradition of staging mainly English plays there, despite the demand for plays of American origin and significance. Before reaching America, however, Lester Wallack had spent some time in Dublin, experiencing the 'outspoken criticism, shrewdness and humour' of the Dublin gallery what Gordon Craig (Ellen Terry's son) later called, less diplomatically, 'the roughest public known to the northern world'.

I remember one particular occasion when a man named Morrison, who led the chorus, a gigantic fellow and very ugly, afforded no little amusement to the audience and his fellow-singers. We had at that period what are called 'Ticket Nights'. After the benefits of the regular performers the underlings of the theatre, the leader of the chorus, the ushers in front and the ticket takers, would have a benefit in common, when it was the custom to give them half the receipts; the manager doing it because he knew perfectly well that the house would be jammed full to the ceiling, as the beneficiaries sold their tickets among their friends and in great quantities. The curious part was the fact that the ushers and ticket takers, who, of course, never played anything themselves, made up for it by pestering the management for some particular play which they preferred. The people on the stage, chorus singers, etc., naturally wanted to do something, to get a chance they never had in any other part of the season. This man Morrison, who, by the way, was known as 'Nigger Morrison', because of his dusky complexion, had a baritone voice

thought how curious it was that in a first-class club there should be only one snuff-box. The characters, as they got excited, kept taking the snuff-box off the table. The Old Member is reading the paper all the time. Presently he looks for the snuff-box, and it is gone. He calls out to the waiter 'Waiter, the snuff-box!' and the servant goes to Blount, or whoever has taken it, and puts it back on the table. Hunt never was perfect in the words of anything he played; but on this occasion he had before him, inside the newspaper, all the cues and his own part; so he had nothing to do but read it, and he was determined to be right for once. When the scene is culminating, in the midst of all the confusion and the roar that is caused by certain necessities of the play, the last thing that is heard is this Old Member shouting: 'Waiter, the snuff-box!' There was a momentary pause, when Hunt hallooed out: 'Waiter, the buff-snox!' Of course, the scene closed with more laughter than ever before.

Another very curious thing of that sort occurred to me when I was playing Charles Surface at Wallack's theatre. An actor named H.B. Phillips was Crabtree, and in the scene in which Crabtree and Sir Benjamin Backbite come on with the mass of scandal and stuff and a lot of information with regard to what has previously occurred in the four acts, they proceed to say, 'Have you heard the news?' and so on. They are describing this thing, and, of course, telling all sorts of stories that are not a bit true; and Sir Benjamin Backbite, who is the first to enter has to say, 'Then Charles and Sir Peter began to fight with swords,' and Crabtree rushes on, 'Pistols, nephew; pistols, nephew,' all of which is, of course, false. Sir Benjamin says: 'Oh, no, no, no, no; then Sir Peter was wounded. I know it was swords, because he was wounded with a thrust in the *seconde.*' 'No, no, no, no,' the other says; 'a bullet in the thorax, a bullet in the thorax,' and he was so anxious that he said, 'No, no, no, no, a thullet in the borax!' Very curious to say, the audience hardly noticed this then, and would not have noticed it at all but for John

Brougham, who never spared anybody (he was playing Sir Oliver Surface), and who said directly: 'What the devil is his borax?'

SOURCE
Lester Wallack, *Memories of Fifty Years* (1889)

J. B. HOWE
(1828–1908)

602

This string of disasters is recounted by Howe in his autobiography, A Cosmopolitan Actor.

When the 'bus arrived at the Eyre Arms, I saw several of the company waiting to receive me. It was now twenty-five minutes past eight.

'What's the meaning of this? Not dressed? My G—!'

Judge of my horror when I alighted being saluted with—'Oh, my boy, my dear fellow! We were just giving you up altogether. Wherever have you been?'

'Where? Don't ask me now,' I gasped; 'but why are you not dressed?'

'What was the use of dressing without Hamlet?'

'What are they doing, then?' I asked, and Crauford answered:

'Why, there's a Mr — (I forget the name now) on the stage reciting the soliloquy upon death.'

He had already got through several others.

'There is! Well, of all the infernal impudence!'

This was said while we were running along towards the Abbey, out of breath, indignant, furious, raving. I arrived at the top of the balcony at the entrance door facing the stage, when I saw and heard the gentleman named uttering the last three or four lines of the soliloquy.

I shouted at the top of my voice—

'Go off, sir; go off! How dare you?'

And there ensued, as might be expected, a perfect babel of tongues in an instant. Suffice that I mounted to the stage and claimed the attention of the audience for a few minutes while I briefly stated the dilemma I had been placed in by the untimely arrival of the wardrobe, and politely claimed their indulgence while the artists were fitly costumed, and then we would go through the entire tragedy from beginning to end.

This announcement was received with *éclat*, and I descended to the 'realms of darkness' beneath the stage to dress with the rest, when—Well, can you imagine?—no, of course you can't—my torture on being told that Mr Frank Huntly, who had promised so faithfully to get permission from his manager at the Bower to do the Ghost, had given it up at the last moment. What was I to do?

'I'll do the Ghost,' said Crauford, 'and here is a young gentleman, who knows almost every line of the piece, who can go on for Laertes.'

This was 'his nibbs' who had been spouting during my absence, and for whom I did not feel at that moment the most cherished friendship. However, what was I to do? I consented. The piano and cornet had been going it ever since the announcement. The audience were getting more impatient every instant. Crauford took off his Laertes dress and began to put on the 'complete steel' (made of grey glazed lining) of the Ghost, the helmet was at least a little more real (papier maché); and while we were thus engaged he loquaciously informed me that he didn't know a line.

Here was another crusher!

Never mind. I was equal to the occasion. I knew every line of at least the 'Platform Scene', so I told him simply to go on at the proper cues, and I would speak for him as well as myself. After a long delay—it was now nine o'clock—the little bell went, and by my direction the bed curtains were drawn from the centre to the sides, and all the artists clung to each other as far out of sight as the gap between the tables and the wall would allow.

When the play commenced in earnest everything went swimmingly. When your humble servant made his appearance—well, my 'natural modesty forbids, &c.'; however, it was, candidly speaking, all right.

Mind, I am supposing that you here know the first, second, and third scenes are over; we are now into the 'Platform Scene'. The dialogue went all right, and I believe not one of the spectators ever dreamt but that it was Crauford himself speaking the Ghost's lines, as I artfully turned my head to the back each time I had to do the ventriloquial for him, and as persistently faced the audience whilst uttering the heart-rendering speeches of the melancholy Dane.

When I had to speak the last lines of the Ghost, 'Adieu! Adieu! remember me,' I put in an aside to every word thus—'Adieu! (step back) Adieu! (farther) remember (go on) me.' Crauford took step after step as instructed, until, not thinking of the treacherous gap at the side of the wall, he fell backwards off the edge of the table stage, and as a drowning man will clutch at a straw so did the poor Ghost clutch at the bed curtains, and down came the whole of the proscenium, exposing to view all the company, who at once tried to rush off the tables through the door at the back in the wall leading to the private house of the proprietor.

I have heard laughter in my time, and have often been the means of creating it in the various roles I have assumed; but no shout ever greeted my ears equalled for length or strength the continued roar of that night. And the incident appeared so ludicrous to me that, notwithstanding the former annoyance I had been subjected to, I literally had to hold my sides with laughter, while poor Will

Crauford lay in the gap, with his helmet off, part of his body down the gap and his heels in the air, the chintz curtains tightly clutched in his hands forming a sort of tent over him. Whether he was enjoying the fun underneath I could not say.

After the roaring was over, I put in an amendment to the text thus—

'Remember thee? Yea, thou poor ghost; I shall never forget thee!'

Nor have I, as the above lines, I hope, fully prove.

SOURCE
J. B. Howe, *A Cosmopolitan Actor* (1888)

JOAN LITTLEWOOD (1914–2002) & GERRY RAFFLES (1928–1975)

603

London's Theatre Royal, Stratford East, became famous under the management of Gerry Raffles, who worked with his partner, Joan Littlewood, who was the artistic director there from 1953 to 1974 and whose celebrated 'Theatre Workshop' productions included A Taste of Honey *and* Oh, What a Lovely War! *Among the many notable actors whose careers were enhanced by their time with Littlewood's Theatre Workshop were George A. Cooper, Brian Murphy, and Harry H. Corbett, who each feature in this collection of theatrical calamities.*

Theatre Workshop had many adventures, particularly on the road: Gerry Raffles plugging into the local grid and blacking out the entire town, the pantechnicon, containing cast and set, breaking down in the Welsh mountains, and, in Europe, some actors on one train, others on another going in the opposite direction and the set still on the platform, they are not stories that can be told neatly in a few sentences.

I think stories told by actors, rather than directors, work best because actors are the ones up against it. Joan told me that, at a time when she was trying to pull out of acting, she was sitting in her usual position as director, on the steps at the back of the gallery in the Theatre Royal, scribbling notes, when she stabbed right through her block of paper writing: 'What silly born bitch has missed her entrance?' It was her.

Harry Greene, father of Sarah Greene [theatre owner and producer], told me that, during a performance of *Volpone*, George A. Cooper, playing Volpone, was sitting in a wheelchair under the proscenium arch when the iron curtain fell to the stage floor. Only Harry pulling George back saved his life.

Brian Murphy told me that, at a first preview of *Ned Kelly*, performed in front of two rows of long suffering nurses, the show so overran that Gerry Raffles had to come on stage before the end and tell the audience that, if it wanted to catch the last bus, it had better leave.

The end was the deep stage filled with smoke, which Gerry stood in front of while Harry H. Corbett as Ned, right at the back, wearing his sound muffling bucket helmet waited to make his entrance. Having waited longer than he thought necessary and, thinking his cue must have come, he strode downstage, through the smoke, to say his most famous line: 'Such is life!' Everyone had gone home.

SOURCE
Peter Rankin, unpublished manuscript (2018)

PETER BOWLES (1936–)

604

Many years before his own stardom, Peter Bowles appeared in a minor part in an Old Vic production of Macbeth, *in which the leading men were Paul Rogers and John Neville.*

After a short London season [in 1956] the Old Vic Company, before flying off to America, went on some dates in England. The one thing I remember of this is that at a matinée in Manchester, during the sword fight between Macbeth and Macduff, which was played with real steel claymore swords so that sparks flew as they clashed, Macbeth's sword blade literally flew off its handle. I was on stage at the time and we all froze as we heard very clearly the swish, swish, swish as the steel blade spun into the darkened packed auditorium. It must have gone right to the back of the stalls, after what seemed like a life-time there was a horrible scream from someone 'out there'. The fight continued Paul Rogers quickly pulled out his dirk and retreated with John Neville's Macduff into the wings.

Everyone was very worried and concerned as to the damage inflicted by the deadly blade. A man had been rushed to hospital with a cut head, we were told. But there was another performance that evening to take our minds off it. Paul Rogers must have felt awful, but at the end of that evening's performance, a gentleman turned up at the stage door smiling but heavily bandaged. Was he going to sue, and take the Old Vic for every penny it had, as would probably happen today? No, he just wanted permission to keep the sword blade that he had with him, as a memento, and would Mr Paul Rogers please give him his autograph. We were a lucky company, and he was a very lucky man, who it seemed had had the best theatrical experience of his life.

SOURCE
Peter Bowles, *Ask Me If I'm Happy* (2010)

DAVID WESTON

(1938–)

605

Something in the air... David Weston noticed it when he was playing the Gentleman (and understudying Ian McKellen in the title role) in King Lear *at Stratford.*

The Gentleman sits at the back of the stage for most of the long first scene, supposedly writing down Lear's edicts. Gerald and young Richard, as attendants, stand a few feet away. Tonight I hear Richard sniffing and become aware of a noxious smell. I look up and think I see a faint suspicion of guilt creep across Gerald's handsome face, or is it drifting in from the wings? At that very moment Romola [Garai as Cordelia] breaks away from Lear and walks straight into the miasma—I'm certain she thinks it is me. Farting on stage is not altogether uncommon. I remember the line of soldiers that used to stand on guard under the night sky in the interminable French camp scene in *Henry V* at the National. They became so bored that each night they managed to fart in sequence. When I was young, I heard old actors tell tales of a renowned Dame—perhaps the aptly named Marie Tempest—who would never quit the closed confines of a box set without leaving a pungent remembrance behind.

SOURCE
David Weston, *Covering McKellen: An Understudy's Tale* (2011)

feinted exit, a deft hurl, and then a return to the stage without missing a beat.

SOURCE
Dominic Dromgoole, *Hamlet: Globe to Globe* (2017)

DECLAN DONNELLAN
(1953–)

607

Touring often throws up peculiar challenges for acting companies. Here Declan Donellan, Artistic Director of the touring company Cheek by Jowl, remembers one particular incident during a world tour of As You Like It. *The production was played by an all-male company, with Adrian Lester taking on the part of Rosalind to great critical acclaim.*

Once, the baggage truck broke down at the Romanian frontier. So that evening's performance would have no set, no props and no costumes. The actors improvised as best as they could forage. The first-night audience was more than forgiving, they stood and cheered, and at the next morning's press conference the critics enthused: 'Amazing!—and later today your truck will arrive?' 'Yes!' the actors replied, swelling with their inventiveness. The Romanians continued: 'Also you will have the set tonight?' 'Yes, yes!' 'Also the costumes tonight?' '... Yes, yes yes!' '... And also the actresses? ...'

SOURCE
Declan Donnellan, 'All You Need is Love: Adrian Lester and the Miraculous All-Male *As You Like It*', *The Guardian* (12 November 2014)

TIM PIGOTT-SMITH
(1946–2017)

608

Occasionally an unforeseen circumstance actually helps the play along. Here actor Tim Pigott-Smith describes one particular night at the National Theatre in 1988. The production was The Winter's Tale; *Tim Pigott-Smith was playing Leontes, and was directed by Peter Hall as part of his final season as Artistic Director. The story recounts the circumstances of the final scene of the play in which Hermione's 'statue' comes to life.*

I'll never forget one night when we were performing in the Cottesloe [now the Dorfman Theatre, the smallest of the National Theatre's stages], and there was a blackout over the whole of Waterloo. One of the actors, who was about to come on and describe the statue by Giulio Romano, suddenly found his dressing room corridor in complete darkness. He had to feel his way down three floors and along to the studio, and missed his entrance. But it meant that we played the last scene with the statue entirely in candlelight. And of course it was absolutely gobsmacking. Because the point about candlelight is that it flickers [...] It was a phenomenal experience to play that last scene just with two huge candelabra.

SOURCE

Tim Pigott-Smith, interviewed by Julian Curry, *Shakespeare on Stage* (2010)

ACTORS IMPROVISING

WILLIAM PINKETHMAN

(*c*.1660–1725)

609

William Pinkethman was an English comic actor with a reputation for playing to the crowd.

It must be confessed, that the actors, termed low comedians, are too guilty of adding to their author's text. Sometimes, indeed, it happens, that the wit, or happy imagination of the actor, is of service to the situation in which he is placed, and unexpectedly gives a relief or embellishment to that which would otherwise be neglected, or perhaps disapproved.

The contrary practice is, however, much more common... Will Pinkethman, of merry memory, was in such full possession of the galleries, that he would hold discourse with them for several minutes. To fine him for this fault was in vain; he could not abandon it, and the managers were too generous to curtail him of his income. At length, I was told, he and Wilks came to this whimsical agreement: Pinkey consented, that whenever he was guilty of corresponding with the gods, he should receive, on his back, three smart strokes of Bob Wilks's cane.—This fine, however, was, I believe, never exacted. I shall give the reader one specimen of his unseasonable drollery.

In the play of the Recruiting Officer [by George Farquhar], Wilks was the Captain Plume, and Pinkethman one of the Recruits. The Captain, when he enlisted him, asked his name: instead of answering as he ought, Pinkey replied, 'Why! don't you know my name, Bob?

I thought every fool had known that!' Wilks, in rage, whispered to him the name of the Recruit, Thomas Appletree. The other retorted aloud, 'Thomas Appletree! Thomas Devil! My name is Will Pinkethman:' and immediately addressing an inhabitant of the upper regions, he said, 'Hark you, friend: don't you know my name?'—'Yes, Master Pinkey (said a respondent) we know it very well.' The playhouse was now in an uproar; the audience, at first, enjoyed the petulant folly of Pinkethman and the distress of Wilks; but, in the progress of the joke, it grew tiresome, and Pinkey met with his deserts, a very severe reprimand in a hiss; and this mark of displeasure he changed into applause, by crying out, with a countenance as melancholy as he could make it, in a loud and nasal twang, *Odsfo! I fear I am wrong!*

SOURCE
Thomas Davies, *Dramatic Miscellanies* (1785)

DAVID GARRICK
(1717–1779)

610

For nearly thirty years, until his retirement in 1776, Garrick, though small in stature, dominated the London stage, both in tragic roles such as Hamlet and Richard III and in comic roles such as Abel Drugger in Ben Jonson's The Alchemist. *Here Garrick gets himself into hot water on account of his powers of mimicry.*

When Garrick first undertook to play Bayes in *The Rehearsal* [by George Villiers, the 2nd Duke of Buckingham], he had some doubts of the propriety of taking-off his brother performers, and therefore made a proposal to Giffard the manager of the theatre in Goodman's

Fields, to permit him to begin with him, as a kind of an apology for the rest. Giffard supposing that Garrick would only just glance at him to countenance the mimicry of the others, consented: but Garrick hit him off so truly, and made him so completely ridiculous, at rehearsal, that Giffard, in a rage, sent him a challenge; which Garrick accepting, they met the next morning, when the latter was wounded in the sword arm.

The comedy of *The Rehearsal* had been during this time advertised for the Saturday night ensuing; but the duel intervening (which none but the parties and their seconds knew of at that time, and very few ever since), the play was put off for a fortnight longer, *on account of the sudden indisposition of a principal performer.* At the end of that time it came out, with imitations of most of the principal actors, but Giffard was totally omitted.

SOURCE

Thomas Davies, *Memoirs of David Garrick*, ed. Stephen Jones (2 vols 1808)

EDMUND KEAN
(1787–1833)

611

The version [of *Richard III*] I played was of course, Shakespeare's, not Cibber's. It is amazing how long the bombastic fustian of Cibber held the stage, and how hard his version was to dislodge from it. Edmund Kean, who made his great success in Cibber's version, revolted at last and tried to force Shakespeare, pure and unadulterated, upon the public; but they would have none of it, and he had to return to Cibber. The oft-quoted line 'Off with his head! So much for Buckingham!' which according to tradition never failed to bring down the house was Cibber's. (I think Irving was the first to win over the public for Shakespeare's unspoiled, original version?)

The applause which followed this absurd line was naturally very precious to the actor who was playing 'Richard'. Harry Loveday, whose father had played with Kean, told me a good story. One night a small part player [Yarnold] from sheer nervousness, rushed on to the stage and shouted 'My Lord, the Duke of Buckingham is taken and we've cut off his head.' Kean, absolutely nonplussed, could only murmur: 'Oh!...then there's nothing more to be said.'*

Or, in other accounts and better iambics: 'Then bury him! So much for Buckingham.'

SOURCE
Sir John Martin-Harvey, *Autobiography* (1933)

WILLIAM CHARLES MACREADY (1793–1873)

612

When playing Macbeth one night at Manchester his servant, who should have been in the wings with a bowl of cochineal which Macready used to smear on his hands to represent blood, failed to put in an appearance. Macready's exit was only a very momentary and rapid one, and finding that the blood he relied on for the next scene was not there, he rushed up to an inoffensive commercial traveller, who had been allowed as a great treat by his friend, the local stage-manager, to come and watch the mighty star from the side, and without any warning struck him a violent blow on the nose, smothered his hands in the blood that flowed freely, and ran on to the stage again to finish the Act.

When the curtain fell he apologised to the commercial for his apparent rudeness, as he put it, in the most courtly and chivalrous manner, at the same time presenting the object of his attentions with a five-pound note.

SOURCE
Sir Seymour Hicks, *Me and My Missus* (1939)

J. W. COOKE
(*fl.* 1850s)

613

The celebrated American tragedian, Mr Cooke, was always fond of frolic on his benefit night, declaring he never took liberties with his friends at any other time.

It once happened during an engagement at Philadelphia that on such an occasion he was short of money and at a loss to know where to raise the wind for the accustomed breeze. In this dilemma he started up the town in a speculative mood, determined to inspirit himself in some way or other.

Having reached the corner of Callow Hill and Eighth Street, he perceived one of those enticing signs of three golden balls. He turned the corner and entered the fatal door, and addressed the man behind the counter thus:

> 'My name is Cooke. This is my benefit night. The manager can't do without me. I am up for Richard III. I want something to eat. I have no money. Now I propose to pledge myself for ten dollars, and you may lay me upon one of your shelves.'

The joke was a queer one. The pawnbroker paid the ten dollars, and Cooke was laid up. The theatre that night was crowded, and at seven o'clock the manager came forward to apologise, stating that with the permission of the audience, the performance would commence with a farce.

He had sent in different directions, but was unable to find Cooke in the city. He promised that the tragedian would be forthcoming in the course of half an hour.

As the manager retired, he was told that a boy wished to see him in the green-room. He found the boy, who presented a note written in cipher, which he at length translated thus:—

> MY DEAR JONES,—I am pawned for ten dollars; send and redeem me, or it will be impossible for Richard to be himself to-night.
>
> Yours, &c.,
> W. COOKE.

The manager started immediately after the fixed star, and found him nicely shelved with a plate of biscuits and cheese. In the button-hole of his coat was a piece of paper marked 'No. 1,473; pawned for ten dollars.'

The amount was paid, a cab called, and Mr Cooke and the manager returned to the theatre, where the former had just time to dress and commence, 'Now is the winter of our discontent.' It is said that he never acted better or received more applause.

SOURCE
J. B. Howe, *A Cosmopolitan Actor* (1888)

JOHNSTON FORBES-ROBERTSON
(1853–1937)

614

Apropos of mishaps upon the stage, I recall one that happened to that greatly gifted woman, Miss Elizabeth Robins, during a performance of Miss Constance Fletcher's play of *Mrs Lessingham,* at the Garrick. It was in a scene where I, as her husband, was trying to soothe her distressed condition. She had bought for the part a necklace of imitation diamonds and pearls, which she wore clasped firmly round her throat. Suddenly, to my consternation, the necklace broke, and the jewels, that I knew had cost her a considerable sum, began to drop on the carpet. While trying to comfort her, I managed to get most of the jewels into my joined hands. So far so good, but we were both in evening dress, and, my hands being full, I could not stow the things into my pockets without exposing the mishap to the audience, as we were standing in the middle of the stage. She at that moment gave a deep sigh which caused a momentary hiatus between her bodice and her chest. With what I consider a magnificent inspiration, I quickly poured the whole lot into that slight gap and got from her a stifled, gasping 'Thank you,' and we continued the scene.

SOURCE
Sir Johnston Forbes-Robertson, *A Player under Three Reigns* (1925)

OLIVER BURCHETT CLARENCE

(1870–1955)

615

There was one place of entertainment called 'Botting's Stores and Music Hall' where we got full measure of song, music and drama for sixpence. Here one night we were treated to a thriller and towards the finale the evil man had a terrific struggle with the heroine, in the midst of which he caught sight of a friend of his in the audience. Still struggling and in the middle of his protestations that she must and will be his, he called out to his pal, 'Wait for me 'Arry. Shan't be long now.'

SOURCE

O. B. Clarence, *No Complaints* (1943)

MARTIN JARVIS

(1941–)

616

In 1960 a young Martin Jarvis was working as Assistant Stage Manager at Pembroke Theatre in the Round in Croydon. The play was Lady Barker's Last Appearance.

During performances there was no place for a prompter to hide, so my only task, apart from setting out a few props beforehand, was to ring the telephone bell in the final scene. This was vital to the plot as it was meant to be the bank manager ringing with an answer to the important question: who is masquerading as Lady Barker? On stage the phone had to be answered by the old housekeeper, played

story about an off-stage phone bell that never rang and some awful ASM who wasn't there when needed.

SOURCE
Martin Jarvis, *Acting Strangely* (1999)

IAN OGILVY
(1943–)

617

Aged 17, Ian Ogilvy was working as a 'student' stage manager at the Royal Court Theatre in London's Sloane Square.

I don't recall much about the run of *The Keep*. It's in the nature of things in the theatre (and indeed much to be desired) for exactly the same events to happen every night, so only occasions of a fairly catastrophic kind stick in the mind. I remember a small catastrophe: one night, when setting the props on stage for the performance, I managed to leave the telephone on the prop table in the wings. In the middle of the play the absent phone rang, as it was supposed to do. The sound came from a hidden speaker inside the sideboard where the telephone, in all its squat, black Bakelite glory, should have been squatting but wasn't. Miss Jessie Evans reached for it. Saw it wasn't there. Glared into the prompt corner with a look of incandescent hatred. Turned back and looked out over the audience with the air of a woman who was deciding whether or not to be bothered answering the bloody thing at all. The non-existent phone continued to shrill. Miss Evans came to a decision. She took the breath of an actress close to the end of her tether. 'I'll take it in the hall,' she said imperiously and stalked into the wings.

SOURCE
Ian Ogilvy, *Once a Saint* (2016)

ROBIN SOANES
(1947–)

618

Actor Robin Soanes remembers working at the Bush pub fringe theatre in West London. The theatre was located in an upstairs room which had no facilities.

When we did *A Bed of Roses* in 1978, once we were backstage there was no way back to the dressing room, or, indeed, the lavatory. If we needed a pee during the performance it was either a ladder onto the roof and down the drainpipe, or down the backstairs and across the road to the 'cottage' on the corner of Shepherd's Bush Green. I found during the dress rehearsal that I was bursting for a piss and opted for the 'cottage'. The only thing was I was playing a vicar and at the time was dressed in full surplice, cassock and dog collar. I entered the brick toilet where forty men in tight jeans were fiddling with or eyeing each other's willies. On the appearance of a man of the cloth in their midst, there was a mass zipping up of zips and within five seconds I had the entire bank of urinals to myself.

SOURCE
Neil Burkey, *Close-Up Magic: 40 Years at the Bush Theatre* (2011)

ACTORS CORPSING

SAMUEL PEPYS
(1633–1703)

619

'Corpsing' is a British slang expression for unintentionally laughing during performance. In America they use the term 'breaking'—as in 'breaking character'. The origin of the term 'corpsing' is unclear, but generally reckoned to come from provoking an actor to laughter while they are portraying a corpse.

Samuel Pepys, a regular theatre-goer, deplored uncalled for laughter, both from the audience and from the players.

To the Duke of York's playhouse, and there saw 'Mustapha': which, the more I see, the more I like; and is a most admirable poem, and bravely acted; only both Betterton and Harris could not contain from laughing in the midst of a most serious part, from the ridiculous mistake of one of the men upon the stage; which I did not like.

To the Duke of York's House, and there saw 'Heraclius', which is a good play; but they did so spoil it with their laughing, and being all of them out, and with the noise they made within the theatre, that I was ashamed of it, and resolved not to come thither again a good while, believing that this negligence, which I never observed before, proceeds only from their want of company in the pit, that they have no care how they act.

SOURCE
Diary of Samuel Pepys, ed. John Warrington (1953)

LAURENCE OLIVIER
(1907–1989)

620

In 1937, Olivier played Hamlet at the Old Vic.

At one performance the most 'dweadful' thing happened during the duel. Laertes fell splendidly on his back, legs akimbo, but his codpiece burst open. He raised a downstage knee to hide his manhood from the audience and the play continued. The problem was next evening's performance: the very first scene on the battlements of Elsinor, when the soldiers were expecting the ghost to appear.

'What,' Marcellus asked, 'Has this *thing* appeared again tonight?' It was no good. The actors' convulsed laughter brought the curtain down, long before the 'Crowing of the Cock'.

SOURCE
Tarquin Olivier, *My Father Laurence Olivier* (1992)

'DRYING' AND 'NERVES'

JOHN PALMER
(?1742–1798)

621

Upon the subject of this representation of Lord Russell [the title role in a play by William Hayley], Palmer's brother once told me a ludicrous anecdote, to which I incline to give some credit. It seemed that Palmer had done with Lord Russell, as he did with many other characters, that is, totally neglected to study the words of the part; and in this dilemma he bethought himself of an expedient, which answered astonishingly, and, indeed, by the audience was never suspected. As much of Lord Russell was unlearned on the night of its performance, he thought it was better to speak from some character that he did know, than one that he did not; whenever, therefore, he felt himself at a loss, he dexterously introduced some passages from the Earl of Essex, which he contrived to fit into the cues received by Lord Russell; and thus, really giving some parts, and masking others, he gained another day to perfect himself in the character. It will be remembered that to his audience this play was completely new; while the dialogue was in progress, and not seemingly irrelevant, there were no means of detection.

SOURCE
James Boaden, *Life of John Philip Kemble* (1825)

GLENN MELVYN
(1918–1999)

622

Glenn Melvyn was a Manchester-born English actor, director, and, later, film and television scriptwriter, who worked with the young Ronnie Barker in repertory at the Oxford Playhouse in the early 1950s.

He [Glenn Melvyn] told me of a very young lad in his first speaking part on the boards who was so petrified that before the curtain rose on the first night, he dropped to his knees in the wings and began to pray to his Maker. He felt a tap on the shoulder. He looked round to see the imposing, cloaked figure of the leading man. 'Don't rely on him too much in the third act, laddie, he's helping me with a quick change.'

SOURCE
Ronnie Barker, *Dancing in the Moonlight* (1993)

MICHAEL SIMKINS
(1957–)

623

Michael Simkins is a RADA-trained British actor who has appeared in the West End, on television, and in film, but is probably best-known as a writer. His best-selling memoir, What's My Motivation?, *described the life and travails of a jobbing actor.*

I was once with a company of actors who were about to do a production of Shakespeare's *Twelfth Night*, for which a much older actor was being recruited to play the part of the aged priest. While discussing the new arrival, one of our number asked the inevitable question surrounding any actor of particularly mature years. 'But can he still do the dickies, darling?'

The 'dickies' are the words. He was asking in his oblique way if the ancient recruit would still be able to remember his lines. Or if he'd even be able to learn them in the first place.

[...]

[E]very actor has experienced the awful sensation of 'drying' on stage—that moment when, inexplicably, a line or word refuses to come to hand when you need it. Once you've gone through your first 'dry', you're never quite the same cocky bugger you were before, however much you try to laugh it off. And you can't rely on someone helping you from the side of the stage these days. Prompters went out with Sir Donald Wolfit.

The stage manager is supposed to keep an eye on the script in case of emergencies, but they have other calls on their time. A friend of mine appearing in Swansea, who once pleaded three times for a prompt from the wings, received the answer: 'Hang on, I'm doing something.'

[...]

I was in the audience on the opening night. Two hours in and the priest entered on cue to confirm the marriage vows. 'A contract of eternal bond of love...' I knew he'd dried. My buttocks instinctively clenched and my eyes refocused from his taut features up on the stage to the back of the cardigan worn by the audience member in front of me.

I couldn't look. I knew deep within me that the rest of his speech had vanished into the dark recesses of his mind, lost and irretrievable, at least until later on. By which time it would be of no use.

The actors grouped around him looked on helplessly. The silence was deafening. After what seemed an age but was probably only a couple of seconds, his voice, quavering with anxiety, blurted out the only thing his scrambled mind could come up with.

'And I see from my watch that it's time to arrange the nuptials.'

He walked off. He'd been on stage for about 15 seconds.

SOURCE

Michael Simkins, 'An Actor's Life', *The Guardian* (5 September 2001)

THE DEMON DRINK

WILLIAM DUNLAP
(1766–1839)

624

William Dunlap was a playwright, author of The History of the American Theatre, *and manager of New York's Park Theatre.*

On the last day of October a new drama from Dunlap's pen, 'The Mysterious Monk', was performed with Hodgkinson in the leading part. Its reception was not enthusiastic. Quiet now seems to have prevailed in the greenroom, but the theatre was not to be the abode of tranquillity. One night in November, two sea captains became drunk (it was then permissible to bring liquor into the house), and began calling for 'Yankee Doodle' during the overture. Not receiving the desired solace for their patriotic ears, they hurled missiles at the orchestra and defied the indignant audience. A riot ensued which resulted in the ejection of the offenders; but returning later with a number of sailors, they assailed the doors of the play-house until the city watch took them into custody. This fracas resulted in the prohibition of intoxicants until the end of the first piece.

SOURCE
Oral Sumner Coad, *William Dunlap* (1917)

RIVALRY

EDWIN FORREST
(1806–1872)

628

Edwin Forrest was the leading American tragedian of his day, and the first American actor to challenge the masters of the English stage. In spite of a tendency to rant in his early years he won a popular and devoted following at home and rivalled Macready for the plaudits of London's audiences when he appeared at Drury Lane in 1836–7. A second visit, however, in 1845–6 led to an open feud, sparked by Macready's jealousy and Forrest's competitive spirit. To appreciate the extraordinary sequence of events surrounding this feud, we start with a passage from Macready's Diaries *which describes the occasion when Forrest hissed him on stage in Edinburgh. The piece of business that offended Forrest was Macready's introduction of a pas de mouchoir (a dance with a handkerchief) during the play scene in* Hamlet.

Edinburgh, March 2nd.—Acted Hamlet really with particular care, energy, and discrimination; the audience gave less applause to the first soliloquy than I am in the habit of receiving, but I was bent on acting the part, and I felt, if I can feel at all, that I had strongly excited them, and that their sympathies were cordially, indeed, enthusiastically, with me. On reviewing the performance I can conscientiously pronounce it one of the very best I have given of Hamlet. At the waving of the handkerchief before the play, and 'I must be idle,' a man on the right side of the stage—upper boxes or gallery, but said to be upper boxes—hissed! The audience took it up, and I waved the more, and bowed derisively and contemptuously to the individual. The audience carried it, though he was very staunch to his purpose. It discomposed me, and, alas, might have ruined many; but I bore it down. I thought of speaking to the audience, if called on, and spoke to Murray about it, but he very discreetly dissuaded me. Was called for, and very warmly greeted. Ryder came and spoke to me, and told me that the hisser was observed, and said to be a Mr W—, who was in company with Mr Forrest! The man writes in the *Journal*, a paper, depreciating me and eulogizing Mr F., sent to me this place.

March 3rd.—Fifty-three years have I lived, to-day. Both Mr Murray and Mr Ryder are possessed with the belief that Mr Forrest was the man who hissed last night. I begin to think he was the man.

SOURCE
Macready's Reminiscences, ed. Sir F. Pollock (1876)

629

Macready won considerable sympathy from this episode and public feeling ran against Forrest. When Forrest again visited England in 1845 he was received with marked hostility, which he attributed to Macready's manoeuvrings. It is hardly surprising therefore that Macready's visit to America in 1848 should have aroused similar national passions against him. In the circumstances it was simply asking for trouble.

On the 20th of November, 1848, Mr Macready appeared at the Arch Street Theatre, Philadelphia. It was then, and for the first time, that an unsuccessful attempt was made to drive him from the stage. Upon his being called before the curtain he addressed the audience as follows:

> 'He had understood, at New York and Boston, that he was to be met by an organized opposition, but he had abiding confidence in the justice of the American people.' (Here the noise and confusion completely drowned his voice, and three cheers were attempted for Forrest, and three hearty ones were given

for Macready.) He resumed by saying, 'It was the custom in his country never to condemn a man unheard.' (Cheers and calls, a voice crying out, 'Did you allow Forrest to be heard in England?') He said, 'I never entertained hostile feelings towards any actor in this country, and have never evinced a feeling of opposition to him. The actor alluded to had done that towards him, what he was sure no English actor would do—he had openly hissed him.'

(Great noise and confusion, hisses and hurrahs.) 'That up to the time of this act he had never entertained towards that actor a feeling of unkindness, nor had he ever shown any since.' (Collision in boxes and great uproar throughout the house.) He said, 'That he fully appreciated the character and feelings of the audience, and, as to his engagement, if it was their will, he was willing to give it up at once; (no, no, cheers and hisses;) but that he should retain in his memory the liveliest recollection of the warm and generous sentiments of regard shown him, and should speak of the American people, whom he had known and studied for the past twenty years, with the same kind feelings that he ever had done.'

This, the third speech delivered by Mr Macready, before Mr Forrest had uttered a syllable, called forth from the latter gentleman this scathing card. The editor of the *Pennyslvanian*, of Nov. 22nd, 1848, introduced it thus: 'We received the following card last evening. It is a reply to the speech of Mr. Macready, at the Arch Street Theatre, on Monday evening.'

A CARD FROM EDWIN FORREST

Macready, in his speech, last night, to the audience assembled at the Arch Street Theatre, made allusion, I understand, to 'an American actor' who had the temerity, on one occasion, 'openly to hiss him.' This is true, and, by the way, the only truth which I have been enabled to gather from the whole scope of his address. But why say 'an American actor?' Why not openly charge me with the act? for I did it, and publicly avowed it in the *Times* newspaper of London, and at the same time asserted my right to do so.

On the occasion alluded to, Mr Macready introduced a fancy dance into his performance of Hamlet, which I designated as a *pas de mouchoir*, and which I hissed, for I thought it a desecration of the scene, and the audience thought so too, for in a few nights afterwards, when Mr Macready repeated the part of Hamlet with the same tomfoolery, the intelligent audience of Edinburg greeted it with a universal hiss.

Mr Macready is stated to have said last night, that up to the time of this act on my part, he had 'never entertained towards me a feeling of unkindness.' I unhesitatingly pronounce this to be a wilful and unblushing falsehood. I most solemnly aver and do believe that Mr Macready, instigated by his narrow, envious mind, and his selfish fears, did *secretly*—not *openly*—suborn several writers for the English press to write me down. Among them was one Forster, a 'toady' of the *eminent tragedian*—one who is ever ready to do his dirty work; and this Forster, at the bidding of his patron, attacked me in print even before I appeared on the London boards, and continued his abuse of me at every opportunity afterwards.

I assert also, and solemnly believe that Mr Macready connived when his friends went to the theatre in London to hiss me, and did hiss me with the purpose of driving me from the stage—and all this happened many months before the affair at Edinburg, to which Mr Macready refers, and in relation to which he jesuitically remarks that 'until that act he never entertained towards me a feeling of unkindness,' Pah! Mr Macready has no feeling of kindness for any actor who is likely, by his talent, to stand in his way. His whole course as manager and actor proves this—there is nothing in him but self—self—self—and his own countrymen, the English actors, know this well.

Mr Macready has a very lively imagination, and often draws upon it for his facts. He said in a speech at New York, that there, also, there was an 'organized opposition' to him, which is likewise false. There was no opposition manifested towards him there—for I was in the city at the time, and was careful to watch every movement with regard to such a matter. Many of my friends called upon me when Mr Macready was announced to perform, and proposed to drive him from the stage for his conduct towards me in London.

My advice was, do nothing—let the superannuated driveller alone—to oppose him would be but to make him of some importance. My friends agreed with me it was, at least, the most dignified course to pursue, and it was immediately adopted. With regard to an 'organized opposition to him' in Boston, this is, I believe, equally false; but perhaps in charity to the poor old man, I should impute these 'chimeras dire' rather to the disturbed state of his guilty conscience, than to any desire upon his part wilfully to misrepresent.

The only mistake we think Mr Forrest made in this letter, was the expression calling Mr Macready a 'superannuated driveller'. Mr Macready was born in the year 1793, consequently at the time this article was written, 1848, he was but fifty-five years of age. A man cannot be called or considered superannuated at that age.

To this letter, Mr Macready replied in a card 'to the public', dated Jones' Hotel, Nov. 22nd, 1848:

In a card, published in the *Public Ledger* and other morning papers of this day, Mr Forrest having avowed himself the author of the Statement, which Mr Macready has solemnly pledged his honor to be without the least foundation, Mr Macready cannot be wanting in self-respect so far as to bandy words upon the subject; but, as the circulation of such statements is manifestly calculated to prejudice Mr Macready in the opinion of the American public, and affect both his professional interests and his estimation to suspend their judgment upon the questions, until the decision of a legal tribunal, before which he will prove his veracity, hitherto unquestioned, shall place the truth beyond doubt.

SOURCE
James Rees, *Life of Edwin Forrest* (1874)

630

The quarrel reached fever-pitch within a few months, and when Macready visited New York, to play Macbeth at the Astor Place Opera House, actual tragedy occurred; in the affray outside twenty-two people were killed and thirty-six injured. A pamphlet published shortly afterwards offered this account of the 'Terrific and Fatal Riot'.

On the night of the tenth of May, 1849, the Empire City, the great metropolis of the Union, was the scene of one of those horrors of civilization, which for a time make the great heart of humanity stop in its beatings. In the darkness of night, thousands of citizens were gathered in a central square of the most aristocratic quarter of New York—gathered around one of its most conspicuous and magnificent edifices, the Astor Place Opera House [...]

Around this edifice, we say, a vast crowd was gathered. On the stage the English actor Macready was trying to play the part of MACBETH, in which he was interrupted by hisses and hootings, and encouraged by the cheers of a large audience, who had crowded the house to sustain him. On the outside a mob was gathering, trying to force an entrance into the house, and throwing volleys of stones at the barricaded windows. In the house the police were arresting those who made the disturbance—outside they were driven back by volleys of paving stones.

In the midst of this scene of clamor and outrage, was heard the clatter of a troop of horses approaching the scene. 'The military—the military are coming!' [...] Further on was heard the quick tramp of companies of infantry, and there was seen the gleam of bayonets. A cry of rage burst from the mob. The appearance of an armed force seemed to inspire them with a sudden fury. They ceased storming the Opera House and turned their volleys against the horsemen. Amid piercing yells and execrations, men were knocked from their horses, the untrained animals were frightened, and the force was speedily routed, and could not afterwards be rallied to perform any efficient service.

Now came the turn of the infantry. They marched down the sidewalk in a solid column; but had no sooner taken up a position for the protection of the house than they were assailed with volleys of missiles. Soldiers were knocked down and carried off wounded. Officers were disabled. An attempt to charge with the bayonet was frustrated by the dense crowd seizing the muskets [...] At last the awful word was given to fire—there was a gleam of sulphurous light, a sharp quick rattle, and here and there in the crowd a man sank [...] with a deep groan or a death rattle. Then came a more furious attack, and a wild yell of vengeance! Then the rattle of another death-dealing volley [...] The ground was covered with killed and wounded—the pavements stained with blood. A panic seized the multitude, which broke and scattered in every direction. In the darkness of the night, yells of rage, screams of agony, and dying groans were mingled together. Groups of men took up the wounded and the dead, and conveyed them to the neighbouring apothecary shops, station-houses and the hospital.

The horrors of the night can never be described. We looked over the scene that misty midnight. The military [...] were grimly guarding the Opera House. Its interior was a rendezvous and a hospital for the wounded military and police. Here and there around the building [...] were crowds of men talking in deep tones of indignation. There were little processions moving off with the dead or mutilated bodies of their friends and relations. A husband, uttering frenzied curses, followed his mortally wounded wife to the hospital. An aged mother found her only son [...] in the agonies of death. Many a wife sat watching at home, in terror and alarm for her absent husband [...]

SOURCE
H. M. Ranney, unpublished pamphlet (1849)

EDWIN BOOTH
(1833–1893)

631

One night at supper in the Beefsteak Room, Irving told me an amusing occurrence, which took place at Manchester when Booth played there. He said it was 'about' 1863, so it may have been that time of which I have written—1861. *Richard III* was put up, Charles Calvert, the manager, playing Richmond, and Booth Gloster. Calvert determined to make a brave show of his array against the usurper, and being manager was able to dress his own following to some measure of his wishes. Accordingly he drained the armoury of the theatre and had the armour furbished up to look smart. Richard's army came on in the usual style. They were not much to look at though they were fairly comfortable for their work of fighting.

But Richmond's army enthralled the senses of the spectators, till those who knew the play began to wonder how such an army could be beaten by the starvelings opposed to them. They were not used to fight, or even to move in armour, however; and the moment they began to make an effort they one and all fell down and wriggled all over the stage in every phase of humiliating but unsuccessful effort to get up; and the curtain had to be lowered amidst the wild laughter of the audience.

SOURCE

Bram Stoker, *Personal Reminiscences of Henry Irving* (1906)

DISTINGUISHED VISITORS

WILLIAM EWART GLADSTONE
(1809–1898)

632

The Prime Minister often came to see Henry Irving's productions, usually sitting on the same cushioned seat by the corner of the stage. This particular visit, to a double bill, is described by Bram Stoker, Irving's manager at the Lyceum, and later his biographer, and the author of Dracula.

The Corsican Brothers was, so far as my knowledge goes, the first play—under Irving's management—which Mr Gladstone came to see.* The occasion was January 3, 1881—the first night when *The Cup* was played. He sat with his family in the box which we called in the familiar slang of the theatre 'The Governor's Box'—the manager of a theatre is always the Governor to his colleagues of all kinds and grades. This box was the stage box on the stall level, next to the proscenium. It was shut off by a special door which opened with the pass key and thus, as it was approachable from the stage through the iron door and from the auditorium by the box door, it was easy of access and quite private. After *The Cup* Mr Gladstone wished to come on the stage and tell Irving and Ellen Terry how delighted he was with the performance. Irving fixed as the most convenient time the scene of the masked ball, as during it he had perhaps the only 'wait' of the evening—a double part does not leave much margin to an actor. Mr Gladstone was exceedingly interested in everything and went all round the vast scene. Seeing during the progress of the scene that people in costumes were going in and out of queer little alcoves at the back of the scene he asked Irving what these were. He explained that they were the private boxes of the imitation theatre; and added that if the Premier would care to sit in one he could see the movement of the scene at close hand, and if he was careful to keep behind the little silk curtain he could not be seen. The statesman took his seat and seemed for a while to enjoy the life and movement going on in front of him. He could hear now and again the applause of the audience, and by peeping out through the chink behind the curtain, see them. At last in the excitement of the scene he forgot his situation and, hearing a more than usually vigorous burst of applause, leaned out to get a better view of the audience. The instant he did so he was recognised—there was no mistaking that eagle face—and then came a quick and sudden roar that seemed to shake the building. We could hear the 'Bravo Gladstone!' coming through the detonation of hand-claps.

**Winston Churchill was another Prime Minister who often visited the theatre. He sometimes bought three seats, one for himself, one for his daughter Mary, and one for his hat and coat.*

SOURCE
Bram Stoker, *Personal Reminiscences of Henry Irving* (1906)

QUEEN MARY
(1867–1953)

633

Royalty in the audience sometimes creates a special challenge for the cast of a play. Queen Mary attended the matinée of an Aldwych farce by Ben Travers that starred Ralph Lynn, Tom Walls, and Robertson Hare.

Queen Mary attended a special matinée, which was given for some distinguished charity or other. I was commanded to be received in her box during the second interval. This interval immediately followed a scene in which Ralph and Tom, desirous of keeping Robertson Hare imprisoned in a room, decided that the best way of doing this was to remove his trousers and take them along with them. This was the farce's moment of most blatant frivolity, but a good deal that had preceded it had not been exactly puritanical. I awaited the comments which Her Majesty might graciously be pleased to make with some disquietude.

She said, 'It is very amusing and very interesting.' I bowed my acknowledgement, though I couldn't help wondering whether 'interesting' was a compliment to myself or to Robertson Hare. Then, with a slightly quizzical smile, she added, 'Is it an adaptation from the French?'

SOURCE
Ben Travers, *Vale of Laughter* (1957)

CHARLES CHAPLIN
(1889–1977)

634

Here is another example of the challenges actors face when there is royalty in the audience. One of Charlie Chaplin's earliest stage engagements, before moving to America, was in The Painful Predicament of Sherlock Holmes, *with William Gillette in the title role.*

Holmes was an immediate success. During the engagement Queen Alexandra saw the play; sitting with her in the Royal Box were the King of Greece and Prince Christian. The Prince was evidently explaining the play to the King for, during the most tense and silent moment, when Holmes and I were alone on the stage, a booming voice with an accent resounded through the theatre: 'Don't tell me! Don't tell me!'

SOURCE
Charles Chaplin, *My Early Days* (1964)

JOHN COUNSELL
(1905–1987)

635

Back in Windsor, John Counsell and his wife, actress Mary Kerridge, regularly received royal visitors at the Theatre Royal.

In April to *This Happy Breed* [by Noël Coward] came the King and Queen bringing the sixteen-year-old Princess Margaret with them (her sister was in Belfast launching her first ship). It was their first visit since 1939, security restrictions having ruled out any such possibility during the war. I asked Noël Coward, as author of the play, to help me receive them. As on previous occasions, Lilian Begbie, our Box Office manageress, was stationed in one of the boxes in order to pass on a hand-signal from me to the conductor of the orchestra to play the National Anthem at precisely the right time. This was to be when Their Majesties had reached their seats but had not yet sat down. As I led the Royal party into the auditorium through the side door at the back of the balcony stalls the Queen was on my right. On my left a group of young women in the back row had swung round in their seats to stare, and were thus unaware that the rest of the audience was rising to its feet. I therefore made a quick gesture to them to stand up. Miss Begbie, though mystified, took it to be the awaited signal. The Anthem struck up as the Royal party reached the top of the twelve stairs between them and their seats. Standing at attention with the rest, I had plenty of time to realise in horror what was going to happen next. As the last note died away the director took the cue and the house lights began to go down. I completely panicked and shouted out, 'No,No,No!' The Queen laid her hand on my arm and said, 'Please don't worry; it's all in the spirit of the evening.' These words, meant to comfort, only added to my embarrassment.

The curtain rose and the play began. Mary and John Slater, who opened it, were dimly aware of a kerfuffle in the balcony stalls. They did not realise that the sudden flare of a cigarette lighter came from the King searching for the number of his seat. Meantime, the rest of the party were still standing motionless at the top of the stairs.

'Go on, ma'am, go on,' said Noël.

'I would like to go on, Mr Coward' came the unruffled reply, 'but you are standing on my dress.'

SOURCE
John Counsell, *Counsell's Opinion* (1963)

636

In 1953 the Queen and the Duke of Edinburgh came to a performance of Agatha Christie's new play Witness for the Prosecution *at the Theatre Royal Windsor.*

After the authoress and my fellow directors had been presented, it came to Stanford Holme's turn. The Duke, hearing that he was a member of the staff, asked him many searching questions about the organisation of the company, the actors' salaries, the time given to rehearsals, costs, takings and so forth. Finally, he asked whether the news that the Queen and he were coming had made any difference to business. He was delighted by Stanford's reply:

'Well, sir, to a play by Agatha Christie on a Saturday night, the honest answer must be "No"!'

SOURCE
John Counsell, *Counsell's Opinion* (1963)

DOMINIC DROMGOOLE
(1963–)

637

Dromgoole was Artisitic Director of the Bush Theatre and the Oxford Stage Company before taking the helm at Shakepeare's Globe in London from 2005 to 2016. As the Globe company returned from playing Hamlet *in every country across the world, Dromgoole announced he would be leaving the role of Artistic Director. Here he recounts a visit from 'the least disappointing man in the world', Barack Obama, also shortly to leave his job.*

The President doesn't just drop in. For days armies of visitors checked the place out—security, and press, and protocol organisers. When he did arrive, police and homeland security shut down the whole of Southwark. Robocop-like figures crowded every doorway of the Globe, the brutal modernity of their firepower and protective cloting clashing weirdly with the oak and plaster.

An hour before he arrived we were rehearsing a quick omelette of music and soliloquies to present for him. A helicopter appeared overhead and drowned out all noise (the Globe's lack of roof makes it ever vulnerable to curious helicopters). 'We can't have that,' I shouted over the noise of the blades towards a White House aide. 'Hold on.' She said, 'I'll get the head of security.' She came back instantly with with a man who was extremely civil and taller than

Goliath. I craned upwards and repeated, 'We can't have that', civilly but loudly. 'I'm sorry, sir, but you have to have the helicopter; we need the coverage.' 'Fine,' I said. 'we won't do the show then.' He looked at me briefly, muttered something into his collar, and the helicopter flew smartly away. [...]

The company did great. The music relaxed the air and made the presentation less formal. Obama stood in the yard on one side, almost a hundred press on the other, the actors in the middle, and Matt, Ladi and Naeem [Matthew Romain, Ladi Emeruwa, and Naeem Hayat, who had all played Hamlet during the world tour] steered us through the major speeches. They were crisp, clear and precise and spoke with feeling, and the President was attentive and alert. I invited him to come and join us on stage, and he did, shaking everyone's hand. We chatted of this and that, his honesty and warmth disarming. At the end, he was told I was leaving my post the next day. 'What are you going to do?' he asked. 'I have no idea,' I said. 'Well maybe you can come and hang out on the beach with me.' That just about made my year. We did a photo together, shaking hands. Involuntarily, a noise came out of my gut, which could just about be discerned as me saying, 'Thank you, sir. You have been an inspiration to me and my daughters.' He looked alarmed at first, since the gruff noise sounded more like someone making a discreet pass than a message of gratitude, but he settled, said an uncertain 'Thank you', and was then ushered away. 'That was better than the whole tour,' Ladi said.

SOURCE

Dominic Dromgoole, *Hamlet: Globe to Globe* (2017)

FIRE AND BRIMSTONE

TATE WILKINSON
(1739–1803)

638

Alexander the Great was the play, got up with great attention: I was the Alexander [...] All went off with great eclat till the latter part of the fourth act, soon after the death of Clytus.—Some olive leaves, &c. intended for decorations, being twisted and interwoven with little bits of wax, caught fire from the lights, and the flame continuing to blaze, the burnt particles occasioned a strong stench—an universal cry of 'Fire! Fire!' prevailed, on which every person was alarmed, but not one so horridly aghast as the dead Clytus, who had expired by the rage of Alexander: he rose with the agility of a tumbler that would not have disgraced the Royal Circus; his uprise and exit were so quick that he threw the immortal Alexander on his back. The late noble Earl of Effingham, who was remarkably corpulent, evinced equal alacrity with dead nimble-footed Clytus, and gave evident proofs of superior agility; for instead of making his way to the box-door, he with one spring of the utmost ease, swiftness, and dexterity, vaulted over the side-box, and lighted on his feet on a row in the middle of the pit, standing erect; the seat gave proof to the credit of the carpenter; for it did not yield, but firmly supported its ponderous and noble weight.

In a few minutes the trifling cause that occasioned this universal panic subsided, and was soon extinguished; the audience called to order, the ladies instead of fainting, being surrounded by martial heroes, smiled; Lord Effingham returned to his box, but not by the way he went into the pit: No sooner was his Lordship settled in *statu quo* than all the gentlemen of the army (for he was universally beloved) gave a general salutation, which his Lordship returned, and after a hearty laugh on all sides the play was ordered to go on, and old grey-headed Clytus made his second appearance after death, and prostrated himself once more a victim at the feet of Alexander. It appeared so truly ridiculous, that the convulsive fits of laughter which involuntarily ensued, may easier be conceived than described; it was truly whimsical, and mutually entertaining.

SOURCE
Tate Wilkinson, *Memoirs of His Own Life* (1791)

JOHN PHILIP KEMBLE
(1757–1823)

639

Besides being an actor of note, John Philip Kemble was also known for his efforts, as manager, to defend the increased price of admission to Covent Garden Theatre after it had burned down in 1808. Rebuilt almost immediately, it re-opened in September 1809, provoking the Old Price Riots, an extraordinary battle of wits between the audience and the manager, which Kemble, in the end, lost gracefully.

Covent Garden Theatre was burned on September 19th, 1808, and was now in rapid progress of rebuilding. Its re-opening led to the most extraordinary theatrical riots that this country ever witnessed. Immediately after the destruction of the theatre Kemble solicited a subscription to rebuild it, which was speedily filled up, and the Duke of Northumberland contributing ten thousand pounds. The first stone of the new building was laid by the Prince of

Wales on the last day of the year 1808, and it was completed with such rapidity that on the 18th of September 1809, it was opened with *Macbeth,* Kemble himself appearing in the character of Macbeth. In the new arrangement a row of private boxes formed the third tier under the gallery. The furniture of each box and of the adjoining room was to be according to the taste of the several occupants. To make these extraordinary accommodations for the great the comforts of the rest of the audience were considerably diminished. To crown all, the theatre opened with an increase of the prices, the pit being raised from 3s. 6d. to 4s., and the boxes from 6s. to 7s. The manager said that this was necessary to cover the great expense of rebuilding the theatre; but the public declared that the old prices were sufficient, and that the new ones were a mere exaction to enable Kemble to pay enormous salaries to foreigners like Madame Catalani (who had been engaged at 150*l.* a week to perform two nights only). On the first night of representation, which was Monday, the curtain drew up to a crowded theatre, and the audience seemed to be lost in admiration at the beauty of the decorations until Kemble made his appearance on the stage. A faint attempt at applause got up by his own friends was in an instant drowned by an overpowering noise of groans, hisses, yells, which drove him from the stage. Mrs Siddons then came forward, but met with no better reception. Kemble had declared he would not give in to the popular clamour, but the next night and the nights following it was continued with greater fury. On Wednesday night the manager came forward to address the audience, and attempted to make a justification of his conduct, which was not accepted. On Friday he presented himself again, and proposed that the decision of the dispute should be put to a committee composed of the Governor of the Bank of England, the Attorney-General, and others. On Saturday night this was agreed to, and the theatre was shut up until the decision was obtained, the obnoxious Catalani having in the meantime agreed to cancel her engagement. On the Wednesday following the theatre was re-opened, but the report of the committee being of a very unsatisfactory kind, the uproar became greater than ever. The manager is said to have hired a great number of boxers, and on the Friday night following, the various fights in the pit gave it the appearance of a boxing-school. During this period everything distinguished by the epithet O.P. (old prices) became fashionable. There was an O.P. Dance. Finding it utterly impossible to appease the rioters in any other way, Kemble gave in to them. A public dinner was held, at which no less than five hundred people attended, and Kemble came in person to make an apology for his conduct. After dinner there was a crowded theatre, and amid considerable uproar a humble apology was accepted from the manager. After their demands had been complied with a large placard was unfurled, containing the words, 'We are satisfied.' Thus ended this extraordinary contest.

SOURCE
Wright's Caricature History, quoted in W. Clark Russell, *Representative Actors* (1888)

WILLIAM DUNLAP
(1766–1839)

640

The destruction by fire of the theatre at Richmond, Virginia in 1811 was one of the greatest tragedies in the history of early American theatre. Placide was the actor Alexandre Placide, who, until fleeing the French Revolution, had been rope dancer to Louis XVI.

A new play and pantomime had been advertised for the benefit of Mr Placide. The house was fuller than on any night of the season. The play was over, and the first act of the pantomime had passed. The second and last had begun. All was yet gaiety, all so far had been pleasure, curiosity was yet alive, and further gratification anticipated—the orchestra sent forth its sounds of harmony and joy—when the audience perceived some confusion on the stage, and presently a shower of sparks falling from above. Some were startled, others thought it was a part of the scenic exhibition. A performer on the stage received a portion of the burning materials from on high, and it was perceived that others were tearing down the scenery. Someone cried out from the stage that there was no danger. Immediately afterwards, Hopkins Robinson ran forward and cried out, 'The house is on fire!' pointing to the ceiling, where the flames were spreading like wild-fire. In a moment, all was appalling horror and distress. Robinson handed several persons from the boxes to the stage, as a ready way for their escape. The cry of 'Fire! Fire!' ran through the house, mingled with the wailings of females and children. The general rush was to gain the lobbies. It appears from the following description of the house and the scene that ensued, that this was the cause of the great loss of life.

The general entrance to the pit and boxes was through a door not more than large enough to admit three persons abreast. This outer entrance was within a trifling distance of the pit door, and gave an easy escape to those in that part of the house. But to attain the boxes from the street it was necessary to descend into a long passage, and ascend again by an angular staircase. The gallery had a distinct entrance, and its occupants escaped. The suffering and death fell on the occupants of the boxes, who, panic-struck, did not see that the pit was immediately left vacant, but pressed on to gain the crowded and tortuous way by which they had entered. The pit door, as we have said, was so near the general entrance, that those who occupied that portion of the house gained the street with ease. A gentleman who escaped from the pit among the last, saw it empty, and, when in the street, looked back upon the general entrance to the pit and boxes, and the door had not yet been reached by those from the lobbies. A gentleman and lady were saved by being thrown accidentally into the pit, and most of those who perished would have escaped if they had leaped from the boxes and sought that avenue to the street. But all darted to the lobbies. The stairways were blocked up. All was enveloped in hot scorching smoke and flame. The lights were extinguished by the black and smothering vapour, and the shrieks of despair were appalling. Happy for a moment were those who gained a window and inhaled the air of heaven. Those who had reached the street cried to the sufferers at the windows to leap down, and stretched out their arms to save them. Some were seen struggling to gain the apertures to inhale the fresh air. Men, women, and children precipitated themselves from the first and second stories. Some escaped unhurt—others were killed or mangled by the fall. Some with their clothes on fire, shrieking, leaped from the windows to gain a short reprieve and die in agonies.

'Who can picture,' says a correspondent of The Mirror, 'the distress of those who, unable to gain the windows, or afraid to leap from them, were pent up in the long narrow passages?' The cries of those who reached the upper windows are described as being heart-sickening. Many who found their way to the street were so scorched or burnt as to die in consequence, and some were crushed to death under foot after reaching the outer door.

SOURCE
William Dunlap, *History of the American Theatre* (1833)

HENRY IRVING

(1838–1905)

641

The threat of fire was once a real and present danger in theatres across the world. On the opening night of Henry Irving's Hamlet *in New York in 1883, torches on stage threatened disaster.*

Early in the [play] scene one of these torches got overheated, and the flaming spirit running over set fire to one of the stage draperies. The super-master, Marion, who was 'on' in the scene, at once ran over and tore down the curtain and trampled it out.

Through it all Irving never hesitated or faltered for an instant. He went on with his speech; no one could take it from movement, expression or intonation that there was any cause for concern.

Still a fire in a theatre has very dreadful possibilities; and at the first sign of flame a number of people rose hurriedly in their seats as if preparatory to rushing out. There was all over the house a quick, quiet whisper:

'Sit down!' As if in obedience, the standers sat.

There was but one exception. A lanky, tallow-faced, herring-shouldered, young man, with fear in his white face, dashed up the aisle. It is such persons who cause death in such circumstances. There is a moment when panic can be averted; but once it starts nothing can stop it. The idea of '*Sauve qui peut!*' comes from the most selfish as well as the most weak of human instincts. I feared that this man might cause a panic, and as he dashed up I stepped out and caught him by the throat and hurled him back on the ground. At such a time one must not think of consequences—except one, which is to prevent a holocaust. The rude, elementary method was effective. No one else stirred. I caught the fallen man and dragged him to his feet.

'Go back to your seat, sir!' I said sternly. 'It is cowards like you who cause death to helpless women!' He was so stunned or frightened that he did not make the least remonstrance, but went sheepishly back to his seat.

On the way he had to pass a man who stood a little in front of me—a tall, powerful, black-bearded, masterful-looking man. As the other was passing he put out his hand, and with finger and thumb caught the lappet of the young man's coat and drew him close. Then he said in a low voice, full of personal indignation as at a wrong to himself:

'Do you know that you rushed past me like a flash of lightning!'

Then he suddenly released him and turned his eyes to the stage. I think it was the most contemptuous action I ever saw. The rest of those present moved no more.

SOURCE
Bram Stoker, *Personal Reminiscences of Henry Irving* (1906)

AMBER MASSIE-BLOMFIELD
(1984–)

642

Over time, with the arrival of stringent safety regulations for theatres, building fires became less frequent, but as recently as 2015 the Grand Hall of the BAC (Battersea Arts Centre) caught fire and was totally destroyed, prompting an outpouring of support and generosity from both the local and theatrical communities alike. Arts producer Amber Massie-Blomfield recounts the story.

On 13th March 2015, I was on a train heading southwest from Waterloo station. As we passed through Clapham, I glanced in the direction of Battersea Arts Centre, which can just be made out in the distance from the railway line. The blue air was filled with smoke, thick and heavy on the skyline. It seemed implausible, the contents of a disordered dream. But a scan of Twitter confirmed it: Battersea Arts Centre was on fire.

Artistic director David Jubb learned the news at home on the Kent coast. His colleague made what seemed to be a routine phone call to inform him that the buikding's fire alarms had gone off and that the staff had assembled outside—the sort of thing that happens in theatres when people burn their toast or use the wrong kind of fog machine in a rehearsal room. But then he heard the catch in her throat as she saw flames take hold of the roof of the Grand Hall at the back of the building. The panic rose in her voice when she told him to get here right away.

Within minutes the fire was raging, wind stoking the flames and spreading it across the roof, towards the clock tower. [...] Crowds gathered behind flimsy red and white tape, training their cameras on it, tilting their phones up towards this grim, impromptu tourist attraction. [...] Soon, the roof caved in, the inferno opening up the building's insides to the sky, everything leaning inwards and disintegrating, beams and tiles and scaffolding poles. 'Jesus have mercy God', someone said.

[...] Nobody was hurt in the fire, but for some time it was feared that Pluto, the theatre's much-loved black cat, had been caught inside—until he turned up days later, brazen and unharmed.

[...] On Twitter, a hashtag started—#BACPhoenix—and very quickly it was flooded with stories of days and nights spent at BAC, debates sparked and worldviews changed, friends made and romances kindled.

JOHN COUNSELL
(1905–1987)

649

During the Second World War, John Counsell, actor and for many years manager of the Theatre Royal, Windsor, worked at SHAEF (Supreme Headquarters Allied Expeditionary Force) at Versailles.

One lunch party which sticks vividly in my mind, and for reasons other than the exquisite cuisine, took place after we had been in France only a few weeks.

Our hostess was the very chic wife of the owner of a large department store, who was being held by the police on suspicion of collaborationist activities. There were four other guests, all very charming, and speaking excellent English. Half-way through the meal a conversation on the following lines was initiated by my left-hand neighbour.

'Mon Commandant, I trust that you have succeeded in accommodating yourself with a suitably charming mistress during your stay in France.'

Me (slightly taken aback, but answering gravity with gravity): Do you know, as a matter of fact, I haven't.

My left-hand neighbour: How long has the commandant been here?

Me: Two months.

M.L.H.N: Est-ce possible!

Me: C'est vrai.

M.L.H.N: But this must be remedied, monsieur. The reputation of France for hospitality is at stake. It is necessary that steps should be taken by us to put matter. …

(The rest of the table are informed of the situation, and murmur their agreement.)

Me: (realising that a blunt assertion that I am '*un mari fidele*' would not only sound priggish but would certainly not be believed): Vous etes tout a fait gentilles.

Somebody or other: In the matter of choice, monsieur, do you favour blonde, brune or brunette?

Me: That, monsieur, is a question of mood.

My Hostess: Do you regard of most importance intellectual accomplishment or physical attraction?

Me: Shall we say half and half, madame?

Another Dame: I think the commandant must meet Phi-Phi.

Hostess: She already has a lover, and her intellectual accomplishment does not exist.

M.L.H.N: How about Zu-Zu?

The other Dame: Mon dieu, non! No one could accuse her of having physical attraction.

Hostess: As monsieur is connected with the stage I think it would be plus convenable for him if we chose an actress. There would thus be a common basis of interest.

(General applause.)

There followed a detailed analysis on the lines indicated of many of the leading lights of the French stage. I managed somehow to keep as straight a face as the rest of the company, who evidently viewed the topic as a serious one, which needed the most careful thought. My one attempt to swing the conversation on to different lines by enquiring into the acting ability of one of the candidates was swiftly countered by my left-hand neighbour with:

'Monsieur, do you not require Mlle So-and-so for your *personal* use?'

I lapsed into silence and while names continued to be bandied about, fell to wondering how I was to avoid giving offence after so much care had been taken on my behalf. No suitable choice had been agreed by the time coffee was served, at which we were joined by the author of the two most successful plays then running in Paris. A chap called Anouilh. For the next half hour no one else could get a word in edgeways. He had been asked to meet me, and had come, apparently, with the intention of persuading me to launch his plays in London. Though his interest dropped to zero when he discovered that I was only the director of a 'provincial' theatre, I have him to thank for rescuing me from what was fast becoming a very tricky situation.

SOURCE
John Counsell, *Counsell's Opinion* (1963)

ESMOND KNIGHT
(1906–1987)

650

One sultry Saturday afternoon, just as I burst through the bushes in search of the treacherous Demetrius, the air-raid sirens wailed out in their 'doleful choir'. The people of London were as yet unused to this horrid din and, being absorbed by Shakespeare's poetry, for a moment sat watching, scarcely daring to admit the warning, but when the full significance of that chilling clarion burst upon them they glanced nervously at one another, then snatched up their umbrellas and mackintoshes and bolted for the shelters.

A young actress making her first stage appearance as one of Hippolyta's ladies-in-waiting, seizing this golden opportunity, strode boldly to the edge of the stage and called in a clear ringing voice: 'It's all right, ladies and gentlemen, don't be alarmed, it's only the animals in the Zoo!' And, indeed, in happier days the animals and birds settling down for the night had provided superb atmospheric background effects for the play. Today they were silent, but the young actress's bold endeavour caused those more resolute to remain, and we continued with the play. But the Battle of Britain had begun, and as I woke from a pleasant sleep on the greensward, stuttering the words: 'My Lord, I shall reply amazedly, half sleep, half waking,' I could see, through the trees to the east, an enormous column of yellow smoke rising thousands of feet into the air. The Germans had bombed the Docks.

SOURCE
Esmond Knight, *Seeking the Bubble* (1942)

LAURENCE OLIVIER
(1907–1989)

651

Leaflets now explained what to do in the event of a German invasion: 'Stay inside your homes and on no account try to get away. The roads must be kept clear for our soldiers and tanks to move rapidly against the aggressor.'

Notices were put in theatre programmes commending fortitude and valour, and some managements could not resist printing their own admonishments—'With courage and the strength of the Island Race, you should find it possible to last until the end of the play.'

SOURCE
Tarquin Olivier, *My Father Laurence Olivier* (1992)

ALEC GUINNESS

(1914–2000)

652

Soon after the outbreak of the Second World War, the young Alec Guinness was anxious to 'join up' for military service.

A few days later, somewhere off Piccadilly, I ran into Dennis Price, who was a casual friend from the time we had been together in one of Gielgud's productions. 'You should join us at Sevenoaks,' Dennis said encouragingly, 'It's an anti-aircraft battery and there is simply nothing to do. Major Cazalet is a dear, and there are lots of chums. Johnnie and Jack and Hughie and Sebastian among others. (I won't recall, now, who all those Christian names represented.) You can swing as much leave as you want; all you have to do is say you have a dinner engagement at the Savoy, which you simply can't get out of. I think we should sit out the war very comfortably. Do join us. I'll have a word with Cazzers.'

Dennis looked very smart in his khaki; a sharp crease to his trousers, shiny boots and a rakish tilt to his cap.

So, a week later, I took the train to Sevenoaks and walked from the station, very nervous and undecided, but in my best suit and head held high. I arrived at a large suburban house, which didn't have the air of being occupied by the military; in fact it appeared to be totally deserted. The hall through which I strolled was empty of furniture or any sign of human life. Very gingerly I pushed open a door. There, in a small room, each lolling over his typewriter, sat two sergeants, knitting. They looked up with some surprise but busily continued their two plain one purl.

'Yes?' said one of them, affably enough. 'And what can we do for you?'.

'I am hoping to see Major Cazalet.'

'Are you expected?'

'I think so' I said.

These were not what I had expected sergeants to be like and I wondered, briefly, what Peggy's uncle would have made of them.

'Well, hold on a tick,' said the one nearest the door, 'I'll go and have a peep. What name did you say?'

I gave my name, and the sergeant wearily put down his knitting and left the room. The other eyed me roguishly.

'Going to join us?'

'I don't know yet.'

'What, may I be so bold to ask, do you do in civvy street?'

'I'm an actor,' I said.

'Oh, my Gawd! Not another! My dear, the place is swarming with them. It's a positive snake-pit. You know we've got Dennis and Hugh?'

'So I heard'

The door opened and Sergeant No 1 reappeared.

'She'll see you now, toute suite.' He flipped a wrist in the direction I was to take. As I made my exit I heard No. 2 say to his colleague, but for my benefit I am sure, 'Not exactly a dish, but quite sweet.' I took a deep breath and knocked on the Major's door.

Major Cazalet was a smallish benign-looking man. He rose from his desk and motioned me to a chair opposite him. The room, which was in a Victorian turret, was uncarpeted and almost bare.

'Do sit down,' he said. 'It's luck you've caught us on a slack day. Most of the fellows are out learning about the Bofors gun. Dennis has spoken to me about you. You found your way all right?'

'With no difficulty, Sir.'

'Oh, good.' There was a silence, as if he was searching for something to say. Then he went on. 'We are rather over-manned at present.'

Another silence. 'What do you think? Would you like to join us? Of course, I do realise you've seen nothing. Take your time.'

I shuffled and fumbled before finally saying, 'Might I have a day or two to think it over, sir?'

'By all means. Good heavens, I'd hate to rush anyone. Let's see; it's Tuesday. Could you possibly let me know by Thursday?'

'Yes,' I said, knowing perfectly well I could let him know there and then if I had the courage.

When I left the building both sergeants were peering after me out of a window. One of them waved. As I wandered back to the station I fussed as how to make suitable apologies to Dennis.

Not long after this there were questions in the House of Commons about the Sevenoaks battery; the whole thing was broken up; and Jack and Johnnie and Dennis and Hugh and Co. were dispersed to different and less pleasant duties.

SOURCE
Alec Guinness, *Blessings in Disguise* (1985)

653

In fact, Guinness joined the Royal Navy Vounteer Reserve and in the summer of 1943 took part in the Allied landings on Sicily.

Later in the morning an irate Commander RN appeared, angrily asking why I was so late in landing. I considered he was out of touch. I pointed out that, far from being late, I considered I had been the first to arrive. He clearly didn't believe me and muttered something disparaging about RNVR officers.

'What did you do in civvy street, Sub?'

'I was an actor, Sir.'

The familiar question, and, the equally familiar twisted smile at the answer. My temper has always been short-fused, particularly in those days, and I suddenly saw red and gave way to a cold rage.

'An actor I was, sir, and an RNVR officer I am. My ship was the first to arrive here, leading others—which was not part of my orders—and I beached at exactly the right spot at exactly the time I was told to. And you will allow me to point out, sir, as an actor, that in the West End of London, if the curtain is advertised as going up at 8pm, it goes up at 8pm not an hour later; something which the Royal Navy might learn from.'

SOURCE
Alec Guinness, *Blessings in Disguise* (1985)

SIMON CALLOW
(1949–)

654

Let us begin to bring down the curtain on this act with two anecdotes from actor and writer, Simon Callow. The first is set in Northern Ireland, in Belfast at the height of 'the Troubles'. Callow was appearing in a version of the German comedy Schippel, *presented by Edinburgh's Traverse Theatre company.*

Schippel was the uncontested hit of the season. We detached it from the repertory and started on our travels. First we went to Belfast, and then London. Belfast was a terrible shock. It was never a beautiful city, but this was a vision of hell. Every one of the wonderful bars we used to drink in had been blown up. The streets were lined with barbed wire. Every alleyway was chicken-netted and guarded by soldiers. You were frisked from head to foot in every shop. Armoured cars would suddenly pull up, soldiers would leap out scattering to every doorway, their guns cocked. A small group of them would surround a car, drill a hole in the window, fill it with foam and then detonate it. A muffled boom, and it was dragged away. Throughout the performances, at regular intervals, one could hear the sound of explosions or gunfire. The audience remained imperturbable, while we quaked. We were the first mainland group to play in Belfast since the fighting began. I have never before or since experienced anything like their appetite for theatre, and especially for comedy. They ate us up passionately. It was so moving, their need, and the thought that our work, which can so easily seem like icing sugar, a flourish, an embellishment, could be so deeply, desperately, desired, was deeply moving.

SOURCE
Simon Callow, *Being an Actor* (1984)

655

Simon Callow toured with the Joint Stock theatre company in The Speakers, *a free-form play by Tony Bicat, in which the audience perambulates and is invited to heckle the speakers.*

We were booked for a midnight spot at the Abbey, as part of the Dublin Festival. That means that most of the audience had been drinking since 11.am, just for a start. We, however, were caught up in the crosscurrents of something much bigger. We had decided to do the show with the iron safety curtain down and the audience on stage with us, our great scaffolding lighting tower slap in the centre. So at ten past twelve, we started. Immediately we were heckled as we had never been heckled before: filibustering was more like it. Eventually, when it was impossible to continue or engage the hecklers in any kind of dialogue, I said to one of them, as my lower-middle-class Socialist Party of Great Britain speaker, 'OK, mate, you seem to have a lot to say for yourself, why don't you come up 'ere and tell us all about it.' He clambered up on to the box, opened his mouth, was unable to orate, so said 'Oh fuck off the lot of youse, you're all a load of cunts.' Ironic applause, and I was able to continue. The speaker to my left had hit on the same ploy. His heckler, however, similarly silenced by standing on the box, unzipped his fly and started to urinate on the stage. Mild cries of 'shame' and much mirth. Suddenly, there was an irruption on the other side of the audience. 'That's the bastard that killed Frank Stagg!' A tiny, white-haired gentleman was suddenly surrounded by a posse of tough-looking men, all from the audience. It was Mr O'Dalaigh, the President of the Republic, on an incognito visit, and the posse were his bodyguard. Swiftly, he was removed from the theatre. His accusers, who seemed to be connected with our filibusterers, were jostled by remnants of the bodyguard, to cries of 'Shame, let them alone you pigs', and so on.

Theatre in Dublin has to put up with a lot of stiff competition from life.

SOURCE
Simon Callow, *Being an Actor* (1984)

by permission of Chatto&Windus, an imprint of VINTAGE, Penguin Random House LLC.

26. Anecdote relating to Daniel Day Lewis, *The Guardian*, 29 October 2012: Copyright Guardian News & Media Ltd 2020.
27. Martin Jarvis, Acting Strangely: Copyright © Martin Jarvis, 1999. Reproduced by permission of Greene & Heaton Ltd.
28. *And Furthermore Judi Dench as told to John Miller, Weidenfeld and Nicholson* 2010: *And Furthermore Judi Dench as told to John Miller* (2010). Published by Weidenfeld and Nicolson.
29. Kevin Spacey in *Marie Claire*: TI-Media Limited.
30. 'I'm starting to believe in the universe right now', interviewed by Liz Hoggard, *The Guardian*, 20 December, 2015: Copyright Guardian News & Media Ltd 2020
31. Dominic Dromgoole, *Globe to Globe*: Dominic Dromgoole, *Hamlet: Globe to Globe*. Copyright © 2017, Dominic Dromgoole. Reprinted with kind permission of Canongate.
32. John Dennis, *The Critical Works*: Hooker, Edward Niles. *Critical Works of John Dennis. Vol. I and II*. pp. 405–406, 409–410. © 1943 The Johns Hopkins Press. Reprinted with permission of Johns Hopkins University Press.
33. G. B. Shaw, *Selected Letters*: The Society of Authors, on behalf of the Bernard Shaw Estate.
34. Richard Findlater, Lilian Baylis: Richard Findlater, *Lilian Baylis* (1975). Published by Allen Lane. Reprinted with kind permission of Angela Findlater.
35. Harold Clurman: Excerpt(s) from THE FERVENT YEARS by Harold Clurman, copyright © 1957 by Harold Clurman. Copyright renewed 1985 by Sidney Davis. Used by permission of Alfred A. Knopf, an imprint of the Knopf Doubleday Publishing Group, a division of Penguin Random House LLC.